Springer
Tokyo
Berlin
Heidelberg
New York
Barcelona
Budapest
Hong Kong
London
Milan
Paris
Singapore

T. L. Kunii • A. Luciani (Eds.)

Cyberworlds

Tosiyasu L. Kunii
Professor
Hosei University
3-7-2 Kajino-cho
Koganei City, Tokyo
184-8584 Japan
and
Senior Partner of MONOLITH Co., Ltd.
1-7-3 Azabu-Juban, Minato-ku,
Tokyo, 106-0045 Japan

Annie Luciani
ACROE
INPG-46 av. Félix Viallet
38 031 Grenoble Cedex
France

ISBN 4-431-70207-5 Springer-Verlag Tokyo Berlin Heidelberg New York

Printed on acid-free paper

Printed in Hong Kong

Typesetting: Camera-ready copy from the authors/editors
Printing & binding: Best-set Typesetter, Ltd., Hong Kong
SPIN:10633033

Think. Do we live our life to end up sucked into black holes? Is that the destiny of the human race? Numerous people die on this earth from hunger, from disease, or even through futile hostility. If this is one side of human reality, the other side is presented here. Can we not synthesize better worlds and then make them real? Living in the digital era, a bit in a computer can be transformed into a step movement through devices such as stepping motors, linear cars, and direct control robots. Now we can be the creators of synthetic worlds. Let us cooperate toward a common goal. Cyberworlds is the manifesto and the records of the pioneers in this field. Yes, it is a book of wisdom and an open invitation to synthetic worlds, still very primitive and humble. Further, we should not let fear of failure stand in our way; to err is human.

Tosiyasu Laurence Kunii and Annie Luciani

Preface

The worlds synthesized in the cyberspaces of networked computers are the theme of Cyberworlds. Cyberspaces have come into prominence with the development of the Internet and are expected to expand drastically with the emergence of national and international information systems. The purpose of the book Cyberworlds is to discover the architecture and design of cyberworlds by synthesizing worlds in cyberspaces. The underlying philosophy is crucial to the success of the architecture, and an initial effort is made to delineate it at the beginning of the book. The book's topics are selected to clarify the issues of the philosophy, architecture, and design of cyberworlds through a wide variety of case studies.

The approach presented in the book is thus characterized as synthetic rather than analytic. There already are numbers of books with observations and analyses of cyberworlds. They warn of the danger of widespread crimes and accidents in the cyberworlds, for instance. Without a philosophy and methodologies of how to architecturally design and synthesize the cyberworlds, the worlds in cyberspaces tend to be arbitrarily extended, disordered, and, in extreme cases, criminal.

This book is intended to benefit readers by providing them with a possible direction to take in deciding how to synthesize worlds in cyberspaces. Creating new worlds in new spaces with almost unlimited dimension and scale is an immense challenge. In principle, anyone at any moment can participate in the creation. The book serves as a creator's reference and also as a design guidebook.

Applications of cyberworlds as synthetic worlds are versatile: from cybercorps, electronic commerce, virtual reality, electronic media, and multimedia to cyberpolitics and cyberlaw. This book provides essential materials for living in the real world as well as for living through cyberworlds, for running world politics, planning corporate global strategies, managing research institutions, and planning life on a firm basis.

Cyberworls is thus addressed to anyone interested in information technology and its social impact. No prior knowledge is required. Readers will become familiar with computational technology and the potentials of the Internet. Professionals working in information technology as well as undergraduate and graduate students in computer science, social sciences, and business studies will find this a useful textbook.

Acknowledgments

Cyberworlds has come about through extensive research meetings sponsored by the University of Aizu; The Embassy of France in Japan; the MOVE Consortium supported by Fujitsu, MicroSoft Japan, and Ricoh; and the Aizu Area Foundation for the Promotion of Science and Education. All contributions have been rigorously peer- reviewed more than two times through discussions and editing. Creating the type of book presented here was itself creating a cyberworld. Hence, the final acknowledgment goes to the contributors.

Tosiyasu Laurence Kunii
Annie Luciani

Table of Contents

List of Contributors

Part I

Foundation

Theme 1

Philosophy

1. The Philosophy of Synthetic Worlds – Digital Genesis for Communicating Synthetic Worlds and the Real World –

Tosiyasu L. Kunii*
The University of Aizu, Aizu-Wakamatsu City, Fukushima 965-80, Japan

Summary.
Personal history-based and personal experience-based philosophy of synthetic worlds is expressed in an attempt to construct the general philosophical framework to model and create synthetic worlds and to establish communications with the real world we live. As a ground to characterize the worlds, both synthetic and real, the nonlinear and singular nature of the worlds is researched.
Key words and phrases: philosophy of synthetic worlds, communicating worlds, world modeling, Digital Genesis, CW-complex, homotopy, singularity, nonlinearity, Morse theory

1.1. Synthetic Worlds and the Real World

For us living in the era of digital society, synthetic worlds mean the unlimited and creative dimensions opened up in front of us as the digital worlds, spanning over innumerable numbers of networked computers and covering the entire globe. This is the greatest creation opportunity human beings have ever had. The creation of the worlds demands unlimited creativity. Hence, creativity is the first thing here.

At the same time, unless we are extremely wise, there is a danger that they will grow beyond anyone's control and will create evils. Potentials can be looked at both generally and individually. In the past, human beings have created synthetic worlds in passive forms *per se* such as historical monuments, legends, literature, and religious scripts. Historical perceptions are also essential to associate synthetic worlds with such passive historical forms. The Book of Genesis and Rig Veda of India present splendid legendary worlds. In a Chinese legend, there is a description of the world of the dead named 'the country of yellow springs' that is referred in a Japanese 7th century legend Kojiki. Pyramids, Taj Mahal, Inca ruins and Angkor Wat ruins are historical

* Current Address: Computational Science Research Center, Hosei University, 3-7-2 Kajino-cho, Koganei-shi, Tokyo, 184-8584 Japan (e-mail:tosi@kunii.com)

and religious monuments that remind us of the mentally synthesized worlds of people who created them. All of them have remained passive until we have created active synthetic worlds on networked computers.

Synthetic worlds have the core themes of their own. The first is: the philosophy of synthetic worlds. However, for any philosophy to be an active philosophy, it has to have a sequel to influence the real world. The sequel consists of the second through the fourth themes. The second is: the modeling of synthetic worlds. The third is: the architecture of synthetic worlds. The fourth is: the design and implementation of synthetic worlds in digital spaces. Philosophy should be the first thing we are concerned, in the sense that we first present synthetic worlds as a philosophy, not just as a technique, to foresee the meaning, potential, and effects of synthetic worlds. In this sense, this write up is my personal Digital Genesis, thinking on the creation of digital worlds as active synthetic worlds.

Modeling defines what are synthetic worlds generally and also individually. Architecture defines how synthetic worlds are configured generally and also individually. Design defines how synthetic worlds are actually laid out for realization. Implementation presents general and individual methods to construct synthetic worlds in digital spaces. Having synthetic worlds thus constructed, we can now go into the individual objects and themes of the constructed synthetic worlds. The evolution of any research is recursive. The individual objects and themes of the constructed synthetic worlds later revise and upgrade the philosophy, architecture, design and implementation. This is the nature of the spiral evolution of synthetic worlds.

Science is to understand, and engineering is to synthesize. Both can be combined to create new academic disciplines. However, researches on synthetic worlds and the real world have been separated unfortunately. Science on the real world at the bottom level is physics, and science at the highest level is cosmology and medicine for human bodies called micro-cosmoses. Cosmology has been making advances through the observation of the real world and has made some great discoveries essential for research on the creation process of the cosmos, such as the discovery of the cosmic wrinkles. The cosmic wrinkles were discovered by COBE, a satellite shot out in 1992 as a part of the research project led by George Smoot and his group at the University of California, Berkeley, in 1992[10], to verify certain essential information on the formation of the universe. The wrinkles discovered in space were lying stretched out over a large area, not unlike the Great Wall of China. This discovery is considered one of the major scientific findings of the 20th century. The universe, then, possibly is like a sheet of cloth, named the world sheet[11], woven by space and time as its warp and weft. The wrinkles on this sheet of cloth came about as the universe was formed, just like wrinkles in clothing are created, viz. through the interaction of warp and weft, here: through the interaction of space and time, along with their subsequent collective motions, at the beginning of the universe's formation. Stephen W.

Hawking's research on cosmology with the help of Roger Penrose has been theoretically modeling the real world at the cosmic level[11] .

However, cosmology has not been connected to synthetic worlds. We have to also synthesize our own cosmos in synthetic worlds, which is the entire world largest in scale. In terms of complexity, both cosmos and human bodies have almost equivalent complexity according to our current knowledge. However, an abstraction hierarchy or complexity equivalent to that of material has not been known in synthetic worlds. Furthermore, there has been no general correspondence established between the real world and synthetic worlds.

We are now going into the real interconnection and the complexity hierarchy research of synthetic worlds to understand synthetic worlds first in science and then to synthesize them actually through engineering. That is the way how we are going to create new academic disciplines of synthetic worlds. That should be the real future of computer science and engineering.

1.2. Visual Abstraction for Complexity Modeling - A Case Study through a Naïve Sequence of Q&A -

Q: There are 3D surface warping, 3D surface fitting and 3D animation. What is in common?

A: Homotopy.

Q: What's good in homotopy?

A: It can be an information lossless representation, if we choose to do so.

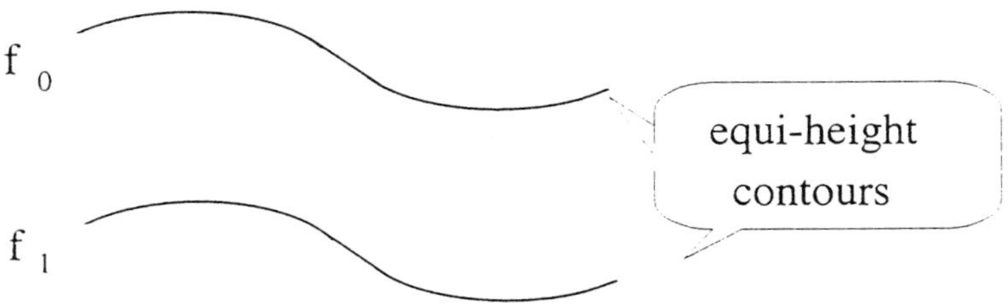

Suppose we have two maps f_0 and f_1 such that

$f_0, f_1 : X \to Y$ where X and Y are metric spaces.

f_0 is defined to be **homotopic** to f_1 and denoted by $f_0 \simeq f_1$ if there exists a continuous map H,

such that

$H : X \times I \to Y$ and $H(x,0) = f_0, H(x,1) = f1$.

H is called a **homotopy** from f_0 to f_1.

Q: How lossless?

A: Correspondences, differentiability and singularity in particular, can be maintained.

triangulation

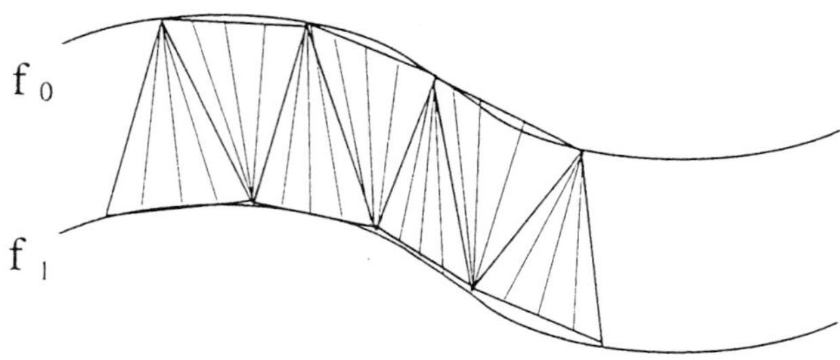

homotopy

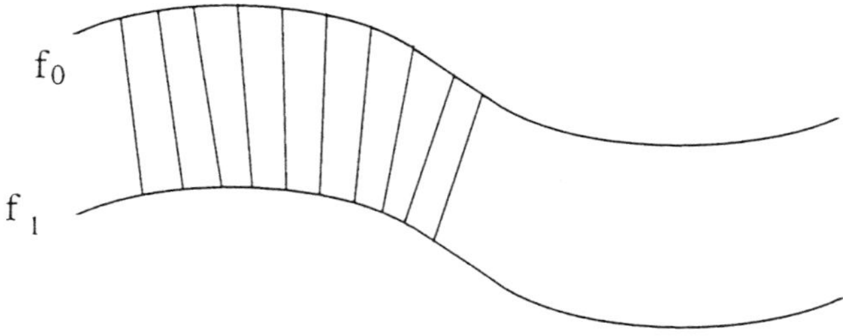

Q: How about a B-spline?
A: It's a linear homotopy.
Originally, the concept of a polyhedron was not necessarily topological. To make it topological, a polyhedron with a homeomorphism onto a metric space is provided and known as a **curvilinear polyhedron**.
A natural extension of a curvilinear polyhedron is a **CW-complex**, natural in a sense homotopy theory can be developed for it in a straightforward manner.
When a CW-complex is locally homeomorphic to an open ball, it is called a **manifold**. To be a little bit more precise, it is locally Euclidean, Hausdorff and hence 2nd countable.
Q: Suppose we carry out the data space visualization of very large and complex images with multiple view points, as often required in the visualization of the workspaces of computer vision-equipped robots and of human

hands, a guide map, and ancient paintings. Can we use Euclidean spaces as the data spaces?

A: Only locally. Globally, we have to use CW-complexes.

Q: Can we reduce complex shapes to elements, such as in the case of matter into elements by Mendeleev and finally into atoms and molecules?

A: Yes, into elementary singularity signs such as folds, cusps, crosses, p++C singularities, in many cases. For example, the elementary singularity signs serve as the indexes in feature restoration such as the restoration of organ shapes from x-ray film images and CT images, and also in the characterization of the beginning of the universe as seen in the Hawking's theory. The study of signs is called **semiotics**. The reduction of shapes into atoms and molecules was done in the Hamiltonian cases by Anatoly Fomenko[21]. General cases are under research.

1.3. Material and Information

In 1969 when I was young and 32, as a new associate professor of the Computer Centre of the University of Tokyo, I happened to propose establishing the Information Science Department at the Faculty of Science. Then, a lot of arguments arose on the quite fundamental issues such as "why information sciences could be a scientific area" and "what should be the discipline." Particularly, physicists, chemists, and biologists were skeptical on why information science could be studied as a discipline equivalent in its academic depth, to material sciences.

Before getting their questions, I questioned the same to myself. The information worlds I was synthesizing inside computers while computing intermolecular electronic interactions with a hope to understand the mechanisms of various intermolecular interactions in diversified areas such as photosynthesis and carcinogenesis, were really thrilling when I faced with them. My original intention was to compute the intermolecular electronic structures of existing materials. What I found myself actually doing was synthesizing hypothetical information worlds which might or might not be associated with the real material world. Computer scientists compute varieties of information turning them into algorithms and data structures. Material scientists study materials having living organisms and the cosmos as the cases of the most advanced forms of materials. Then what is in common between the two categories of research objects: material and information?.

Information science has its own unique research goals including the themes to answer the question above: "What is in common in material sciences and information sciences?" As is well known, in biological science, biological forms are assumed to be generated based on genes which, in a case of human beings, have 6×10^9 adenosines per person. I hypothesized then, at that time in 1969 that information at its highest level should have some gene-type information that generates the rest of information automatically. As a step to prove the hypothesis by discovering the similar entities as genes in information, I took the approach of abstracting algorithms and data structures from higher order botanical trees as published in 1984[2] and also from forests as published in 1991[3]. The result indicated that the most of the information to generate the tree shapes was dedicated to the generic information to define the general tree branching pattern of higher order trees, and that very little amount of information was assigned to determine the species specific forms. That explained the reason why, once a person has developed the cognitive ability to recognize higher order trees as a generic entity, it is so fast for that person to distinguish and identify the individual species of higher order trees. Such information as a whole automatically generated higher order tree shapes to provide an evidence towards the proof of the hypothesis. This work of us published in 1984 was recognized as an early work on artificial life synthesis method in 1989 by Christopher G. Langton[23]. Hugh Ching of Post-Science Institute also provided another evidence by discovering automatic software generating software[22].

1.4. Multimedia and Synthetic Worlds

Animals including human beings have, by nature, sensors dealing with various types of information as multi-media. The information which animals can deal with includes sight (or the sense of vision), hearing, touch, smell, and taste. Current computers can handle only audio and visual information among a variety of multi-media information processing capabilities that animals have. However, during the last two decades, the evolution of multi-media technology has been contributing to the significant expansion of the areas of information science.

Although the boom on multi-media just has come recently, I have been involved in research on multi-media computers since 1968. At that time, I started researches on fashion shows with raster graphics[7], automatic composition and performance by computerized music instruments, and extraction of voice from the recordings of songs accompanied by a piano. These researches were later expanded into a human body inner-trip project[8], the project on analysis of expert techniques of martial arts[6], [17], and the project on development of bi-directional multi-media computer networks[9]. These researches were initiated by the motivation to create synthetic worlds in computers different from the real world. Although synthetic worlds are new and still not well known worlds, they still should have the aspects of multi-media as the means for integrating a number of media in the synthetic worlds.

Computer technologies started from number crunching, and expanded into database management, visualization, and multi-media. However, unbelievably slow progresses have been observed in the evolution of essential researches on computers and computing such as theories and models, for multi-media. Therefore, even if multi-media information can be displayed, it is difficult to recognize and extract its features and to confirm or verify the identities and the validity. Given such information spaces, we will be always lost in synthetic worlds.

Unfortunately, it will take a long time to overcome these difficulties. Below, we describe an approach to visualization based on topological modeling for assisting our understanding of synthetic world structures and functions.

1.5. Topological Modeling for Visualization

A model such as hierarchical abstraction is essential in both visualization and pattern recognition. Visualization synthesizes images and shapes from the model through computer graphics techniques, and pattern recognition extracts, identifies and abstract the features of images as the model. Therefore, visualization and pattern recognition have the model as the common base. Visualization assists our understanding of object structures and functions, and this understanding, in turn, helps us reconstruct the objects from measurements. To represent and understand the structure of 3D objects in computers, we need a method to describe their shapes abstractly. Further, to understand 3D object shape changes, differential topology is essential to know the global structure of the differential spaces. Differential geometry tells the detailed shapes.

We took the singular points approach for describing complex shapes[4] based on the Morse theory and the Reeb graph. We can describe the topology of complex objects by using singular points of a function defined on the object surface[4], [5], in place of the vertices, edges, faces and holes. The critical points are peaks, pits, and saddles. These singular points play significant roles in characterizing objects. According to the Morse theory[16], a one-to-one correspondence exists between the non-degenerate singular points and the cells that constitute the object surface. Suppose an object surface is a C2 two dimensional manifold. Then according to the Morse theory, singular points on the surface can be classified into three types: 0D cells (vertices), 1D cells (chips of strings or edges), and 2D cells (patches or faces)[20]. In other words, the Morse theory tells us that *we can construct the object surface by pasting the cells that corresponds to the singular points.* How it's neat. It has been getting clearer that everybody has to master differential topology, which is highly abstract, as a basic knowledge for use in practice. Therefore, I have been involved in research and education, of differential topology for ten years.

The Morse theory has been proven to be powerful for the visualization of characteristic points. However, we have found problems that cannot be solved by the approach above. New applications always give rise to new requirements which after formalization yield axioms or hypotheses, and then theories and technologies. Suppose that we go on an inner-trip of a human body by a micro-machine using multi-media. In order to properly guide and receive reliable reports of the observations by the dispatched micromachine inside the human body, we need to extract features for characterizing the shape of internal organs with wrinkles which contain many ridges and ravines. If it is possible, a new method can be established for localizing the treatment of the disease areas by the micro-machine instead of giving medicines to the entire human body through injection.

Let us look at an example. How can tumors in the bowel be characterized? A tumor is considered as a type of wrinkles which appear on the inner surface of the bowel. This type of wrinkles require the definition of such features that are still effective even if the direction of the surface gradually changes. Now, our project team at the University of Aizu has finished the first step of definition and theory development[1], [15] in cooperation with the mathematics department of the Moscow State University. The Hessian matrix cannot be used for characterization because it depends on the definition of the direction of height. A wrinkle is likely to be a ridge or a ravine (a series of degenerate peak- or pit- points), and therefore, the Morse theory cannot be applied either, because of the degeneracy of the characteristic points. Our project has invented an effective method for characterizing such complex shapes and for extracting features based on local computation to cut down the computational complexity drastically. The extracted features are invariant with respect to translations and rotations of the surface and it leads to a method of hierarchical description of surfaces that yields new approaches to shape coding, rendering, and design. We are also investigating the problem of analyzing grinding processes and shape analysis of teeth based on this new approach.

The next question is what is the height along the bent stem of a flower. While taking a walk in the garden on the Hongo campus of the University of Tokyo, I presented this problem to Anatoly Fomenko of the Moscow State University. Fomenko was amused with this question because the height always changed along the stem and then branched out. There has been no satisfactory mathematical theory to answer this question and he was interested in it as a new research theme.

Our approach always starts from particular needs and the needs always require innovative theories. In ancient Greece, Pythagoras proved a theorem now known as the Pythagorean theorem based on the knowledge in Egypt derived from the practical needs . Needs-oriented approaches are often much stronger than what is called generalized thinking and have been finding fruitful results along with innovative mathematical theories. In research and education, we have been always emphasizing the needs-oriented approach or, sometimes called a top-down approach emphasizing individual humane needs as the top. Therefore, a popular statement that mathematics is the basis of computer science and engineering or even of information science is unacceptable to us. We consider mathematics an ancestor and a field of information science.

1.6. Mental Modeling of Shapes: A Parallel Mental Process Modeling and Interaction Modeling through CW-Complexes

Shape modeling actually goes through the following three levels:

(a) Mental Shape Modeling.
(b) Prototype Shape Modeling.
(c) Product Shape Modeling.

Mental shape modeling means how a designer models a shape mentally, and remembers it[14]. To interconnect highly parallel mental shapes in highly parallel mental scenes, the modeling space is a CW-complex[15]. Prototype shape modeling is usually a series of processes of the designers interaction with computers to turn the mental shape model into a shape model inside the computers. The prototype shape model needs to be flexible and hence topological, homological and homotopic for it to be useful throughout the entire course of later refinement. Product shape modeling specifies how a prototype shape model is refined into the final product shape model which is manufacturable and hence geometrical in nature. The problems of current shape modeling and commercially available CAD systems are:

(a) for mental shape modeling: no provision or support,
(b) for prototype shape modeling: very little provision or support, except homological invariance in terms of the Euler characteristics in DESIGNBASE[13], and
(c) for product shape modeling: very many and near saturation, but with insufficient quality from the standpoint of product design testing, verification and validation.

Our research indicates the need to promote the importance of the supporting systems for mental shape modeling. Mental shape modeling has been proven to produce drastic results in varieties of areas such as:

(a) effective tropical rain forests growth to recover the lost forests[3],
(b) expert techniques in skiing and martial arts, which shortened the learning time from 3 years to 3 days in deep powder skiing[14] and to 30 minutes in martial arts with around 50 thousand times efficiency increase[6], [17], and
(c) characterizing geographical terrain surfaces for guide map synthesis[18], [19].

Acknowledgments

The author wishes to express heartily thanks to the sponsors of the synthetic world workshops.

References

1. T. L. Kunii, A. G. Belyaev, E. V. Anoshkina, S. Takahashi, R. Huang, and O. G. Okunev, "Hierarchic shape description via singularity and multiscaling," in Proceedings of the Eighteenth IEEE Annual International Computer Software and Applications Conférence (COMPSAC) (Taipei, Taiwan), pp. 242-251, November 9-11, 1994.
2. Aono and T. L. Kunii, "Botanical Tree Image Generation –Theory and System–," IEEE Computer Graphics and Applications, Vol. 4, No. 5, pp. 10-34, 1984.
3. T. L. Kunii and H. Enomoto, "Forest: An Interacting Tree Model for Visualizing Forest Formation Processes by Algorithmic Computer Animation - A Case Study of a Tropical Rain Forest -," Computer Animation '91, Nadia Magnenat-Thalmann and Daniel Thalmann (eds.), pp. 199-213, Springer-Verlag, Tokyo, 1991, [also available as Technical Report 91-008, Department of Information Science, Faculty of Science, the University of Tokyo.]
4. T. L. Kunii and Y. Shinagawa, "Research issues in modeling complex objects shapes," IEEE Computer Graphics and Applications, vol. 14, no. 2, pp. 80-83, 1994.
5. Y. Shinagawa, Y. L. Kergosien, and T. L. Kunii, "Surface coding based on Morse theory," IEEE Computer Graphics and Applications, vol. 11, no. 5, pp. 66-78, 1991.
6. T. L. Kunii and L. Sun, "Dynamic Analysis-Based Human Animation," Computer Graphics Around the World, Proc. of CG International '90, Singapore, June, pp. 25-29, 1989, T. S. Chua and T. L. Kunii (eds.), pp. 3-15 (Springer-Verlag, Tokyo, 1990), [also available as Technical Report 90-008, Department of Information Science, Faculty of Science, the University of Tokyo.]
7. T. L. Kunii, T. Amano, H. Arisawa and S. Okada, "An Interactive Fashion Design System 'INFADS'," Computer and Graphics, Vol. 1, pp. 297-302, 1975, (The Special Issue of the selected papers of the 1st SIGGRAPH Conference); [presented at the 1st Conference on Computer Graphics and Interactive Techniques (the 1st SIGGRAPH Conference), July 15-17, 1974, sponsored by the University of Colorado Computing Center and ACM/SIGGRAPH.]
8. Y. Shinagawa, T. L. Kunii, Y. Nomura, T. Okuno and Y.-H. Young, "Automating View Function Generation for Walk-through Animation Using a Reeb Graph", The Proceedings of Computer Animation '90, Nadia Magnenat-Thalmann and Daniel Thalmann (eds.), pp. 227-237, Springer-Verlag, Tokyo, 1990, [also available as Technical Report 90-002, Department of Information Science, Faculty of Science, the University of Tokyo.]
9. S. Saito, H. Yoshida and T. L. Kunii, "The CrossoverNet LAN System Using an Intelligent Head-End," IEEE Trans. on Computers, Vol. C-38, No. 8, pp. 1076-1085 (August 1989).
10. G. Smoot and K. Davidson, "Wrinkles in Time," William A. Morrow and Company, Inc., New York, 1993.
11. S. W. Hawking, "Brief History of Time - from the big bang to the black holes -," Bantam Books, New York, 1988.
12. T. L. Kunii, "Cognitive Technology and Differential Topology: The Importance of Shape Features, in Cognitive Technology," Barbara Gorayska and Jacob Mey (eds.), North Holland/Elsevier, Amsterdam, the Netherlands, pp. 337-345, 1996, [presented at the First International Conference on Cognitive Technology, 24-27 August, 1995, Hong Kong.]
13. H. Chiyokura, "Solid Modelling with DESIGNBASE - Theory and Implementation -," Addison-Wesley, Reading, Massachusetts, 1988.

14. T. L. Kunii, "Conceptual Visual Human Algorithms: A Requirement-driven Skiing Algorithm Design," The Proceedings of CG International 96, Pohang, Korea, June, pp. 24-29, 1996, IEEE Computer Society Press, Los Alamitos, California, pp. 2-8, June 1996.
15. T. L. Kunii and T. Maeda, "On the Silhouette Cartoon Animation," The Proceedings of Computer Animation 96, Nadia Magnenat-Thalmann and Daniel Thalmann (eds.), IEEE Computer Society Press, Los Alamitos, California, pp. 110-117, June 1996.
16. M. Morse, "The Calculus of Variations in the Large," American Mathematical Society Colloquium Publication, No. 18, Providence, Rhode Island, 1934.
17. T. L. Kunii, Y. Tsuchida, Y. Arai, H. Matsuda, M. Shirahama and S. Miura, "A Model of Hands and Arms based on Manifold Mappings," in Nadia Magnenat Thalmann and Daniel Thalmann, (eds.), Communicating with Virtual Worlds (Proc. CG International '93), pp. 381-398. Berlin: Springer Verlag, 1993.
18. T. L. Kunii, S. Takahashi, "Area Guide Map Modeling by Manifolds and CW-Complexes," in B. Falcidieno and T. L. Kunii, (eds.), Modeling in Computer Graphics (Proc. IFIP TC5/WG5.10 Second Working Conference on Modeling in Computer Graphics), pp. 5-20. Berlin: Springer Verlag, 1993.
19. S. Takahashi, and T. L. Kunii, "Manifold-Based Multiple-Viewpoint CAD: a Case Study of Mountain Guide-Map Generation," Computer Aided-Design, Vol.26, No.8, pp. 622-631, Butterworth-Heinemann, London, 1994.
20. J. W. Milnor, "Morse Theory," Princeton, University Press, N. J., 1963, 1969 (with corrections).
21. A. T. Fomenko, "Topological Classification of All Integrable Hamiltonian Differential Equations of General Type with Two Degrees of Freedom," in The Geometry of Hamiltonian Systems, Tudor Ratiu (ed.), pp. 131-339, Springer Verlag, New York, 1991.
22. Hugh Ching, "Completely Automated and Self-generating Software System," *United States Patent No. 5485601*, January 1996, and Private Communications e-mail: hching@ix.netcom.com.
23. C. G. Langton (ed.), "Artificial Life," p.36, Addison-Wesley, Reading, Massachusetts, 1989.

Theme 2

Architecture

2. The Architecture of Synthetic Worlds

Tosiyasu L. Kunii*
The University of Aizu, Aizu-Wakamatsu City, Fukushima 965-80, Japan

Summary.
This initial research has been carried out to lay down the scientific and engineering foundation of synthetic worlds architecture. The research shows the value of synthetic world architecture to serve as the basis of clarifying a wide range of important problems in a unified manner. The emotion computation aspects of synthetic worlds are explored as a neglected and yet important architectural element.
Key words and phrases: world architecture, synthetic world, real, world power shift, Pax Informatica, cyberspace, virtual reality, world mapping, world transformation, emotion computation

2.1. Architecture

An architecture in general is a global modeling of what we construct. Here, science serves to understand, and engineering to actually build. Architectural modeling in science and engineering serves as the shared core of the theoretical foundation to deliver what understood in science to engineering for construction. Computers serve to truly valuable modeling of worlds. They are more than aids or tools. Computer science and engineering is an academic discipline dedicated to the study of algorithms for automation. An algorithm is a computational sequence, generally based on data structures. In this sense, a model is an abstracted form of algorithms and data structures . Hence, an architecture in our context means an abstracted form of algorithms and data structures for automatically synthesizing worlds by computers.

Now, let us examine the science phase. The core of science consists of the following **three steps of scientific discovery**:

* Current Address: Computational Science Research Center, Hosei University, 3-7-2 Kajino-cho, Koganei-shi, Tokyo, 184-8584 Japan (e-mail:tosi@kunii.com)

1. understanding and hypothesizing through observation,
2. modeling through the generalization and abstraction of what observed, and
3. proving what modeled matches with what observed.

What about the engineering phase? Engineering develops technology to fulfill the social needs, utilizing the results of scientific discoveries in the following **three steps of engineering invention**:

1. The needs have to be discovered. That is the first social step of engineering. As in science, the initial keys to the success are to understand and hypothesize the social needs and the applicability of the scientific discoveries through observation.
2. An engineering model that is expected to satisfy the needs is developed, and then shaped into an architecture for construction.
3. The architecture is tested to prove that it actually does satisfy the needs.

In the last phase, that is the commerce phase, the engineering results are delivered to the society.

2.2. Science of Worlds and World Architecture - Information Science of World Power Shift -

The real world has been the only tangible world for human beings until we have acquired active synthetic worlds on networked computers. For synthetic worlds to be established as architecturally organized entities through engineering, the architectural discipline of synthetic worlds needs to be clarified, understood and validated through the scientific research of the real world we have been living. Hence, information science of world power shift is hypothesized first, then historical data is abstracted and modeled, and finally the theory is validated against the observation of the real world changes. The approach is information scientific, and hence neither the traditional 'economic power theory' nor its predecessor the 'divine power theory.' The conclusion is: we are now living in the era of nonlinear world power shift, and the real world has already started to shift from the great powers to the cooperative powers.

The great powers generally mean military, economical, political, cultural, and/or religious domination. The world is actually nonlinear globally. An example is seen in the shift of the cosmic view from the Ptolemaic theory to the Copernican theory. This is a good example of a shift to a globally correct approximate world model from a locally correct globally wrong world model.

Question on the validity of Paul Kennedy's prediction on the world power shift arose when I read his famous book, 'The Rise and Fall of the Great Powers[1]', immediately after its publication in 1987. First of all, the time period he considered, namely from 1500 to 2000, looked too short to make any valid prediction of the future history. Hence, his prediction of the rise of Japan as the great power after the USA that succeeded the great power from England seemed unrealistic. Here was the 1st order approximation hypotheses of the great power shift I counter proposed the next year in 1988[2] and also in 1989[3] with a proof to invalidate the Paul Kennedys prediction.

Hypotheses	
Hypothesis 1 :	The *power area size* (namely, the size of the major area of a given great power) is in proportion to the information speed (namely, the speed of the information made available to the power).
Hypothesis 2 :	Similarly, the *power period* is in inverse proportion to the information speed

The *Time Period* Considered:	From the Egyptian Dynasties to the current world, namely from 3,100 BC to 2,000 DC.
The *Initial Power Area*:	The Mediterranean Sea and the surroundings, containing Cairo, Athens and Rome with the size of about 2 million km^2

Egyptian Dynasties

3100 BC:	The union of Upper and Lower Egypt by Menes
332 BC:	The acquisition of Egypt by Alexander the Great of Macedon

Roman Empire (Pax Romana)

27 BC:	Octavian became Emperor Augustus
476 DC:	The last king of the Western Roman Empire deposed by the German King Odoacer
1453 DC:	The end of the Eastern Roman Empire

Information speed was 5 km/hour. Just before the battle of Marathon in 490 BC, Phidippides ran 241 km (150 miles) from Athens to Sparta in two days. The validation of the model is against Pax Britanica and Pax Americana. And then, we can predict the nature of the current and future powers (if any!)

Pax Britanica

As the preliminaries of Pax Britanica, there was the age of great voyages 1400 - 1650. Pax Britanica took place as an epoch making social change known as the industrial revolution: British change from agricultural to industrial economies, took place during 1750 - 1850, and then spread out to the Continental Europe and the USA covering the Atlantic cities, London, Paris and New York, with the area size in the order of around 20 million km^2.

The core of the industrial revolution was founded on the British engineering invention of a series of steam engines as typically seen in British engineer Thomas Savery's invention of high pressure steam engine in 1698, and the improvement to the current reliable design with a separate steam condenser and also with the crank and crosshead mechanism by another British engineer James Watt in 1769. From early 1800 steam engine ships and from 1829 locomotives built by a British engineer George Stephenson became popular. In 1829, the Rocket locomotive carried passengers at the speed of 36 mph (58 km/hour).

Pax Americana

The key action taken as the preliminaries to initiate Pax Americana was symbolized in a slogan "to advance knowledge." The real core of the action was the establishments of "research universities" in the USA. In 1990, the formation of the Association of American Universities signified the growth of American research universities during the years of 1900 - 1940, in terms of the numbers of PhDs produced, the volumes in the libraries and dollars expended for research.

The first power symbol of Pax Americana was an aircraft. The Wright Brothers made the first powered and controlled flight in 1903 in North Carolina, and for 45 minutes in 1907. The World War I, 1914 - 1918, saw the beginning of the use of air crafts for wars. In 1924 Imperial Airways in UK gave a birth to a commercial air route. In the World War II, 1939 - 1945, air forces were first intensively used. 1954 Boeing 707 was the first popularly used jet passenger aircraft. Usual speed of passenger flights is now close to 1000 km/hour connecting the Pacific Rim cities, such as San Francisco, Tokyo, Peking, Seoul, Taipei, Hong Kong, Singapore and Sydney, in the area of 12,000 million km^2 as a part of the worldwide networks of commercial air routes. Note that the whole globe surface is 50,000 million km^2.

Computer industry was the second power symbol of Pax Americana, and still is. Here is a brief chronological sketch.

1930-40: The Turing Machine and computability theory were developed by a British mathematician Alan Turing in 1937, known as the Alan Turing's mathematical abstraction of computability.

1943-46: Vacuum tube-based ENIAC was built at Moore School of Electrical Engineering of the University of Pennsylvania by John Mauchly and J. P. Eckert.

1948: William Bradfield Shockley invented transistors at Bell Telephone Laboratories.

1964: IBM 360 dominance of mainframes started.

Mid 1970: UNIX by Dennis Ritchie and Kenneth Thompson at Bell Laboratories initiated the emergence of minicomputers and workstations.

1980: Patterson and Ditzel at University of California, Berkeley invented RISC.

1987: SPARC architecture machines by Sun Microsystems, a derivative of RISC II machines, have ed the down-sizing and occupied 58.8% share in the workstation market in 1991.

1990-: The Intel and Microsoft dominance of PC (personal computer) market share has been leading the world computer industry.

Summary of the Great Power Shift from 3,100 BC to 1987 DC

The Great Powers	Information Carrier	Information Speed	The Power Area Size	The Power Period
Pax Romana	human feet networks	5 - 10 km/hour	2 million km^2	1000 years
Pax Britanica	surface vehicle networks	50 - 100 km/hour	20 million km^2	100 years
Pax Americana	aircraft networks	500 - 1000 km/hour	200 million km^2 (40% of the whole globe surface)	10 years

The hypotheses are validated.

Pax Informatica

Crash: An Economic Crisis and Chaos

The closing of the gold window by Richard M. Nixon on Sunday, August 15, 1971 laid the ground for monetary crisis around the world. The gold window was established in 1946 based on the Bretton Woods Agreement Act, prepared by the representatives of major trading nations, met in 1944 in Bretton Woods, New Hampshire, and signed by Harry S. Truman on Tuesday, July 31, 1945.

Even with a strong economy, on October 19, 1987 called the Black Monday and the next day, October 20, 1987 called the Terrible Tuesday, the entire financial system of the USA came close to a complete meltdown. Computer networks have linked stock exchanges around the world into one market place.

Now, let us add the great power shift from 1988 DC and beyond to the table:

The Great Powers	Information Carrier	Information Speed	The Power Area Size	The Power Period
Pax Romana	human feet networks	5 - 10 km/hour	2 million km^2	1000 years
Pax Britanica	surface vehicle networks	50 - 100 km/hour	20 million km^2	100 years
Pax Americana	aircraft networks	500 - 1000 km/hour	200 million km^2 (40% of the whole globe surface)	10 years
....	....	....	....	....
Pax X	computer networks	0.5 - 1 billion km/hour	500 thousand times of the whole globe surface	5 minutes

Prediction:

- Nonlinear, quality dominant world power shift -

Since the assumptions were validated, how about and what about the prediction of the future of the world? Unlike Paul Kennedy's prediction, X is not Japonica. Now the first time in the human history, not the quantity but the quality takes the lead and will be the master of the stage and scenes of the real world. Computer networks have linked the world at the information speed enough for any power to have the power area size far beyond the whole area of the globe, but with a momentary power period. Through the digital TV technology the USA and Europe have been developing, TV and computer networks can merge together. The hybrid Japanese HiVision technology lacks this potential. Computers become more than theaters. Computer networks can broadcast computer simulated scenes of the "nuclear winter" presented by Carl Sagan of Cornell University in 1983, forcing the power shift from military to economic dominance. The military use of the Prometheus' nucleic fire is now blocked. The power period of 5 minutes causes fast switching of momentary great powers, turning the great powers into cooperative powers. It means no more rise and fall of the great powers. Hence, Pax Japonica is impossible. Japan will be one of the cooperative world powers. The world architectural model has to be changed from a monolithic linear world power shift model such as Pax Romana to a CW-complex model or, when diffeomorphism holds, a manifold model where varieties of coordinates called "cells" or "charts" coexist. The coordinates can represent any values, such as economical, military, cultural, religious, humane or even ethical values. The excess power of computer networks allows the world to select the expert goals out of trivial. Even old analogue TV networks have already caused the world power meltdowns. The domino effect of world power meltdowns took place in the

Eastern Europe in Romania in 1989, in Germany in 1990, and finally in the Soviet Union in the late 1991. Computer networks can cause further extreme power meltdowns. Media events or media shows in the digital cyberspaces of synthetic worlds that I named virtual worlds in 1984[5], [6] will play the central roles in the real world decision makings in the world politics, economics, industry and commerce. Electronic commerce (EC) is a partial example. We are shifting to Pax Informatica that is not any more another great power, but a cooperative power.

The Prediction of the Future of the Real World:
First time in the human history, the thousands of years old and linear **great power architecture** is going to fade out, and a **nonlinear and cooperative power architecture** supported by digital and interactive networks is coming in.

2.3. Assembling Synthetic Worlds and the Design Problem

For any world to be a world socially meaningful and worth synthesized, the number of the components n is usually extremely large. For example, any information system serving as a social infrastructure for digital communication has as the value of n at least a few ten millions. Assembling a synthetic world requires a particular care. Our research result on assembly[4], particularly on assemblability discriminating method and an assembling sequence generating method named SYDEM (*United States Patent No. 5058026*, Oct. 1991)[12] indicates that, given n components, component match steps are:

(a) in the order of 2^n, namely $O(2^n)$, for compositive assembly, and
(b) in the order of n^2, namely $O(n^2)$, for decompositive assembly.

Even for such a small n value n = 50 and the component match step time of 1 micro second, compositive assembly design requires 30 years and decompositive assembly design requires 3 milliseconds. Unless we decompositively design the assembly using architectural design of the world we are synthesizing, we will never come to the completion. After understanding the assembly design process, it is straightforward to understand the difficulty of the initial design of synthetic worlds. Design is essentially an intellectual compositive assembly process at least and it exhibits $O(2^n)$, namely exponential, growth with n, where n is the number of components. "At least" here means simply "without considering the component design process." Therefore, design is a typical nonlinear process and stands for quality.

Japan has built its economic success story for a hundred years, by turning the designs derived from the discoveries and inventions in the rest of the globes into high demand products, and making them available everywhere on the globe. Has Japan returned the earned money back to the design? In a popular industrial field of "a system on a chip where n is one million," the situation of extreme designer shortage in Japan, as often reported in Japanese news papers casts a vast shadow on the future of the real world industry. Even in a relatively simple area of synthetic worlds with only one million components, this is the reality of the situation of Japan. The straightforward explanation of software designer shortage in Japan is given simply by looking at any popular PC operating system that has 10 to 100 times more components than a system on a chip. In the era of quality and nonlinearity, this signifies the problem with a linear and quantity intensive industrial policy, as seen typically in Japanese memory technology. At this turning point of the real world we live, what we human beings truly need is: a policy towards quality higher education, not towards quantity higher education, to advance knowledge in computer integrated education, for example, to teach design for creation of synthetic worlds, not only for CIM. Fortunately, the policy was set and made effective during the past couples of years at the national and regional levels in Japan.

My own plans for a few decades have been targeted towards the design of synthetic worlds for nonlinear world cooperation and coordination. They now have their homes. I can be steady but cannot be relaxed because design is in high order of magnitude expensive process, so is the higher education for it. Further steps we human beings need to take to this end consist of the following:

(a) restructuring the world economy to raise funds for education for design,
(b) restructuring of education to teach mathematics and computation of nonlinearity and cooperation,
(c) development of the core curriculum and the professional education curriculum, and
(d) development of the courseware of nonlinearity, cooperation, coordination and their practices.

2.4. Architectural Bases of Synthetic Worlds

The evolution of computed objects has been taking place, starting from numbers, then to files, and further to multimedia that integrate motion pictures, voices and sounds. The evolution of computer architecture has been hand in hand with the evolution of computed objects, starting from the von Neumann architecture for number crunching, then to virtual storage architecture for file processing, and finally to the current multimedia architecture which includes visual computer architecture. To understand the nature of the evolution one step deeply, let us look at a simple visual element of multimedia: a *surface*. 4D morphological modeling of a surface requires an architectural model which is capable of capturing continuous and irregular shape changes of the surface in the real world, for example a human face as a soft object. The required architectural model is beyond triangulation and mesh control, and is actually based on homotopic modeling. The surfaces of the shapes have to be at least second order differentiable to identify the characteristic points of the Morse theory such as peaks, pits and saddle points[7].

The surface derived from the real world is not necessarily extracted robustly from the measured data sets. Similarly, the surface designed as a part of synthetic worlds are often represented as data sets and hence not necessarily analytic. The issues on the sensitivity of numerical differentiation combined with the identification of the characteristic points have been presenting truly practically large problems to be solved. The problems are theoretical and even philosophical too. Let us look at a couple of cases. Depending on the *required scale range* of the object, when we need to derive a surface of the object from the measured data sets, we choose a few kilometers to microns or even to sub nanometers as the scale range in geographical world modeling. A further larger scale range was needed to establish the cosmic modeling. An example was already seen in the shift of the cosmic view from the Ptolemaic theory to the Copernican theory. As explained before, this was a good example of a shift from a locally correct globally wrong world model to a globally correct approximate world model.

The problem of capturing, extracting and deriving surfaces from the observed data sets (or we often simply call them the 'observation') of the real world objects is, thus, a typical case of transforming or mapping the architecture of the real world through observation as data sets into the architectures of the synthetic worlds through computation as derived surfaces that are often not analytic either. A quite simple cognitive scientific situation will illustrate the case further. Suppose we have a graveled rural road connecting two villages A and B. How to go to B from A? This may sound a foolish question but not really. Any usual human driver can just drive from A to B. Then, what happens when we have an unmanned vehicle contest, and miniature unmanned vehicles are going to compete to reach B starting from B? If a certain unmanned vehicle is equipped with computer vision-based scene cognitive devices to navigate it, it will be lost when the gravels are bigger than the vehicle unless the synthetic world in the computer of the vehicle is installed in such a way that a real world architectural model in the computer matches with the architectural model of the synthetic world and that the global architectural model to represent the road path from the village A to the village B is globally navigating the vehicle passing one gravel particle after another. A rural road is usually winding, and the global architectural model has to count on it. The same situation arises when a micromachine is to be build to get it navigated through a human body so that it doses medicine in higher concentration to the sick part of the body directly instead of giving the medicine to the whole body. Navigating our human visual sense through a computer generated virtual reality world also poses the identical situation. So is a financial trading situation that is a navigation through the real world financial changes in time and space to meet a virtually synthesized 'globally profitable financial trading goal.' The navigators even have their own identity as 'global financial traders.' The whole range of extremely wide open problems of importance can now be handled as a *world mapping problem* or as a *world navigation problem*. The key mapping or navigation indexes are critical points, or more generally singularity signs. They come from differential topology that tells the topological properties of differential spaces. The scale range also needs to be considered and studied carefully as explained above.

2.5. Emotion Computation

Emotion computation is the most important and challenging areas left all the time for future research. Rational information dominance in computation will become clear if we carefully watch what's happening inside computers that have been processing practical applications. Currently, computers process and communicate rational information only. In practice, almost no emotional information has been processed by computers so far for serious major applications.

In the real world, emotional information plays key roles in a wide spectrum of important scenes that range from personal affairs such as marrying somebody, buying expensive things, making friends and enjoying life, to global decisions of national and international policies.

Look at human emotional expressions. In a human body, the major part of emotional information is expressed facially often accompanied with verbal expressions. The human brain dedicates a significant part of it to control facial muscles. Gestural expressions, particularly hand expressions, also heavily serve to convey emotional information. A direct and real-time approach to emotion computation is the key to the architecture of emotion computers that can emotionally interact with human beings at the emotionally intellectual level. For computers to be able to process and communicate emotion directly, it must be observed, understood and responded by computers directly in real-time. To this end, in 1992 we have already developed a stereo photometry to measure human expressions in real time successfully based on our lighting switch photometry[9], [10], [11]. There are categories of emotion. One category of emotion is given morphologically, for example, as photos, paintings, masks, movies or videos bearing certain types of emotion. Other categories are verbal, literal and symbolic. Computer scientific, engineering and commercial study of emotion needs to be conducted from the side of direct observation and modeling of emotion by computers. As mentioned above, physically, emotion takes the forms of facial, gestural and verbal expressions, besides literal, symbolic and pictorial expressions towards which past studies have been inclined.

The morphological observation and understanding of the dynamic change of facial and hand expression by muscular control require 4D modeler-based 4D computer vision. Differential topology as well as differential geometry are the sound framework of morphological modeling. Singularity theory, homotopy theory and Morse theory are the examples.

For relating morphological modeling with emotion modeling, understanding the relationships between the goal-oriented, algorithmic and code-level animation of human emotional expressions is a key to the success as has been studied by Nadia Magnenat and Daniel Thalmann[8]. Goal-oriented animation means the generation of animation algorithms from a given animation goal which in our case is emotional information. A scheme of multi disciplinary cooperation is effective to relate the algorithmic and code-level animation with the goal-oriented animation. For example, the knowledge of experts are crucial on the facial muscle control sequences related to facial and gestural emotional expressions. Further, multi disciplinary cultural research is essential in this area, such as a joint work of theatrical performance experts and model-based computer animation experts with close cooperation with medical doctors working in the related areas, to extend theatrical semiotics research[13].

References

1. P. Kennedy, "The Rise and Fall of the Great Powers," Random House, 1987.
2. T. L. Kunii, "Pax Japonica," (in Japanese), President Co., Ltd., Tokyo, October 1988.
3. T. L. Kunii, "Creating a New World inside Computers - Methods and Implications -," Proc. of the Seventh Annual Conference of the Australian Society for Computers in Learning in Tertiary Education (ASCILITE 89), G. Bishop and J. Baker (eds.), pp. 28-51, Gold Coast, Australia, December 11-13, 1989, [also available as Technical Report 89-034, Dept. of Information Science, The University of Tokyo].
4. T. L. Kunii, T. Noma, and Kyu-Jae Lee, "SYDEM: A New Approach to Computer-Aided Design of Assemblies and Assemblability Testing," Visual Computing: Integrating Computer Graphics with Computer Vision (Proc. CG International 92), T. L. Kunii (ed.), pp. 469-479, Springer, Tokyo, 1992.
5. T. L. Kunii and T. Noma, "Computer Graphics as a Tool to Visualize Virtual Worlds," Video Culture Canada's Second Annual International Festival "The New Media," November 2-6, 1984, Toronto.
6. T. L. Kunii, "Electronic Alice's Wonderland," Graphics Interface 85, May 27-31, 1985, Montreal.
7. T. Ikeda, T. L. Kunii, Y. Shinagawa, and M. Ueda, "A Geographical Database System Based on The Homotopy Model," Modern Geometric Computing for Visualization, T. L. Kunii and Y. Shinagawa (eds.), pp. 193-206, Springer-Verlag, Tokyo, 1992.
8. D. Thalmann and N. M. Thalmann, "Computer Animation," Springer, Heidelberg, 1985.
9. H. Saji, H. Hioki, Y. Shinagawa, K. Yoshida, and T. L. Kunii, "Extraction of 3D shapes from the moving human face using lighting switch photometry,"

Creating and Animating the Virtual World (Proc. Computer Animation '92), Nadia Magnenat-Thalmann and Daniel Thalmann, (eds), pp. 69-86, Springer-Verlag, Tokyo, 1992.

10. H. Saji, Y. Shinagawa, T. L. Kunii, H. Hioki, K. Hara, N. Asada and M. Yasumoto, "Characterization of Object Shapes by Singular Points - with an Application to Feature Extraction of Human Facial Expressions - ," Visualization and Intelligent Design in Engineering and Architecture (Proc. VIDEA'93), pp. 29-43, Computational Mechanics Publications and Elsevier Science Publishers, Amsterdam, the Netherlands, 1993.
11. H. Saji, Y. Shinagawa, S. Takahashi, H. Hioki, and T. L. Kunii, "Measuring Three- Dimensional Shapes of Human Faces by Incorporating Stereo Vision with Photometry Using Blending Functions," Fundamentals of Computer Graphics (Proc. of Pacific Graphics '94, August 26-29, 1994, Beijing, China), Jiannan Chen, Nadia Magnenat Thalmann, Zesheng Tang, and Daniel Thalmann (eds.), pp. 3-18, World Scientific, 1994, [also available in: Proceedings of the 4th International Conference on Computer-Aided Drafting, Design and Manufacturing Technology (CADDM'94), Tang Rongxi (chief editor) pp.3-10 (International Academic Publishers, 1994)].
12. T. L. Kunii, T. Noma and K. Lee, "Assemblability discriminating method and assembling sequence generating method," United States Patent No. 5058026, Oct. 1991.
13. E. Fischer-Lichte, "The Semiotics of Theater," Indiana University Press, Bloomington and Indianapolis,1992.

3. Influence of Emerging Synthetic Worlds on System Architecture

Jean Bellec
Director of System Engineering, ex-Bull, France
(e-mail:JBellec@compuserve.com)

The goal of this presentation is not to present new applications of virtual reality, but rather to evaluate the impact of the popularity of these types of applications on the architecture of systems and more particularly on the specifications of the ubiquitous workstation. I believe that one of the major motivations for pushing the investment into technology of information is the requirement of world synthesis.

I will initially take some examples of applications that are implemented as simulation of reality and that are already available in games for affordable personal computers.

In the example of the commercial program named Flight Simulator^{TM}, the program implements the laws of aerodynamics on models of airplanes.

A data base of the topography and of the geomorphic characteristics of the world is used for showing the landscape visible from the cockpit, as a base for the navigation map. It is used for detection of terrain collision or landings in the sea! The data base is extracted from the official maps and new releases of the program introduce satellite photography for improving the realism of the landscape texture. Special monuments such as the Statue of Liberty, Arc de Triomphe , Notre Dame, Nishi Shinjuku buildings are recorded as 3D models. Obviously, this data base has a potentially unlimited size and more realistic conditions will lead to a gigabyte size for a relatively limited area of the world.

In addition to this visible representation of the world, a data base of the radionavigation facilities is required for the simulation of IFR navigation. This data base includes the characteristics of the radio-navigation aids, such as frequencies, geographical position and 3D features of the directional aids as ILS. The position of the virtual airplane vis à vis those navigation aids is shown in the same way as in real airplanes in a virtual instruments panel.

The flight simulator has been coupled (i.e. a communication link connects two personal computers) with Air Traffic Control simulator where the simulated plane competes for air space with simulated traffic under the orders of an ATC controller who instructs pilots with direction, speed and altitude levels. Pilots reaction to instructions is not necessarily complying and ATC has to give new instructions as it would be the case in reality.

Communications between Flight Simulators can also display the image of other airplanes that are " piloted" by other computers users.

Flight Simulator also includes simulation of wind (direction and speed at miscellaneous altitudes), turbulence and clouds. Aerodynamics of airplanes and outside visibility are modified according to those weather conditions. Weather fronts have been recently introduced. It is now possible to make the weather of the flight Simulator real through a communication link to weather bureau forecast network.

It would not be a big problem to add real planes trajectories inside a traffic controller program if judged useful for controllers training.

This example may help to identify some desirable specifications of the workstation of the future, by pointing out the limitations of the today PC in front of the potential improvements of the application.

While simulators by companies like France's Thomson-CSF and several British or American companies have been available for a long time using several minicomputers and reconstructions of aircraft cockpits, the gap between the FS game and the professional devices is closing and FS is used in aviation schools for amateur pilots. The purely electronic simulation allows easily to change conditions, as well the parameters of the environment or the parameters of the airplane and an add-on of the FS game allows now to change some characteristics of the Concorde or the Airbus to test if changing the power of engines or the width of the wing may improve or deteriorate the performances of the plane. Obviously, the game is far from reproducing accurately the real aircraft characteristics and professional pilots have observed many differences from the reality. But, we are not far of being able to host the CAD drawings of the real airplane inside a personal workstation.

I have spent much time about airplane simulation, but the approach may be the same for other modes of transportation, such as train networks or cars. In addition to fun, such reality simulation has a major application in training, from driving to repairing. Publication of real drawings and characteristics of real machines may lead to interesting property rights issues and may delay some applications of accurate simulators.

Another area of applications may come from the consequences of the globalization of the economy. It becomes desirable to allow a person to work in an environment that is a reconstruction of the environment existing in a remote site. Existing networks to day allows intellectual work to be done on various sites. Astronomers in France are accessing and controlling directly a real telescope located in Chile. Programmers from Bull located in France and others in India work on the same software procedure. Now, virtual reality allows teleworking to be extended to many more activities than simple abstract subjects. Co-working with a person on a different continent will require that several difficult problems be overcome: from the need for synchronizing asynchronous processes required by the time differences to achieving automatic translation of spoken languages.

Globalization might lead to wider competition for salaries and might lead to lower affluence in presently developed countries. It is possible that virtual traveling will replace at least partially the "golden week" crowds of Japanese people visiting western museums and shops, while it would be more difficult to emulate in a computer beach combing or spa relaxing. In a few years, it is probable that visiting museums on computers may achieve the same success as canned music compared to live music attending.

After those considerations on some dimensions of applications, we will now address the requirements that the real world simulation have on the specifications of the **workstation of the future**. By workstation, we name the computing device serving as the interactive mediator with the human. That is not limited to the desktop personal computer or professional UNIX workstation, but also includes different types of mobile devices, some probably yet to be invented.

The workstation has essentially to emulate human **senses**. The sense the closest to be emulated is certainly the view. Stereoscopic view has not received yet an indisputable solution but the problems of color and even the field of view are solved. We have prototypes for the sense of touch and the sense of ear has received satisfactory solutions. Some work on odor analysis and synthesis has been published, but technology has to make significant progresses before applications may reach the general public. The sense of taste seems the hardest to simulate and we are not likely to find to morrow the reproduction of the taste of Beaujolais wine or that of Japanese rice.

We will examine some aspects of the architecture of the most important components of the **workstation**.

By memory, I intend both the main storage and secondary storage. A major characteristics of the real world simulation is that such applications can always use a little bit more **memory** than you have available in your workstation. Eventually, a general purpose VR workstation should store the whole remembrance of the world. Obviously, you may store a part of this memory on some network server, but there are some restrictions of usage, due to the desire for privacy and there is above all the cost (time and money) of accessing your data through a network. Universities and workers in big companies can easily afford high bandwidth networks. I think that we have also to address the needs of private researchers or of small business and the disc storage industry has proven its capability to provide enormous storage capacity at a price that is now less than half a dollar per megabyte. In addition, the majority of applications can use compression algorithms that save more memory.

The most constraining data are images. Presently the definition of images are determined by the capacity of graphic displays. CD photo is based on the television set definition. However, with improvements on displays, we would like to store images at the definition of color slides, such as 3600x3600 with 24bits of color. Even with high compression factors such as 100x, the display of animated video with theater-like definition will require huge amount of secondary storage. We may expect that future fiction movies will be entirely synthetic and may requires far less memory, but I think that we should be prepared not to forget the memory of the past, nor the capture of nature pictures that will probably be mixed with artificial reality in the movies of the future. The requirements of digital sound is also a problem if we wants to store music in its raw format. The conversion of Bela Bartok piano recordings or of Furtwangler interpreted symphonies in some MIDI format, without losing any information is probably an area of your research. Anyway, the storage of a collection of 200 CDs of classical music is likely to occupied 100GB of memory.

Recording real digitized speech raises a similar challenge, but speech handling should require recognition and I do not expect vast collections of real speech except for special applications such as authentication of stock transactions that may be the role of specialized servers. Most applications will use synthesized voice without too much inconvenience.

Finally, the capacity of storage will be what will be financially affordable. I will guess that around year 2000, a workstation will include one gigabyte of main memory used essentially as cache of objects and methods located in secondary writable disc storage of around 16 GB. In addition to that, the workstation will host a copy of books and music of a part of the "world memory" as a library of around 100GB of CDROM.

The major challenge that VR raises to the workstation is presently the **processing** power. All of us have a desire of being able to do 3D rendering of high definition images in a fraction of second. The best artificial pictures we have seen may require a dozen hours of R4000 in your workstations. With what the technology improvements are preparing fo us, we may expect to obtain by year 2000, a processing power of 250 MIPS per processor. The CPU limitations are due to the heat dissipation of faster devices and above all to the economics of the industry that needs money and time to build finer definition devices and to design efficient superscalar processors

I believe that the solution to your problems may come from parallel processing. It will be possible to group 4 (perhaps 16) processors of the present complexity of a Pentium or a 601 PowerPC in a single chip at a comparable cost to the present microprocessors. However, the challenge will be the software at the system level and at the application level. The industry is just starting to invest heavily in those technologies, applying parallel processing to object oriented software and I believe that it may become popular at the workstation a few years after 2000.

Workstations processors receive **inputs** from human actuated devices or from automatic sensors. Existing input devices from keyboard to sensitive gloves through different kinds of mice, trackballs or joysticks are able to solve the needs of the majority of virtual reality applications. Their response time, their inertia and the bandwidth needed for transmission to the system are quite satisfactory. Sensors are also available from the process control industry or from consumers goods. The integration into the workstation of industry originated sensors particularly from the chemical industry may yet raise unsolved cost problems.

To be able to recreate the artificial reality, it is extremely useful to "see" real things. The connection of video cameras is extremely useful to complement artificial objects or persons. The existing technology of videophone and teleconferencing will be used in conjunction with high definition still cameras that may replace flat bed scanners limited to flat 2D objects. An interesting problem is encountered in to day teleconferencing: the capability for different viewers to access a specific field of view. A solution to that problem could be around purely electronic zooming of a wide angle picture produced by HD-TV camera which is likely to be stereoscopic for recording 3D objects.

The most difficult problems to be solved are related to sound (and speech) recognition and selective filtering to isolate one voice in a non random noisy environment. An interesting problems would be to isolate Latin people (French and also Italian) arguing in a meeting without too much listening at each other. The solution probably has to rely on software when several directional microphones is not available

After voice has been recognized or if the computer wants to speak, it is desirable to record the parameters of the voice of the speaker to be able to emulate it and make indistinguishable the voice of real people and the voice of the computer. To avoid abusing, it will be necessary to protect those parameters by encryption keys and also by enforcing legally that protection.

A long dream of Japanese scientists is the computer interpreter able to generate real time translation of foreign languages, decreasing the need to learn foreign vocabulary and grammar and treating all people of countries as equal.. Obviously Europe can also take a big advantage of that technology also.

More serious problems are encountered in the area of **displays.**

The definition available in graphics now currently reach 1200x800 on professional workstation and is 1024x768 on simpler PC. Such a resolution is adequate for LCD or LCD displays having a 20 inches in size, but is very far from eye separation if we had very large screens with a wider angle of view. There is many technological progresses that will find customers as soon they are available, specially for large flat LCD type devices.

Another need to address is the widening of the field of view. Virtual Reality experiments favor integrated helmets or goggles. Some applications, for example military or biking will not object to helmets, It is yet not certain that wearing those devices for the whole day will gain wider acceptability. I believe that there is a good incentive for solving technological challenges, given in account the potential of research sharing with the requirements of HDTV. Color stereoscopic views is still at the experimental level and in quest of innovative solutions for large public affordability.

Other challenges are set in front of architects and engineers. Simulation of features like temperature and humidity is required for a realistic simulation of the user being inside the synthetic world and not in front of its TV set. if the creation of an hot and humid environment is possible with air conditioning, it is not so obvious to change this environment as fast in the reality, and furthermore with the rhythm of some movies.

The control of robotics, related to seat movements and reproduction of some physical sensations seems to be available from the industrial robotics technology.

An stand alone workstation will not be to host many synthetic world applications. There is also some probability that a single user needs to use simultaneously several workstations. The **interconnection** bandwidth differs according to the type of application. We may expect that the bandwidth necessary for numeric HD-TV will be able to satisfy the requirements. Teleconferencing on a mix of real conversation and virtual users may require independent telecommunications lines: dialoguing with real users requires some adaptation to their communications devices.

About **software**, I will like to make a comment about the presentations that we have seen during this week. The majority of programs are independent. The only software common between them are limited to the library offered by the manufacturer of the workstation. It would be desirable that the applications programs you are producing be linkable together, so that the plants growing in a program could be mixed with the virtual landscape subject of an architectural project. Common format for description data bases, use of a common system of coordinates, uniform conventions for linkage conventions are some of the constraints for integration. Independently from research in advanced technology fields and in new subjects of synthesis which could proceed in universities relatively free from economic constraints, the output of your work should be made available to many people. The affordability of the software is extremely dependent on the decrease of its production cost by the reuse of basic software between developers from the industry as well as from universities.

In conclusion, I should say that the success of the technology you are working about is deeply dependent on the cost of the station. At the present time the majority of you works on still expensive workstations that are not affordable to the majority of potential users. When the retail price of the hardware you work for will reach the level of a standard microcomputer or a television set, say around \$1,000, we will see a wide spreading of the virtual reality technologies.

My guess about the potential of hardware technology is that seems achievable by the middle of the next decade, taking in account it takes some years between a design is announced and a computer in a box is available on the shelf of your favorite toy shop.

Building synthetic worlds does not require a big infrastructure breakthrough such as the TV networks did in the 50's, such as the revamping required by digital TV. Obviously, VR is able to use and to take benefit from the "information highways" that are announced for for the next future, but it does not require them, so their pace of development is independent.

Finally, I believe that the processing requirements of the world synthesis favors investments of information technology in parallel processing. It might be the prime customer for parallel processing units affordable by a single individual, which is for the moment recognized as justifying big investments for the important, but limited in size, supercomputer market.

Part II

Design and Implementation: Case Studies

Theme 1

Artificial Life

4. The Meaning of Life – Real and/or Artificial

James M. Goodwin
Department of Computer Software, The University of Aizu,
Aizu-Wakamatsu City, Fukushima 965-80, Japan
(e-mail: james-g@u-aizu.ac.jp)

Summary.

The boundaries between life and inanimate but complex systems are not obvious, even though people commonly think that anyone can instantly distinguish living from non-living systems. This paper attempts to identify those features which "define" life, but presents a number of examples of ambiguous lifelike systems, emphasizing presence or absence of these critical features. Thus we try to understand the meaning of life "as it could be" not only life as we know it. The paper discussses what the purpose to life, if any, might be. It examines the "artificial" nature of artificial life. Noting that it is not always evident how to separate "real" ("natural") life from "artificial" life, we consider whether several systems – both actual and fictional – qualify as life forms, so that we may clarify the issues suggested. New social, political, and legal issues to be considered in light of the probable existence (development?) of artificial life are discussed, referring to examples from current fiction. The paper pays particular attention to computer based life forms, and the use of so-called genetic operators to support synthetic evolution. It then discusses the possible applications of artificial life forms and methods, using goal directed synthetic evolution, to problems for the benefit of humanity. It finally examines the limitations of current methods and the benefits to be obtained by the use of life-derived computer methodology, both in the construction of synthetic worlds and in the real world.

Key words: Artificial life, genetic operators, genetic algorithms, genetic programming, evolutionary programming

4.1. Introduction

This paper is not intended to be either a definitive or a new description of artificial life. That is too large a task. There have been many conferences [1], [2], books [3] and papers devoted to artificial life or to its aspects, but as yet there is no definitive understanding of the field. Nor is there general agreement on even a definition of life, or of features by which it could be recognized, for example if discovered on some distant planet. Even the word "artificial" is a cause for concern. Some have gone so far as to suggest that if we develop new life forms, even they must be regarded as natural, since they would themselves be an outgrowth of evolution.

This paper is, instead, devoted to exploring the ambiguity of the definition of life, real or artificial, and to the exploration of some of the directions that are indicated by the acceptance of the biological paradigm. Although this introduces many philosophical questions, this paper is not intended to explore in detail the large (and confused) philosophical literature. On the other hand, such questions can not be avoided.

Life, if it is anything, is adaptive. It is the result of complex and nonlinear processes, which are not amenable to the reductionist methodology which has been the basis for most past scientific advances. Such often used and previously powerful tools as superposition are not appropriate to such processes, nor are the heretofore highly valuable approaches such as perturbation theory. Once this is recognized, it is then possible to look for new tools which can be used to explore this subject, and which can be turned outward and used in the solution of difficult problems.

4.2. The Distinction between Living and Nonliving

The three categories. We need to consider the distinction between *living* things, *dead* things (things that were once living but are no longer), and *non-living* things (those which never satisfied the conditions for life). It is the familiarity which people have with instances which clearly belong to one or another of these categories that leads to their surprise at the suggestion that the distinction may not always be clear. But closer examination leads to the conclusion that the boundary between these categories is often fuzzy, and the definition of membership is not easy. As we look at ambiguous cases, we are led to the realization that the distinction is not always evident. This leads to the conclusion, growingly more pragmatic than philosophical, that methods used by living things and by life as a class may be applicable to the solution of difficult problems if used by nonliving things, such as computer programs and mathematical theory.

The three views.

(a) The "life is obvious" view
This common position holds that there is a clear distinction between living and non-living things; and though it may be difficult to codify criteria, it is clear, given an example, whether it is living or not. In this view, it is not possible to change from Not-Life to Life.

(b) The weak claim [9]
This view holds that computer processes and the like, and artificially

created chemical or biochemical entities, even if they have the behaviors attributed to life, are only simulations of life, but not instances of life. This follows the same line of reasoning that says that a blueprint of an airplane is not an airplane, and can never become one. Nor can a computer simulation of an airplane ever become an airplane. The missing physical attributes are critical, and essential to the real airplane or real life. On the other hand, their presence may not be sufficient to establish life.

(c) The strong claim [9]
Any list of criteria, or any definition which is sufficiently rich to include all biological life as we know it, will be unable to exclude certain classes of computer or physical processes; so they MUST be considered to be alive. Similarly, physical systems such as robots, or biochemical systems which meet the defining properties well enough, must be considered to be alive.

The importance of boundaries. We must consider how to define the extent of an organism. Are complex organisms alive or just conglomerates? In particular, we should ask if humans should be regarded as living things or just as communities of living and nonliving parts. Conversely, we must ask if there is a transition between life and non-life in supposedly living organisms, and if so, where that transition occurs. In particular, if a person is alive, does that imply that his cells are also alive, or at least capable of being alive? If a cell is alive, does that imply that its DNA is also alive, or at least capable of being alive? And if the DNA is alive, does that imply that its carbon atoms are also alive, or at least capable of being alive? Is the air (especially the O_2) and the CO_2 we exhale a part of us? Is it therefore alive? What about our toenails, or our bones? If in fact a living organism is composed of nonliving things, we must ask what essential point makes something alive?

Temporal boundaries are also important. Must a candidate organism perform life functions all the time? Can it rest or cease some functions and still be considered alive? Must it perform all of the functions together at least some of the time? The answers to these questions is far from obvious. They have been studied for a very long time without notable resolution.

John Von Neumann [13] suggested that the essence of life was the ability to reproduce a copy of the organism from a "soup" of material without assistance. To that end he suggested a cellular automaton model which could perform the task assigned. (Cellular automata models have become a fruitful field of investigation and Conway's *Game of Life* has spawned its own community of investigators.) Simpler solutions have been developed since Von Neuman's work was completed, notably by Langton [8], but all such solutions have the same question to answer: where are the boundaries of the organism? The cellular automaton model depends on states and locations outside the organism's apparent bounds for its state updating. It is *not possible to separate the organism from the environment* and still have it reproduce.

The implications of these models are, first, that life is not separable from the environment; second, that life is not separable from the non-living material from which it is made; and thirdly, that the essence of life lies not in its materials or in vitalistic natural forces, but rather in nonlinearity, complexity, and self-organization. Thus the building of artificial life models has the promise of harnessing the power and the flexibility of those now active areas of study, and of passing beyond the restricted successes of our older analytic tools. Computer modeling is, of course, one of the essential tools of these new fields.

Necessary properties of life: Candidates and counter-examples.

Metabolism - eating. Eating can be defined as taking in materials from outside which are modified for the use of the organism - e. g. to build its *self*. If eating is necessary, we must ask if we don't eat, are we no longer alive? For how long can we fast? It has been pointed out [12] that some seeds can remain dormant for thousands of years without metabolizing yet, under appropriate conditions, are capable of germinating, much as a computer process, temporarily swapped out, can remain dormant for long periods only to become active again when conditions warrant.

How broadly can eating be interpreted? Stars absorb hydrogen from "outside" and use it to produce energy by nuclear fusion and even to grow in size or mass by accretion. Galaxies "eat" other smaller galaxies and also "eat" intergalactic hydrogen molecules or dust, to make new stars (grow to become bigger or "better" galaxies?). Are they to be considered alive? Plywood objects have been exhibited [10] which "eat" by attaching to other objects by hooks, and use the other objects to make new and more sophisticated forms. Do they meet the criterion? If not, why not?

Metabolism - waste ejection? The metabolic process includes waste product rejection. Is it necessary to eject waste to be considered alive? If so, it is important to define waste in a general manner to avoid overly restrictive interpretations.

When an organism metabolizes, that non-equilibrium process results in a decrease in the entropy of the organism, but in a net increase in the entropy of the universe. The increased entropy, whether in the form of solid garbage or disordered energy (heat) is what is generally called waste. In fact, there is some possibility that efficient and rapid production of garbage and of increased entropy may be the ONLY hallmark of life. The more sophisticated the life form, the faster it seems to create entropy.

Waste production is not special to life. Even Penrose's plywood creatures can produce waste. Figure (1) shows examples of complex Penrose creatures. The left panel shows two identical plywood objects, with levers, hooks, etc. The right panel shows them joined, making a "creature".

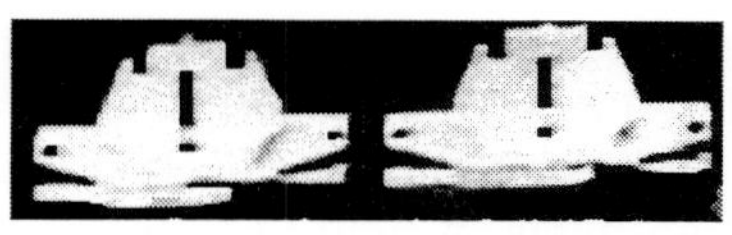

FIGURE 1. Complex Penrose creature

FIGURE 2. Penrose creature eating and making waste

Figure (2) shows Penrose creatures as they take in "food", make it part of their "body" and eject material (out the back) as waste. The left panel of figure (2) shows an object on the left of the creature, approaching it. The center panel shows the object absorbed into the creature, and the creature ejecting an unneeded waste component out the back. The right panel shows yet another object being absorbed and the last original part of the creature being ejected. What remains is a creature, identical to the original, but with all new components, and some unneeded waste.

Metabolism - growth. Is it necessary to grow to be alive? Does growth refer to the whole organism growing, or to just some parts growing? Is a single cell enough? It should be noted that fingernail growth continues in clinically dead people. Are the nails alive? Are the people not yet dead? Again, Penrose's plywood objects can grow by accretion, as can crystals. Figure (3) shows such growth. The simple symmetrical objects shown are subjected to shaking, to simulate thermal agitation. The objects, by themselves, do not come together, but bounce apart.

FIGURE 3. Penrose creatures, growing by accretion

The top panel of figure (3) shows the system with two of the objects joined by an external experimenter, and placed as a *seed* among the objects. Agitation causes adjacent objects to tilt, and eventually the hooked parts engage, linking objects together. The bottom panel of figure (3) shows the process after linkup. Even though the initial pair is extremely unlikely to be formed by agitation, once a pair is formed, the formation of the extended object becomes very easy. If the pair creature is an example of life, then "life begets life" is an accurate description of the process above. It is an example of an autocatalytic process, in which a very improbable process, once it occurs, makes it easy for other similar processes to occur. The result is replication, in apparent violation of the laws of chance. This will be discussed in more detail later in this paper.

Mobility. Although mobility is normally considered important, and most animals are mobile, most plants, such as trees, are not. An obvious case where mobility is not needed for life is the case of paralyzed people. Mobility thus seems not to be necessary.

Reproduction. Even this critical function is not essential to categorize a candidate as alive. Mules are unable to reproduce, but are regarded as alive. People cannot reproduce except for certain periods during their lives. Single cells reproduce by division, so such methods must be considered acceptable. But even Penrose's plywood creatures can reproduce, making copies of themselves from materials in a *soup* of objects, driven only by random agitation, akin to heat energy.

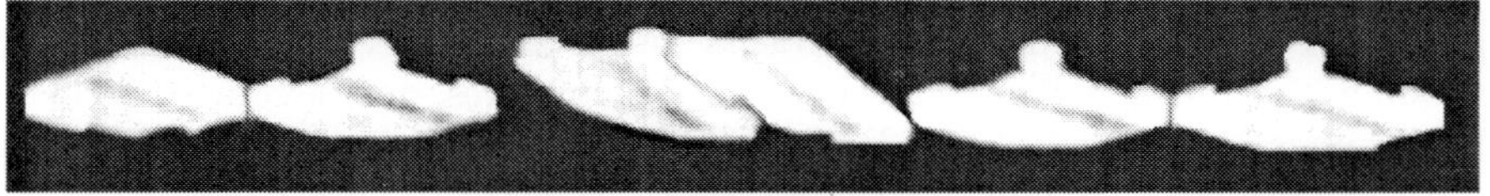

FIGURE 4. Penrose creatures, in a soup of components

FIGURE 5. Penrose creatures, reproducing in the soup of components

Figure (4) shows objects of two kinds mixed in a linear soup of "nutrient", together with an already linked pair as a seed. Figure (5) shows the system after agitation. A "child", in this case identical to the parent seed, has formed. Notice that the process happens by itself due to random shaking in the soup, catalyzed by the presence of the seed, which is no way changed in the process.

FIGURE 6. Penrose creatures, uniting prior to reproducing

A more complex plywood object which has a more complicated, but also more compelling, reproductive pattern is shown next. In figure (6), the left panel shows two objects, linked to form a creature. The center panel shows an object approaching from the left, and the right panel shows the object absorbed into the creature, while a fourth object approaches from the left. In figure (7), the left panel shows the fourth object being absorbed into the creature, and the right panel shows the creature, divided automatically into two creatures identical to the original. This is akin to the way that many "real" single cell creatures reproduce.

FIGURE 7. Penrose creatures, reproducing by division

Evolution. This seems to be essential, but the case of the mule is again striking. Since it can not reproduce, it can not evolve. In fact, one can make a case that mules ARE artificially created life forms. But they were created from already living parents by normal means.

For evolution to occur, reproduction *must* be *corrupt* rather than producing an exact copy of the parent. This is what is often used to eliminate crystals as life forms. Furthermore, in the case of sexual reproduction, it is not possible to exactly duplicate *both* parents. But then the meaning of *reproduction* must be examined more carefully. It is less than clear what is being preserved by nonfaithful reproduction.

If an environment is static, an organism may *solve* the problem of coping with its environment so well that it need not, and does not, evolve, it would seem odd to deny that such an organism were alive simply because of its success.

On the other hand, rocks, mountain ranges, landscapes, stars, and even galaxies change and evolve through time. Since these are not normally considered to be alive, evolution is not unique to life.

Thus it seems that evolution is neither unique to life nor is it a property necessary to categorize something as living.

Mortality? Is this definable? If we can't say what "alive" means, how can we define "no longer alive"? Nor is it clear that all living things die. When cells reproduce by division, is seems hard to decide when "it" dies or even what "it" is after many generations. It would be very odd to claim that an object that never dies can never be considered alive, just because of that. Again, this would rule out success.

Life and the Second Law. One trait that seems common is the creation of waste, loosely defined as the increase of unusable items. Since usable items have some distinguishing trait which makes them suitable for some purpose, they are examples of order. Unusable items are in this sense disordered. Thus making waste implies increasing disorder, raising the entropy of the universe. The Second Law of Thermodynamics says that real processes increase the entropy of the universe. Living beings, by metabolism, increase their own order, but do so at the expense of adding even more disorder to the rest of the universe. Living things are typically not in thermal equilibrium with their environment, and the more "advanced" species are further from equilibrium. Mammals, for example, maintain a rather constant temperature, independent of their environment. Thus, an objective observer might be tempted to say that more advanced life forms make entropy faster than less advanced or nonliving forms. One might even say that life appears to have one definable goal: the creation of waste at the greatest rate possible.

Properties sufficient to establish "aliveness". It is tempting to ask if there are *any* properties sufficient to establish a thing as being alive. Creating waste, while characteristic, is not sufficient since all processes create net waste. But some have claimed that all intelligent creatures are also alive, or that all self-aware creatures are alive. Let us consider whether these properties are really sufficient.

(a) Intelligence
It seems as difficult to define intelligence as life, if not more so. So there is no unique way to recognize intelligence, nor is it clear any more if all intelligent things are alive. As an example, skillful chess playing was once a mark of intelligence. We now have computer programs which play chess skillfully, but are not regarded as living. So intelligence may not be sufficient.

(b) Self awareness
Again it seems as difficult to define self-awareness as life, if not more so. There is no unique way to recognize self-awareness. One method is to ask the candidate if it is self-aware. But computers can be programmed to reply "yes", but dogs can not. Since this test may well give the wrong answer, and since there seems no other sure way to establish self awareness, self awareness seems also not to be sufficient to categorize something as alive.

4.3. Life "as it could be"

Chemical approach. A number of investigators have begun to look at reconstruction of the building blocks of natural life - DNA, RNA, and the like - from the basic chemical constituents contained in a "soup". Others have looked at the conditions required to produce such elements spontaneously, and have speculated that the existence of autocatalytic interacting sets of components are the necessary ingredients to create self-organization, even with members that are extremely unlikely to occur by themselves.

For example, consider a set of three components, A, B and C, with A occurring commonly, but B and C occurring only rarely due to chance perturbations, such as cosmic rays striking A. If B can act as a catalyst making the formation of C from A more likely than if B were not present, and C can similarly act as a catalyst for the formation of B from A, then it is possible to produce large quantities of both B and C.

The two charts in figure (8) show such a situation. The left chart shows the quantities of the three components present as a function of time. The right chart shows only the "rare" components, B and C. It should be noted that there are negligible quantities of B and C present for a long time, but at some point the amounts rise rapidly, and with suitable rate parameters, stabilize.

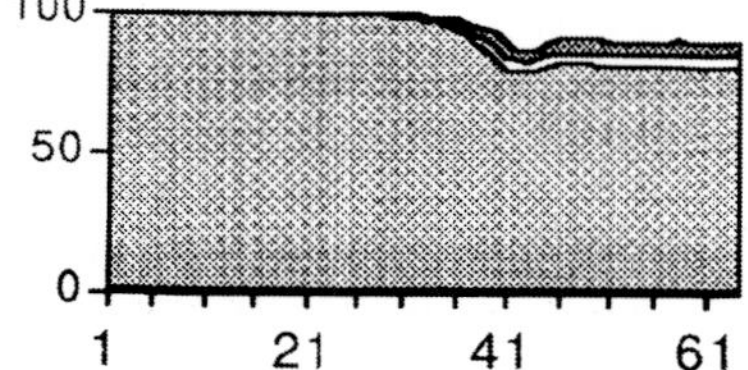

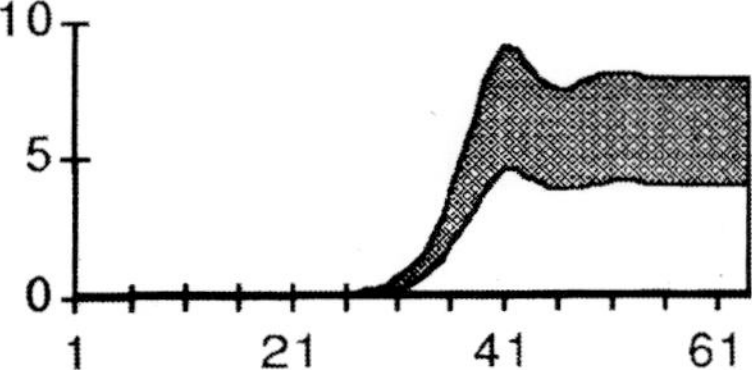

FIGURE 8. Time development of autocatalytic system

The iterative equations governing the system shown are:

$$B_{i+1} = A_i R_B C_i + \mathrm{RAND}()/K$$
$$C_{i+1} = A_i R_C B_{i+1} + \mathrm{RAND}()/K$$
$$A_{i+1} = (A_i - B_i - C_i)/(A_i + B_i + C_i)$$

Here $R_B = 0.012$ and $R_C = 0.013$ are the rates for producing B and C respectively with A present. RAND() is a uniformly distributed random variable with $0 < \mathrm{RAND}() < 1$, and $K = 1{,}000{,}000$.

The charts show that the 'final' levels of B and of C are each about 4. But if A were absent, the occurrence of B or C would be about $1/1{,}000{,}000$.

If B were not able to catalyze the production of C (i. e. if $R_C = 0$), the occurrence of C would be about $1/1,000,000$.

Similarly if $R_B = 0$ then the level of B would be about $1/1,000,000$. Note that raising or lowering the level of noise, K, only changes the time until the onset of macroscopic production of B and C. Qualitative changes of the behavior of the system are due only to changes in the rates, R_B and R_C.

Biological but not carbon. The argument above made no reference to DNA, RNA or carbon based life, and so would be true for any naturally occurring autocatalytic set, or for that matter, one that was constructed. (Much as the set A B C was constructed; this simple set is not life, but it shows at least one aspect of life, the spontaneous emergence of unlikely systems from a soup.) Furthermore, the discussion above was not restricted to biological systems.

Computer viruses. This is one of the most ambiguous forms. The similarity to real viruses is almost total, but even real viruses are ambiguous. They cannot function but look much like a crystal if they have no host. But given a host they become active, and reproduce. Computer viruses are similar. One suggestion on coping with computer viruses is to create (or even breed) "search and destroy" programs to selectively kill them. Then one must ask about the status of these programs as living entities.

The methodology of computer based artificial life.

Genetic algorithms and genetic operators. The serious study of artificial life may be credited to the development and use of so-called genetic operators [5] and genetic algorithms. These methods were couched in the terminology of biology, but were strictly defined computational approaches. Creatures are formed based on instructions in their "genetic codes", often a simple binary string. These creatures are assigned a task, and evaluated for "fitness" based on how well they achieve the task. A genetic pool is created by replicating the most successful members in numbers proportional to their individual fitness. Pairs are chosen at random from the pool to serve as "parents" for the next generation. Then genetic operators are applied to create new members, forming the next generation of programs. Their fitness is evaluated and the cycle is repeated. There are two commonly used genetic operators:

(a) Mutation
Each parameter of the program is changed to a new randomly chosen value. The change is done, in successful applications, only rarely, using an average probability of changing a value, called the mutation rate. The effect of the mutation operation is to produce diversity in the gene pool,

causing the overall search to have the opportunity to try solutions far from the current "good" area.

(b) Crossover (sexual mating)
A random point is chosen in the descriptor of each of the two programs being mated. The programs are cut into front and back halves. The front of the first is attached to the back of the second to make a new "organism" and vice versa to make another. These programs are the children which form the next generation. They resemble, but are not identical to, their parents. The effect of crossover is to keep some properties which hopefully contributed to the fitness of each parent, and combine them in the hope of producing a more fit child. If successful, the child will then continue and contribute to the next gene pool heavily. If the combination is not fit, as is often the case, the child is simply not allowed to reproduce, and those unfit characteristics die out. This produces an adaptive and usually convergent search.

It should be noted that neither genetic algorithms nor evolution itself evaluates the appropriateness of *individual parts* of the genetic material. Nor is the fitness the sum of fitness of the individual components. Instead, fitness and likelihood of survival is evaluated based on the performance of the organism resulting from the genetic code in the task required. Individual bits are *not* evaluated and purposefully manipulated, but changed stochastically. The *results* of these changes are evaluated, not the changes themselves. At first this appears rather wasteful and inefficient, and one is tempted to believe that careful analysis could do much better. This seems not to be the case in complex problems.

Artificial ants finding artificial food in artificial mazes. As an example of the application of genetic algorithms to problem solving, consider the problem of locating objects in a region with unknown structure. An instance of this problem [7] places food along an irregular, bent, and even broken trail through a 32 X 32 toroidal grid (one step up from the top goes to the bottom; similarly for right and left). The goal is to "breed" an artificial ant capable of running the trail and finding all the food in minimal time.

An ant has a single binary "sensor" which can only detect presence or absence of food in the square directly in front. An ant can turn right (90°), turn left (90°), move one square forward, or do nothing. The sensory input and the possible actions were encoded as a bit string description of a finite state automaton (453 bits long in this case).

Genetic algorithms were applied to randomly chosen strings (in parallel since there is no interaction except for the choice of the breeding pool) and produced an ant capable of running the trail within a time limit, and getting all the food. The authors also considered "smart" ants, represented as multilayer neural networks. The values and weights were encoded as a bit string and genetic algorithms were applied. They again succeeded in producing an artificial ant capable of running the trail within the time limit, and getting all the food, obtaining a totally different kind of solution.

But the fitness function chosen did not give a reward to speed, only a penalty for "timing out". Better ants could have been obtained with a better fitness function. Similarly, the successful ants got very good at the trail presented, but had little luck with a new trail. They had mastered the problem given, but could not generalize to other trails. This is because the problem space was not rich enough to reward the development of general methods for searching trails. If several similar trails to the given one were presented to the ant being evaluated, it would have been successful and chosen for breeding if it could have developed a method that would work on all of those trails, perhaps internally encoding the common features of the trails given. Then an ant capable of running all of the trails presented might be able to run a new trail with similar properties.

This is a lesson learned from life: a challenging, but not too difficult, environment discourages lazy life forms and produces clever ones. The lesson can be applied to computing as well, if the adaptive paradigm is adopted.

Evolutionary computations as life forms. There have been a number of efforts to use genetic operators and genetic algorithms to direct the parallel development of sets of programs [6], beginning with randomly constructed programs. There are two major approaches, directed and undirected evolution.

Directed evolutionary programs. A goal is chosen and programs generated are evaluated on how well they achieve the goal ("fitness"). A *genetic pool* is formed by replicating, in proportion to their fitness, the tree structures underlying the programs, removing the ones with least fitness, and choosing trees at random from this pool to be "parents". Genetic operators are then applied to these parent trees. For example, crossover is done by picking points on the parent trees, and exchanging subtrees. Of course, most programs so generated are terrible at achieving the goal since they are constructed randomly, with no concern for their objective.

However, perhaps surprisingly, this method can generate some quite successful, and apparently imaginative, solutions to a wide variety of problems. The method can be described as an adaptive search through the space of programs, to locate programs which are good or even optimal at their task, as evaluated by the fitness function. Such evolved programs seem to have made purposeful developments and adaptations, require sustenance (machine cycles), adapt to their environment, and produce offspring that are not simple clones. The old codes "die" and the dead codes are waste material that needs to be dealt with.

Undirected evolving codes. An alternate form of "computer program as life form" has been suggested [11], in which a pseudo machine code is used to prepare a program whose *sole function* is to make a working copy of itself (thus *reproducing*) somewhere in memory. Once created, the copy is allocated its own machine cycles, and its code space is write protected. When multiple organisms are present in memory, the external computer program, "Tierra", allocates machine cycles (food) to each on a round robin basis. The programs are subject to occasional mutation. At the time of creation, an entry for the program is placed in a "Reaper Queue", and if memory is full, the program at the top of the queue is "killed". It no longer gets machine cycles, and its code space can be written on by others. Anytime a program generates an error (e.g. as a result of a bad mutation) it is advanced in the Reaper Queue. There is no explicit fitness function, and no crossover.

Even without these typical tools, this simple set of principles produces a rich array of evolving codes which develop a wide variety of techniques to more efficiently reproduce and survive. The Tierra creatures can *move* to new locations, invade other creatures and use their cycles, and even utilize "dead" code segments from unsuccessful creatures if their programs (produced by random modification) so dictate. Notice that the round robin resource allocation puts a premium on smaller and more efficient programs. Bizarre programs evolve, including parasites and cooperating societies. The author calls the programs "creatures" and the implication is that they are in some sense alive.

Coevolution of multiple species. A variant on the directed evolution was suggested [4] in which the goal was to breed a good sorting program using genetic operations. While the attempt succeeded, the resulting program was not as good at sorting lists of numbers (prepared by the experimenters) as were some available methods. In an attempt to improve the result, the *lists* were also treated as organisms to be bred, with a quite different fitness function from that of the sorters: a *fit* list was one that took a long time to be sorted, one that "broke" the sort programs. The sorters and the lists were allowed to evolve together. The lists became trickier to sort and the sort programs got better at sorting. The best sorter was comparable with the best hand coded programs. As a bonus, the method provided a test set of hard to sort lists, which could be used as sorting benchmarks. The lesson was that in a competitive environment, there was more pressure to improve, and *both* artificial life forms took advantage of that pressure.

A rather interesting side point should be noted. Although the evolved program code was efficient, the method used was more or less unintelligible; the pattern of swap and compare steps, rather than being neat and orderly as in a "programmed" sort routine, looked fractal. The evolved lists, on the other hand, seemed to contain bits and pieces of worst case lists for a variety of typical programmed sorters.

Computer Robots. We now have industrial robots that slavishly follow a set of instructions to do a preassigned task. On the other hand, artificial neural net based industrial robots have been developed which were able to locate and reject "bad" bottles from an assembly line. These were not programmed, but were adaptively trained by having an expert at the task pick bottles and "tell" the computer (which used a video camera to sense the bottles, caps, labels, etc.) whether the bottle was good or bad. No reasons were explicitly stated for the decisions of the expert, which in some cases were wrong or at least unrepeatable. The robot learned to do the task, faster and sometimes *better* than the expert, and was used commercially until the originating *company* died. This robot showed intelligence but not life, in some views.

But it appears possible in the future to evolve programs to design robots, to evolve the robots themselves, or to evolve robots which design and build new and better robots. At that point the question of whether they are reproducing or of whether they are alive could become irrelevant, or could become the source of moral dilemmas. But the bits and pieces needed to build such worker robots (e. g. adaptive neural network learning and genetic algorithms) seem to exist now.

Judging the criteria: ambiguous candidates. The table below lists in abbreviated form a number of candidate life forms, some natural and some artificial, some obviously alive and others obviously (to most people) not alive. Consider how well they satisfy the suggested criteria.

The examples considered are: crystals, rocks, DNA molecules, viruses, computer viruses, Tierra computer program creatures, chain letters, coral reefs (made largely of dead coral), Penrose's plywood creatures, automobiles, television sets, garbage dumps, national economies, bureaucracies, political systems, stars, galaxies, and computer programs produced by directed evolution. Some of these have already been discussed. Chain letters, which have not been discussed yet, are surprising.

A chain letter is a recursively defined creature – a list of names (sent to the person at the bottom of the list) together with a request that:

(a) an "award", usually cash, be sent to the top person on the list;
(b) the name of the top person then be deleted;
(c) multiple copies of the list be sent to new recipients with the recipient's name added to the bottom.

The request indicates the benefit for participation – getting multiple awards when one's name reaches the top of the lists. Chain letters *eat* names, paper, and cash; they *grow* as names are added; they *reproduce* at an alarming rate; they change and *evolve* at the hands of current recipients who try to increase their benefits; they *move* rapidly through the mails; and they leave used copies of themselves and their paper as *waste*. Individual letters *die* when they are received and discarded, and even the species can die out when the exponential growth is seen to be a problem. Chain letters are, of course, aided by people in their growth and reproduction cycle, but in that sense they are like a virus. Moreover, *no* life form can survive in isolation; in the same sense, *people* can be regarded as a virus, with the earth as the host.

Only humans and chain letters, among those listed in the table, get a perfect score. Chain letters are surprisingly as good a match as humans, but are hardly regarded as alive. While this must call the criteria into question, it seems difficult to formulate better ones. Perhaps the good result for humans is only chauvinism by the human creating the categories and the evaluation. It may reflect the common attitude that "life is what *we* do".

Note that automobiles also do quite well, although their reproduction, like the chain letter, is the result of a symbiotic relation with humans. An alien observer might regard automobiles as the dominant life form on the planet, subject to an infestation of humans, seen as parasites which use the automobile-hosts to carry out important functions such as food gathering, mobility, and even sexual reproduction.

Note also that stars and galaxies seem to fit the criteria about as well as humans. Since their motion is complex and unpredictable, probably being chaotic, it may be possible to claim that they are travelling according to their desire, rather than blindly following physical laws. On the other hand it is hard to make the contrary argument, that humans are NOT bound by physical laws, but instead have some mystical "life force" which distinguishes living beings from nonliving things.

Unless we accept the position that atoms and even subatomic particles are alive, we must conclude that either living things can be made from a sufficiently rich or complex combination of nonliving things (which makes the drawing of the boundary difficult) or else that nothing is really alive.

It should be noted that evolving is not a property of individual organisms, but of the species. On the other hand, since members of a species are normally somewhat different from one another, it is sometimes hard to define what is meant by species, and just what it is that is evolving, and what is being preserved.

SYSTEM	EAT	WASTE	GROW	MOVE	REPRODUCE	EVOLVE	DIE
crystals	accrete	yes[a]	yes	may	accrete	NO	dissolve
rocks	accrete	erode	some	may	division	shape	erode
DNA	?	?	NO	with cell	yes	yes	?
biological viruses	yes	yes	some do	yes	yes in host	yes	can
computer viruses	yes	yes	NO	yes	yes in host	can	can
Tierra creatures	yes code	cycles[b]	NO	to new memory	yes	yes	yes
plywood creatures	yes	yes	yes	random	yes	NO	NO
coral reefs	coral?	itself?	yes	NO	can	yes	dead
cars	gas, oil	lots	rare	yes	seem to	yes	yes
garbage dumps	yes, new garbage	sca-venge[c]	yes	by[d] growth	seem to	NO	NO
television sets	electri-city	total?	NO	rare	seem to	yes	yes
chain letters	yes	yes	yes	yes	yes	yes	yes
trees	yes	yes	yes	NO	yes	yes	yes
mules	yes	yes	yes	yes	NO	yes	yes
humans	yes	yes	yes	yes	yes	yes	yes
bureau-cracies	yes - forms	yes - time	yes	yes	yes	yes	NO
national economies	yes	unclear	yes	NO	some have	yes	maybe
political systems	yes	yes	yes[e]	yes	NO	yes[f]	yes
stars	yes (H)	yes-us[g]	yes	yes	divide[g]	yes	yes
galaxies	yes-stars	yes	yes	yes	divide	yes	yes
evolved programs	new code	yes	yes	NO	yes	yes	perhaps

Table 1. Summary of criteria for life, as applied to candidates

(a) Some materials from the nutrient bath are unused in the crystal.
(b) In addition to time for cycles, electricity is needed and heat is ejected as waste also.
(c) Material removed from the dump by scavengers is no longer useful to the dump as garbage, and can be considered as its waste.
(d) As the dump grows it moves, much as an amoeba extrudes pseudopodia.
(e) Growth of countries by expansion at borders or by conquest also produces extension of its political system.
(f) Popular political systems are copied, e.g. "exporting democracy".
(g) We are produced using heavy elements created only during supernova explosions during stellar life cycles; new stars are also born from the ejected material.

4.4. Morality: the Rights of Life

Existence - endangered species laws. The smallpox disease was nearly eliminated from the earth a few years ago. A group of people came forward, asking that some representative of the smallpox virus be kept alive, since it had become an *endangered species.* Their argument was that humans did not have the *right* to wipe out an entire species, and, secondarily, that there might come a time when the virus could prove useful in coping with some as yet unknown problem. (The moral problem solved itself – the virus managed to rebound by its own actions.)

This calls to mind another moral question: why is it considered somewhat acceptable to kill a number of members of a species, but less acceptable to destroy the whole species? Is this not in fact a tacit acknowledgement that the *species* is an organism with its own rights, and perhaps goals and desires? Similarly, a few cells or even body parts may be destroyed without the action being called murder. But annihilation of a race is commonly treated as a more severe crime than simple murder. We should consider whether life forms, real or artificial, have any inherent rights, and if so, why.

We often judge the rights of life forms based on their intelligence. A sheep seems less intelligent than a dog (dogs herd sheep but not vice-versa), so it is more danger of being eaten. Fish seem still less intelligent, and are killed with impunity. Vegetables show still less intelligence, and are eaten by nearly everyone. We do not even use the word "kill" in this context, but instead such words as "harvest", which have no negative feeling. Of course we may be using a poor measure of intelligence, or merely dismissing life forms unlike ourselves. But in the case of computer viruses or evolved programs, the question of the basis for "having rights" needs to be addressed.

Non-exploitation. One possible right is continued existence. Another is non-exploitation. Most people now consider slavery as immoral, but have few qualms about using animals to pull plows or guard homes, regarding animals as possessions. Plants are given even less concern, even though trees are sophisticated biochemical factories which cause insects to do their bidding by use of odor and imagery. How then should we treat artificial life forms if we create (or discover) them? The problem has been addressed in science fiction, but may soon become a real concern.

The problem has been treated often in the popular television series "Star Trek", in which the avowed mission is to seek out new life forms. Needless to say, when found, these lead to moral questions if considered carefully. A few problems of this nature are mentioned briefly.

(a) Data the android
The series "Star Trek, the Next Generation" features an android named "Data", supposedly built by a scientist, complete with a "positronic brain" and an ultra strong body. He is supposed to hold in his brain a collection of the life experiences of the destroyed race from the planet of his construction. In one episode, a computer scientist (the villain) wanted to shut Data off, download his memories into a mainframe computer, and dissect and study his brain with the goal of replicating the construction. Data was not pleased with this offer, and declined to be shut off. A court trial ensued, to determine whether Data was a living being with the right to refuse, or a possession of Star Fleet, like a toaster.

(b) The worker robots
Another episode featured newly designed worker robots, whose performance was good enough to convince Data (who had won his case) that they had become intelligent life forms who should not be forced into "slavery", doing dangerous tasks in lieu of the (not always human) crew. Data won again.

(c) The nanites
A school experiment gone awry allowed nanometer sized crystal-like objects to have the opportunity to evolve. Since they were so small, their life processes and development advanced at a rapid rate, until they began to cause problems with the starship. An attempt to destroy them failed and they responded in kind. Data allowed himself to be used to negotiate a truce with the nanites, which had evolved to the point where they were the more advanced form, able to dictate terms if they so chose. At such a point, the concept of intrinsic rights for life forms began to look appealing to the formerly dominant species.

(d) The rock mother
The older Star Trek series considered the case of an apparently malevolent living rock that could move by melting the less alive rock around it, and that was killing human miners exploiting a newly developed planet. When it was discovered that the rock was the last of the race, and designated mother to the next generation of its species, guarding and protecting its bowling ball like babies, many of which had been smashed during the mining, negotiation and compromise took over. It turned out that the progeny, when hatched, *liked* to dig, and when not endangered, helped the mining operation immensely.

Commentary. These moral and ethical issues must be faced eventually if the development of artificial life progresses until its *creatures* show the traits of living systems. Similar problems, associated with successful research, occurred in physics when the atomic bomb became a reality, in chemistry when massive production of poison gas became easy, in biochemistry with the development of gene splicing, and in medicine when it became possible to keep bodies alive by "heroic" means. It is probably best to consider such questions early, so that we are better prepared to deal with them when needed.

4.5. Conclusions and Future Directions

I have considered cases which show ambiguity between life and non-life, indicating that a clear dichotomy between the two is not defensible, but instead that there is a rather continuous transition. As the result of discrete evolutionary processes, the transition is not necessarily smooth in any sense, nor is it necessarily complete. It often exhibits features of punctuated evolution, in which a better solution, once discovered, can become completely dominant over a population in a short time or for a narrow range of external parameters.

The genetic search process of *real* evolution is massively parallel. Genetic search is, in a sense, an autocatalytic process. Even though it may be extremely unlikely to produce a reasonable solution by random selection, it is much more likely to produce *small pieces* of good solutions randomly. Once parts of a good solution are discovered, the genetic operators can produce a population richer in those parts, which can form the nucleus for building larger pieces, even more suitable than the originals. The process proceeds recursively.

The success or failure of any individual is not important in this process, nor is the preservation of the identity of the species which tries to solve a problem. Thus the substitution of computer modeling (after consideration of ethical and moral issues, discussed above), can avoid the damage to individuals or species possible in real evolution (and, of course, it can also be done more quickly).

The finding of an optimal solution is not essential either – any decent solution will do. The search is therefore *solution driven* not problem driven (even a misunderstood or badly stated problem can be solved if an acceptable *solution* can be recognized or roughly evaluated) nor driven by the searcher. Even if many search methods fail, some may contain or approximate the features needed for success, and the genetic operators may then produce a reasonable solution.

Once the blurred boundary between life and non-life is accepted and life is no longer treated as having unachievable, special, almost mystical properties, it becomes promising to consider the utilization of techniques and methodologies associated with life to solve such problems. Evolution and learning have in fact been able to produce sophisticated solutions to problems that are just beginning to be dealt with using conventional mechanical and computational methods. *Artificial* evolution and *artificial* learning may produce similar benefits, but have the advantage of higher speed than the corresponding biological processes.

The power of artificial life based methods. Problems such as image recognition, image understanding, sound recognition and understanding, all in the presence of noise, have been solved by living systems in sloppy but remarkably effective ways, using massive parallelism despite slow inaccurate hardware. Problems such as one shot learning, associative recall of information from insufficient clues, and the learning of complex motor and control skills such as ice skating, walking erect, or maintaining constant (more or less) body temperature in a changing environment, have been difficult at best for our traditional methods, but satisfactory solutions have been found in the natural living world.

We have seen that *life based* methods such as artificial neural networks (aided by physical based methods such as annealing), genetic algorithms, genetic programming, together with more mathematical methods such as fractal and chaotic analysis, cellular automata and fuzzy logic, have been effective in dealing with a number of hard problems. They find solutions which are often not perfect, but still quite good.

Particularly as computers get better, faster, and bigger, we can see the limitations of the traditional architectures and traditional computing approaches, based on explicit programming and the attempt to find precise and provably correct solutions. As the machines get better, the problems we *wish* to solve get bigger and less precisely defined. We need to develop methods to cope with inaccurate and incomplete data, and with inability to determine, even, if a proposed solution is correct. Such solutions appear to be obtainable using methods such as learning (both supervised and unsupervised), evolutionary search, and coevolution implying both competition and cooperation.

The essence of such *soft computing* methods is nonlinearity, feedback, adaptiveness, and the use of data which is normally inaccurate, incomplete, and noisy. It is necessary for success to regard these not as drawbacks, but as strengths. For it is the very sensitivity of nonlinear feedback systems, and their ability to amplify noise that is the source of their strength, since they can quickly reveal incorrect solutions by failure. They become a *sieve*, which lets bad solutions through the mesh, while keeping an ever richer mix of "not too bad" solutions, perhaps even including an optimum solution. Because these methods are *adaptive*, they can *track* a changing problem domain, unlike preprogrammed methods. This is a new and critically needed capability.

The weakness of artificial life based methods. Computer science already has accepted some methods used by living things for computational purposes. The field of artificial neural networks, which bases its approach on emulating the structure and function of the brain, has already begun to produce useful results and insights. Genetic algorithms have been successful in solving a number of practical problems such as job shop scheduling. The acceptance of ideas from the field of artificial life, particularly the use of genetic algorithms, evolutionary computational methods, and parallel stochastic search restricted in scope by genetic operations can lead to another computational paradigm shift. The new approach is basically the adaptive search through a solution space to a problem specified by way only of a fitness function.

But before we can really take full advantage of these methods, it will be necessary to explore and thoroughly understand the mathematical structure of the problems addressed, the methods of solution, the topology of the spaces being searched, and the reliability and applicability of the approaches.

In particular, there is no general proof yet that evolutionary programs will find the proper solution, or even any solution at all. The method uses *soft constraints* with a penalty for violation but no prohibition. This is both a weakness and a strength. The weakness is that it is not possible to guarantee convergence; the strength is that alternative, perhaps superior, approximate solutions are rarely ignored, which allows tracking of changing environments.

Furthermore, there is as yet no understanding of *why* some problems are solved readily while others do not yield any solution, but fail to converge. Nor is there any general principle for determining the best way to *represent* a given problem to take advantage of these methods. It is not clear that there really exists a method to get good solutions for arbitrary problems. In the case of neural networks, for example, it has been shown that learning by the most commonly used method, error back propagation, can be chaotic and produce fractal structure in the search space with only a part leading to correct solutions. This may well be true of genetic search as well. It may turn out to be undecidable in advance if a particular problem can be solved with a given choice of parameters.

Another problem is that there are no automatically obtainable criteria for the choice of a fitness function, which is now typically hand tooled. Too restrictive a fitness function can force the methods to ignore some regions of the search space, and solutions to the actual problem being considered. They find, instead, results consistent with a special fitness function which could have been obtained by misunderstanding the true essence of a problem, but simply seeing some details as very important.

Traditional artificial intelligence seems to have fallen victim to that difficulty. By breaking a task into "obvious" subgoals, recursively, until the final steps are trivial to realize, AI methods ignore and even reject better and more elegant solutions which have a completely different subgoal structure, or none at all. The approach taken by traditional computer science has similar problems. It insists on a method which works in all cases with any input data set. But one lesson learned by studying evolutionary methods, is that solutions are data dependent and even dependent on the order of data presentation.

Even such advanced computational approaches as virtual reality suffer from problems associated with prescriptive programming. A user is limited to the environment provided by the programming. As an example of this limitation, consider a virtual reality presentation of the interior of an artery, to be used for training medical students to cope with defects such as aneurysms. If the cases provided by the programmers are exhausted or the range of parameters provided is exceeded, no more can be done. Even random selection of new parameters is inadequate since those may be inconsistent or undesired.

If that environment could adapt or evolve, in cooperation with the objectives and activities of the learner, it can become a synthetic world with inherent variability and flexibility. The programmatic restrictions would disappear, providing a better tool for the user. But we have not, as yet, determined the conditions and requirements for such techniques to converge, nor any way to estimate, *a priori* the quality of solutions which may be discovered.

Future directions. In *natural* life as we know it, DNA, which seems clearly *not* to be alive but merely to be a complex molecule, supplies the structure to support complexity, variability, and adaptation. These factors are the strengths of living systems. They provide the power to solve many difficult tasks including:

(a) obtaining massive amounts of sensory data over huge dynamic ranges, rapidly and simultaneously from multiple sensors of many types;
(b) understanding context from sensory inputs including at least sight, sound, odor, touch, and taste, even in noisy backgrounds;
(c) associative memory recall and rapid access to data from incomplete or even incorrect clues;
(d) being able to move stably but flexibly, apparently at the volition of the organism, even over unfamiliar terrain.

Such tasks are very hard for current prescriptive programming methods. Traditional mathematical analysis is also inappropriate, since the necessary equations are hard to obtain and often essentially impossible to solve.

The computational equivalent of DNA and the processes that it supports is now available in the form of adaptive learning, genetic algorithms, evolutionary programming, fuzzy set theory, fuzzy logic, and massive parallelism. These can provide the support for complexity, variability, and adaptability, although sometimes at the expense of sacrificing precision or optimality in favor of solutions which meet the needs of the problem, but which need not be the best ones. It is necessary to regard imprecision, complexity, and lack of provability as *virtues* which allow flexibility and power, not as problems.

Regarding life as a set of *processes* rather than as a state indicates that there is little to prevent the utilization of life based approaches. The lack of sharp bounds between life and non-life indicates that the proper structure can provide for lifelike capabilities and, by including user (just another life form) preference in the models, can develop tools for the construction of synthetic worlds which are to the liking of the constructors and the users as well.

Thus it seems essential to pursue and investigate these methods, both from the practical and the theoretical point of view. In many problems now coming to our attention, superposition of results and reductionist approaches, which have worked so well for linear systems, now fail. It is critical that such problems be studied by all possible means, and not just ignored as being "too messy". The mathematical descriptions of this class of problem, although complicated, show promise of elegance, as in the case of other nonlinear and complex systems.

References

1. *Artificial Life*, C. Langton ed., Addison-Wesley 1989
2. *Artificial Life II*, C. Langton et al., eds., Addison-Wesley 1992
3. *Genetic Algorithms in Search, Optimization and Machine Learning*, D. E. Goldberg, Addison-Wesley 1992
4. Hillis, W. Daniel, Coevolving Parasites ..., in *Artificial Life II*, C. Langton et al., eds., Addison-Wesley 1992
5. *Adaptation in Natural and Artificial Systems*, J. Holland, MIT 1992
6. *Genetic Programming*, J. Koza, MIT 1992
7. D. Jefferson et al., Evolution as a Theme in Artificial Life, in *Artificial Life II*, C. Langton et al., eds., Addison-Wesley 1992
8. C. G. Langton, Studying Artificial Life with Cellular Automata, *Physica* 22D, 1986
9. C. G. Langton - Introduction, in *Artificial Life II*, C. Langton et al., eds., Addison-Wesley 1992
10. L. S. Penrose, *Scientific American* Vol. 200, 105 (1959); *Artificial Life II Video Proceedings*, Addison-Wesley 1992
11. T. Ray, An Approach to the Synthesis of Life, in C. Langton et al., eds., *Artificial Life II*, Addison-Wesley, 1992
12. C. Taylor, "Fleshing Out" Artificial Life II, in C. Langton et al., eds., *Artificial Life II*, Addison-Wesley, 1992
13. *Theory of Self Reproducing Automata*, J. Von Neumann, University of Illinois Press 1966

5. Artificial Life as Synthetic Biology

Paul Bourgine
Cemagref, Parc de Tourvoie, 92185 Antony Cedex, France
(e-mail:bourgine@cemagref.fr)

Eric Bonabeau
Santa Fe Institute, 1399 Hyde Park Road, Santa Fe, NM87501, USA
(e-mail:bonabeau@santafe.edu)

Summary.

Artificial Life (AL) can be seen as synthetic biology since it is aimed at abstracting the dynamical properties of the living and at synthesizing systems which exhibit life-like behaviors. In AL, Life is considered as a property of the organization of matter and not as a property of matter itself. This research program will allow a better understanding of such processes and properties as autopoiesis and autoreproduction, evolution and learning, morphogenesis and development, collective intelligence and the emergence of cooperative processes. It also constitutes a framework to study how these processes and properties can be combined to provide the autonomy and adaptivity characteristic of the living. Artificial Life's experiments resort most often to systems which (rarely) evolve in (and interact with) real environments, or (most often) evolve in (and interact with) computational synthetic worlds.

Key words: Artificial life, synthetic biology, emergence, autonomy, functionalism, boundary conditions, bottom-up/top-down approaches

5.1. Introduction

Artificial Life (AL) is an emerging field of research gathering various disciplines - biology, cognitive science, computer science, chemistry, epistemology, physics, ...- into a unified polymorphic program whose goal is to study life in a synthetic way. Artificial Life can be seen as synthetic biology since it is aimed at abstracting the dynamical principles of the living and at synthesizing systems which exhibit life-like behaviors.

The bet of AL is based on the idea that it is possible to study life as a property of the organization of matter rather than a property of matter itself. AL is thus concerned with the formal basis of life whereas biology is more concerned with the analysis of life based on organic matter. *"AL is not restricted to the medium of carbon chain chemistry in its attempts to synthetize biological phenomena. Rather it uses whatever medium is most appropriate and convenient for the synthesis of the phenomena under study"*.

In this sense, AL provides a large class of scientific experimental techniques to study emergent processes and properties like autopoiesis and autoreproduction, evolution and learning, morphogenesis and development, collective intelligence. By helping to understand these properties, it contributes to theoretical biology and leads to a renewal of engineering applications, inspired by the living. AL'ss methods can be fruitfully applied to many domains. If you are dealing with systems which are too complex to be studied with traditional scientific tools, AL can certainly help. You should not forget your primary goals and get lost in AL's immensity. If you are a biologist seeking new modeling tools, AL is a general toolbox which offers you a broad spectrum of new techniques of experimentation, from computer simulations of evolution to models of how decentralized systems can collectively perform biologically relevant tasks. If you are looking for ways of getting out of classical AI's dead end, AL can help by providing you with ways of making symbols emerge out of low-level sensory-motor processes. If you are a computer scientist, not necessarily involved in AI, AL gives you the pleasure not only of playing god, but also of finding new distributed algorithms for optimization, control or prediction. If you are a philosopher, AL will give you the opportunity to think about new issues in ethics, epistemology, and so on, and will provide you with years of work to unravel the ontological status of life: you will be able to think over life as no other philosopher before. If you are an engineer, AL constitutes an almost inexhaustible source of ideas for the design of a bunch of new machines. Finally, if you are an artist, AL opens a world of new experiences to you: it complements the traditional artistic techniques by extending the scope of art-as-it-is to the wider scope of art-as-it-could-be, where everything which is in your imagination, even deep inside your subconscious, can be recreated in alternative media.

In the first part of this paper, we will present some tentative definitions of AL as well as its scope and topics. In the second part, some difficulties in studying emergent properties of the living are discussed. Finally, we shall define AL as a framework to study how these properties can be combined to provide the autonomy and adaptivity characteristic of the living.

5.2. Artificial Life and Synthetic Biology

Tentative definitions of AL. What is Artificial Life? It is interesting to notice that there has been an evolution in the definitions of AL given by its founders during the last five years. After AL I, Langton wrote [1]: *"AL is the study of man-made systems that exhibit behaviors characteristic of natural living systems. It complements the traditional biological sciences* *concerned with the analysis of living organisms by attempting to synthesize lifelike behaviors within computers and other artificial media. By extending the empirical foundation upon which biology is based beyond the carbon-chain life that has evolved on Earth, AL can contribute to theoretical biology by locating life-as-we-know-it within the larger picture of life-as-it-could-be."* This constitutes quite a broad, loose definition, but it definitely shows the global ambition of AL: being able to synthesize lifelike behaviors and not being restricted to 'life-as-we-know-it' but rather extending investigations to 'life-a! ! s-it-could-be'. This second point may be considered just a side effect of the first one, since synthesis leads to a wide spectrum of possibilities obviously not taken into account by classical analytical approaches.

The very same ambition can be found in the words of Langton after AL II [2]: *"AL is a field of study devoted to understanding life by attempting to abstract the fundamental dynamical principles underlying biological phenomena, and recreating these dynamics in other physical media -such as computers- making them accessible to new kinds of experimental manipulation and testing. (...) In addition to providing new ways to study the biological phenomena associated with life on Earth, life-as-we-know-it, AL allows us to extend our studies to the larger domain of the 'bio-logic' of possible life, life-as-it-could-be, whatever it might be made of and wherever it might be found in the universe. Thus AL is not only about studying existing life, but also about the possibility of synthesizing new life, within computers or other 'artificial' media. The life that is realized in these alternative media will force us to broaden our understanding of the proper domain of biology to include self-organizing, evolving, and even 'living' machines, regardless of the ! ! specific physical stuff of which they are constituted, or whether or not they are based upon the same chemical and physical principles as the life that has evolved here on Earth."* We can see that this definition is more accurate than the previous one, thus more cautious in some sense, but it is also more dangerous in that it makes a lot of implicit as well as explicit controversial reductionist assumptions. It also clearly locates AL on a 'functionalist scale': life, defined as a function (or as a set of functions) *"can be studied in an abstract way, without bothering about what sort of bits and pieces actually implements* "[3], that is AL's research strategy is 'functional synthesis' (rather than functional analysis).

The third definition seems more reasonable, since it equates AL and synthetic biology and gives epistemological justifications (scientific experiments, engineering applications, and contributions to theoretical biology) to the existence of the field: *"AL is synthetic biology. It involves attempts to put together life, evolution, and other biological phenomena from first principles for the purpose of scientific experiment and engineering applications. As such, AL is not restricted to the medium of carbon chain chemistry in its attempts to synthesize biological phenomena. Rather, it uses whatever medium is most appropriate and convenient for the synthesis of the phenomenon under study. (...) It is extremely important for theoretical biology that we explore the en-*

semble of what could have evolved, not just what did evolve. Thus the scope of AL is broader than traditional biology. AL is an attempt to extend the theory and practice of biology beyond life as we know it to the! ! domain of life as it could be, in any of its possible incarnations. "

Synthesizing lifelike behaviors. In the diagram below, two axes allow for the description of the models of AL: one dimension is dedicated to the representation of the levels of description and is very similar to the levels of Popper's World I that describe biological systems and their parts: ecosystems, populations, high-level organisms, tissues and organs, populations of cells and unicellular organisms, cells and unicellular organisms, organelles, liquids and solids, molecules, atoms, elementary particles, sub-elementary particles. The other dimension represents the degree of abstraction, i.e. the distance from the phenomenological world.

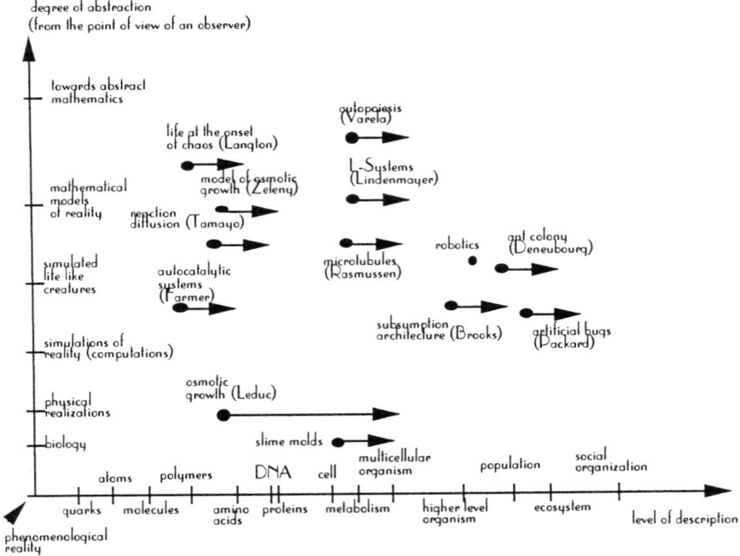

The little black circles indicate the locations of the models in the plane, and the arrows show the type of dynamics that AL is mostly concerned with: horizontal moves on the diagram. In effect, AL models and simulations are most often intended to produce some kind of higher-level structure or organism from a set of elements or individuals interacting with one another and with their environment.

The phenomena producing the higher-level structures are of similar nature: the behavior exhibited by the system of elements as a whole is never explicitly programmed by the experimenter, it is the result of a set of micro-interactions generating macro-structures that Forrest calls epiphenomena. The process by which non-prespecified behaviors appear -usually but not necessarily at another level of description - is emergence. By breaking things down, analytical biology studies the components of life and misses its emergent properties. As opposed to this reductionist, top-down approach, AL concentrates on how a population of interactive components is capable of producing these emergent properties. Thus emergence is a central concept of AL: It is naturally and closely related to its synthetic nature, and generates all the methodologies used in the field, namely bottom-up approaches to the study of life. In fact, feedback loops are also of great importance in the appearance of higher-level phenomena: most of the arrows on the diagram should be double-sided arrows, to account for the existence of 'strange loops' between higher-level and lower-level structures.

The fact that the horizontal axis approximately represents Popper's World I is not pure chance. Popper suggests four levels of emergence, the first two clearly referring to the constitution of World I: *"on the first level, there is the theory of emergence of heavy atomic nuclei in the center of big stars, and (...) the evidence for the emergence somewhere in space of organic molecules. On the next level there is the emergence of life.(...) life creates something that is utterly new in the universe: the peculiar activity of organisms; especially the often purposeful actions of animals; and animal problem solving. All organisms are constant problem solvers; even though they are not conscious of the problems they are trying to solve. On the next level, the next great step is the emergence of conscious states. With the distinction of conscious and unconscious states, again something utterly new and of greatest importance enters the universe. It is a new world: the world of conscious experience. On the next level, this is followed by the emergence of products of the human mind, such as the works of art; and the works of science; especially scientific theories".* Of course AL is more concerned with the second aspect -the emergence of life-, and somewhat with the third one, while one could say that cognitive science is concerned mostly with the third and fourth aspect -the emergence of consciousness- and somewhat with the second one. We see here that AL and cognitive science overlap and that is of utmost importance.

This diagram is far from perfect since the 'emergent' quality may not be a property representable within the two suggested dimensions: for instance, it is hard to represent the 'emergence' of communication.

We did not care too much about the second axis so far. But this second axis is crucial, not only for AL, but for science in general. There is a constant feedback from experiments to models, and from models to theories, while theories shape the way we build our models, which in turn channel the experiments we wish to carry out. One should not forget to look at the lower part of the diagram which is a source of empirical constraints, and one should not forget to look for theories and for general abstractions. One flaw of AL in its actual configuration -different from its stated ideals- is the lack of vertical moves on the diagram, that is the absence of empirical constraints, and the weak number of theories compared to the bunch of simulations we are facing. Now it is true that the confessed goal of AL is to build-up a general theory of life, thus the vital élan of AL theoretically tends to locate it in the upper part of the diagram. On the practical side however, this is not at all true. As regards the lower part, it is lost in the 'quest for the essence of life-as-it-could-be'.

Since it seems to be more difficult to start from manifestations of life and try to find its fundamental principles by top-down analysis, than to start from computational simulations and physical observations and try to synthesize more and more complex behaviors which in turn might capture the nature of some aspects of life, AL thus focuses on ways of achieving emergence to generate these more and more complex behaviors.

"The most surprising lesson we have learned from simulating complex physical systems on computers is that complex behavior need not have complex roots. Indeed, tremendously interesting and beguilingly complex behavior can emerge from collections of extremely simple components", [1] Langton says. This is the main justification of the approach: theories of complex systems give rise to fantastic hopes, and most of the models in the diagram of the previous paragraph constitute successes in reproducing aspects of living systems. L-systems, catalytic nets, etc..seem to confirm these hopes: one further step to take consists in betting on even more spectacular successes of theories of complex systems, and one doesn't see why such a bet should not be taken.

The question of knowing whether AL will be able to capture the essence of life by applying this methodology is more philosophical, and even if AL is unable to do so, it obviously does not mean that it won't be able to achieve anything at all. The existing models have already achieved something: they can explain or give some insights about some aspects of living systems and thus are relevant to science. In that sense, AL is perfectly possible (it is even useful): any model of a natural system is partial and exists at a given level of description, therefore only some aspects of the system can be captured by the model -this is a common feature of all sciences having to deal with natural systems. AL is such a science and has been able to reproduce (using several kinds of media, the parameters of which are usually not included in the model) aspects peculiar to life: AL does not need any other epistemological justification.

In fact, we can consider AL as a general toolbox in which one can find a set tools appropriate for synthesis. These tools can be applied to the study of biological phenomena, or can be used for engineering purposes, or can even serve artistic creation. But since the source of inspiration of AL is obviously the living (i.e. the living-as-we-know-it), AL is related to some kind of biology. Since the lifelike behaviors generated within AL are synthesized, it is natural to think of AL as synthetic biology, which it is indeed. Note that almost everything is synthetic in AL: not only are the agents artificial, but also their environments (except in robotics, where the goal is precisely to plunge artificial creatures into real environments). The artificial environment of an artificial creature, however virtual it might look to us, is the only reality that the creature 'knows': thus in a sense, AL is aimed at synthesizing creatures which live in virtual worlds!

5.3. Synthetic Biology and Emergence

As we have already mentioned, the notion of emergence seems to be a central idea in Cognitive Science and a key concept of Artificial Life. It generally involves some kind of levels, and states that emergence occurs when a property is absent at a given level and is present at another. It is loosely summarized in Lewes's definition (1874!): "Theory according to which the combination of entities of a given level realizes a higher-level entity whose properties are entirely new".

Even if there is no real agreement on what it should imply for a phenomenon to be emergent, some people have attempted to give somewhat formal definitions of emergent computation.

Emergent computation and AL. In order to understand the concept of emergent computation, one should first define a set of agents, their behavioral rules, i.e. how each agent reacts to some features of its environment or to some other agent(s) which which it may communicate. The iterative application of the local rules generates a global emergent behavior or structure.

The behavior of the global system is never preprogrammed by the experimenter. It is the result of a set of micro-interactions generating macro-structures which Forrest named 'epiphenomena'. Let us summerize the conditions under which an emergent computational structure appears:

- There must be a set of agents following local rules
- Interactions between agents must exist. These interactions produce global patterns named "epiphenomena", at the macro-level.
- These epiphenomena must be interpretable as some computation they perform.

Likewise, one could define emergent functions in general by replacing the word computation by the word function: an epiphenomenon would then have to be interpretable as a function implemented at the collective level by the agents. We see here that in any case, emergence is a concept related to an observer, since an interpretation is needed. This conception of emergence is the most commonly shared one.

The notion of emergent computation is central AL for it generalizes the notions of genotype and phenotype. The local rules which specify the behaviors of the elements play the role of genotype, whereas the equivalent of the phenotype is the structures and behaviors which emerge. Thus we can say that the local rules (the genotype) generate the global behavior or structure (the phenotype).

But the emergent pattern may not be only due to the local rules but also to 'external' boundary conditions. In order to convince us of the difficulty one has to find the appropriate rules necessary to generate a particular (functional) pattern, one may think of partial differential equations which play the role of local rules: the solutions of such equations crucially depend on boundary conditions, which together with the equations (to which they are external) determine the actual shape of the solutions. Likewise, a global behavior may not be well-defined by the local, lower-level laws only (which constitute internal boundary conditions), but may as well necessitate external 'explanations'. In AL, there is an implicit assumption that the boundary conditions can be self-generated: not too many exogenous factors need be taken into account in order to generate the expected higher-level behavior from lower-level laws.

The notion of boundary condition has been introduced by Polanyi [4] in his "Life's irreducible structure", a neo-vitalistic manifesto containing a lot of interesting objections against reductionism. The idea behind boundary conditions is that the functioning of a system (say a machine) is highly underdetermined by lower-level considerations (say physical laws). It is true that the higher level has a behavior which is compatible with physical laws, but physical laws alone are "unspecific", they cannot determine the behavior of the higher level. Polanyi's conviction is that life cannot be reduced to physical and chemical processes because irreducible boundary conditions are needed to make the link between physics, chemistry and life. This concept of boundary conditions is rather important, because among the huge number of possible states of the world allowed by physics, only a few are compatible with life: therefore, we need some guide towards these few possibilities.The idea of boundary condition is closely linked to Elsasser's immensity, to Pattee's non-holonomic constraints and to Rössler's privileged zero property, nicely summarized in [5]. One of the major tasks of AL's epistemologists is to justify this idea of self-generated (or intrinsic) boundary conditions. AL has to prove that intrinsic boundary conditions are good enough at reducing (drastically) the space of behaviors to the interesting ones.

It must be noticed that it seems reasonable to resort to endogenous explanations first, since they are in some sense the simplest ones. Moreover, from a computational point of view, it is certainly more efficient to simulate an artificial world with simple local rules which generate complicated pattern: one specific example is the obstacle avoidance behavior of Craig Reynolds' boids [1]. Boids are flocking artificial creatures moving in an artificial world. In order to maintain the coherence of the flock, they do not need any kind of global information: each boid obeys three simple local rules which are (i) 'maintain a minimal distance from other objects, (ii) 'match velocities of neighboring boids, (iii) move toward flock's perceived center of mass'. These rules alone allow the boids to form a flock which re-aggregates after an obstacle has been met. In very much the same spirit, Sims' images [6] generated by equations and selected by genetic algorithms constitute a beautiful example of how powerful AL's methods can be at synthesizing artificial worlds. Peter Oppenheimer's artificial Menagerie is yet another argument in favour of AL's methods applied to the creation of artificial universes.

To be aware of some dangers when synthesizing lifelike behaviors. One question which may be asked about a synthetic research program such as the one proposed by AL is: How can synthetic models be validated in AL? AL is one of the sciences of the artificial, as defined by Simon. The artificial object can be so similar to a natural one that observers can not distinguish it from outside, even if their functioning is very different: *"This kind of imitation is possible because differently organized physical systems can produce quasi identical behaviors"*. This definition by Simon is very important because it implies both the possibility of functional abstraction and of a phenomenological validation of synthetic models. But we have to be very careful with these two matters.

First, functionalism can be very dangerous. It leads to the belief that two processes on two very different substrates can exhibit close behaviors. For instance, classical AI is based on the idea of a symbolic computation independent of any substrate and that intelligence can be simulated on a traditional computer. Connectionnist AI rejects this hypothesis and reintroduces a more realistic substrate, i.e. artificial neural networks. By claiming that AL has to abstract dynamical principles of the living independently from carbon chain molecules, AL takes a functionalist position similar to that of classical AI.

Conversely, a radically realist (vs functionalist) position leads to giving up simulations. Since it is widely acknowledged that simulations are an important method of scientific investigation, we have to take a medium position between functionalism and realism, which allows to abstract the principles underlying living phenomena and to model them while still being grounded in the biological inspiration.

Second, because the kind of validation AL resorts to is not biological but only phenomenological, there is a risk to accept some very vague similarity as validation. Furthermore, if AL consists in the study of life-as-it-could-be, no constraint other than phenomenological is necessary. This could make scientific explanation in AL quite weak, but on the other hand this is excellent for synthetic Art which has to invent some unknown forms of living, free from (almost) any constraint: Aesthetic constraints seem to be the only ones (beside the limits of our imaginations).

AL's project is strongly influenced by the idea that one could study life-as-it-could-be as opposed to life-as-we-'know'-it (by the way, do we really know it ?). But such a large ambition is dangerous: in particular, it seems that no constraint can be imposed on AL, since life-as-it-could-be has by definition no ontological status, and life-as-it-could-be could be anything. Thus AL needs some constraints - empirical or others. A vague resemblance with some aspects of living systems is too weak a constraint. There are other sciences dealing with life, adaptation, evolution, ..., which can provide sufficient constraints. The best bottom-up approach needs some kind of validation by top-down data. Purely synthetic approaches are doomed because it means proceeding from *"the bottom to the top, and trying to reobtain the lost information by reconstruction, while recognizing from the beginning of the climb that no information will appear"* if it was not available to the climber from the start.

Studying life-as-it-could-be may also constitute an intractable task, all the more as 'real life' already covers a large spectrum of possible behaviors: *"Life is self-organizing in the sense that it leads to very special forms, i.e from a wide basin of attraction it leads to a much narrower set of meaningful states. But this alone would not yet be surprising: the surprising aspect is that this attraction is not at all rigid. Although the attractor is very small compared to full phase space, it is still huge and it therefore allows for a wide spectrum of behaviors"*.

The synthetic (bottom-up) approaches of AL are to be opposed to analytic (top-down) approaches. The failure of classical AI to simulate intelligence by top-down approaches shows that the only possible solution is to study cognition not by using bottom-up approaches alone, but by using a combination of both top-down and bottom-up approaches. This principle can be applied to the study of life as well. AL has bottom-up methodologies but uses implicit top-down confirmations. AL's simulations have to be judged on how well they simulate aspects of the living, simply because simulating implies simulating something: it is a sort of 'intentionality' of simulations, simulations are 'about something'. But these top-down confirmations must be made much more explicit, under the form of empirical constraints. Quoting Pattee: The main criticisms of neuroscientists against AI is that it has *"for the most part neglected the fundamental biology of the nervous system. This criticism will undoubtedly be aimed at AL as well"*.

5.4. Artificial Life as a Framework to Study Autonomy

Putnam asked whether AI had taught us anything of importance about the mind, and he was *"inclined to think that the answer is no"*, because AI has no Master Program, because AI *"doesn't really try to simulate intelligence at all. Simulating intelligence is only its notional activity; its real activity is writing clever programs for a variety of tasks"* [7]. The same criticism holds for AL, if one replaces intelligence by life. We propose a Master Program for AL, and we believe that it is essential if AL is to teach us anything of importance about life: one possible master program consists in studying autonomy.

And it is also true that AL could easily become the largest collection of computer simulations ever. Hence the necessity for building theories. The unifying theme of autonomy is one way of trying to develop theorie: autopoiesis, organizational and operational closure are prototheories that need be completed, tested. AL should not be a bunch of simulations without theories: like Pattee, we shall say that simulations are judged on how well they reproduce the features of phenomena they are supposed to simulate (only phenomenological resemblance), while theories can be *"judged by a much more comprehensive range of criteria: from the concrete test of how well they can predict specific values for the observables of the system being modeled, to abstract tests such as universality, conceptual coherence, simplicity and elegance (...) We accept the idea that there are many valid simulations and realizations of a given behavior, but we think of a theory more exclusively as the best we have at any given time"*. Using Putnam's words, the only way for AL not to be *"one damned thing after another"* is to have a Master Program, otherwise we would be tinkers, - like evolution-, and the number of *"damned things"* we may think of may be *"astronomical"*.

Autonomy as a synthetic property of lifelike systems. One may think of AL as a field devoted to the study and the realization of lifelike systems. By 'lifelike system' we mean a system exhibiting some (but not necessary all) emergent properties of the living. If a system is to be autonomous, it has to exhibit most of such properties. In particular, autonomous systems are capable of regenerating and self-producing their own boundary conditions. In that sense, studying autonomous systems is a more ambitious task than studying 'lifelike' ones, and at the same time it constrains AL's perspectives without impoverishing them.

Autonomy can be seen as the synthetic property of both living and lifelike systems. A Master Program on autonomy can thus be seen as an enhancement of AL as synthetic biology.

With this program, AL becomes concerned with theories of autonomous sytems. No theory of autonomous systems is well-formed today, despite some loose characterizations. It is worth noticing that such characterizations apply to a much wider class of systems than that of the biological systems by which they were inspired. Other characterizations of autonomy may reveal fruitful in order to make the concept of autonomous system both more accurate and richer.

Anyway we need to characterize, even loosely, what aspects of biology are relevant to the study of life, and then to focus on these aspects. Pattee said that *"the crux of the issue (...) is who decides what is fundamental about biology. This is where a theory of life is needed"*. We cannot disagree with this, but we shall even restrict the field of investigation: this is where a theory of autonomy is needed. Once again, we believe that the study of autonomous systems can give great insights on the nature of life, while at the same time dramatically reducing our space of investigation. Far from diminishing the richness of the very large field defined by Langton, this restriction just implies focusing on what is the gist of (artificial) life: autonomy, defined as *"the basic and fundamental capacity of living creatures to be, to assert their existence and to bring forth a world that is significant and pertinent without being pre-digested in advance"* [8]. It is not pure coincidence if almost all the features suggested by Farmer and Belin to characterize life are relevant in this context: a living organism is a pattern in space-time, composed of many interdependent parts, with a metabolism, with the ability to store information (of a 'self-representation'), having functional interactions with its environment, and being stable under perturbations. All these features can be summarized in one sentence: a living organism is capable of maintaining its viability in dynamic, varying environments.

AL and cognitive science. Studying autonomous systems also implies dealing with the problem of embodiement [9], which we consider the equivalent of the problem of 'background or commonsense knowledge' in AI. In that sense, the master program we propose bridges the gap between AL and Cognitive Science, just as does the "Animat's approach" to which it is very close not only in principle but also in practice. Cognition being an important property of living organisms -we do not refer only to human cognition but also to all the cognitive abilities of simple organisms-. Even if *"life=cognition"* is an equation which need be taken cautiously, studying cognition from the point of view of autonomy belongs to AL. Moreover, AL has to become 'cognitive' in that sense. Alternative approaches to cognitive science, seeing as much intelligence in the capacity of a simple insect to survive as in the ability for playing chess, will be insightful for cognitive science, while they can obviously be classified into AL's approaches.

5.5. Conclusion

Artificial Life as synthetic biologyIn conclusion, we should first remember that while top-down approaches usually forget to obey lower-level constraints and laws, purely bottom-up approaches usually forget to look at higher-level constraints, and this leads in both cases to considerable flaws. AL, being 'very bottom-up', needs constraints. We propose that both empirical constraints originating from biology and other natural sciences, and pragmatic constraints oriented by the design of useful, viable, efficient, robust, flexible, decentralized, lifelike systems should be taken into account. Second, by focusing on the study of autonomy -the ability to live-, AL will naturally be led to obey these constraints. Therefore we propose the following for AL's Master Program: "AL is a field of study devoted to developping theories of autonomous sytems by abstracting their fundamental principles".

References

1. C.Langton, ed., *"Artificial Life"*, Addison-Wesley, 1989.
2. C.Langton, *"Computation at the edge of chaos"*, in Artificial Life II, C.Langton, C.Taylor, D.Farmer, S.Rasmussen, eds., Addison-Wesley, 1991.
3. E.Sober, *"Learning from functionalism - Prospects for strong AL"*, "-Artificial Life II, Addison-Wesley, 1992.
4. M.Polanyi, *"Life's irreducible structure"*, Science 160, 1308-1312, 1968.
5. G.Kampis, *"Emergent Computations, Life and Cognition"*, in World Futures, vol.31, pp 33-48, Gordon and Breach Science Publishers S.A, 1991.
6. K. Sims, Video Proceedings of Artificial Life II, Addison-Wesley, 1991.
7. H.Putnam, *"Much Ado About Not Very Much"*, in The Artificial Intelligence Debate, S.R.Graubard ed., MIT Press, 1988.
8. F.Varela, P.Bourgine, *"Towards a practice of autonomous systems"*, Proceedings of ECAL 91, MIT Press, 1992.
9. F.Varela, E.Thompson, E.Rosch, *"The Embodied Mind"*, MIT Press, 1991.
10. P.Cariani, *"On the design of devices with emergent semantic functions"*, Ph.D dissertation, State University of New York at Binghamton, 1989.
11. P.Cariani, *"Adaptivity and emergence in Organisms and Devices"*, in World Futures, vlo.31, pp.49-70, Gordon and Breach Science Publishers S.A, 1991.
12. C.Emmeche, *"Life as an Abstract Phenomenon: Is AL Possible?"*, Proceedings of ECAL 1991, MIT Press 1992.
13. W.Elsasser, *"Principles of a New Biological Theory: A Summary"*, J.Theor.Biol., 89, 131-150, 1981.
14. P.Grassberger, *"Problems in quantifying self-generated complexity"*, Helvetica Physica Acta, 62, 489-511, 1989.
15. D.Hillis, *"Intelligence as an Emergent Behavior; or, The Songs of Eden"*, The Artificial Intelligence Debate, S.R.Graubard ed., MIT Press, 1988.
16. B.-O.Küppers, *"Information and the origin of life"*, MIT Press, 1991.
17. C.Langton, *"Studying Artificial Life with cellular automata"*, Physica D, 22, North-Holland, 1986.
18. J.-A.Meyer, S.Wilson, eds., *"From Animals to Animats"*, MIT Press, 1991.
19. G.Nicolis, I.Prigogine, *"Exploring Complexity: An Introduction"*, R.Piper GmbH & Co. KG Verlag, 1989.
20. H.Putnam, *"Reductionism and the nature of psychology"*, Cognition, 2, 131-146, 1973.
21. M.Resnick, *"Overcoming the Centralized Mindset: Towards an Understanding of Emergent Phenomena"*, Epistemology and Learning Memo No.11, November 1990.
22. E.Schrödinger, *"What is Life ?"*, Cambridge University Press, 1944.
23. P.Schuster, *"Dynamics of molecular evolution"*, Physica D, 22, North-Holland, 1986.
24. R.Solomonoff, *"A formal Theory of Inductive Inference"*, Inf. & Control., 7, 1964.
25. R.Thom, *"Modèles mathématiques de la morphogenèse"*, Christian Bourgois, 1980.
26. C.H. Waddington (ed.), *"Toward a Theoretical Biology"*, Edingburgh University Press, 1968.
27. W.Weaver, *"Science and Complexity"*, Am. Scientist, 36, 536-544, 1968.
28. P.Weiss, *"Das lebende System: Ein Beispiel für den Schichtendeterminismus"*, in Das Neue Menschenbild, Ed. A.Koestler & J.R.Smythies, Vienna, 1970.

6. Simulation of the Growth of Plants – Modeling of Metamorphosis and Spatial Interactions in the Architecture and Development of Plants –

F. Blaise, J.-F. Barczi, M. Jaeger, P. Dinouard and Ph. de Reffye
Unité de Modélisation des Plantes, CIRAD-GERDAT, BP 5035 34032 Montpellier CEDEX 1, France (e-mail: blaise@cirad.fr)

Summary.

In the past, numerous techniques have been used in the representation of plants. The Plants Modeling Unit of CIRAD developed an original method of plant growth simulation based on botanical notions of plant architecture. But in simulating metamorphosis, the notion of a reference axis which shows all the stages of differenciation in a branch throughout its growth is needed. Also, if we consider the simultaneity of biological events which characterize a plant's functioning, we can study the environmental (nutrition and precipitation needs) and spatial (crowding, light influence) interactions. The reference axis is structured like a finite automaton and the discrete events simulation (scheduler) is used for the parallel simulation of the growth.

Key words: natural phenomena, plant architecture, botany, reference axis, growth simulation, ring simulation, finite automaton, scheduler, environmental and spatial interactions.

6.1. Introduction

For several years, the use of different techniques has resulted in remarkable outcomes in the simulation and representation of trees: geometric models of branching [11] [25] [1], graftals [38], particle systems [32], fractals [29] [22], L-systems [31] [30] [27], combinatory trees [10] [39], cones-spheres [28], program of pseudo-genetic evolution [37], translucid ellipsoids [14]. A detailed description of these different methods appears in [12] and [13].

A different approach, which more particularly concerns trees, was developed at CIRAD. It uses the qualitative knowledge provided by Hallé *et al.* in plant architecture [21] and the quantitative methods perfected within the Plants Modeling Unit [33][4] [34] [15]. These methods are based on the description of the functioning of buds (growth, death, branching) through stochastic processes. The growth software, still called growth engine, stemming from these theories allows for the construction of realistic plant models in which the topology (the arrangement of the plant's parts) and the geometry (the layout of the parts in space) are simulated using the parameters of the model, which are themselves estimated with experimental data taken from the trees. These models primarily allow for 3-D visualization of the tree's architecture, but also serve as a basis for different applications. They permit, for example, the simulation of the sun's rays which penetrate a plant covering and the calculation of their radiative transfers [8].

Once the architecture of a plant is defined, other parameters can have an effect on its growth. Thus, calculating the presence of a new element in a plant is not sufficient. An external event can change the result of the calculation of a new element's role and can affect the functioning of normal growth. Two types of interaction can be distinguished: environmental interaction and spatial interaction. The first refers to the different types of stress (hydric, nutritional and climatic) that disrupt the normal organization of events at any given time during growth. Spatial interaction takes into account the obstacles that a bud can encounter (a wall, a neighbouring tree, another branch from the same tree, a zone of shade). In other words, there can be an interaction between the topology (organization of elements that make up a plant as they affect each other) and the geometry of a plant.

The Plants Modeling Unit developed several generations of growth software that differ in their botanical knowledge, or in their implementation in the computer. The use of the prefixed order in a plant's growth which was characteristic of the old growth engine does not allow for consideration of interactions. This is why a parallel control of the elements was introduced in the new generation in order to take into account the simultaneity of events in a bud's functioning.

6.2. Botanical Concepts, Basis for Modeling

Morphology. The elementary structure used in the description of the plant's aerial architecture is the plant axis (Img.I.1), otherwise known as the stem or branch. It is made up of a stem or axis carrying leaves and ending in an embryonic part, the apical meristem, at its tip. The leaves are inserted into the stem at the nodes and are positioned along the axis according to the geometrical rules of phyllotaxy (Img.I.1). The part of the stem situated between two consecutive nodes is the internode.

The growth in length of a plant axis is made up of two phases: fabrication of the internodes in the meristem (apical growth), and their growth after a variable amount of time (internodale growth). The part of the stem that is put in place during a lengthening period is called growth unit (G.U.) (Img.I.2). In temperate trees, the first internodes during spring growth correspond to the forms fabricated the previous year, and define the preformed part of the G.U. If new forms are fabricated and lengthened during the same period of lengthening, they will be called neoformed parts.

Continued growth (Img.I.3) is when the apical meristem never ceases functioning. On the other hand, if the meristem experiences a succession of lengthening and rest periods, it is rythmic growth (Img.I.4).

The aerial apparatus of the plant is generally made up of several plant axes which branch out from each other. Lateral branching is done with lateral meristems situated at the leaf axils. If the apical meristem continues to function and the branched structure has a dominant central axis, it is called monopodial branching (Img.I.4.a). But, if the apical meristem dies or is transformed, and if the remaining lateral branches take over, it is called sympodial branching (Img.I.4.b). Furthermore, the development of an axillary meristem can be immediate (sylleptic branching) (Img.I.3.a) or differed (proleptic branching) (Img.I.3.b).

The branching order is an important aspect in the description of a branched structure. Normally, the first formed axis, issued from the seed, is order 1. The branches that it carries are order 2, and so on (Img.I.5).

In a plant, all axes do not present the same morphological characteristics. The most obvious differences between them concern the direction of their growth. In simple terms, axes with erect, vertical growth are called orthotropic, and axes with horizontal or oblique growth, are called plagiotropic (Img.I.6).

A plant can be subdivided into two subsets: the plant apparatus (stems, leaves, roots) and the reproductive apparatus (flowers and inflorescences). The flowers appear on the plant axes at the apical (Img.I.4.b) or lateral (Img.I.4.a) plant meristems, then affecting the growth in length of the axes if they form at the extremities. The plant's sexuality can thus determine the sympodial or monopodial character of the future branched system (Img.I.4).

Notions of plant architecture. A thorough study of tree structure allowed Hallé and Oldeman [20] to clarify the notion of an architectural model. The architectural model is defined as being the ideal spatial structure created by a plant during its growth, in a non-traumatic environment.

The goal of architectural analysis is to describe the form of plants when taken as a whole [21]. The necessary observations for this analysis depend on:

- the growth mode,
- the branching mode,
- the morphological differenciation of the axes,
- the sexuality.

Based on these primary morphological characteristics, Hallé classified the entirety of the known plants into less than thirty models (Fig.1).

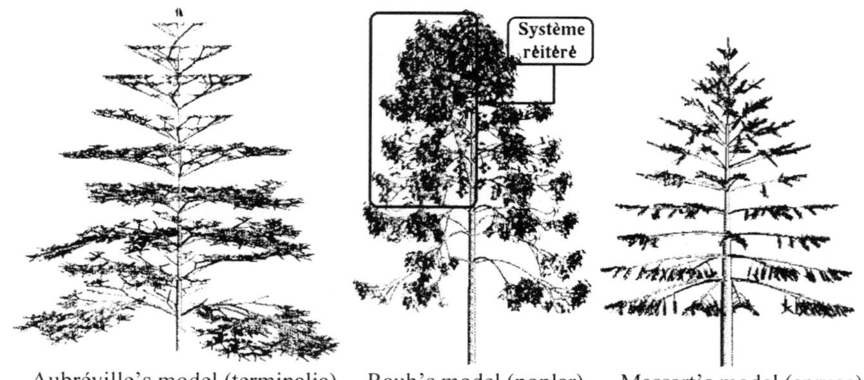

Aubréville's model (terminalia) Rauh's model (poplar) Massart's model (spruce)

FIGURE 1. Examples of architectural models.

The grouping together of the different axes of a tree is also done according to their morphological characteristics. Describing axes through the use of categories helps to define the architectural unit of a tree [5].

Other phenomena affect the architectural structure of a plant. Such is the case with the reiteration process which causes duplication of its own architectural unit within a single plant.

It is important to note that only young trees are considered in this theory since they correspond to a stage of development where the morphology of the axes according to branching order can be differentiated. Their architectures exist in a hierarchy. Thus a particular homogeneous functioning can be related to the founding bud of a plant axis from a given order. The Hevea is a good example of this type of architecture (Fig.2.a).

However, with trees of a temperate climate, the strength of the axes that appeared in a same year is not linked to the notion of branching order most of the time. Thus, on a cherry-type trunk, one can distinguish zones which are alternated with long and short axes from a same branching order (Fig.2.b). In adult trees, the differences between branching orders progressively decrease from the lower to the higher parts where we find structures made up of short axes piled up along the edges. In other words, the architecture of a tree goes through changes as it develops. One must be aware of this notion of metamorphosis in modeling the phenomena of alternance and ageing in plant axes if botanical realism is desired.

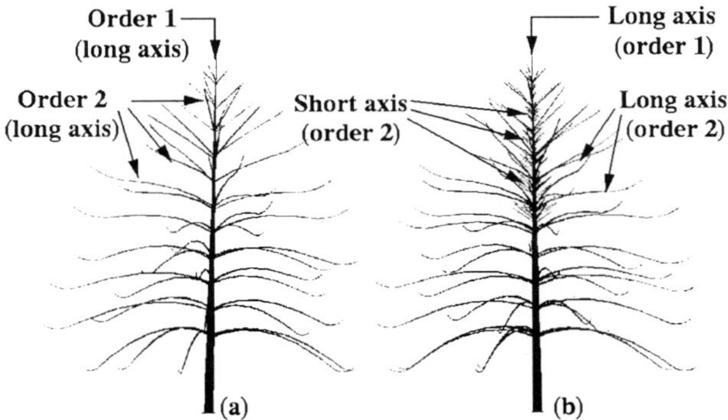

FIGURE 2. Ramification order and axis morphology.

Plant metamorphosis: notion of physiological age. The German writer, Goethe, had a passion for botany and in 1790, he published a work on the metamorphosis of plants [16]. He notes that stems undergo a progressive transformation from the plant stage to a final floral stage. Thus the founding meristem fabricates first a leafy zone which will progressively transform into inflorescence. If the phenomenon occurs rapidly, a herbaceous flowering plant results. If it is very delayed, a tree results. This phenomenon of progressive differentiation of tissue is irreversible.

Daniel Barthélémy defines the concept of automatic flowering in his thesis [3]. He shows that, with all trees, the architecture of a basic model goes through a metamorphosis as it ages which is correlated with the progressive appearance of flowering over all the structure of the plant.

In his studies of types of buds and branches, Rivals [36] notes that two ages co-exist in a tree. He distinguishes the real age and the physiological age. Therefore, the short and flowered outer branches of an adult tree are physiologically old even though they are recently formed. In young trees, growths of the same age can co-exist on an axis although some are physiologically young (main branches) and others are physiologically old (short flowered axes). Thus a bud can be born old! The notion of physiological age is, in fact, the key to the organization of a plant's architecture and of its development.

Physiological age markers in tree organization levels. There are at least four levels of organization in a tree:

- the internodes,
- the growth unit (G.U.),
- the plant axis,
- the architectural unit.

The growth unit is the basis for rhythmic growth of plant axes. These axes are made up of G.U.'s which themselves are made up of internodes that correspond to a plant growth. The juxtaposition of successive G.U.'s thus gives the impression of rhythm. The number of internodes in a G.U. can be fixed or variable and follows a distribution. This is studied in more detail in [18] and [19].

It is in the unit of growth that the notion of physiological age manifests itself the most. In this presentation, we will take an average G.U. and will concern ourselves only with the modeling of the physiological age.

We consider that a G.U. put forth over a year is not yet branched. The branches appear only on the G.U. of the preceding year (Fig.3). Most often, a G.U. is made up of two parts: one of which is preformed; and the other of which is distal and neoformed. The neoformed part is not systematic. The studied G.U.'s have a predominant neoformed part that is absent in the short

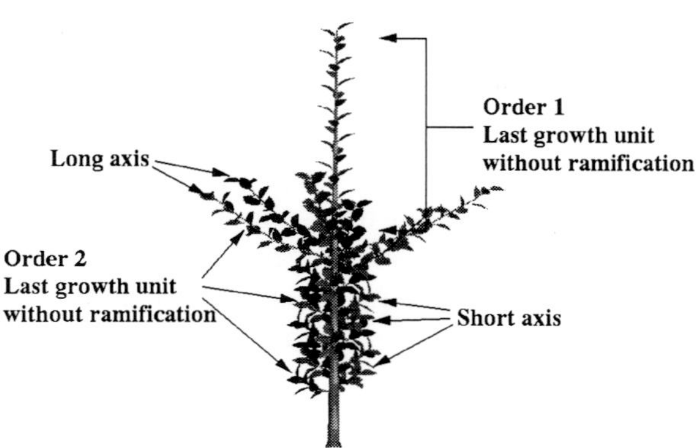

FIGURE 3. Ramification gap on the last G.U.

G.U.'s. The development of the neoformed part is linked to its physiological age.

In general, the strength of axis G.U.'s diminishes as one descends from the top of the carrying G.U. to the preformed part. This phenomenon is called acrotony. The branches are thus ordered according to a physiological age gradient. The short axis G.U.'s of the middle carrying G.U. have an older physiological age while the branching axis G.U.'s at the top are young although older than the carrying G.U.

When the G.U.'s have physiologically aged, they become shorter and shorter and there are fewer differences between the axis and the carrier which reach a terminal physiological age. This fundamental mechanism permits an explanation of the architectural methamorphosis of plants as they develop.

6.3. The Notion of Reference Axis: the Basis for Modeling Architectural Metamorphosis

Definition of the reference axis. One can create a theoretical plant axis which involves all the different possible stages of buds from the seed to the flower (from birth to death). The evolution along this axis is progressive. With each stage that corresponds to a given physiological age, the characteristics of morphological evolution in the bud are made known. We call this plant axis, the reference axis.

The characteristics of evolution in a bud involve, in particular, the stochastic laws of its functioning: processes of growth, death, and branching. The functioning of the apical bud of an axis implies a physiological ageing. The growth is thus marked by an evolution to the stage which leads to flowering in the reference axis. The process of death is marked by the end of evolution in the current stage of the reference axis. Branching implies the development of an axillary bud physiologically older than the principal bud. The initial stage of the axis bud is thus obtained by a jump in stage from the principal bud to the flower in the reference axis.

Only these processes lead to the modification of physiological age. This principle of organization was presented in [24] and [2].

Properties of the reference axis. The notion of reference axis unites the concepts of order and reiteration, and allows for pruning and for the metamorphosis of a plant structure. A reiteration is a certain kind of branching. It is marked by a jump 0 from the physiological age of the axillary bud in the reference axis. Axillary and carrying buds are then the same.

The notion of reference axis allows for automatic pruning of structures. The buds die in the final stage of the reference axis. If all the buds of a branch are at the last stage, the branch can be removed as it is dead and will remove itself .

The metamorphosis is intrensic to the reference axis. It permits a functioning that differenciates little by little as the plants grows. The growth itself, the branching, and the death of the buds are marked by evolutions from one stage to another. The pruning accentuates the change in the physionomy of the plant as it develops.

The description of models based on Hallé's typology of order is marked by a particular reference axis. It is made up of as many stages as branching orders, from order 1 to the ultimate order. The functioning of an apical bud is marked by a jump 0 (it does not age) and the branching is marked by a jump 1.

The image II.1 depicts a plant metamorphosis in 15 stages with a strategy of reiteration and automatic pruning quite well. As a reminder, with temperate climate trees, one stage in the reference axis corresponds to one year in general: the growth is a jump 1.

Automaton, a computer programming structure for the reference axis. The reference axis is thus marked by a finite group of stages and by evolutions that allow passage from one stage to another. If one associated a computer programming entity called *state* to each stage and expressed the evolution using a *transition function*, the structure of an automaton would then be defined (Fig.4). The stages of the reference axis being ordered and the evolution oriented, the associated automaton is said to be *left to right*.

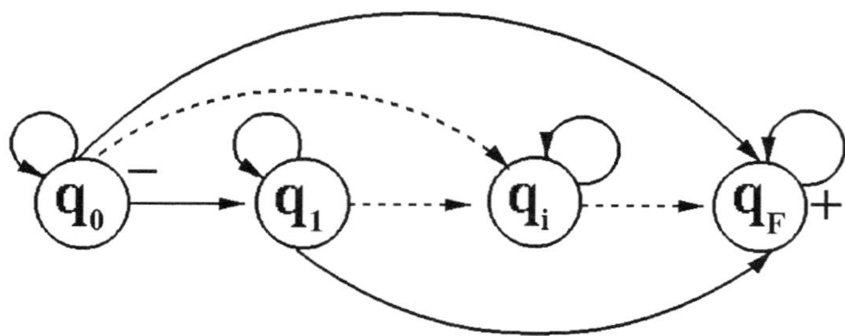

FIGURE 4. The reference axis: a finite automaton.

A state is characterized by three parameters:

- topological parameters (growth, branching, and death laws),
- geometrical parameters (length, angle),
- parameters of the transition function.

In practice, describing certain *key* states could suffice. The parameters of the undescribed states would be deduced from the uniformed states through interpolation. This renders the method particularly efficient.

This finite automaton system is sufficient for determining the tree growth.

Applications. Plate II presents several real plants simulated by an automaton standardized with measured data (Img.II.2, II.3, II.4 and II.5).

Note that this automaton allows for production of fractal like patterns. In this case, the reference axis is limited to one single state. The developement of the plant, in growth and in branching, is characterized by an evolution 0 and a decreasing scale in the plant's geometry.

6.4. Evolution of the growth engine

Introduction. The prefixed engine used in [23] can only simulate free growth in homogeneous conditions and does not take possible external interactions into consideration. This is why we are presenting a new use of bud functionings which permits simulation of their simultaneity in time and

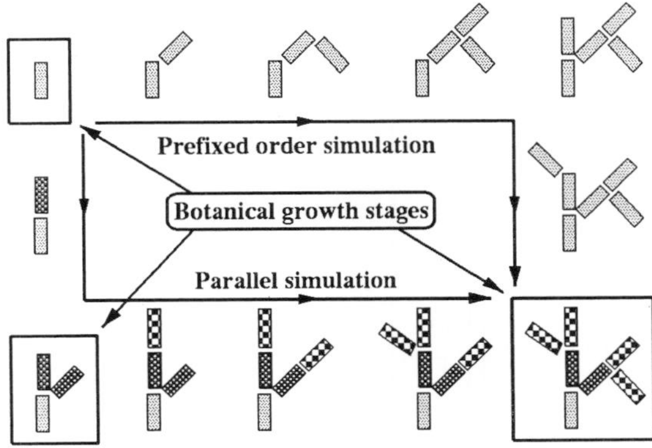

FIGURE 5. Prefixed order and parallel growth engine.

exact control of their given spatial environment: the parallel growth engine. Fig.5 simulates the functioning of a prefixed engine and a parallel engine using a simple example.

One can distinguish three important notions in the simulation of plant growth:

(a) the topology: describes the arrangement of the elementary entities that make up the plant,
(b) the geometry: allows for a link between simulation and visualization of a plant,
(c) growth dynamics: important aspect which allows for the organization of the events that characterize plant growth in time.

These notions are concretely marked by a structure of data and programs that tend to follow the organization of the plant itself.

Computerized method of controlling the simultaneity of events in the plant.

Topology and geometry of the plant. Keep in mind that four specific levels of organization in the plant can be distinguished: the internode, the G.U., the axis and the plant. In fact, this last level permits simulation of growth not only of one isolated plant, but it gives the possibility of considering a group of plants and controlling their possible interactions. This is a new aspect to the parallel growth engine.

For each entity in the structure, the topological links are defined (Fig.6).

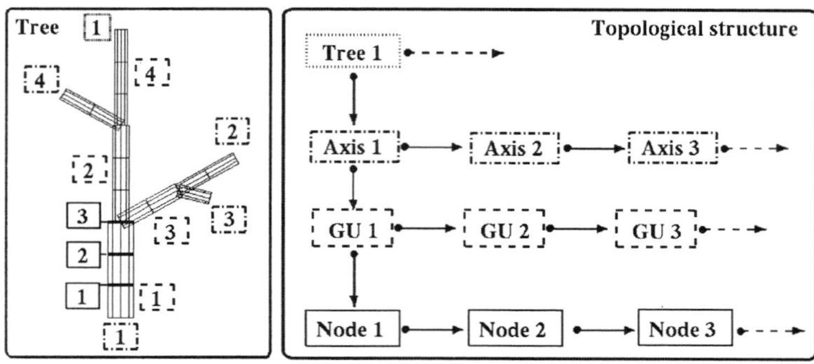

FIGURE 6. Topology hierachical scheme.

Also, this hierarchical structure permits a regrouping of certain data at specific levels according to their significance in order to limit redundancy. For example, the branching order will be stored at axis level instead of at each G.U. level.

There are multiple uses for this topological structure. First of all, it allows us to store the plant's geometry at the lowest level of the hierarchy. Each new internode that appeared during growth is geometrically defined in order to represent the plant at the end of simulation. Then, it allows for control of the pruning. In fact, as soon as an axis is dead and pruned off, all of the entities that were a part of it are suppressed from the topological structure and will not be taken into consideration throughout the rest of growth. Finally, it provides access to the reference axis data. Each internode is linked to a stage in the reference axis corresponding to its physiological age and provides for consultation of the plant's functioning parameters.

Growth dynamics: real time and physiological time. The parallel control of the buds on a sequential machine is made by using the technique of simulation with discrete events [26] [6]. The only accessible times are the times of the events and the incrementation of time is done from one moment to another. The control of time in the simulation is thus assured by a scheduler (Fig.7). It is important to realize that, except for the current event, the other events are only potential as their apparition can be affected as the events that precede them are treated.

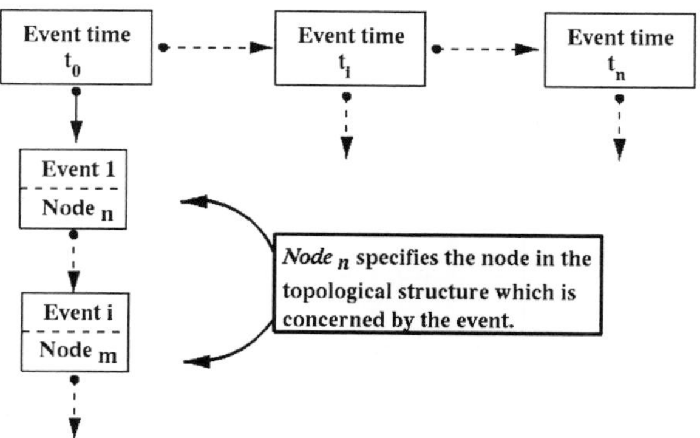

FIGURE 7. Scheduler scheme.

At each moment of occurrence in the scheduler, the simulation will treat a list of events wich concern the creation of new vegetative organs. Their functioning occurs according to their position in the reference axis.

The organ can be inhibited. Thus, the creation event is put off for later in time. This inhibition can result from an endogenous function of the plant or can be the consequence of environmental conditions that are not favorable to the plant at that particular moment. In the case of a death of the organ, we erase its treatment from the scheduler.

When the organ is successfully created, its geometric parameters (position in space and dimensions) are calculated using the parameters defined in the reference axis for the physiological age of the organ. However, spatial interactions (intervening contact in general) can cancel the creation for geometrical reasons.

The creation of a new element involves the updating of the structure of topological data and the scheduler. In addition, a link between it and the stage in the reference axis corresponding to its physiological age will be created.

When a new internode appears, it carries, by definition, a terminal bud and potential axillary buds. Each of these buds can give birth to new event at a specific moment in time. The updating of the scheduler involves determining the times of occurrence of these events and placing them at the adequate moment in the scheduler. These times of occurrence are calculated according to the endogenous functioning parameters of the plant defined in the reference axis.

The updating of these different structures implies the existence of links that permit access to the different parameters and structures involved (Fig.8).

Once all the events at the top of the scheduler's list are treated, we go on

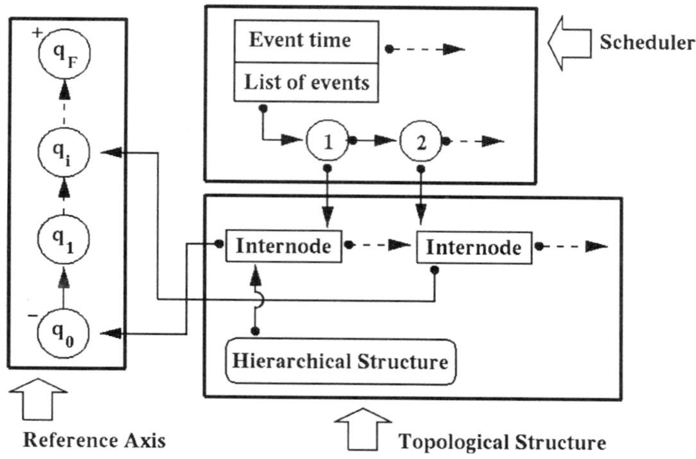

FIGURE 8. Entities and their links.

to the time of occurrence for the following events. The simulation stops as soon as all event times in the scheduler have been treated.

Simulation of the growth in thickness of the axes.

Modeling the diffusion of assimilates. In a temperate climate, the terminal buds put a new leafy G.U.into place, and the diameter of the branches increases by another ring. Only the leafy G.U.'s provide the assimilates that are necessary for growth in length and in thickness of the tree thanks to photosynthetic activity. If one wishes to calculate the thickness of the formed rings at all points on a tree, one must, on the one hand, have a model that takes all knowledge of growth and plant architecture into account, and, on the other hand, one must have use of the laws of production, diffusion, and consumption of the assimilates within the architecture in order to calculate the uniform thickness of the formed rings. One can then explicitely treat the allocation of assimilates according to different laws, and establish a formal link between the internal structure of the branches and the external architecture of the growing tree [35].

Simulation of the diffusion of assimilates model. However complicated a given tree may be, the simulation has access to all the exact characteristics of its architecture at all times, thanks in particular to its topological structure. Specifically, the number of leafy G.U.'s susceptible to produce assimilates through photosynthesis is known.

Let us now consider that the diffusion of assimilates takes place according to a law of uniform distribution. This means that the quantity of

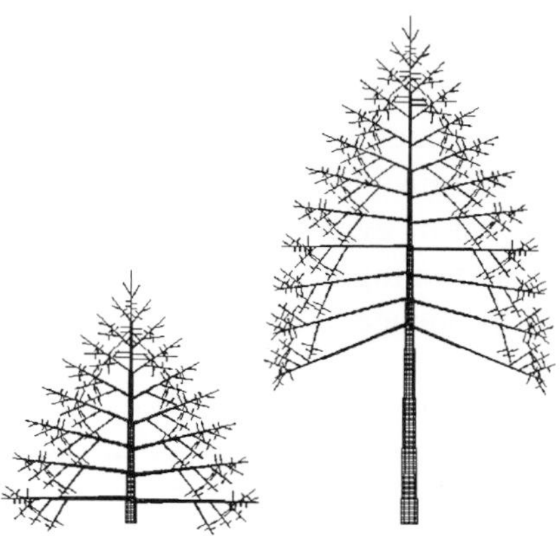

FIGURE 9. Two stages of growth (10 and 20 years).

assimilates sent out by a leafy G.U. each year is constant and is equally distributed into cylindrical rings on each previous G.U. down to the base of the trunk. Using this hypothesis, we are going to study several aspects of the internal structure of a simulated tree's trunk.

Figure 9 shows the architecture of a tree simulated at two stages of its growth (10 years and 20 years). The dominance between carrier axes and carried axes automatically caused by the uniform diffusion is clearly visible when one considers their diameter.

The visualization of the layering of rings can be done longitudinally or radially. The longitudinal section is voluntarily condensed in order to better visualize the profile (Fig.10).

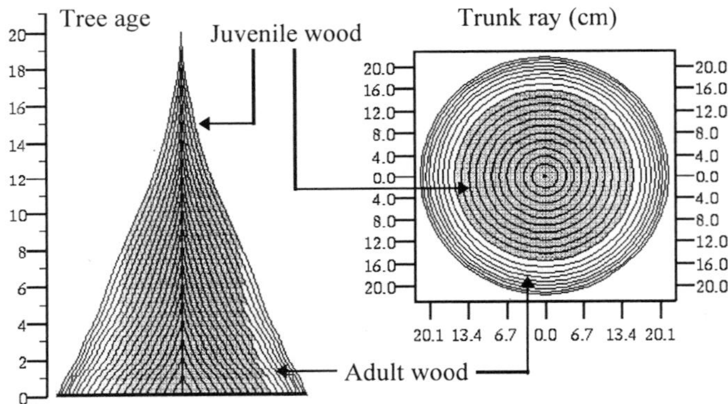

FIGURE 10. Longitudinal and radial sections to the trunk basis (20 years).

6.5. Influence of Climate on Annual Growth

The dynamics of tree growth, such as the ordering in time of the events that are characteristic of the architectural formation, is maintained by a scheduler. This structure allows for the discretization of real time. For each discrete date, there is a list of events to be treated. Supposing that climatic conditions during the functioning of the buds concerned by these events are equally available, the influence of stress on their activity can also be simulated.

Thus, a "stress" data file, that describes the influence of climatic conditions on primary and secondary growth of internodes throughout the growth of a tree, can be defined. This data file is made up, for each discrete date, of two "climatic factors", between 0.0 and 1.0, which permit the balancing of the length of the internode and the quantity of assimilates produced by the leaves or needles by reducing their assimilatory capacity. A factor of 1.0 defines optimal conditions.

Figure 11 shows the results obtained for different stress data files on a 15 year-old pine tree. The left pine, which experienced no stress, shows growth units with 5 internodes on the trunk, the last of which is a short internode.

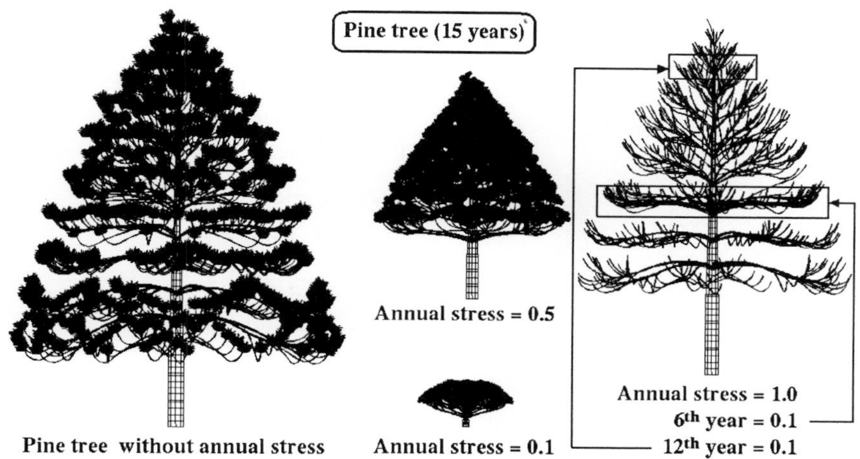

FIGURE 11. Climatic influence on pine tree's growth.

Two other simulations utilize stress data files where climatic conditions remain homogeneous throughout growth, both for lengthening and for production of the assimilates. The first, with a climatic factor of 0.5, particulary modifies the G.U.'s of the trunk that, at that point, have 2 or 3 internodes. The balancing of assimilate production limits secondary growth. A modification in the assimilative capacities of the needles is a consequence of the reduction in their size. The second simulation utilizes a climatic factor of 0.1. In this case, the trunk is made up of G.U.'s with only a single short internode: one obtains a natural "bonzai". There is also great reduction in the diameter of the trunk. Climate conditions in mountains could cause such an architecture.

The last simulation is the result of optimal climatic conditions growth except for the 6th and the 12th years when the climatic factor is 0.1. During these two years, the G.U. of the trunk will only be made up of a single, short internode. This explains the short distance separating the verticils of the axes with a branching order of 2 between the 6th and 7th years and the 12th and 13th years.

We are now going to look at the influence of climatic conditions on the formation of the rings in greater detail. Take, for example, the previously presented 15 year-old pine, that experienced two unfavorable (the 6th and the 12th) during its growth. The pine tree on the right in figure 11 shows the architecture of the tree in question.

The longitudinal and radial sections of the trunk show a small width of the rings for the unfavorable years (Fig.12). Keep in mind that the pine tree is 15 years old, and that the 6th year corresponds to the 10 year-old rings and the 12th year corresponds to the 4 year-old rings.

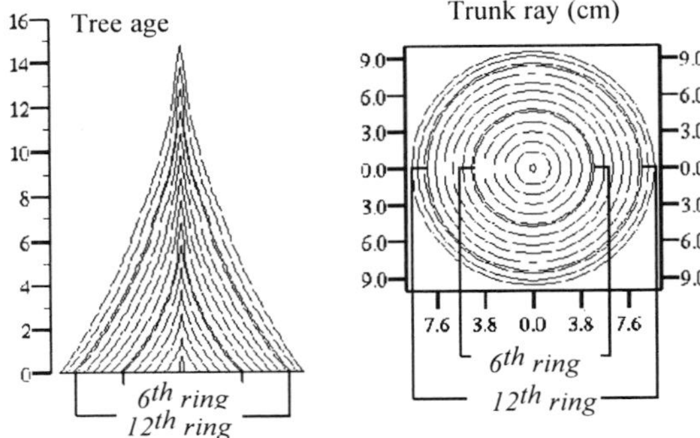

FIGURE 12. Longitudinal and radial sections of the stressed pine tree.

6.6. Simulation of the Tree/Environment Interactions

The tree and its environment. Architectural studies are always done on populations of individuals in a given agro-climatic context. Statistical analysis of the functioning of the buds thus allows for the reproduction of the studied trees' architecture in all its variability. The effect of the environmental factors (soil, fertilization, water supply, lighting...) can be taken into consideration by analyzing the architectural parameters at different stages or when receiving different treatments.

Reconstituating the plant formations is not just a matter of the positioning, within a given space, of trees that were simulated independently from each other: the competition between neighboring trees should be taken into consideration [6] [7]. As a reminder, the growth engine, by utilizing plant level of the topology hierarchical structure, allows for the growth simulation of several trees at a time. This competition intervenes at different levels. We will not discuss the competition between the roots at this time, but we are interested in the competition between the aerial parts. This competition is especially linked to the penetration of sunrays into the canopy.

Besides the action of the light, other physically impeding phenomena within the crown of a tree or between the crowns of neighboring trees can cause a "pruning" of the plant axes.

Discretization of space and trees. One problem resides in the resolution of the collisions between entities with known geometries. The most direct solution is to use the analytic geometry that, with the help of classic tools, will be entirely satisfactory in most cases. This approach can only be used for scenes composed of a limited number of volumes and surfaces with simple geometries. It is not, however, conceivable in treating plant formations with a great number of elements. We have also used the voxel space technique which has already been created to manage the interactions between a tree and its environement (obstacles, shading) during its growth [17].

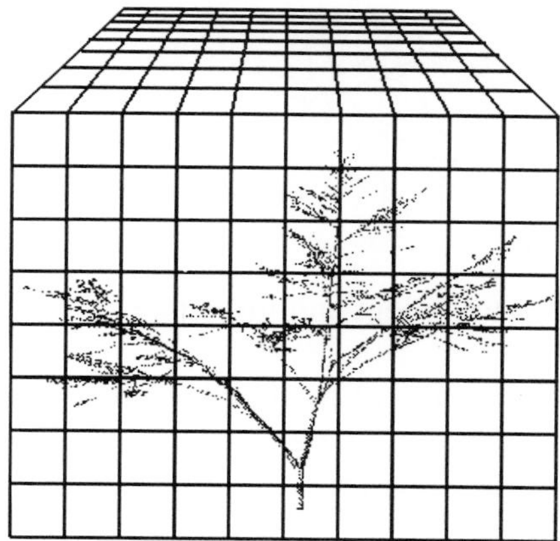

FIGURE 13. Voxel space and discretization of trees.

Voxel space is defined as a region in 3-D space which becomes discrete by following a regular mesh of parallelograms or voxels. The dimension of the voxel is still called discretization pace. Thanks to this discrete space, it is easier and quicker to determine certain relationships, such as proximity or intersection between geometrical objects, than with the use of analytical geometry. Indeed, the objects to be treated are plant organs that are considered not as geometrical entities, but as groups of voxels (Fig.13). A voxel is thus considered occupied once it is crossed by an organ.

Detection and treatment of the impediment. An impediment intervenes each time that an axis penetrates into a voxel that is already occupied. Depending on the case, different treatments can, nevertheless, be carried out. Indeed, for mecanical reasons, the probability of collision between two axes depends on their "topological spacing". For example, two axes carried by the same G.U. are minimally susceptible, despite their proximity, to mutually impeding each other. On the other hand, two geometrically similar axes belonging to different main branches, *a fortiori* different trees, have a strong chance of collision. Once the eventual collision is detected, and the impediment demonstrated, an adequate treatment must still be completed. It is not important to determine the exact intersections between the internodes. Only the absence or existence of a collision interests us. This would mean inhibition or continuation of growth. In other words, in the case of impediment, the bud dies.

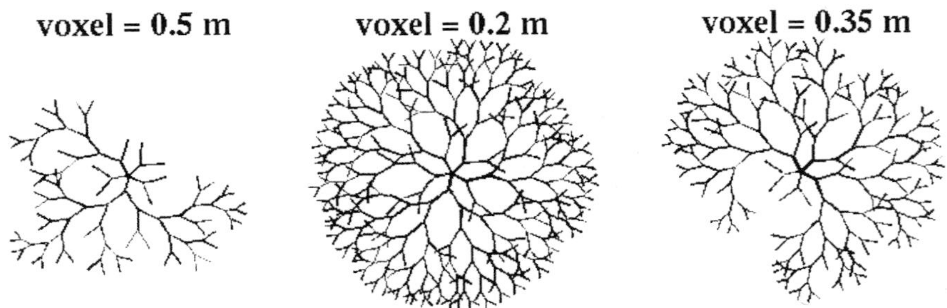

FIGURE 14. Impediment treatment and influence of the discretization pace.

Figure 14 shows the results of treatment of the impediment of branches at the first level of a terminalia. The dimension of the voxel discreting space can greatly modify the resulting architecture, of course. But it is not for this reason that one should consider the principle of discretization of space as a method with undependable or even random results. Indeed, the different architectures obtained with voxels of different dimensions gradually evolve and converge towards a "limit" topology that corresponds to an asymptotic value for the pace of discretization. In other words, a minimal pace value exists under which the obtained architectures are similar [6].

Another phenomenon is known as architectural shyness in plants. It expresses the capacity in certain species to avoid the crowns of neighboring trees by limiting development of their own branches before contact. It is manifested by the formation of open spaces between neighboring crowns (Fig.15).

FIGURE 15. Simulation of two tropical trees with shyness effect.

Light influence.

Trees and light. The influence of light is considered to intervene in two different manners:

- by modulating the growth and bud branching processes according to the quantity and the quality of the locally-received light,
- by orienting the plant axes in order to intercept the maximum amount of light (phototropism).

The penetration of light depending on its direction must be calculated. This problem of the priveleged direction of light brings us to the problem of selecting the different directions to be analyzed.

Model of light penetration. The penetration of light can only be calculated in a limited number of discrete directions. Each direction is associated with an angular sector. So that all the angular sectors can have the same solid

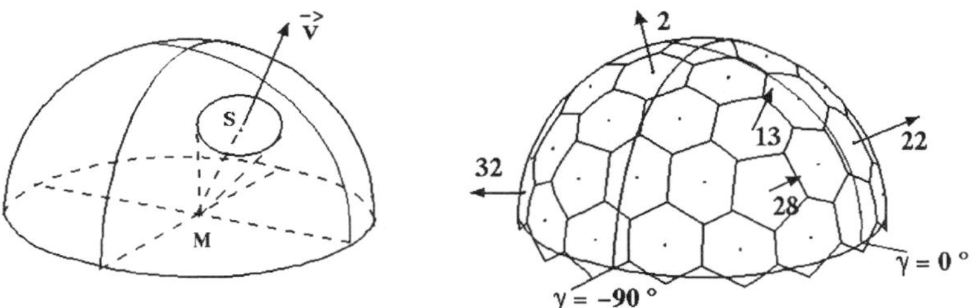

FIGURE 16. Discretization of the canopy of heaven using the TURTLE model.

angle, a particular discretization of the canopy of heaven is necessary. In this case, 46 directions are defined in the hemisphere, each at around 24 away other adjacent angles [9] (Fig.16).

In order to calculate the amount of light that arrives in a voxel, one should cover all of the voxels crossed in each defined direction (Fig.17). The amount of light that crosses each voxel is determined by its contents. The percentage of incident rays in a given direction is the product of the rate of transmission of the crossed voxels. We assume that the light of the sky is identical for all 46 sectors.

Searching for light. Each new portion of the axis put in place in voxel space has an original direction determined by the orientation of its carrier axis. The intensity of the rays received from the 46 sectors can induce a deviation from this original direction. The importance of each sector in this calculation depends on the difference in angle between its direction and the original direction of the axis. The resulting deviation can be modulated according to the parameters of light sensibility. Figure 18 shows the reaction of a tree that is very sensitive to the shade of an opaque wall.

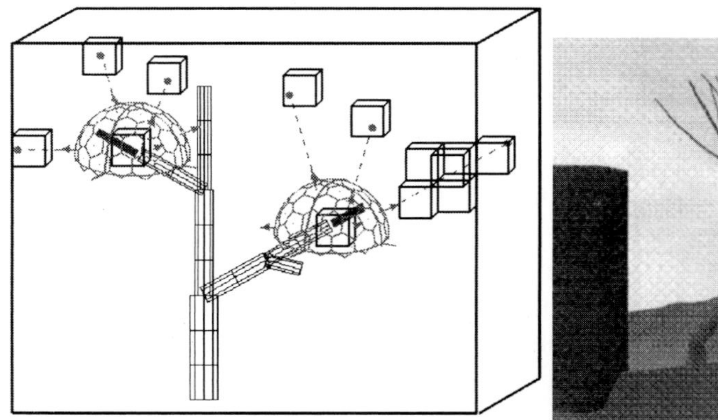

FIGURE 17. Amount of light in a voxel.

FIGURE 18. Search for ligtht.

Influence of inter-crown interactions on secondary growth. Figure 19 presents an overhead view of a grove of 6 spruce trees in competition and one isolated spruce that developed without any hindrance from neighbors and that will serve as a reference. An influence by the neighboring trees on the development of the crown of the central tree is noticeable, as well as a general tendency by the surrounding trees to develop towards the exterior in order to benefit from open space.

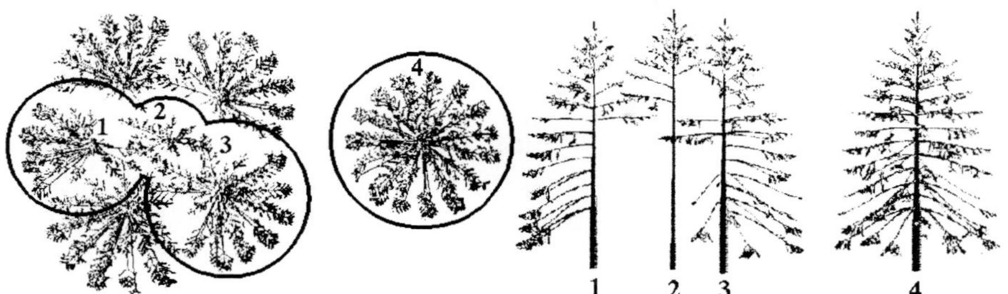

FIGURE 19. Influence of the self-pruning on the secondary growth.

In the right half of this figure, we selected 4 spruce trees in particular: 3 from the grove, including the central tree, and 1 isolated tree. This image shows a great difference in the thickness of the trunks, especially between the isolated tree and the central tree. This is explained by the "pruning" of numerous branches from the grove trees, as a consequence of the phenomena of impediment between crowns. Indeed, by disappearing, these branches, or leafy growth units, stopped producing assimilates and caused a great reduction in the width of the trunk rings.

Figure 20 shows the longitudinal and radial sections at the base of the trunk for the isolated tree and the central tree of the grove. The concentric rings of the isolated tree are more regular than those of the central tree. This is explained by the relative homogeneity of the isolated tree's crown all throughout its growth.

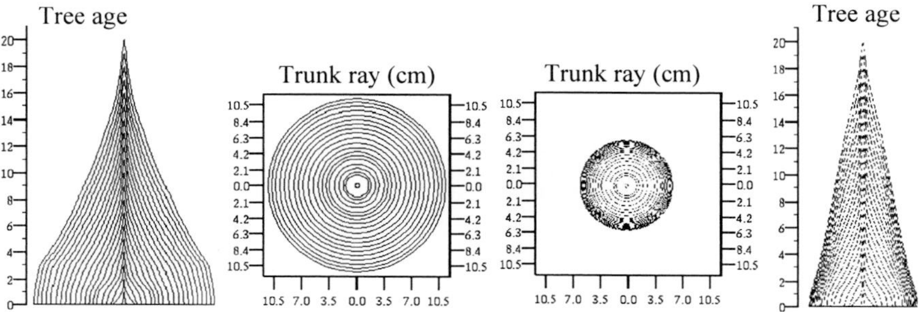

FIGURE 20. Longitudinal and radial sections at the base of the trunk for the isolated and the central trees.

6.7. Technical Aspects

The growth engine, developed in C language, is implemented on UNIX workstations. The result of the simulation is a data structure which describes the 3-D geometry of each element of the plant with a transformation matrix [24].

The definition of simple graphical objects (internodes, leaves, fruits, flowers) allows for a representation of the simulated plant. In addition, a program for composing lanscapes allows for productions with plants, terrains and buildings (defined by usual CAD/CAM softwares). A realistic rendering (including texture mapping, shadows and light reflection) is thus calculated using the Open_GL library of Silicon Graphics (Img.III.1, III.2 and III.3).

In particular, the *landmaker* software allows for an interactive description of complicated plantations using specific tools. This possibility will be used in the conception of groves for the parallel engine.

Finally, an animation package allows for description of the path of an observer in the landscape, and the definition of a growth interval for the trees.

This set of tools makes up the AMAP program. The realistic images in this paper have been generated by AMAP.

6.8. Conclusion

The notion of reference axis allows us to define a continuum of morphological differentiation (ageing), and thus to express metamorphosis. Therefore, the typology created by Hallé becomes a result of plant functioning and not an initial cause. The fundamental notions of order and reiteration become visual notions induced by the functioning. The methods for measuring the G.U. defined in [2] allow for the standardization of reference axes in the studied species. If we use a finite automaton structure to represent the notion of reference axis, other techniques among those evoked in the introduction can certainly simulate plant metamorphosis.

The simultaneity of events during plant growth is simulated by a scheduler. This new use of growth dynamics permits numerous applications that are operational in agronomy from now on. Also, the parallelism in the growth engine offers the possibility of simulating plant growth while taking into consideration spatial and environmental interactions.

The result of the simulation is a three-dimensional model where one can both count the fabricated topological entities and visualize the resulting geometry, especially the aerial architecture of the tree and the layers of rings in the trunk caused by migration of the assimilates according to the chosen mode of diffusion. However complex the tree's architecture may be, the diffusion of the assimilates can be simulated.

Because of the parallellism of active buds and the discretization of space, simulation of growth of not just one tree, but a group of plants, and the treatment of interactions between their crowns is possible. All reduction in the volume of leaves, no matter its origin, will have an implication on the production of assimilates and thus on the quantity of wood produced. Use of the TURTLE model, in discreting the sun's light into prefered directions, allows one to estimate the quantity of light received by the leaves and thus precisely calculate their photosynthetic capacity in order to model the production of assimilates.

Other applications are made possible by parallelism in the generation of buds and by the treatment of interactions. Thus, the quantity of wood produced by the diffusion of assimilates is spread out along the whole architecture and mechanically responds with it. It is thus possible to create mechanics of a rooted tree; study the equilibrium of the tree, according to the density of the wood and the laws of diffusion; and even contemplate mechanical or architectural reactions. Futhermore, the simulation of multi-specific or non-aged plantations would be possible, which would optimize lighting strategies with chosen constraints for the optimal ligneous result. The developed models should, indeed, inspire very pertinent simplications that would allow for the calculation of interactions within the population.

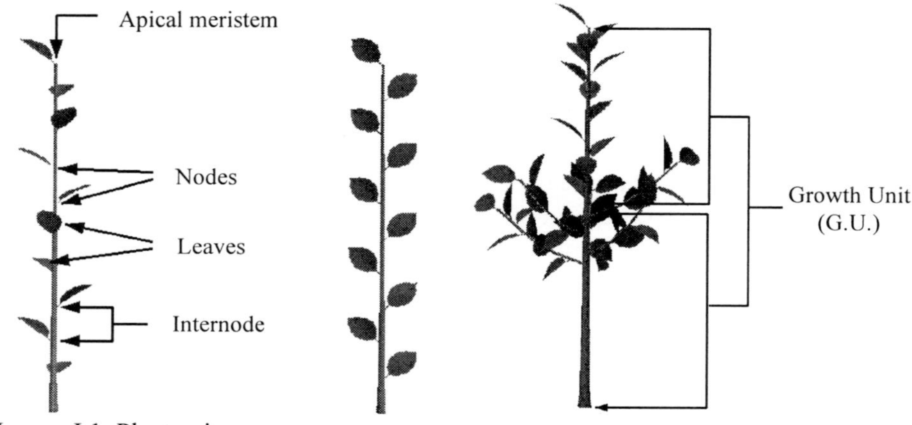

IMAGE I.1. Plant axis.

IMAGE I.2. Growth unit (G.U.)

(a) Sylleptic branching (b) Proleptic branching

IMAGE I.3. Continued growth.

(a) Monopodial branching and lateral flowering (b) Sympodial branching and terminal flowering

IMAGE I.4. Rythmic growth.

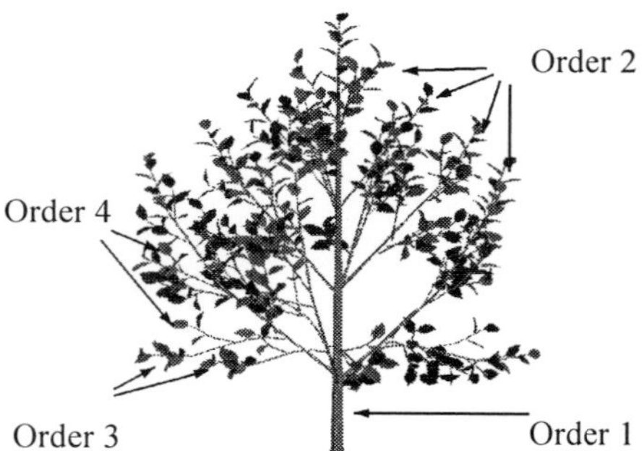

IMAGE I.5. Ramification order.

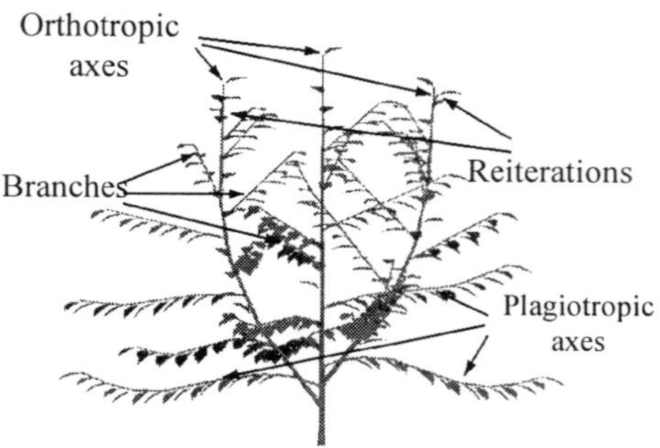

IMAGE I.6. Direction of growth.

Plate I

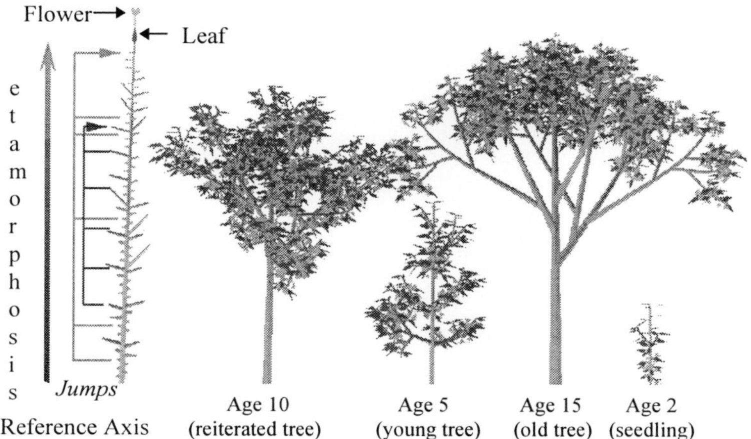

IMAGE II.1. Growth and metamorphosis of a theoritical plant.

IMAGE II.2. Growth and metamorphosis of a cotton tree.

IMAGE II.3. Plantation of rubber trees.

IMAGE II.4. Growth and metamorphosis of Japonese Elm (*Zelkova serrata*).

IMAGE II.5. Close-up of palm tree plantation.

Plate II

IMAGE III.1. Landscape with CAD/CAM objects and plants.

IMAGE III.2. Shadow effect in a forest.

IMAGE III.3. Light reflection on water.

Plate III

References

1. Aono, M., Kunii, T.L., 1984. *Botanical tree image generation.* IEEE Computer Graphics and Applications, Vol.4(5), pp 10-33.
2. Barczi, J.F., Reffye (de) Ph., Caraglio, Y., 1997. *Essai sur l'identification et la mise en oeuvre des paramètres nécessaires à la simulation d'une architecture végétale : le logiciel AMAPsim.* In Bouchon J., Reffye (de) Ph. & Barthélémy D. (Eds), *Modélisation et simulation de l'architecture des végétaux*, INRA, Science Update, pp. 205-254.
3. Barthélémy, D., 1988. *Architecture et sexualité chez quelques plantes tropicales: le concept de floraison automatique.* Thèse Doct., Physiologie, Biologie des Organismes et des Populations, Montpellier, France.
4. Barthélémy, D., Blaise, F, Fourcaud, T., Nicolini, E., 1995. *Modélisation et simulation de l'architecture des arbres : bilan et perspectives.* Revue forestière française, n° spécial "Modélisation de la croissance des arbres forestiers et de la qualité des bois", 71-96.
5. Barthélémy, D., Caraglio, Y., Costes, E., 1997. *Architecture, gradients morphogénétiques et âge physiologique chez les végétaux.* In Bouchon J., Reffye (de) Ph. & Barthélémy D. (Eds), *Modélisation et simulation de l'architecture des végétaux*, INRA, Science Update, pp. 89-136.
6. Blaise, F., 1991. *Simulation du parallélisme dans la croissance des plantes et application.* Thèse 3ème cycle, spécialité informatique, N°1071, Université Louis Pasteur, Strasbourg, France.
7. Blaise F., Houllier F., Reffye (de) Ph., 1996. *Simulation of tree architecture and growth in a forest stand: AMAPpara software.* In G. Nepveu (Ed.), *Connection between silviculture and wood quality through modelling approaches and simulation softwares*, IUFRO WP S5.01.04 Workshop (Hook, Sweden, 13-17/06/94), INRA, Nancy, pp. 46-55.
8. Dauzat, J., Eroy, N.M., 1996. *Simulating light regime and intercrop yields in coconut based farming systems.* European Society for Agronomy, 7-11 July, Wageningen, The Netherlands, 16 pp.
9. Dulk (den), J.A., 1989. *The Interpretation of Remote Sensing, a feasibility study.* Master's thesis, Wageningen Agricultural University, Neederland.
10. Eyrolles, G., Viennot, G., Françon, J., 1986. *Combinatoire pour la synthèse d'images réalistes de plantes.* 2ème Semaine de l'Image Electronique, Nice, France.
11. Fisher, J.B., Honda, H., 1979. *Branch geometry and effective leaf area: a study of terminalia branching pattern -1- theoretical trees. -2- survey of real trees.* Amer. J. Bot., Vol.66, pp 633-644,645-655.
12. Fournier, A., 1987. *Prolegomenon* in *Modeling of Natural Phenomena.* Course notes #16, Siggraph'87, Anaheim.
13. Françon, J., 1990. *Sur la modélisation informatique de l'architecture et du développement des végétaux.* 2ème Colloque International "L'Arbre", Institut de Botanique, Montpellier, France.

14. Gardner, G.Y., 1984. *Simulation of Natural Scenes using Textured Quadrics Surfaces*. Computer Graphics, Vol.18(3), pp 11-20.
15. Godin, C., Guédon, Y., Costes, E., Caraglio, Y., 1997. *Measuring and analysing plants with the AMAPmod software.* In Marek T. Michalewicz (ed.), *Advances in computational life sciences: Plants to ecosystems*, CSIRO, Australia: 53-84.
16. Goethe (von), J.W., 1790. *La métamorphose des plantes.* Traduction de Bideau, H., 1975, Editions Triades, Paris.
17. Green, N., 1989. *Voxel space automata: modeling with stochastic growth processes in voxel space*. Computer Graphics, Vol.23(3), pp 175-184.
18. Guédon, Y., 1997. *Modélisation de la séquence d'événements décrivant la mise en place d'éléments botaniques.* In Bouchon J., Reffye (de) Ph. & Barthélémy D. (Eds), *Modélisation et simulation de l'architecture des végétaux*, INRA, Science Update, pp. 187-202.
19. Guédon Y., Costes E., 1997. *Modélisation de la croissance d'un axe végétatif.* In Bouchon J., Reffye (de) Ph. & Barthélémy D. (Eds), *Modélisation et simulation de l'architecture des végétaux*, INRA, Science Update, pp. 173-185.
20. Hallé, F., Oldeman, R.A.A., 1970. *Essai sur l'architecture et la dynamique de croissance des arbres tropicaux.* Masson and Cie.
21. Hallé, F., Oldeman, R.A.A., Tomlinson, P.B., 1978. *Tropical Trees and Forests.* Springer Verlag, Berlin, Heidelberg, New-York, 441p.
22. Hart, J.C., DeFanti, T.A., 1991. *Efficient Antialiaised Rendering of 3-D Linear Fractals*. Computer Graphics, Vol.25(4), pp.91-100.
23. Jaeger, M., 1987. *Représentation et Simulation de Croissance des végétaux.* Thèse 3ème cycle, spécialité informatique, N°328, Université Louis Pasteur, Strasbourg, France.
24. Jaeger, M., Reffye (de), Ph., 1991. *Basic concepts of computer simulation of plant growth.* Journal of Biosciences, Vol.17(3), pp 275-291.
25. Kawagushi, Y., 1982. *A morphological Study of the Forme of Nature*. Computer Graphics, Vol.16(3), p 223-232.
26. Leroudier, J., 1980. *La simulation à événements discrets.* Monographies d'informatique de l'AFCET, Hommes et Techniques Edition.
27. Mech, R., Prusinkiewicz, P., 1996. *Visual Models of Plants Interacting with their Environment*. Proceedings of SIGGRAPH 96 (New Orleans, Louisiana, August 4-9, 1996). In *Computer Graphics* Proceedings, Annual Conference Series, 1996, ACM SIGGRAPH, pp. 397-410.
28. Nelson, M., 1990. *Cone-Spheres*. Computer Graphics, Vol.24(4), pp. 59-62.
29. Oppenheimer, E., 1986. *Real time Design and Animation of Fractal Plants and Trees*. Computer Graphics, Vol.20(4), pp 55-64.
30. Prusinkiewicz, P., James, M., Mech, R., 1994. *Synthetic topiary*. Proceedings of SIGGRAPH 94 (Orlando, Florida, July 24-29, 1994). In *Computer Graphics* Proceedings, Annual Conference Series, 1994, ACM SIGGRAPH, pp. 351-358.
31. Prusinkiewicz, P., Hammel, M., Mjolsness, E., 1993. Animation of Plant Development. Proceedings of SIGGRAPH 93 (Anaheim, California, August 1-6, 1993), In *Computer Graphics* Proceedings, Annual Conference Series, 1993, ACM SIGGRAPH, pp. 351-360.

32. Reeves, W.T., Blau, R., 1985. *Approximate and Probabilistic Algorithms for Shading and Rendering Structured Particle Systems.* Computer Graphics, Vol.19(3), pp 313-322.
33. Reffye (de), Ph., Dinouard, P., Jaeger, M., 1990. *Basic concepts of computer plants growth simulation.* NICOGRAPH'90 Computer Graphics: "Where do we go now that we've arrived?", Tokyo, pp 219-234.
34. Reffye (de) Ph., Houllier F., Blaise F., Barthélémy D., Dauzat J., Auclair D., 1995. *A model simulating above- and below- ground tree architecture with agroforestry applications.* Agroforestry Systems, 30: 175-197.
35. Reffye (de) Ph., Houllier F., Blaise F., Fourcaud T., 1997. *Essai sur les relations entre l'architecture d'un arbre et la grosseur de ses axes végétatifs.* In Bouchon J., Reffye (de) Ph. & Barthélémy D. (Eds), *Modélisation et simulation de l'architecture des végétaux*, INRA, Science Update, pp. 255-423.
36. Rivals, P., 1965. *Essai sur la croissance des arbres et sur leurs systèmes de floraison.* Journée d'Agriculture Tropicale et de Botanique appliquée. Vol.XII(12), pp 655-686, Vol.XII(1-2-3), pp 91-122, Vol.XIV, pp 67-102.
37. Sims, K., 1991. *Artificial Evolution for Computer Graphic.* Computer Graphics, Vol.25(4), pp 329-328.
38. Smith, A.R., 1984. *Plants, fractals and formal languages.* Computer Graphics, Vol.18(3), pp 1-10.
39. Viennot, X., Eyrolles, G., Janay, N., Arques, D., 1989. *Combinatorial Analysis of Ramified Patterns and Computer Imagery of Trees.* Computer Graphics, Vol.23(3), pp.31-40.

7. Synthetic Animals in Synthetic Worlds

Agnès Guillot and Jean-Arcady Meyer
Ecole Normale Supérieure, Animatlab, 75230 Paris Cedex 05, France
(e-mail:guillot@wotan.ens.fr, meyer@wotan.ens.fr)

Summary.
This paper provides an overview of various research efforts that aim at designing adaptive *animats*, i.e. synthetic animals able to survive in synthetic worlds. The control architectures of these animats are either programmed by a human designer or, more or less, automatically determined by means of nature-mimicking processes such as learning, evolution and development. The paper concludes with a brief discussion of the directions in which future animat research should be oriented.
Key words: Animats, Control architecture, Development, Evolution, Learning

7.1. Introduction

Synthetic worlds are inhabited by synthetic animals - or *animats* - which live, feed, reproduce and die in these worlds. Animats are equipped with sensors, with actuators and with control architectures that endow them with more or less sophisticated adaptive abilities. They are at the heart of a significant number of research programs [7], [14], [16], [18] in both fundamental and applied perspectives. On the one hand, indeed, the synthesis of animats can be expected to help in understanding how real animals manage to survive in real worlds. On the other hand, the corresponding mechanisms and working principles may prove to be effective in devising truly autonomous and adaptive robots.

The literature on animats falls into four broad categories [9], [15], [17], [19], according to whether it concerns animats whose control architectures have been *programmed* by a human designer, or animats whose behavioral plasticity is due to biologically-inspired automatic processes - like the processes of *learning, evolution* or *development.*

In order to illustrate the diversity and the originality of the animat approach, this paper will describe several research efforts drawn from the corresponding literature. It will conclude with a brief discussion of the directions in which future work should be oriented.

7.2. Preprogrammed Behaviors

Many animats exhibit adaptive behaviors because they have been purposely preprogrammed by a human designer. The work of Beer [3], for instance, belongs to the field of "neuroethology", which aims at reproducing as faithfully as possible available knowledge about the nervous systems of actual animals. Beer has elaborated a model enabling an artificial cockroach to display sequences of behaviors that ensure its survival in a simple simulated environment - a rectangular area with obstacles, walls and food patches. The whole control architecture of the insect consists of four interconnected neural networks that control locomotion, edge-following and both appetitive and consummatory behaviors involved in feeding (Figure 1).

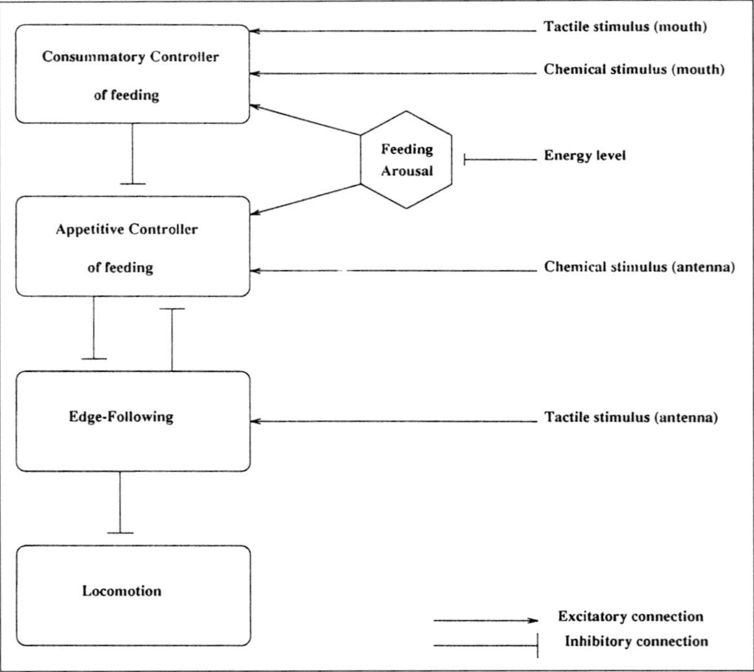

FIGURE 1. Global control architecture of Beer's artificial insect. After [3].

Neurons correspond to sensory units, motor units, motivation units or interneurons. The network depicted on Figure 2a, for instance, ensures the insect's locomotion and governs the rhythmic motion of its legs. This network calls upon three motor neurons: the neurons involved with *stance* and *swing* determine how forcefully the leg is propelled forward or backward, while the *foot* motor neuron determines whether or not the foot is set down. Motion's periodicity is due to a *pacemaker* neuron P, and the force applied in each stance phase, together with the periodicity of P discharges, depends on a general level of excitation controlled by the *command* neuron C. The sensors essential to the operation of such a network are two neurons that emit a signal whenever a leg reaches an extreme angle. Lastly, a central connection between the pacemakers (Figure 2b) synchronizes the movements of the insect's legs, thus guaranteeing its stability. In addition, other neurons not described here allow the insect to make use of its motor equipment for specific purposes, such as avoiding obstacles.

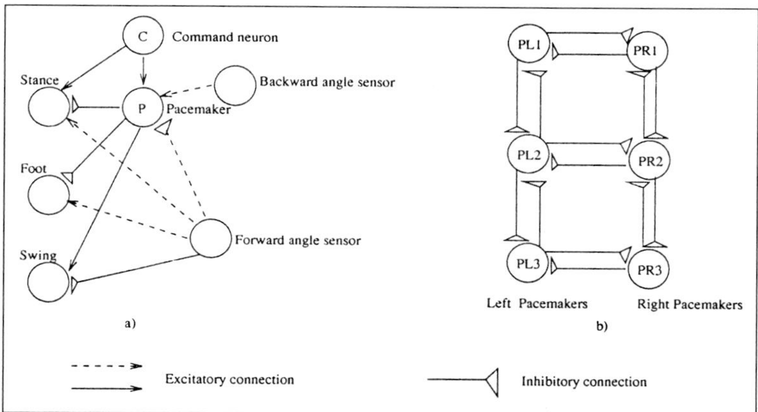

FIGURE 2. Beer's artificial insect circuits. a) leg controller. b) central coupling between pacemakers. After [3].

Another neural network enables the insect to reach food patches when it is hungry (Figure 3a). The odors detected by the chemical sensors located on each antenna (ACS) are compared by two neurons, LOS and ROS. The difference detected is used to generate a rotation towards the strongest odor caused by the excitation of an appropriate interneuron -LT or RT- governing the lateral extension of the front legs. When the energy rate of the insect decreases, the activity of an *energy sensor* neuron (ES) also diminishes, thus disinhibiting a *feeding arousal* neuron (FA) that otherwise would be spontaneously active. This neuron then excites a *search command* neuron (SC), that will decide whether or not to head for food.

A third network (Figure 3b) governs food ingestion. When the chemical (MCS) and tactile (MTS) sensors in the mouth indicate that food is present (FP), and when the insect is motivated enough to feed (FA), the *consum-*

matory command neuron (CC) is activated and forces the *pacemaker* neuron (BP) to produce rhythmic signals that make the *motor* neuron (MO) open and close the mouth. When the energy rate increases, the activation level ES inhibits FA, which in turn ends up by suppressing the activity of BP and causes the feeding to stop. Moreover, a positive feedback loop between FA, PB and MO modulates realistically the frequency of chewing during a meal.

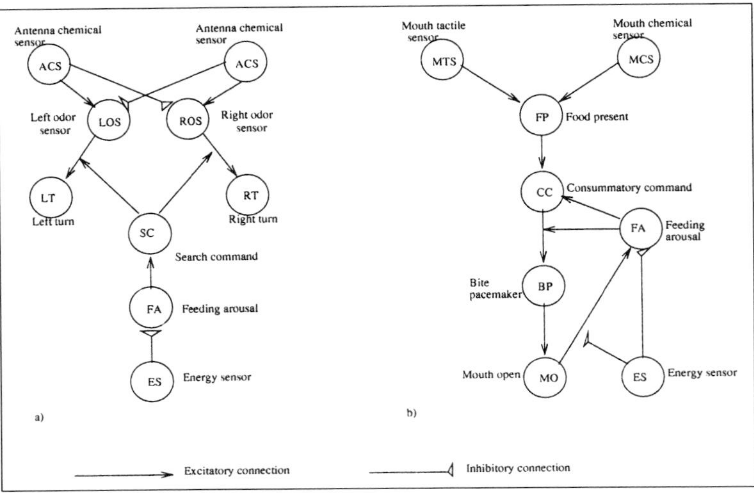

FIGURE 3. Beer's artificial insect circuits. a) appetitive controller of feeding. b) consummatory controller of feeding. After [3].

Considering that the same neurons are involved in the initiation and control of these behaviors, a specific organization must preclude the simultaneous occurrence of incompatible acts - i.e., those calling upon the same motor units. The solution retained is a *hierarchical organization*, where the consummatory part of feeding takes precedence over the orientation towards food, which in turn is dominant with respect to the obstacle avoidance (Figure 1). According to such an organization, exploration is the behavior engaged in by default, while locomotion is activated in the course of every behavior entering into this hierarchy.

This architecture allows an artificial insect to perform realistic successions of behaviors such as those illustrated in Figure 4: at point A, the insect detects food, but cannot reach it; instead of staying there, it edge-follows the obstacle (point B); at point C, it looses the food odor, wanders and edge-follows the wall (point D); at point E, it detects food again and finally reaches it (point F).

This work demonstrates that adaptive behavioral sequences can emerge in an animat endowed with a very simple nervous system connected in a

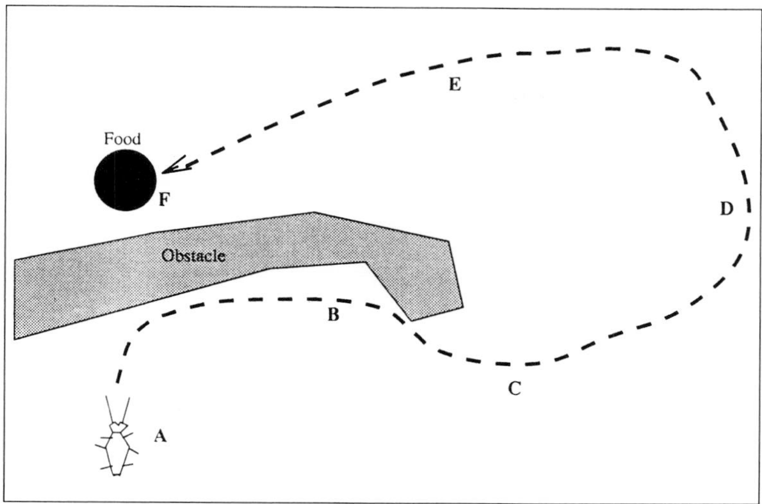

FIGURE 4. An adaptive behavioral sequence of Beer's artificial insect. After [3].

clever way by its designer. The insect architecture is totally distributed, but not uniformly: it must be structured so as to ensure an adapted alternation between behaviors in response to changes in the animat's internal state or in the external environment.

7.3. Learned Behaviors

To reduce the role of a human designer to a minimum, many studies address the way animats can autonomously improve the adaptiveness of their behaviors while experiencing new situations in their environment. In particular, in the situation of *reinforcement learning*, the animat has to discover, by trial and error, how to coordinate its actions in order to maximize a cumulative reward over time. Such a reward is either a positive or a negative signal coming from the environment.

The Barto and Sutton model [2] allows an animat to learn to orient itself in a two-dimensional environment, using odorous landmarks . This environment contains one central landmark (C) surrounded by four others (N,S,W,E). Each landmark emits an odor the gradient of which decreases with distance. The task of the animat is to learn how the four peripheral landmarks are associated to the central one, and to navigate toward this goal even if it ceases to emit its odorous signal. The architecture of the animat is a neural network with special neurons inspired from Klopf's "hedonistic" neuron concept [11]. As an input, this network receives a combination of four odorous signals (XN, XS, XW, XE) associated with the peripheral landmarks (N, S, W, E), and furnishes, as an output, a combination of motor signals (YN, YS, YW, YE) associated with the four spatial directions. The reinforcement signal Z corresponds to the odour of the central landmark C, a signal that the animat seeks to maximize (Figure 5).

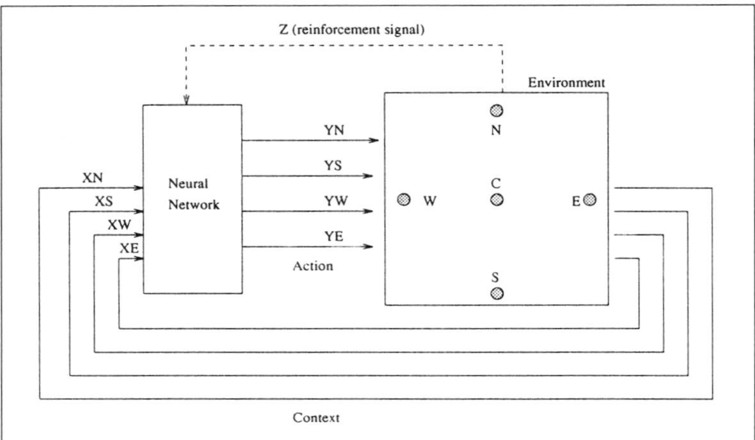

FIGURE 5. Neural architecture of Barto and Sutton's animat interacting with its environment. After [2].

Learning takes place as the animat moves in the environment. The neurons' synaptic strengths are updated so that, when the activation of a motor neuron at a given spot brings about a motion in a direction where Z increases, this neuron will have a better chance of being activated on the same spot in the future. Conversely, a motion in a direction where Z decreases will decrease the probability of activating the corresponding neuron.

After training, the animat gradually learns what direction it must move in from any given point in order to reach the goal. It thus can find the goal from any starting point by selecting the correct displacement at each intermediate point. This kind of adaptive ability is known as *route-navigation* [8].

Barto and Sutton's animat illustrates a typical *behaviorist* architecture: it doesn't need to build an internal representation of the environment to be able to navigate adaptively. On the contrary, the DYNA architecture proposed by Sutton [24] includes a world model and adds some planning abilities to a reinforcement learning process. DYNA is composed of four modules (Figure 6):

- the real environment, that changes state in relation with the animat's movements and that distributes a reward signal,

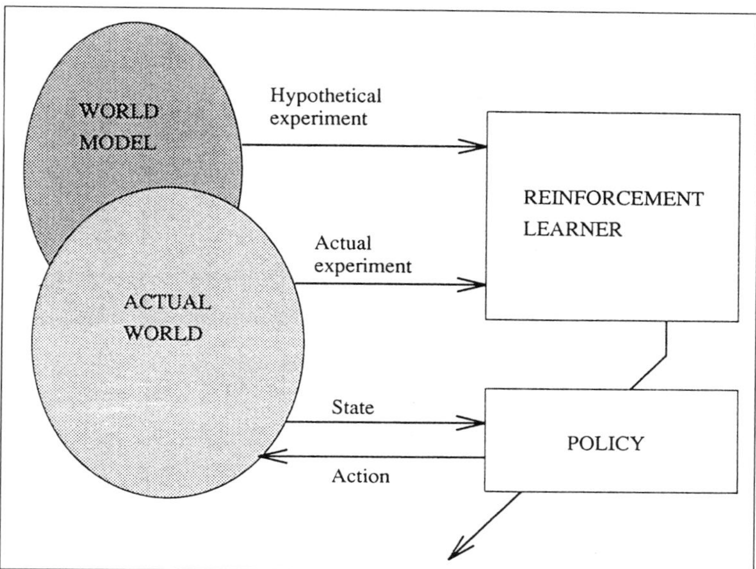

FIGURE 6. Dyna architecture. After [19].

- the internal world model, that the animat elaborates for itself and that is intended to represent the one-step input/output transitions of the real world,
- the policy function, relied on by the animat to determine what action to initiate in response to each possible state of the real environment,
- a primitive reinforcement learner that improves the policy function over time.

The world model and the policy function are progressively modified as the animat experiments with the operational laws of its world. These modifications depend on two types of experiments that the animat may alternate between: *actual* experiments, carried out on the real environment and *fictitious - or hypothetical-* experiments, that make use of the internal world model. Such hypothetical experiments endow the animat with planning abilities and make its behavior depend on its expected consequences.

Simulations effected on various DYNA architectures indicate that the corresponding animats are able to learn the shortest path leading from the starting state S to the goal state G, in the obstacle-encumbered environment on Figure 7. Moreover, such trial-and-error learning is expedited when animats avail themselves of the planning possibilities afforded by their internal world model and interleave one or more hypothetical experiments with actual experiments. What is more, some of these architectures exhibit generalization capabilities in changing environments.

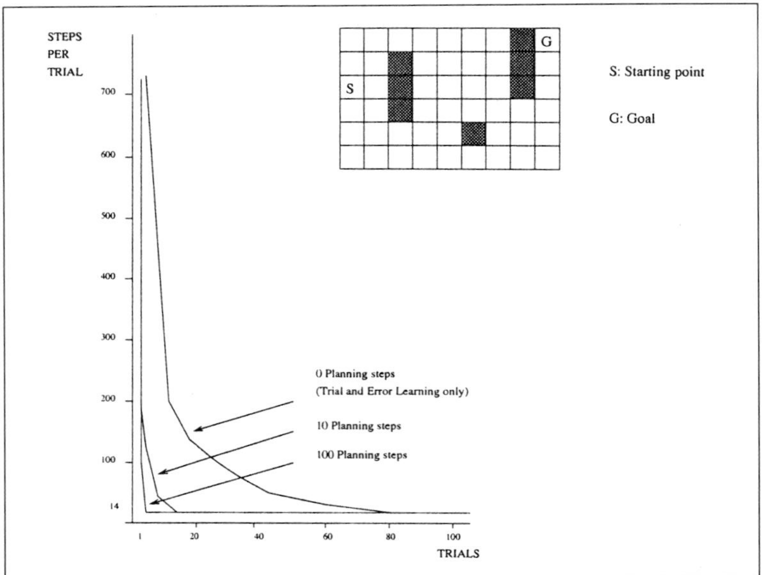

FIGURE 7. An example of the learning curves obtained in a specific navigation task with Dyna. The more hypothetical experiments (k planning steps) using the world model, the faster the optimal path is found. After [19].

7.4. Evolved Behaviors

Cliff et al. [6] have simulated an evolving process during which the neural architecture and the sensors' properties of each individual in a population of animats are improved over successive generations. During this process, *genotypes* of offspring are inherited from those of their parents and altered under the influence of mutation and crossing-over operators. At each generation, the adaptive value of each *phenotype* -called its *fitness*- is evaluated by a test of the aptitude of each animat to generate the behavior sought by the experimenter, thereby allowing the genotypes that perform best to reproduce from one generation to the next, as well as eliminating those genotypes that perform most poorly.

Instead of generating explicit control programs, Cliff et al. [6] make evolve the architecture of neural networks that directly link the sensors and actuators of an animat. The animat is equipped with various sensors: two forward and two backward whiskers, a front and a back bumper, and two photoreceptors. It is also equipped with actuators: two wheels and a trailing rear castor. The wheels have independent drives allowing turning on the spot and fairly unrestricted motion across a flat floor.

The architecture of the nervous system is general: the neurons are noisy linear threshold units, variable in number. If eight of them are input neurons

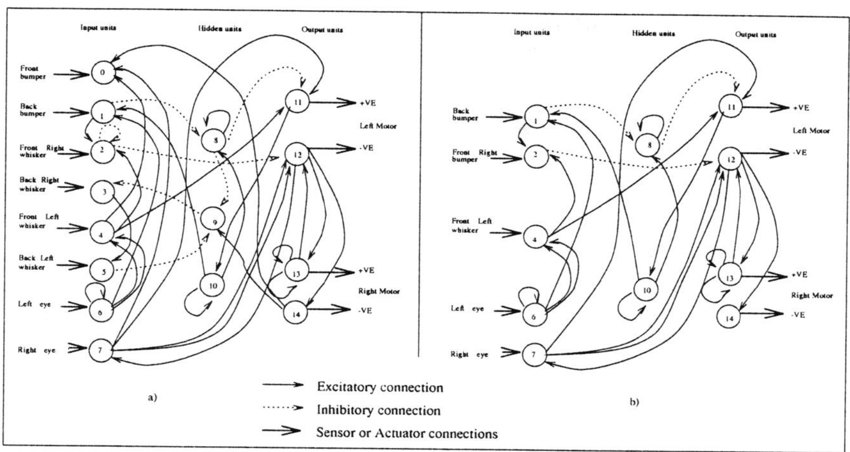

FIGURE 8. a) An evolved neural controller. b) The same network as on Figure a), with redundancies removed. After [5].

-one neuron per sensor- and four of them output neurons -two neurons per motor- the number of interneurons is variable and is determined genetically. Likewise, if certain connections may interconnect two neurons, other connections result in temporarily preventing any transfer of information along specific direct connections. The number and nature of these various connections are genetically determined: the genotype of each animat consists of two chromosomes, one coding for the neural architecture, and the other coding for the properties of the visual sensors, i.e. the angle of acceptance and the eccentricity of the two photoreceptors.

The results show that it is possible to cause an animat's nervous system to evolve in such a way as to enable it to use its visual perception capabilities to avoid collisions with the wall of an empty cylindrical room prior to making physical contact with the wall via one of its tactile sensors. Thus an animat can evolve in such a way as to be able to predict, from visual data alone, that a collision is likely in a near future, and to initiate appropriate evasive action. Examination of the evolved networks that generate such behavior reveals a complex connectivity with numerous redundancies. In earlier generations, the tactile sensors are widely used. Later, vision becomes progressively more dominant, and the tactile sensor input units are essentially used as internal neurons which process visual information (Figure 8).

7.5. Behavioral Development

If learning and evolution have already often been used for the automatic design of control architectures of animats, such is not the case with development- a point stressed by Meyer and Guillot [19]. However, a few applications combining development, evolution and learning have recently been published [12] and [13].

The work of Nolfi and Parisi [22], for instance, is concerned with the evolution of animats that consume food randomly distributed within a simple 2-D environment. Each animat is equipped with a sensory system that allows it to perceive the direction and the distance of the nearest food element and with a motor system that provides the possibility of turning any angle between 90 degrees left and 90 degrees right, and to move forward 0 to 5 steps. The nervous system of each animat is a bidimensional network with up to 40 neurons, whose development is coded in the animat's genotype. This genotype is a fixed-length string of 40 blocks, each block being made up of eight genes that describe the developmental fate of a given neuron. The first five blocks in the string correspond to sensory neurons, the last five blocks to motor neurons and the 30 intermediate blocks to internal neurons, which can be arranged in a maximum of 7 layers.

Within a given block, the first gene is the *temporal expression* gene, and specifies when, during development, the corresponding neuron will be expressed. Neurons scheduled to appear after the animat's death are non-expressed neurons. Two *physical-position genes* represent respectively the x and y spatial coordinates of the corresponding neuron. The *branching-angle gene* and the *segment-length gene* respectively control the angle of each branching of the neuron's axon and the length of each branching segment. The *synaptic-weight gene* determines the synaptic weight of each connection established by the corresponding neuron. In other words, in this model, all connections originating in a given neuron have the same weight. The *bias gene* represents the activation bias of the corresponding neuron. Lastly, the *neuron-type gene* specifies, in the case of a sensory neuron, whether this neuron reacts to the angle or the distance of food and, in the case of a motor neuron, whether this neuron determines the angle of turn or the length of a forward step.

While, in approaches like that of Cliff et al. evocated above, there is a direct mapping between genotype and phenotype, in the work of Nolfi and Parisi, the nervous system of each animat changes during the animat's lifetime, according to the developmental instructions coded in the genotype. Thus, some neurons are created at birth, others appear later, and connections are established between two neurons when the growing axonal branch of a particular neuron reaches the soma of another neuron (Figure 9).

The results obtained by Nolfi and Parisi suggest that pairing an evolutionary with a developmental process is an efficient means for providing adaptive behavior in animats. The results also suggest that the architectures evolved tend to be structured into functional sub-networks.

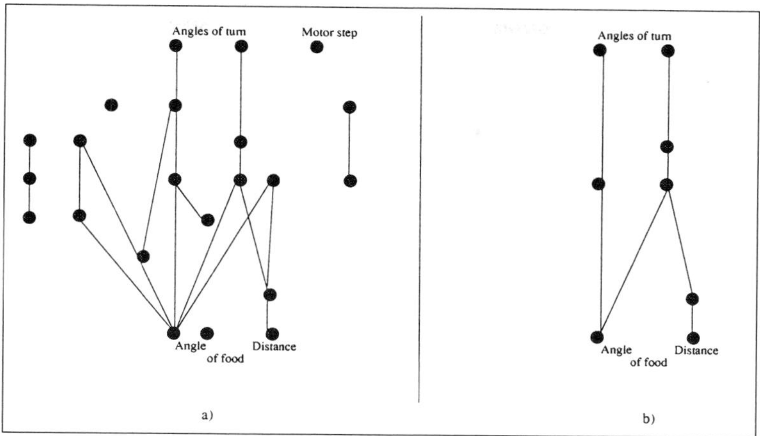

FIGURE 9. Growth process resulting from a randomly generated genotype. The lowest layer corresponds to sensory neurons, central layers to internal neurons and the upper layer to motor neurons. a) Connections established during the developmental process. b) Functional network mapping sensory input into motor output obtained after elimination of redundancies or unused neurons. After [18]

7.6. Discussion and Conclusion

The various examples described above demonstrate that complex functionalities can arise out of simple models. In particular, it is now accepted that a few hundred neurons can be sufficient to control the motivational system and the behavioral sequences of a simple animat. These examples also demonstrate the fact that it is possible to analyze situations that are inaccessible to traditional observational and experimental methods, particularly when these implement an evolutionary process. They also suggest that the animat approach should help in assessing the adaptive value of learning, evolution and development processes and in specifying how these processes interact with and complement each other. Finally, because research on animats seems to be an effective tool for studying how the highest intellectual abilities of man might derive from the simplest adaptive behaviors of animals, there is hope that this research will ultimately contribute to our understanding of the adaptive value and working principles of human cognition [20], [21] and [23].

Nevertheless, the animat approach does present some limitations. For instance, the proof of principles that it yields are rarely used to best avail. Virtually never has research been conducted to ascertain whether a given simple solution to a problem is actually the simplest possible. Nor has it been demonstrated that any given adaptive capacity can be expressly ascribed to a specific global architecture rather than to a particular operational detail. Only a systematic comparison of several different versions of the same problem with as varied as possible a range of solutions can allow the respective advantages and the degree of originality of these solutions to be effectively evaluated.

More generally, it can be seen that, as of today, the animat approach is essentially empirical in nature and that it would gain from a broadening of its theoretical perspective. Fortunately, several research efforts have recently been initiated in such a direction [19]. For instance, the work of Wilson [25] or Horswill [10] on the characterization of environments and the adaptational problems to which they give rise, and that of Agre [1], Chapman [5] or Beer [4] on the theory of interactions between organisms and environments, constitute a valuable groundwork.

References

1. P.E. Agre. *The dynamic structure of everyday life.* Cambridge University Press. 1991.
2. A.G. Barto and R.S. Sutton. Landmark learning: an illustration of associative search. *Biological Cybernetics.* 42:1-8. 1981.
3. R.D. Beer. *Intelligence as adaptive behavior: an experiment in computational neuroethology.* Academic Press. 1990.
4. R.D. Beer. A dynamical systems perspective on agent-environment interaction. *Artificial Intelligence.* 72:173-215. 1995
5. D. Chapman. *Vision, Instruction and Action.* The MIT Press. 1992.
6. D. Cliff, I. Harvey and P. Husbands. Explorations in evolutionary robotics. *Adaptive Behavior.* 2,1:71-108. 1993.
7. D. Cliff, P. Husbands, J.A. Meyer, and S.W. Wilson (Eds). *From Animals to Animats 3: Proceedings of the Third International Conference on Simulation of Adaptive Behavior.* MIT Press/Bradford Books. 1994.
8. C.R. Gallistel. *The organization of learning.* The MIT Press. 1990.
9. A. Guillot and J.A. Meyer. Computer simulations of adaptive behavior in animats. *Proceedings Computer Animation'94.* IEEE Computer Society. 1994.
10. I. Horswill. Characterizing adaptation by constraint. In F. Varela and P. Bourgine (Eds).*Toward a practice of autonomous systems. Proceedings of the First European Conference on Artificial Life.* The MIT Press. 1992.
11. A.H. Klopf. *The hedonistic neuron: a theory of memory, learning and intelligence.* Hemisphere. 1990.
12. J. Kodjabachian and J.A. Meyer. Development, learning and evolution in animats. *Proceedings of the PerAc'94 Conference.* IEEE Computer Society. 1994.
13. J. Kodjabachian and J.A. Meyer. Evolution and development of control architectures in animats. *Robotics and Autonomous systems.* 16: 161-182. 1995.
14. P. Maes, M. Mataric, J.A. Meyer, and S.W. Wilson (Eds.) *From Animals to Animats 4. Proceedings of the Fourth International Conference on Simulation for Adaptive Behaviour.* MIT Press/Bradford Books. 1996.
15. J.A. Meyer. From natural to artificial life: Biomimetic mechanisms in animat designs. *Robotics and Autonomous Systems.* In press. 1997.
16. J.A. Meyer and S.W. Wilson (Eds). *From Animals to Animats: Proceedings of the First International Conference on Simulation of Adaptive Behavior.* MIT Press/Bradford Books. 1991.

17. J.A. Meyer and A. Guillot. Simulation of adaptive behavior in animats: Review and prospect. In [16].
18. J.A. Meyer, H.L. Roitblat, and S.W. Wilson (Eds). *From Animals to Animats 2: Proceedings of the Second International Conference on Simulation of Adaptive Behavior.* MIT Press/Bradford Books. 1993.
19. J.A. Meyer and A. Guillot. From SAB90 to SAB94 : Four Years of Animat Research. In [7].
20. J.A. Meyer. The animat approach to cognitive science. In H. Roitblat and J.A. Meyer (Eds). *Comparative Approaches to Cognitive Science.* The MIT Press. In press. 1995.
21. J.A. Meyer. Artificial life and the animat approach to artificial intelligence. In M. Boden (Eds). *Artificial Intelligence.* Academic Press. In press. 1995.
22. S. Nolfi and D. Parisi. Growing neural networks. *T.R. PCIA-91-15. Institute of Psychology. Rome.* 1991.
23. H. Roitblat and J.A. Meyer. (Eds.) *Comparative Approaches to Cognitive Science.* MIT Press/Bradford Books. 1995.
24. R.S. Sutton. Reinforcement learning architectures from animats. In [16].
25. S.W. Wilson. The animat path to AI. In [16].

8. Simulating Autonomous Life for Virtual Actors

Nadia Magnenat-Thalmann
MIRALab, CUI, University of Geneva, 24, rue du Général-Dufour, CH 1211 Geneva, Switzerland (e-mail: thalmann@cui.unige.ch)

Summary.
Several very complex problems must be solved in order to create true three-dimensional virtual humans in their environment. In this paper, we explain several of these problems and present solutions. First, we try to simulate autonomous actors, that means actors who can exist and live (virtually) by themselves. That means that we develop procedural methods for allowing these synthetic actors to be animated when necessary. Virtual actors should possess in themselves all the knowledge of changing appearance and reacting both to the virtual environment and real world. This is a long term research and in this paper, we present three aspects of this research: first, how to create virtual 3D humans, second, models for simulating expressions and talk, third 3D interaction with real humans and third, simulating cloth deformations while moving.

Key words: virtual actors, synthetic worlds, facial communication, cloth animation, virtual reality, artificial life

8.1. Introduction

The ultimate reason for creating virtual humans (also called synthetic actors) who have autonomous behaviors and who seem real is to be able to interact with them in any virtual scene representing the real world. Anyway, a virtual scene, beautiful though it may be, is not complete without people...virtual people that is. Scenes involving virtual humans imply many complex problems that we try to manage since several years [10]. We slowly come to the point of simulating 3D real- looking virtual humans, taking into account body, face and cloth deformations. Any environment could be simulated and consequently, we will be able to experiment in real-time any virtual environment, and to communicate with virtual humans rather naturally. The main problem is this research is to avoid special effects, 2D effects and direct kinematics techniques like keyframe and rotoscopy. We look after procedural methods to simulate the appearance and the functions of life. If our simulation is based on procedural methods, it is then possible to interact with these actors in virtual reality. In this case, our actors have in themselves a description of their look and also know how to behave and respond to stimuli of their virtual environment and also to stimuli or interaction with the real world.

8.2. Creation of Virtual Humans

The synthesis of realistic virtual humans leads to obtain and include the specific features of the character of interest. For the universally known personalities (actors) such as Marilyn, Humphrey, and Elvis, there is a less scope to make mistakes as the deviations will be very easily detected by the spectator. In spite of this ambition to make realism, or better, imitation, this type of realism should not be confused with the photographic or the cinematographic realism.

Sculpting the shape of a virtual actor. Creating a body for a virtual human is only the first step, his particular character depends on his body movements and his personality is defined by the subtle changes of his facial expressions and other gestures.

To construct these shapes, we propose the use of an interactive sculpting approach. The surfaces of human face and body are irregular structures implemented as polygonal meshes. We have introduced a methodology [11] for interactive sculpting using a six-degree-of-freedom interactive input device called the SpaceBall. When used in conjunction with a common 2D mouse, full three dimensional user interaction is achieved, with the SpaceBall in one hand and the mouse in the other. The SpaceBall device is used to move around the object being sculpted in order to examine it from various points of view, while the mouse carries out the picking and deformation work onto a magnifying image in order to see every small detail in real time (e.g. vertex creation, primitive selection and local surface deformations). In this way, the user not only sees the object from every angle but he can also apply and correct deformations from every angle interactively.

Typically, the sculpting process may be initiated in two ways: by loading and altering an existing shape or by simply starting one from scratch. For example, we will use a sphere as a starting point for the head of a person and use cylinders for limbs. We will then add or remove polygons according to the details needed and apply local deformations to alter the shape. When starting from scratch points are placed in 3D space and polygonized. However, it may be more tedious and time consuming.

With this type of 3D interaction, the operations performed while sculpting an object closely resemble traditional sculpting. The major operations performed using this software include creation of primitives, selection, local surface deformations and global deformations.

The selection process. To select parts of the objects, the mouse is used in conjunction with the SpaceBall to quickly mark out the desired primitives in and around the object. This amounts to pressing the mouse button and sweeping the mouse cursor on the screen while moving the object with the SpaceBall. All primitives (vertices, edges and polygons) can be selected. Mass picking may be done by moving the object away from the eye (assuming a perspective projection) and careful, minute picking may be done by bringing the object closer.

Local surface deformations. These tools make it possible to produce local elevations or depressions on the surface and to even out unwanted bumps once the work is nearing completion. Local deformations are applied while the SpaceBall device is used to move the object and examine the progression of the deformation from different angles, mouse movements on the screen are used to produce vertex movements in 3D space from the current viewpoint. The technique is intended to be a metaphor analogous to pinching, lifting and moving of a stretchable fabric material. Pushing the apex vertex inwards renders a believable effect of pressing a mould into clay.

Global deformations. These tools make it possible to produce global deformations on the whole object or some of the selected regions. For example, if the object has to grow in a certain direction, it can be obtained by scaling or shifting the object on the region of interest.

In the construction of a certain category of figures like realistic human bodies, it is often preferable to keep certain irregularities on the surface. A very smooth skin, for example, does not necessarily guarantees a more realistic appearance. In very delicate parts like shoulders or cheeks the imperfections are visible and generally we have to get rid of them right away, but we can keep some others small irregularities in order to create a figure which seems less plastic and robotized and in order to attenuate the feeling we often feel in front of computer generated human bodies. This kind of imperfections in a realistic figure give the impression of a human figure which has not been conceived only in the "designer's" head but has really been observed from the reality.

8.3. Simulation of Facial Expressions and Talk

It is difficult to create a model for facial animation that is physically realistic confirming to the anatomical details of facial topology while convenient for animators to use and manipulate. We use a multi-level approach, which divides the facial animation problem into a hierarchy of levels that are independent of each other. The higher levels use higher degree of abstraction for defining the entities such as emotions and phrases of speech, by those facilitating animators to manipulate these entities in a natural and intuitive way. From the highest to the lowest, the levels of abstraction encompassed in our system are illustrated in figure 1. A synchronization mechanism is provided at the top level that requires animators to specify the highest level entities: emotions, sentences and head movement with their durations. The system provides default values for durations in case they are not specified. These entities are then decomposed into lower level entities and sent through the pipeline of control at lower levels of the hierarchy. The temporal characteristics of animation are generally controlled at higher levels and the spatial characteristics are controlled at lower levels in our multi level system.

Various facial animation approaches have been proposed: parameterized models [12], muscle model for facial expressions [14],[17],[9]. Several authors have also provided a new facial animation technique based on the information derived from human performances [15],[3], [18]. The information extracted is used for controlling the facial animation. These performance driven techniques provide a very realistic rendering and motion of the face.

Although all movements may be rendered by muscles, the direct use of a muscle-based model is very difficult. The complexity of the model and our poor knowledge of anatomy makes the results somewhat unpredictable. This suggests that more abstract entities should be defined in order to create a system that can be easily manipulated. A multi-layered approach [6] is convenient for this. In order to manipulate abstract entities like our representation of the human face (phonemes, words, expressions, emotions), we propose to decompose the problem into several layers. The high level layers are the most abstract and specify "what to do", the low level layers describe "how to do". Each level is seen as an independent layer with its own input and output.

For our facial deformations, we have extended the concept of Free Form Deformations (FFD) introduced by Sederberg and Parry, a technique for deforming solid geometric models in a free-form manner. It can deform surface primitives of any type or degree, for example, planes, quadrics, parametric surface patches or implicitly defined surfaces. FFD involves a mapping from R^3 to R^3 through a trivariate tensor product Bernstein polynomial. Physically, FFD corresponds to deformations applied to an imaginary parallelepiped of clear, flexible plastic in which are embedded the objects to be deformed. The objects are also considered to be flexible so that they are deformed along with the plastic that surrounds them. A grid of control points is imposed on the parallelepiped. For any point interior to the parallelepiped, the deformation is specified by moving the control point(s) from their undisplaced latticial position.

As an extension to the basic FFDs, we provide the option of including rational basis functions in the formulation of deformation [5]. These rational basis functions allow incorporation of weights defined for each of the control points in the parallelepiped grid. The advantage of using rational FFDs is that

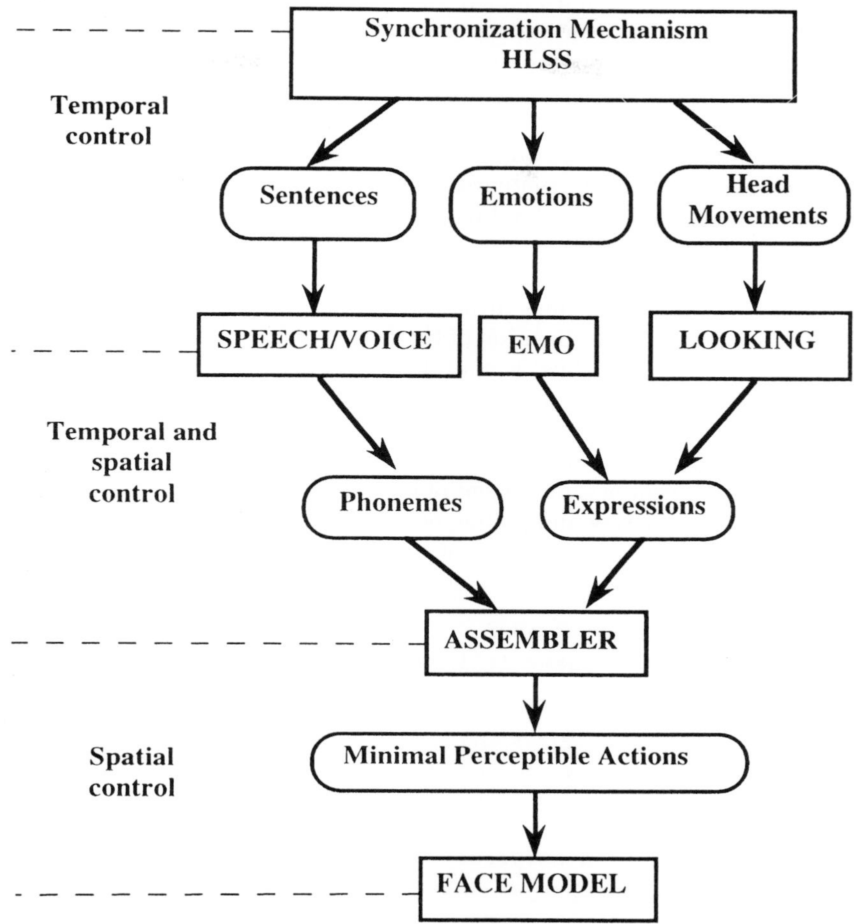

FIGURE 1. Hierarchical Structure of the Multi-level Facial Animation System

they provide one more degree of freedom of manipulating the deformations by changing the weights at the control points.

Region build-up is accomplished by interactive selection of polygons. These regions on the human face generally correspond to their anatomical descriptions, such as nose, lips, eyes, etc. The selection process can be further hastened by attaching the color attributes of the polygons. The magnitude and direction of the muscle pulled is interactively adjusted by changing the position and weight of the control points on the control-unit of a region.

Certain points in a defined region can be set "anchored" meaning they will not deform when the deformations are applied on the region. The physical characteristics of facial mesh points can also be set interactively.

The free-form deformations correspond to the lower level of our multi-layer system SMILE where, at each level, the degree of abstraction increases. The defined entities correspond to intuitive concepts such as phonemes, expressions, words, emotions, sentences and eye motion, which make them natural to manipulate. The top level requires direct input from the animator in the form of global abstract actions and their duration, corresponding to the intuitive and natural specifications for facial animation [7].

Expressions and phonemes in our system are considered as facial snapshots, that is, a particular position of the face at a given time. For phonemes, only the mouth portion (lips) is considered during the emission of sound. A facial snapshot consists of one or more minimal perceptible actions (MPAs) with their intensity specified. A minimal perceptible action is a basic facial motion parameter. Each MPA has a corresponding set of visible features such as movement of eyebrows, movement of jaw, or mouth and others which occur as a result of contracting and pulling of muscles associated. The set of MPAs included is general enough to account for most possible facial expressions. A generic expression can be represented as follows:

```
[expression <name>
     [mpa <name-1> intensity  <i-1>]
     [mpa <name-1> intensity  <i-1>]
     ...
]
```

Example of an expression

```
[expression surprise
     [mpa openjaw intensity  0.17]
     [mpa puffcheeks intensity  -0.41]
     [mpa stretch\_cornerlips intensity  -0.50]
     [mpa raise\_eyebrows intensity  0.40]
     [mpa close\_lower\_eyelids intensity  -0.54]
     [mpa close\_upper\_eyelids intensity  -0.20]
]
```

Example of a phoneme

```
phoneme ee
     [mpa stretch\_cornerlips intensity  -0.29]
     [mpa openjaw intensity  0.50]
     [mpa lower\_cornerlips intensity  -0.57]
     [mpa raise\_upperlips intensity  -0.20]
]
```

The specification of expressions and phonemes is analogous to macros used in a program. The intensity of expression is directly influenced by the intensity of contained MPAs. A strong or feeble expression can be created by appropriately changing the intensities of the associated MPAs. This helps the spatial control of facial animation.

These facial snap shots representing expressions and phonemes can be built up in an interactive expression editor provided inside the system. Users can construct, edit and save the static expressions and thus build a library of pre defined expressions. This library can then become available for a later sequence of animation. By design, the expression editor is independent of the low level realization of muscles and their actions. This scheme of independence makes it plausible to use entirely different simulation models for each MPA separately without affecting the high level control.

The system also allows to compose or blend two or more expressions. This is attained by integrating the MPAs in the respective expressions. This can be interpreted as summing up two or more signals of MPAs where the resulting intensity is the normalized sum of the individual intensities (see Fig.2).

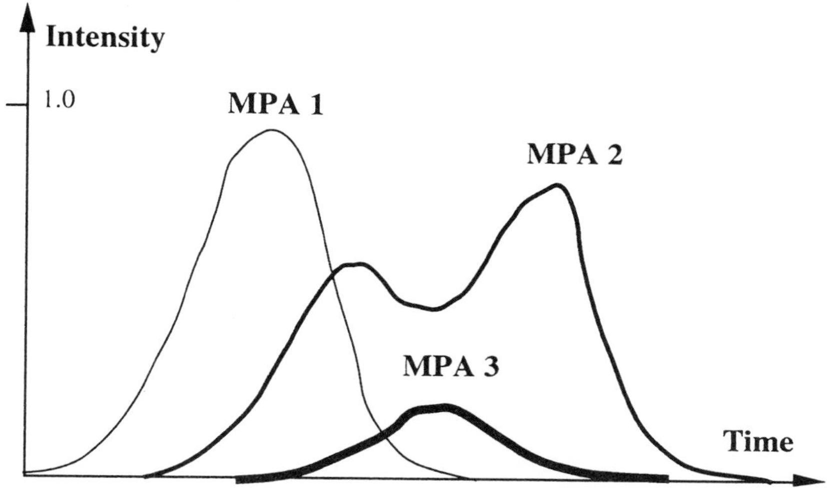

FIGURE 2. MPAs' curves

All facial expressions do not necessarily correspond to emotions and phonemes. Some expressions are exhibited as secondary expressions that differentiate one expressive mode from the others. For example, raising eyebrows may signify termination of a sequence of a speech and may not be a signal of surprise, similarly turning head may symbolize negation for an issue. The animation thus can incorporate such expressions once created and defined in the expression editor.

We need a mechanism of synchronization to ensure smooth flow of emotions and sentences with head movements. A language HLSS (High Level Script Scheduler) is used to specify the synchronization in terms of an action and its duration. From the action dependence the starting time and the terminating time of an action can be deduced. The general format of specifying an action is as follows: while <duration> do <action>.

The duration of an action can be a default duration, a relative percentage of the default duration, an absolute duration in seconds or a deduced duration from the other actions preceding or succeeding to the present action.

The starting time of each action can be specified in different ways, for example, sequentially or parallel using the normal concepts of 'fork' and 'end fork' employed in a scheduling problem. Figure 3 shows some examples of how starting time can be specified in the system. Plates 1 to 3 show facial expressions.

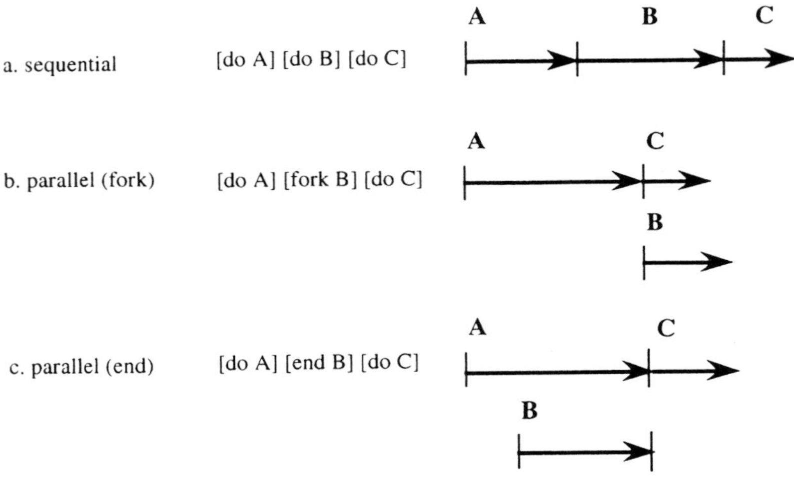

FIGURE 3. Sequential and parallel actions

8.4. Simulating 3D Clothes

In most computer-generated films involving virtual humans, clothes are simulated as a part of the body with no autonomous motion. For modeling more realistic clothes, two separated problems have to be solved: the motion of the cloth without collision detection and the collision detection of the cloth with the body and with itself. A flexible or deformable object is different from a rigid object because it cannot be considered as a whole and its movement cannot be computed from a small set of its points. The flexible object must be divided into small parts and each point is submitted to a set of local and global constraints. These constraints create forces which prevent the violation of these constraints. Solving the dynamic system requires finding an equilibrium between all these forces. Recent research deals with dynamic models for flexible or deformable objects.

After some comparisons, Terzopoulos' elastic surface model [16] was chosen for our system with the damping term replaced by a more accurate. The fundamental equation of motion corresponds to an equilibrium between internal forces (Newton term, resistance to stretching, dissipative force, resistance to bending) and external forces (collision forces, gravity, seaming and attaching forces, wind force):

$$\rho(\mathbf{a})\frac{d^2\mathbf{r}}{dt^2} + \frac{\delta}{\delta\mathbf{r}}\int\!\!\int_{\Omega} \|\mathbf{E}\|^2 da_1 da_2 + \frac{\delta}{\delta\mathbf{v}}\int\!\!\int_{\Omega} \|\dot{\mathbf{E}}\|^2 da_1 da_2 + \frac{\delta}{\delta\mathbf{r}}\int\!\!\int_{\Omega} \|\mathbf{B} - \mathbf{B}_0\|^2 da_1 da_2 = \Sigma\mathbf{F}_{ex}$$

$$\dot{\mathbf{E}}_{ij}(\mathbf{r}(\mathbf{a})) = \frac{d}{dt}\mathbf{E}_{ij} = \frac{1}{2}\dot{\mathbf{G}}_{ij} = \frac{\partial\mathbf{r}}{\partial a_i}\cdot\frac{\partial\mathbf{v}}{\partial a_j} + \frac{\partial\mathbf{r}}{\partial a_j}\cdot\frac{\partial\mathbf{v}}{\partial a_i}$$

We choose to replace the third term (dissipative force) because the one used by Terzopoulos et al. is scalar. So, no matter where energy comes from, it will be dissipated. For example, gravitational energy is dissipated, resulting in a surface which achieves a limiting speed and is not continually accelerated. In our case [2], we use Raleigh's dissipative function generalized for a continuum surface [13]. As $\mathbf{E}$ is the strain (a measure of the amount of deformation), $d\mathbf{E}/dt$ is the "speed" at which the deformation occurs. This means that the surface integral may be considered a rate of energy dissipation due to internal friction. This implies that the variational derivative with respect to velocity of the surface integral will minimize the "speed" of the deformation. With this approach, no dissipation occurs when the surface undergoes rigid body displacement like when falling in an air-free gravity field. This improves the realism of motion.

To apply the elastic deformable surface model, the polygonal panel should be discretized using the finite difference approximation method. We have proposed a new algorithm to calculate the elastic force on an arbitrary element. This algorithm is effective for discretizing not only an arbitrary polygonal panel (concave or convex), but also other kinds of polygonal panels with holes inside them.

In the animation of deformable objects consisting of many surface panels, the constraints that join different panels together and attach them to other objects are very important. In our case, two kinds of dynamic constraints are used in two different stages. When deformable panels are separated, forces are applied to the elements in the panels to join them according to the seaming information. The same method is used to attach the elements of deformable objects to other rigid objects.

After the creation of deformable objects, another kind of dynamic constraint [13],[1] is used to guarantee seaming and attaching. For the attaching, the elements of the deformable objects are always kept on the rigid object, so they have the same position and velocity as the elements of the rigid object to which they are attached. For the seaming and joining of the panels themselves, two seamed elements move with the same velocity and position, but the velocity and position depend on those of the individual elements. According to the law of momentum conservation, total momentum of the elements before and after seaming should remain the same.

Basically, collisions are detected before a cloth's vertices come through the body's polygons and we have to find the position of the point of impact on the polygon, the velocity, and the normal of that point. Moreover, all forces (including internal forces) acting on vertices should be computed.

We have also described a method of collision avoidance that creates a very thin force field around the surface of the obstacle to be avoided. This force field acts like a shield rejecting the points. Although the method works for a simple case of a skirt, use of this type of force is somewhat artificial and cannot provide realistic simulation with complex clothes. In fact, the effect degrades when the force becomes very strong, looking like a "kick" given to the cloth. To improve realism, we have proposed using the law of conservation of momentum for perfectly inelastic bodies. This means we consider all energy to be lost within a collision. The collision detection process is almost automatic. The animator has only to provide a list of obstacles to the system and indicate whether they are moving or not. For a walking synthetic actor, moving legs are of course considered a moving obstacle. Plate 4 and 5 show cloth animation.

8.5. Interaction with Virtual Humans

We should also consider the relationship between the virtual human and the rest of the world. We distinguish four basic cases:

(a) the virtual human is alone in the scene, there is no interaction with other objects.

(b) the virtual human is moving in an environment and he is conscious of this environment.

(c) actions performed by a virtual human are known from another virtual human and may change his behavior
(d) not only may the animator communicate information to the virtual human but this virtual human is also able to respond it and communicate information to the animator.

Virtual humans are moving in an environment comprising models of physical objects. Their animation is dependent on this environment and the environment may be modified by these actors. Moreover several virtual humans may interact with each other. Several very complex problems must be solved in order to render three-dimensional animation involving virtual humans in their environment. For example, we introduced a finite element method to model the deformations of human flesh due to flexion of members and/or contact with objects [4]. The method is able to deal with penetrating impacts and true contacts. Simulation of impact with penetration can be used to model the grasping of ductile objects, and requires decomposition of objects into small geometrically simple objects. All the advantages of physical modeling of objects can also be transferred to human flesh. For example, the hand grasp of an object is expected to lead to realistic flesh deformation as well as an exchange of information between the object and the hand which will not only be geometrical.

In the context of interactive animation systems, the relationship between the animator and the virtual humans should be emphasized. With the existence of graphics workstations able to display complex scenes containing several thousands polygons at interactive speed, and with the advent of such new interactive devices as the SpaceBall, EyePhone, and DataGlove, it is possible to create computer- generated characters based on a full 3D interaction metaphor in which the specifications of deformations or motion are given in real-time. True interaction between the animator and the virtual human requires a two-way communication: not only may the animator interact to give commands to the virtual human but the virtual human is also able to answer him. Finally, we may aspire to a virtual reality where virtual humans participate fully: real dialog between the animator and the virtual human. The animator may now enter in the synthetic world that he/she has created, admire it, modify it and truly perceive it. Finally, computer-generated human beings should be present and active in the virtual world. They should be the synthetic actors playing their unique role in the theater representing the scene to be simulated.

8.6. Communication between the Virtual Human and the Animator

For the communication between the animator and the virtual humans, we have developed a prototype system [8]. As shown in Fig. 4, this system is mainly an inference system with facial and gesture data as input channels and face and hand animation sequences as output channels.

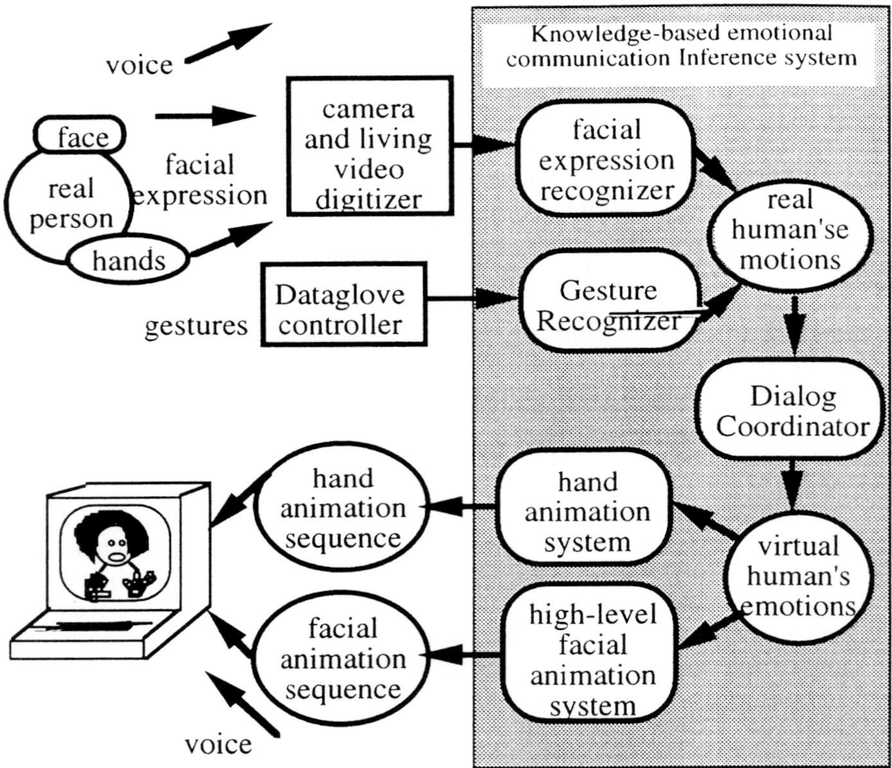

FIGURE 4. Organization of the proposed system

The development of the inference system is divided into three subsystems:

i) a subsystem for the recognition of emotions from facial expressions, head-and-shoulder gestures, hand gestures and possibly speech
ii) a subsystem for the synthesis of facial expressions and hand motions for a given emotion and speech
iii) a subsystem for the dialog coordination between input and output emotions

This last subsystem is a rule-based system: it should decide how the virtual human will behave based on the behavior of the real human. The dialog coordinator analyzes the humor and behavior of the user based on the facial expressions and gestures. It then decides which emotions (sequences of expressions) and gestures (sequence of postures) should be generated by the animation system. For the design of correspondence rules, our approach is based on existing work in applied psychology, in particular in the area of non-verbal communication.

For the recognition of emotions, our method is based on snakes as introduced by Terzopoulos and Waters [1991]. A snake is a dynamic deformable 2D contour. A discrete snake is a set of nodes with time varying positions. The nodes are coupled by internal forces making the snake acting like a series of springs resisting compression and a thin wire resisting bending. The expression forces is introduced into the equations of motion for dynamic node/spring system. Our approach is different from Terzopoulos-Waters approach because we need to analyze the emotion in real-time. Instead of using a filter which globally transforms the image into a planar force field, we apply the filter in the neighborhood of the nodes of the snake.

We only use a snake for the mouth; the rest of the information (jaw, eyebrows, eyes) is obtained by fast image-processing techniques. For the jaw, we consider that the lower part of the lower lip (using information given by the snake) is moving with the jaw i.e. if the law opens, the lower part goes down with the jaw. For the nose, we use the center point of the upper part of the mouth (also using the snake) and we scan upwards until an edge is detected. As we assume that the illumination is very strong, the edge should belong to the shadow of the nose. For the eyebrows, we use the same principles as the nose. We start from the forehead and scan downwards until we detect an edge. This should be the eyebrow. For the eyes, we define a rectangular region around the eyes (using the position of the nose and eyebrows) and we count the number of white points in the region. If the number of white points is under a threshold value, we consider the eye as closed. Plate 6 shows an example.

8.7. Conclusion

We have presented a few main problems to simulate autonomous virtual actors. Several important problems have to be solved to incorporate 3D real-looking actors which possess their own knowledge of their movements and reactions to the virtual and real environments. If we think about applications such as interacting with these actors in virtual reality, we still have a long way to go. This is the challenge of this research for the coming years.

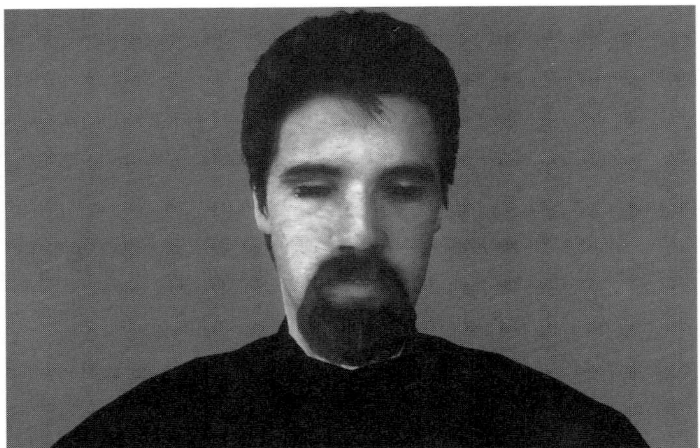

Plate 1. Facial animation with beards and mustaches

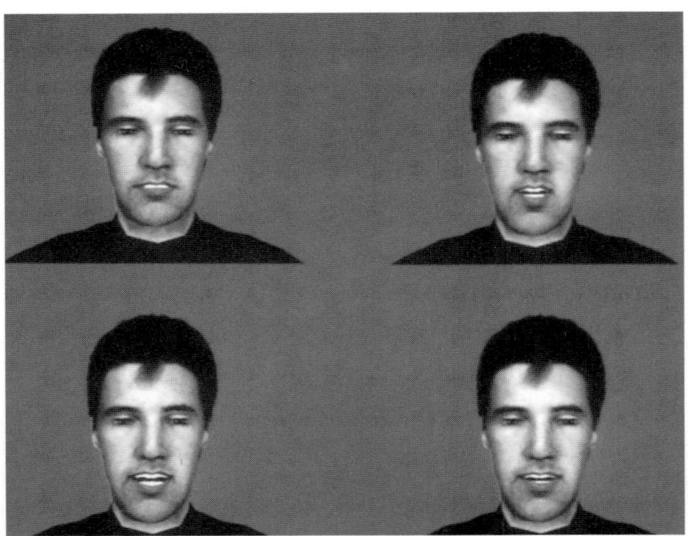

Plate 2. Facial animation with texture mapping

Plate 3. Facial animation with hairstyles

Plate 4. Cloth modeling

Plate 5. Walking sequence with clothes

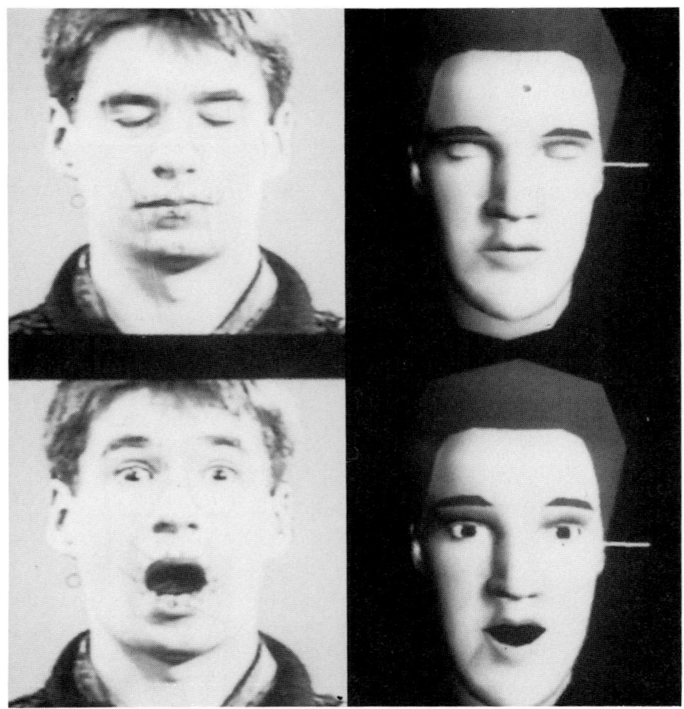

Plate 6. Animator and virtual human

References

1. Barzel R, Barr Alan H (1988) A Modeling System Based on Dynamic Constraints. In Proc. SIGGRAPH '88, Computer Graphics, Vol. 22, No4, pp.179-188.
2. Carignan M, Yang Y, Magnenat Thalmann N, Thalmann D (1992) Dressing Animated Synthetic actors with Complex Clothes, Proc. SIGGRAPH'92, Computer Graphics, Vol. 26, No 2, Chicago, pp. 99-104.
3. deGraf B (1989) in State of the Art in Facial Animation, SIGGRAPH '89 Course Notes No. 26, pp. 10-20.
4. Gourret JP, Magnenat-Thalmann N, Thalmann D (1989) Simulation of Object and Human Skin Deformations in a Grasping Task, Proc. SIGGRAPH '89, Computer Graphics, Vol. 23, No 3, pp.21-30
5. Kalra P, A. Mangili, N. Magnenat Thalmann, D. Thalmann (1992) Simulation of Facial Muscle Actions Based on Rational Free Form Deformations, Proc. Eurographics '92, Cambridge, pp. 59-69.
6. Kalra P. Mangili A, Magnenat-Thalmann N, Thalmann D (1991) SMILE: a Multilayered Facial Animation System, In: Kunii TL (ed) Modeling in Computer Graphics, Springer, Tokyo, pp.189-198.
7. Magnenat Thalmann N, Kalra P (1992) A Model for Creating and Visualizing Speech and Emotion, in: Dale R. et al. (eds) Aspects of Automated Natural Language Generation, Lecture Notes in Artificial Intelligence, Springer-Verlag, Heidelberg, pp.1-12.
8. Magnenat-Thalmann N, Cazedevals A, Thalmann D (1993) Modelling Facial Communication between an Animator and a Synthetic Actor in Real Time, In: Falcidieno B and Kunii TL (eds), Springer, Heidelberg, pp. 387-396.
9. Magnenat-Thalmann N, Primeau E, Thalmann D (1988), Abstract Muscle Action Procedures for Human Face Animation, The Visual Computer, Vol. 3, No. 5, pp. 290- 297.
10. Magnenat-Thalmann N, Thalmann D (1991) Complex Models for Animating Synthetic Actors, IEEE Computer Graphics and Applications, Vol.11, No5, pp.32-44.
11. Paouri A, Magnenat Thalmann N, Thalmann D (1991) Creating Realistic Three-Dimensional Human Shape Characters for Computer-Generated Films, Proc. Computer Animation '91, Springer-Verlag, Tokyo, pp.89- 100
12. Parke FI (1982) Parameterized Models for Facial Animation, IEEE Computer Graphics and Applications, Vol.2, No 9, pp.61-68.
13. Platt JC, Barr AH (1989) Constraints Methods for Flexible Models. In Proc. Siggraph '89 , Computer Graphics, Vol.23, No.3, pp.21-30.
14. Platt S, Badler N (1981) Animating Facial Expressions, Proc. Siggraph '81, Computer Graphics, Vol.15, No3, pp.245- 252.
15. Terzopoulos D, Waters K (1991) Techniques for Realistic Facial Modeling and Animation, in: Magnenat Thalmann N, Thalmann D, Computer Animation '91, Springer- Verlag, Tokyo, pp.59-74
16. Terzopoulos D, Platt J, Barr A, Fleischer K (1987) Elastically Deformation Models. Proc. Siggraph'87, Computer Graphics, Vol. 21, No.4, pp.205-214.
17. Waters K (1987) A Muscle Model for Animating Three- Dimensional Facial Expression, Proc. Siggraph '87, Computer Graphics, Vol.21, No4, pp.17-24.
18. Williams L (1990), Performance Driven Facial Animation, Proc Siggraph '90, pp. 235-242.

9. Towards Autonomous Synthetic Actors

Hansrudi Noser and Daniel Thalmann
Computer Graphics Lab, Swiss Federal Institute of Technology, Lausanne, CH 1015, Switzerland
(e-mail:noser@di.epfl.ch, thalmann@di.epfl.ch)

Summary.

This paper describes an animation approach with autonomous actors reacting to their environment and taking decisions based on perception systems, memory and reasoning. With such a system, we should be able to create simulations of situations such as virtual humans moving in a complex environment they may know and recognize, or playing ball games based on their visual and touching perception. In particular, the paper describes an animation approach where synthetic vision is used for navigation by a synthetic actor. The vision is the main channel of information between the actor and its environment and offers a universal approach to pass the necessary information from the environment to an actor in the problems of path searching, obstacle avoidance, and internal knowledge representation with learning and forgetting characteristics. For the general navigation problem, we propose a local and a global approach. In the global approach, a dynamic occupancy octree grid serves as global 3D visual memory and allows an actor to memorize the environment that he sees and to adapt it to a changing and dynamic environment. His reasoning process allows him to find 3D paths based on his visual memory by avoiding impasses and circuits. In the local approach, low level vision based navigation reflexes, normally performed by intelligent actors, are simulated. The local navigation model uses the direct input information from his visual environment to reach goals or subgoals and to avoid unexpected obstacles. A more complex example of vision-based tennis playing is also presented.

Key words: autonomy, synthetic actor, navigation, synthetic vision, visual memory, octree, obstacle avoidance, tennis

9.1. Introduction

The main goal in our approach is to build intelligent autonomous virtual humans or actors. By intelligent we mean that virtual humans are able to plan and execute tasks based on a model of the current state of the virtual world.

By autonomous, we mean that actors do not require the continual intervention of a user. Our autonomous actors should react to their environment and take decisions based on perception systems, memory and reasoning. With such a system, we should be able to create simulations of situations such as virtual humans moving in a complex environment they may know and recognize, or playing ball games based on their visual and touching perception. To achieve our goals, actors should be able to move freely in the environment and change their motion in real-time. They should also perceive the environment through sensors. We already worked extensively on vision-based behavior; in the future, we intend now to generalize to various sensors and include production and reaction to sounds. Finally, in order to make the simulations truly interactive, the user should be able to communicate with actors moving in Virtual Environments.

This kind of research is strongly related to the research efforts in behavioral animation as introduced by Reynolds (1987). Reynolds introduces a distributed behavioral model to simulate flocks of birds, herds of land animals, and schools of fish. Several other authors have described experiments in "behavioral animation." Haumann and Parent (1988) describe behavioral simulation as a means to obtain global motion by simulating simple rules of behavior between locally related actors. Lethebridge and Ware (1989) propose a simple heuristically- based method for expressive stimulus-response animation. Wilhelms (1990) proposes a system based on a network of sensors and effectors. Ridsdale (1990) proposes a method that guides lower-level motor skills from a connectionist model of skill memory, implemented as collections of trained neural networks.

Our more specific goal is to allow the actor to explore an unknown environment, and to build mental models and cognitive maps from this exploration. While or after the maps are built, the actor can successfully do path-planning, navigation, and place-finding. A system with such functionalities may be used in different domains. In architecture, it can display the flow of people in a building. In artificial intelligence, it can be used both as the input and the output of an emotion system or other broad agents (Bates et al. 1992). In artistic animation, it allows the animator to direct the motion of the actor at a high level, either with script or task (e.g. "go to the kitchen"), or by defining keyframe location to be passed through.

9.2. An Architecture for Animating Autonomous Synthetic Actors

Autonomous synthetic actors should be based on the three key components:

- the locomotor system, concerned with how to animate physical motions of one or more actors in their environment
- the perceptual system, concerned with perceiving the environment.

- the organism system, concerned with rules, skills, motives, drives and memory; it may be regarded as the brain of the actor.

For the locomotor system, there is no general method applicable to complex motions like skiing or playing tennis for example. Only a combination of various techniques may result in a realistic motion with a relative efficiency. Consequently, only a locomotor system based on integrated methods may support these complex movements. The TRACK system (Boulic et al. 1993), has two major goals, first integrating a wide range of motion generators within the unified framework of multiple track sequences, and second, providing a set of tools for the manipulation of these entities.

We have proposed the following methodology: first, the output produced by any generator is adequately sampled in the joint space and each value is recorded and becomes a key value within a track. Then, a set of tools can manipulate the resulting multiple track sequences. Among these tools, we may mention:

- a compression filter used to reduce the key value to minimum within a predefined error rate
- the Coach-Trainee (Boulic and Thalmann 1992) method which allows the kinematics correction of joint-space based motion with respect to Cartesian constraints.

A perceptual system is concerned with perceiving the environment. Our objective was to integrate only three modes of attention: orienting, touching, and looking. For the orientation, we have modeled the ability to stabilize the posture of the body with respect to the gravitational force. The simulation of the touching system consists in detecting contacts between the actor and the environment. The most important perceptual subsystem is the vision system. Our synthetic vision system has been developed in order to deal with complex environments. Until now, we were only able to simulate actors in a corridor (Renault et al. 1990). Now, our actors are able to navigate in complex environments like forests, mazes, flower fields. To create complex environments, like forests, we have extended the formal concept of L-systems for animation (Noser et al. 1992; Noser and Thalmann 1993). In particular, an appropriate vector force field allows physical simulation and behavioral group animation of objects generated by the L-system.

We have modeled the actor brain with a visual memory and a limited reasoning system allowing the actor to decide his motion based on knowledge. The movement decision procedure is the central coordinator to determine further movement. The 3D visual memory allows the actor to memorize the environment he sees and to adapt it to a changing and dynamic environment. His reasoning process allows him to find 3D paths based on his visual memory by avoiding impasses and circuits. The actor's visual memory is defined using an occupancy octree grid, implemented using paging with a hashing function based on the location of the point to be inserted. In order to simulate real situations, we have also introduced possibilities of forgetting, corresponding to the deleting of subtrees in the octree.

9.3. Vision-based Navigation

Global and local navigation. The task of a navigation system is to plan a path to a specified goal and to execute this plan, modifying it as necessary to avoid unexpected obstacles (Crowley 1987). This task can be decomposed into global navigation and local navigation. The global navigation uses a prelearned model of the domain which may be a somewhat simplified description of the synthetic world and might not reflect recent changes in the environment. This prelearned model, or map, is used to perform a path planning algorithm.

The local navigation algorithm uses the direct input information from the environment to reach goals and sub-goals given by the global navigation and to avoid unexpected obstacles. The local navigation algorithm has no model of the environment, and doesn't know the position of the actor in the world.

Once again to make a comparison with a human being, close your eyes, try to see the corridor near your room, and how to follow it. No problem, your were using your "visual memory," which corresponds to the global navigation in our system. Now stand up and go to the corridor near your room, then close your eyes and try to cross the corridor... There the problems begin (you know that there is a skateboard in front of your boss's door but...). This is an empirical demonstration of the functionalities of the local navigation as we define it in our system.

The global navigation needs a model of the environment to perform path-planning. This model is constructed with the information coming from the sensory system. Most navigation systems developed in robotics for intelligent mobile robots are based on the accumulation of accurate geometrical descriptions of the environment. Kuipers and al. (1988) give a nearly exhaustive list of such methods using quantitative world modeling. In robotics, due to low mechanical accuracy and sensory errors, these methods have failed in large scale area. We don't have this problem in Computer Graphics because we have access to the world coordinates of the actor, and because the synthetic vision or other simulations of perception systems are more accurate. We develop a 3D geometric model, based on grid, implemented as an octree. Elfes (1990) proposed a 2D geometric model based on grid but using a Bayesian probabilistic approach to filter non accurate information coming from various sensor positions. Roth-Tabak (1989) proposed a 3D geometric model based on a grid but for a static world.

In the last few years, research in robot navigation has tended towards a more qualitative approach to world modeling, first to overcome the fragility of purely metrical methods, but especially, because humans do not make spatial reasoning on a continuous map, but rather on a discrete map (Sowa

1964). Kuipers et al. (1988) present a topological model as the basic element of the cognitive map. This model consists of a set of nodes and arcs, where nodes represent distinctively recognizable places in the environment, and arcs represent travel edges connecting them. Travel edges corresponding to arcs are defined by local navigation strategies which describe how a robot can follow the link connecting two distinct places. These local navigation strategies correspond to the Displacement Local Automata (DLA) implemented in the local navigation part of our system. These DLAs work as a black box which has the knowledge to create goals and sub-goals in a specific local environment. They can be thought of as low-level navigation reflexes which use vision, reflexes which are automatically performed by the adults.

Synthetic Vision. Our approach using synthetic vision provides the actor with a realistic information flow from the environment (Renault et al. 1990). To simulate human behavior, i.e. the way a human reacts to his environment, we should simulate the way the actor perceives the environment. Moreover, in systems such as L-systems, where there is no 3D geometric database of the environment because the world exist only after the execution of production rules, synthetic vision gives an elegant and fast way to provide information about the environment to the actor.

Artificial vision is an important research topic in robotics and artificial intelligence. But the problems of 3D recognition and interpretation are not yet generally solved (Gagalowicz 1990). With synthetic vision, we don't need to address these problems of recognition and interpretation.

Each pixel of the synthetic vision input has the semantic information giving the object projected on this pixel, and numerical information giving the distance to this object. So, it is easy to know, for example, that there is a table just in front at 3 meters. With this information, we can directly deal with the problematic question: "what do I do with such information in a navigation system?"

The octree as visual memory representation. We use an octree as the internal representation of the environment seen by an actor because it offers several interesting features. With an octree we can easily construct enclosing objects by choosing the maximum depth level of the subdivision of space. Detailed objects like flowers and trees do not need to be represented in complete detail in the problem of path searching. It is sufficient to represent them by some enclosing cubes corresponding to the occupied voxels of the octree . The octree adapts itself to the complexity of the 3D environment, as it is a dynamic data structure making a recursive subdivision of space. Intersection tests are easy. To decide whether a voxel is occupied or not, we only have to go to the maximum depth (5-10) of the octree by some elementary addressing operations. The examination of the neighborhood of a voxel is immediate, too.

Another interesting property of the octree is the fact that it represents a graph of a 3D environment. We may consider, for example, all the empty voxels as nodes of a graph, where the neighbors are connected by edges. We can apply all the algorithms of graph theory directly on the octree and it is not necessary to change the representation.

Perhaps the most interesting property of the octree is the simple and fast transition from the 2D image to the 3D representation. All we have to do is take each pixel with its depth information (given by the z-buffer value) and calculate its 3D position in the octree space. Then, we insert it in the octree with a maximum recursion depth level. The corresponding voxel will be marked as occupied with possible additional information depending on the current application.

The octree has to represent the visual memory of an actor in a 3D environment with static and dynamic objects. Objects in this environment can grow, shrink, move or disappear. In a static environment (growing objects are still allowed) an *insert* operation for the octree is sufficient to get an approximate representation of the world. If there are moving or disappearing objects like cars, other actors, or opening and closing doors, we also need a *delete* operation for the octree. The *insert* operation is simple enough. The *delete* operation however, is more complicated. Our approach follows.

At a given instant, each pixel is inserted into the octree and the corresponding voxel is marked with the actual time stamp. After the insertion of all image pixels, all the voxels in the vision volume are tested whether they have disappeared or not. The principle of such a test is shown in figure 1.

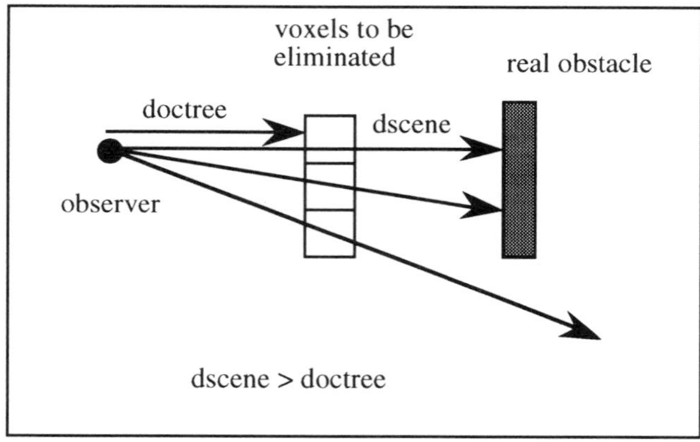

FIGURE 1. Object removal in the octree.

An occupied voxel has to be deleted only if there is no real object either at its position or in front of it. This condition is expressed by equation (1).

$$d_{scene} > d_{octree} \qquad (distancesfromtheobserver)$$

The distance of the voxel of the octree from the observer has to be smaller than the distance of a real object or the background. To get the distance of the voxel from the observer you have to transform the observer into the octree coordinate system and apply the corresponding modeling and perspective transformation to the voxel. Doing this with all voxels in the vision volume, we get the image of the memory in normalized coordinates and can compare it directly with the z buffer values of the 2D synthetic world image .

The algorithm of path finding is based on path searching in a graph. Each free voxel not occupied by an obstacle is interpreted as a node of the graph. All the neighbor voxels are considered to be connected by an edge. So, the octree represents a graph with nodes and edges. The algorithm of path searching uses the principle of backtracking and memorizes all tested nodes in a sorted list. With this list of already tested nodes, circuits can be avoided, and situations without a path from a given source to a given destination can be detected. In a first approach, a path is represented by a sequence of free nodes. To avoid a combinatorial explosion of possibilities in graph searching, we use a heuristic depth first search. The first type of heuristic is characterized by the choice of the neighbors of the current voxel. For example, if we know that the search is done in a plane (2D), we will only examine the neighbors in that plane. So, we can reduce the numbers of new voxels to be tested from 26 to 8. The second type of heuristic is determined by the order of the new neighbors to be tested. If we are searching a path from the current position to an aim, we will sort the list of the new neighbors according to their distance from the aim and we will continue the depth first search with the nearest neighbor to the aim. The third type of heuristic is determined by some additional conditions on the new neighboring voxels to be examined. If we want, for example, that the actor is bound to the ground (if he/she cannot fly) in a 3D environment with stairs, ramps, bridges, holes, etc., we can use only neighbors which have an occupied voxel beneath themselves. With these simple condition, our actor is now able to avoid holes, use bridges and mount or descend stairs and ramps.

The path finding procedure is a mental process of the actor, which is based on the contents of his visual memory (octree). This means that during his reasoning on a possible path, he does not move. Very often, though, he is placed in an unknown environment, which he has still not seen and memorized. In this case, he cannot find a path using, for example, some conditional heuristic. So, he is forced to explore his environment guided by his vision and a heuristic. This exploring is an active process and the actor has to walk and memorize what he sees. In this case, an heuristic depth first search step can be used to guide the actor to guarantee that he finds a way if one exists.

If the actor, for example, is enclosed in a house, there will be no path to a destination outside the house. In this case, he will explore the parts of the interior accessible to him according to the heuristic. He will finish his search by having memorized the interior of the house and the conclusion that he is enclosed. He should avoid turning infinitely in a loop and he can recognize that he has checked all possibilities to find an exit.

To illustrate the capabilities of the synthetic vision system, we have developed several examples. First, an actor is placed inside a maze with an impasse, a circuit and some animated flowers (Plate 1). The actor's first goal is a point outside the maze. After some time, based on 2D heuristic, the actor succeeds in finding his goal. When he had completely memorized the impasse and the circuit, he avoided them. After reaching his first goal, he had nearly complete visual octree representation of his environment and he could find again his way without any problem by a simple reasoning process. We have also implemented a more complex environment with flowers and butterflies (Plate 2); the complex flowers were represented in the octree memory by enclosing cubes.

Local Navigation System. The local navigation system can be decomposed into three modules. The *vision* module, conceptually the perception system, draws a perspective view of the world in the vision window, constructs the vision array and can perform some low level operation on the vision array. The *controller* module, corresponding to the decision system, contains the main loop for the navigation system, and decides on the creation of the goals and administrates the DLAs. The *performer*, corresponding to the task execution system, contains all the DLAs.

The Vision module

We use the hardware facilities of the Silicon Graphics IRIS to create the synthetic vision, more precisely we use the flat shading and z-buffer drawing capabilities of the graphic engine. The vision module has a modified version of the drawing routine traveling the world; instead of giving the real color of the object to the graphic engine, this routine gives a code, call the *vision_id*, which is unique for each object and actor in the world. This code allows the image recognition and interpretation. Once the drawing is done, the window buffer is copied into a 2D array. This array contains the vision_id and the z-buffer depth for each pixel. This array is referred as the view.

The Controller module

In local navigation there are two goals. These two goals are geometrical goals, and are defined in the local 2D coordinate system of the actor. The actor itself is the center of this coordinate system, one axis is defined by the direction "in front", the other axis is defined by the "side" direction. The global goal, or final goal, is the goal the actor must reach. The local goal, or temporary goal, is the goal the actor creates to avoid the obstacles encountered in the path towards the global goal. These goals are created by the Displacement Local Automata (DLA), or given by the animator or by the global navigation system. The main task of the controller is to create these goals created and to make the actor reach them.

Goal creation and actor displacement are performed by the DLAs. The controller selects the appropriate DLA either by knowing some internal set-up of the actor, or by visual by analyzing the environment. For example, if the actor has a guide, the controller will choose the DLA *follow_the_guide*. Otherwise, from a 360 look-around, the controller will determine the visible objects and then determine the DLA corresponding to these objects. No real interpretation of the topology of the environment (as in Kuipers et al. 1989) has yet been implemented. The choice of the DLA is hardcoded by the presence of some particular objects, given by their *vision_id*.

The actor has an internal clock administrated by the controller. This clock is used by the controller to refresh the global and local goal at regular intervals. The interval is given by the *attention_rate*, a variable set-up for each actor that can be changed by the user or by the controller. This variable is an essential parameter of the system: with a too high attention rate the actor spends most of his time analyzing the environment and real-time motion is impossible; with a too low attention rate, the actor starts to act blindly, going through objects. A compromise must be found between these two extremes.

The Performer module

This module contains the DLAs. There are three families of DLA: the DLAs creating the global goal (follow_the_corridor, follow_the_wall, follow_the_visual_guide), the DLAs creating the local goal ball's(avoid_obstacle, closest_to_goal), and the DLAs effectively moving the actor (go_to_global_goal). The DLAs creating goals only use the vision as input. All these DLAs have access to a library of routines performing high level operations on the vision. A detailed algorithm of the use of vision to find avoidance goal is described by Renault et al. (1990) .

9.4. Tennis Playing

Our second example is concerned with the simulation of vision-based tennis playing. The example shows the universal character of the synthetic vision approach, we modeled beside the "navigation and collision avoidance" behavior a "tennis playing" behavior. Tennis playing is a human activity which is severely based on the vision of the players. In our model, we use the vision system to recognize the flying ball, to estimate its trajectory and to localize the partner for game strategy planning. The geometric characteristics of the tennis court however, make part of the players knowledge.

For the dynamics simulation of the ball, gravity, net, ground and the racquet we use the force field approach developed for the L-system animation system. The tracking of the ball by the vision system is controlled by a special automaton. A prototype of this automaton is already able to track the ball, to estimate the collision time and collision point of ball and racquet and to perform successfully a hit with given force and a given resulting ball direction. In a first step, we have a prototype where only two racquets with synthetic vision can play against each other, in order to develop, test and improve game strategy and the physical modeling. Plate 3 shows the prototype system. The integration of the corresponding locomotor system of a sophisticated actor is under development as seen in Plates 4 and 5.

The two actors play in a physically modeled environment given by differential equations and supported by the L-system. In this "force field animation system" the 3D world is modeled by force fields. Some objects have to carry repulsion forces, if there should not be any collision with them. Other objects can be attractive to others. Many objects are both attractive at long distances and repulsive at short distances. The shapes and sizes of these objects can vary, too. Space fields like gravity or wind force fields can greatly influence animation sequences or shapes of trees.

Ball and player recognition. In the navigation problem each colored pixel is interpreted as an obstacle. No semantic information is necessary. In tennis playing however, the actor has to distinguish between the partner, the ball and the rest of the environment. The ball has to be recognized, its trajectory has to be estimated and it has to be followed by the vision system. At the beginning of a ball exchange, the actor has to verify that its partner is ready. During the game the actor needs also his partner's position for his play strategy.

To recognize objects in the image we use color coding. The actor knows that a certain object is made of a specific material. When it scans the image it looks for the corresponding pixels and calculates its average position and its approximate size. Thus each actor can extract some limited semantic information from the image.

Once the actor has recognized the ball, it follows it with his vision system and adjusts at each frame his field of view. As the vision image resolution is very small (50×50 pixels) the ball risks to disappear at far distances or to become too big at near distances. Thus, if the number of "ball" pixels is smaller than a given lower limit the field of view angle is decreased. On the other hand, if the number of "ball" pixels exceeds an upper limit, the field of view angle is increased. By this dynamic adjusting of the field of view angle the low resolution problem of the vision image can be solved.

The trajectory estimation. To play tennis each partner has to estimate the future racket-ball collision position and time and to move as fast as possible to this point. At each frame (1/25 sec) the actor memorizes the ball position. So, every n-th frame the actor can derive the current velocity of the ball. From this current velocity and the current position of the ball it can calculate the future impact point and impact time. We suppose that the actor wants to hit the ball at a certain height h. As the vertical velocity component of the ball is in general not too big, we can neglect air damping and assume the ball moving according to equation 2.

$$m \cdot \dot{v} = m \cdot g$$

$$\Rightarrow x(t) = v_0 + 0.5 \cdot g \cdot t^2$$

with m: mass of the ball
g: gravity acceleration
v_0: initial vertical speed of the ball
t: time

So the impact time at height h can easily be calculated from the quadratic equation. With this solution however, an actor never lets jump the ball. It will play before the ball will touch the ground. To estimate the x and z components of the impact position, we can use the impact time and the solution of the differential equation of the ball movement with linear air resistance given in the following equation .

$$m \cdot \dot{v} = -m \cdot v$$

$$\Rightarrow x(t) = v_0 \cdot \frac{m}{b}\left(1 - e^{-\frac{b}{m} \cdot t}\right)$$

with b: air damping
m: mass of the ball
v_0: initial speed of the ball
t: time

The impact point estimation is performed every n-th frame (n=4, par example). If the ball is close enough to the actor (1 meter) the estimation can be stopped as the impact point is precise enough.

In the next phase the actor has to play the ball. Now he has to determine the racket speed and its orientation to play the ball to a given place.

Figure 2 summarizes the geometrical situation of the racket-ball collision. **a** is the wished resulting ball velocity after the hit, **v** is the arriving ball velocity and **r** its reflection vector. With some geometrical considerations the necessary racket speed **c** can be determined.

Game strategy. Before playing the ball the actor has to decide where to play. In our simulation approach he looks where his partner is placed and then he plays the ball in the most distant corner of the court. This corner determines the x and z direction of the vector **a** in Figure 2. To simplify the strategy we held the inclination of vector a (vertical direction) constant. Thus we can estimate the speed of the resulting ball velocity with a heuristic distance dependent function.

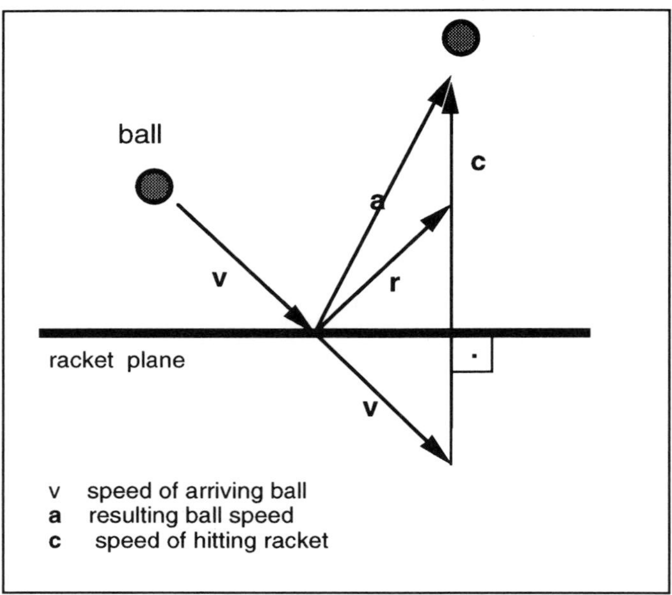

FIGURE 2. Ball-racket collision

The playing automaton. All the above features are coordinated by a specialized "tennis play" automaton. First an actor goes to his start position. There he waits until his partner is ready. Then he looks for the ball, which is thrown into the game. Once the vision system has found the ball, it always follows it by adjusting the field of view angle. If the ball is flying towards the actor, it starts estimating the impact point. Once the ball has passed the net, the actor localizes his partner with his vision system during one frame. This information is used for the game strategy. After playing the ball, the actor goes back to his start point and waits until the ball comes back to play it again.

This simplified automaton does not treat playing errors. In our current version the actor is a with synthetic vision equipped racket, moving along a spline with no speed limitations. The aim of the project was to show the feasibility of a vision based tennis playing. Error free simulations of tennis playing during several minutes have been performed. It is planned in a future extension to integrate synthetic actors with walk and hit motor and to add some error treatment.

9.5. Conclusion

In this paper, we have presented a new approach to implement autonomous synthetic actors in synthetic worlds based on perception and synthetic vision. As vision is a very important perceptual subsystem of an actor, it is an ideal approach for modeling a behavioral animation and offers a universal approach to pass the necessary information from the environment to an actor in the problems of path searching, obstacle avoidance, game playing, and internal knowledge representation with learning and forgetting characteristics.

We think that this new way of defining animation is a convenient and universal high level approach to simulate the behavior of intelligent human actors in dynamics and complex environments.

Acknowledgments

The authors are grateful to Olivier Renault for the development of local navigation and Zhyang Huang and Mrs. Japon for the tennis sequence. This research was sponsored by the Swiss National Foundation for Scientific Research.

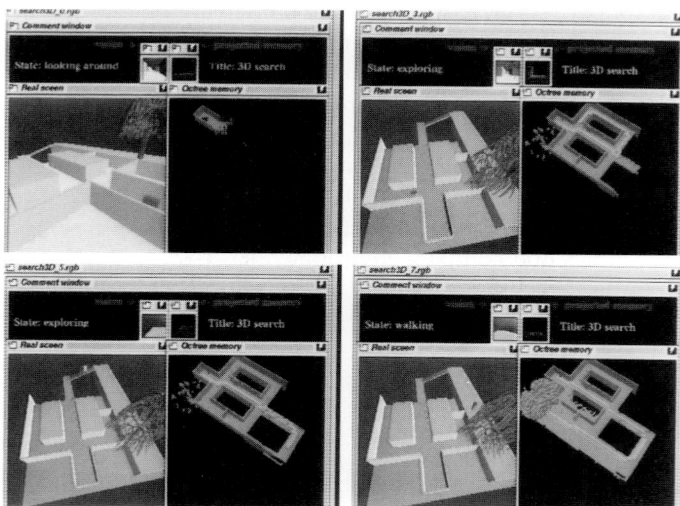

Plate 1: Vision-based navigation in a 2-floor maze

Plate 2: Vision-based navigation for butterflies among flowers

Plate 3: Vision-based tennis playing

Plate 4: Synthetic actress playing tennis

Plate 5: Synthetic actress playing tennis

References

1. Bates J, Loyall AB, Reilly WS (1992) An architecture for Action, Emotion, and Social Behavior. In Proceedings of the Fourth Europeans Workshop on Modeling Autonomous Agents in a multi Agents World, S. Martino al Cimino, Italy.
2. Boulic R, Thalmann D (1992) Combined Direct and Inverse Kinematic Control for the Correction of Predefined Motions, Computer Graphics Forum, October 92.
3. Boulic R, Huang Z, Magnenat Thalmann N, Thalmann D (1993) A Unified Framework for the Motion Manipulation of Articulated Figures with the TRACK System, Proc 3rd Conf. on CAD/CG, Beijing, pp.45-50.
4. Crowley JL (1987) Navigation for an Intelligent Mobile Robot, IEEE journal of Robotics and Automation, Vol. RA-1, No. 1, pp 31-41.
5. Elfes A (1990) Occupancy Grid: A Stochastic Spatial Representation for Active Robot Perception, Proc. Sixth Conference on Uncertainty in AI.
6. Gagalowicz A (1990) Collaboration Between Computer Graphics and Computer Vision. In D. Thalmann, Ed., Scientific Vusualisation and Graphics Simulation, Wiley, 1990, pp 233-248.
7. Haumann DR, Parent RE (1988) The Behavioral Test-bed: Obtaining Complex Behavior from Simple Rules, The Visual Computer, Vol.4, No 6, pp.332-347.
8. Kuipers B, Byun YT (1988) A Robust Qualitative Approach to a Spatial Learning Mobile Robot, SPIE Sensor Fusion: Spatial Reaoning and Scene Interpretation, Vol. 1003.
9. Lethebridge TC and Ware C (1989) A Simple Heuristically-based Method for Expressive Stimulus-response Animation, Computers and Graphics, Vol.13, No3, pp.297-303
10. Noser H, Thalmann D (1993) L-System-Based Behavioral Animation, Proc. Pacific Graphics '93, pp.133-146.
11. Noser H, Thalmann D, Turner R (1992) Animation based on the Interaction of L-systems with Vector Force Fields, Proc. Computer Graphics International, in Kunii TL (ed): Visual Computing, Springer, Tokyo, pp.747-761.
12. Renault O, Magnenat Thalmann N, Thalmann D (1990) A Vision-based Approach to Behavioural Animation, The Journal of Visualization and Computer Animation, Vol 1, No 1, pp 18-21.
13. Reynolds C (1987) Flocks, Herds, and Schools: A Distributed Behavioral Model, Proc.SIGGRAPH '87, Computer Graphics, Vol.21, No4, pp.25-34
14. Ridsdale G (1990) Connectionist Modelling of Skill Dynamics, Journal of Visualization and Computer Animation, Vol.1, No2, 1990, pp.66-72.
15. Roth-Tabak Y (1989) Building an Environment Model Using Depth Information, Computer, 85-90.
16. Sowa JF (1964) Conceptual Structures, Addison-Wesley. Wilhelms J (1990) A "Notion" for Interactive Behavioral Animation Control, IEEE Computer Graphics and Applications , Vol. 10, No 3 , pp.14-22

Theme 2

Synthetic Art

10. Sound Synthesis in Computer Music

Naotoshi Osaka
Information Science Research Laboratory, NTT Basic Research Laboratories, 3-1 Morinosato Wakamiya Atsugi-Shi, Kanagawa 243-0198, Japan (e-mail:osaka@idea.brl.ntt.co.jp)

Summary.

This paper surveys the sound synthesis technology used to create computer music as a new art form. The sound synthesis models referred to here are the additive sinusoidal, phase vocoder, FM synthesis, and physical models. Various types of classification from different viewpoints, including "creative synthesis" newly defined here, allow us to easily understand the features of each synthesis model. Moreover, computer application systems for sound synthesis are introduced, including our new system "O^t*kinshi*". As an example of creative synthesis, sound materials used in the author's own piece are described. In closing, the possibilities for present and future sound synthesis studies are discussed.

Key words and phrases: Sound synthesis, FM synthesis model, additive synthesis, subtractive synthesis, phase vocoder, analysis/synthesis

10.1. Introduction

Computer music has been recognized as an independent genre of music for only the last two decades. It has its origin in musique concrète and electric music from the 1940s. Technology has always been together with this new art. In past years, composers such as John Cage recognized that running a disk backwards creates a musically pleasing sound. In those days new electro-acoustic equipment such as disks and tape recorders became new instruments for some contemporary composers. Since then collaboration has continued between electro-acoustic researchers with musical minds and composers with technical minds. Musicians first used various electro-acoustic equipment such as function generators, filters, and equalizers, which were all available in a broadcast studio. Since digital signal processing techniques have become popular, researchers have also paid more attention to speech transmission technology. Various kinds of distortion coming from vocoders or new coding algorithms looked very attractive. Nowadays, digital computers have become the most common tool used for sound synthesis; computer musicians use it to create new sound materials.

There are other areas in computer music besides just sound synthesis. One is computer-aided composition on the note level, that is, algorithmic composition. This has nothing to do with sound synthesis, but instead the generation of notes. One example of this is Leonard Isaacson and Lejaren Hiller's "Illiac suit for String Quartet" presented in 1956. Another area is interactive computer music. This is computer-realized music rather than computer-aided music. When the speed of the processor was not sufficient, real-time computing was not fulfilled. Furthermore, listeners were insufficient with tape music in a live concert. Progress in the speed of the processor makes it possible to operate digital signal processing in real time, so that computer responds to performers on a stage.

Computer music has enlarged its performance realm such that it also includes visual factors. Interactive music is a newly developed area in such a situation. For a computer to respond to human movement, several sensor technologies are used, such as infrared and magnetic sensors. Other areas include music language development and computer music systems. Therefore, research areas are fairly broad, ranging from sound synthesis to information processing.

This paper focuses on sound synthesis, giving an overview of typical synthesis methods and new possibilities for future studies in the various areas.

10.2. Sound Synthesis

Musical sound synthesis is used primarily 1) to propose sound materials for new computer music, 2) to clarify the acoustical features of instrumental sounds, and 3) to construct an information processing system that understands and synthesizes sounds. We will focus on the research involved in category 1). Number 2) can be addressed as an early stage of category 1).

Figgure 1 depicts the main sound synthesis models and their relations each other. In sound synthesis, there are various model classifications, such as the analysis/synthesis, additive, subtractive, abstract, and physical.

In analysis/synthesis, the model framework provides a model parameter estimation algorithm, given any sound, and resynthesizes the original sound from the model parameters. A phase vocoder [1], sinusoidal model, and LPC are representative analysis/synthesis models.

The rest are classified by the synthesis model itself, which is different depending on whether or not a model is an analysis/synthesis type.

The additive synthesis model expresses sound as a composite sound of each partials, the harmonics of a sound. The subtractive synthesis model reduces spectral information from noise that has spectrally wide information so that it approaches the target spectral characteristics of a particular sound.

Mathews first used additive synthesis in his sound synthesis program "Music III" in 1960 [2] using unit generators.

In the 60s, "analysis" always meant spectral analysis. Risset and Mathews analyzed time-amplitude characteristics of the harmonics of trumpet sound and implemented a linear approximation of these charcteristics into Mathew's newer sound synthesis program "Music IV". It was reported that they achieved almost the same timbre as that of the instrument [3]. In the 70s, analysis meant the same as it did in speech coding theory; that is, arithmetic analysis algorithms enabling original signal reconstruction. In this sense, Moorer first applied an analysis/synthesis technique, the phase vocoder, to sound synthesis for computer music [11], and analysis-based sinusoidal models have taken the lead in additive synthesis.

The abstract model is a signal model whose notation is given mathematically to express various classes of sound, that is, a wide variety of spectra. The FM synthesis model is one representative of abstract models.

In the meantime, physical models aim to express physical sound generation processes as precisely as possible. For in instrumental sound, a vibration description model based on the physical configuration and operation is used. In speech signal representation, the model includes both articulatory and voice source models.

In the history of commercial products, sine functions or unit generators used in the hardware of additive synthesis models have been rather steady. Furthermore, the concept of analysis-based parameter estimation from a natural sound and its hardware implementation has never been fulfilled. Therefore, sound quality was not as sufficient as desired by musicians. The proposal of the FM synthesis model [4] was a revolution in the field, and has brought great improvements in sound quality. Consumer product DX7 by YAMAHA uses FM synthesis. It has become widely spread for both academic and personal use.

However, the sound quality was still not sufficient for all classes of timber. To make the quality more natural, many researchers have felt the necessity of a physical model. In 1993, the first physical model-based product was released by YAMAHA. Many musicians desire further development of this new type of synthesizer.

We would like to add a new classification of perceptual analysis/synthesis and creative synthesis.

Perceptual analysis/synthesis is a synthesis framework whose parameters are found by hand, given natural sound, so that the sound timbre approaches that of the original sound. This does not physically reconstruct any of the original sound; neither wave nor spectrum. The only evaluation method is a subjective test. Abstract models are all said to be perceptual analysis/synthesis models.

Creative synthesis is not a method from the standpoint whether or not the model can simulate a real sound, but aims to develop sound materials

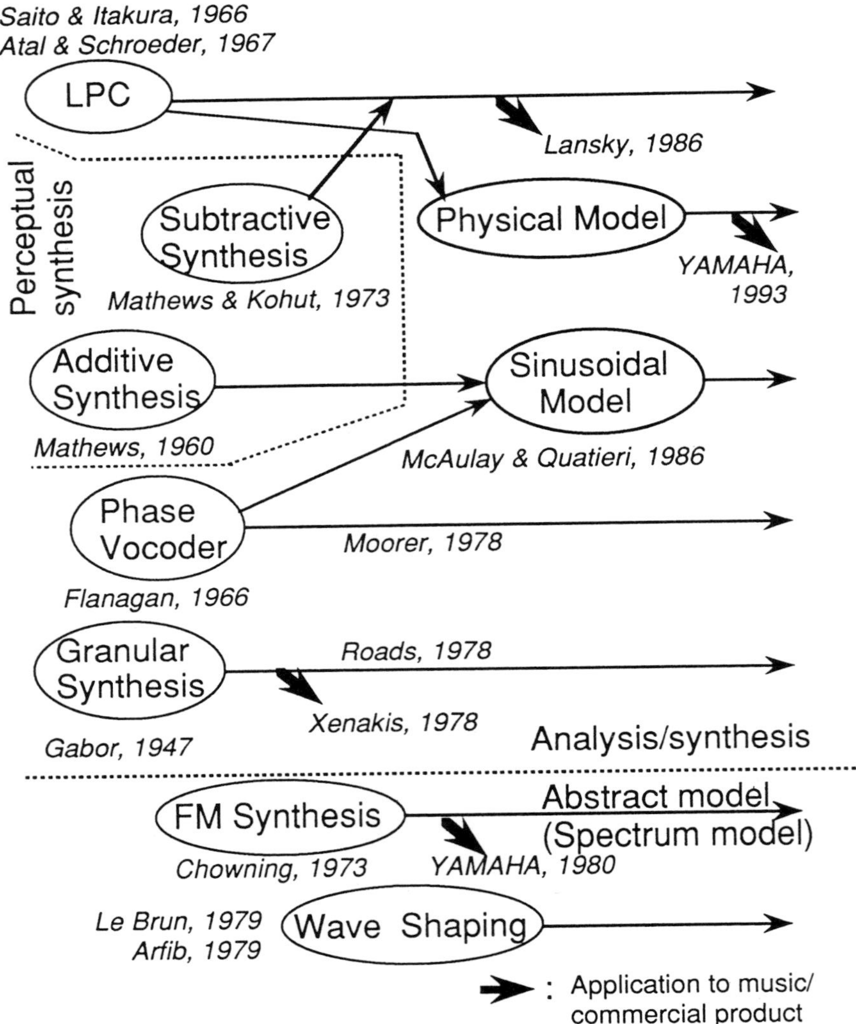

FIGURE 1. Various sound synthesis models for computer music

for new computer music. Some researchers doubt if this activity is explained in the framework of the classical sense of research; however, this is of great importance to the computer musicians.

10.3. Analysis/synthesis

Additive synthesis. Harmonics are very important in the initial approximation of musical sound representation. Therefore, additive synthesis is an intuitive, natural formulation of a musical sound.

Moorer introduced early progress in his overview of the model[5]. A simpler form, used in the 60s and in commercial synthesizers without analysis, is as follows:

$$x(n) = \sum_{l=1}^{N} a_l(n) \sin(\omega_l n) \qquad \textbf{10.3.1.}$$

where $x(n)$ is the signal at sample n, l is the harmonic number, N is the number of harmonics, $\omega_l n$ is the steady-state frequency of harmonic l , and $a_l(n)$ is the time-variant amplitude of harmonic l. $a_l(n)$ is an envelope function which changes very slowly. It is controlled with a few parameters, such as some combination of linear functions. The better sound quality of FM synthesis brought about the demise of earlier versions of additive synthesis without analysis.

Analysis-based additive synthesis is called the sinusoidal model, and is formulated as follows.

$$x(n) = \sum_{l=1}^{N} a_l(n) \sin(\theta_l(n)). \qquad \textbf{10.3.2.}$$

Here, $\theta_l(n)$ denotes the instantaneous phase of harmonic l at sample n, and the rest of the symbols are the same as in Eq. (1). The analysis algorithm [5] is influenced by that of the phase vocoder, but is rather complicated. $\theta_l(n)$ is composed of the constant frequency ω and frequency deviation. It was not until the McAulay and Quatieri (MQ) algorithm [9] was proposed that the analysis and synthesis method was widely spread. However, because there are so many parameters to control, musicians cannot make use of analysis-based synthesis either with or without parameter modification. The next generation of additive synthesis is being designed to have more user-friendly interface involving a limited number of parameters to control timbre.

Phase vocoder. The phase vocoder was developed by Flanagan and Golden [10], and Portnoff has discussed the implementation of the digital phase vocoder [1]. Moorer discussed musical applications of the model, and used it to introduce his own program code to musicians. Musicians have been using the phase vocoder ever since, making it one of the most common models in the field now. The basic formulation below is taken directly from Portnoff. Let $x(n)$ be samples of a signal waveform. Then, the discrete time-dependent Fourier transform is defined as

$$X_k(n) = \sum_{r=-\infty}^{\infty} x(r)h(n-r)W_N^{-rk} \qquad \textbf{10.3.3.}$$

for $k = 0, 1, \cdots, N-1$, where $W_N = exp[j(2\pi/N)]$ and $h(n)$ is an appropriately chosen window. By properly choosing $h(n)$, $x(n)$ is exactly recoverable from its short-time transform, as defined in Eq. (3) and $x(n)$ is given by

$$x(n) \quad = \quad \frac{1}{N}\sum_{k=0}^{N-1} X_k(n)W_N^{nk} \qquad \textbf{10.3.4.}$$

For the analysis-synthesis system defined in Eqs. (3) and (4) to be identical, the only condition is that $h(n) = 0$ for n being all integer multiples of N.

This definition gives us an interpretation of instantaneous frequency. Since its computation for each sample is costly, an interpolation algorithm using FFT was proposed by Portnoff. This makes computation less costly, and less complicated. Moorer chose magnitude and instantaneous frequency as the control parameters, making the phase vocoder easier for musicians to use.

Subtractive synthesis. Both additive and subtractive synthesis are rather misleading terms. These refer to the addition and subtraction of spectral information. In particular, subtractive synthesis represents a filtering operation used to synthesize a sound given noise, which has power over a whole band. It is also used to create physical model by simulating acoustic sound vibration as presicely as possible according to the sound source's physical features. LPC (Linear Predictive Coding), a standard technique in the speech research community [13], is a standard technique of subtractive synthesis. Music researchers have not contributed much to LPC, but many musicians have applied it to their own music pieces. Paul Lansky was the first composer to use it. His opinions about musical applications of LPC are given in ref. [12]. Cross synthesis became popular, where residual of one sound and the vocal tract transfer function of another sound were synthesised. With this tequnique, a sound like speaking clarinet could be realized.

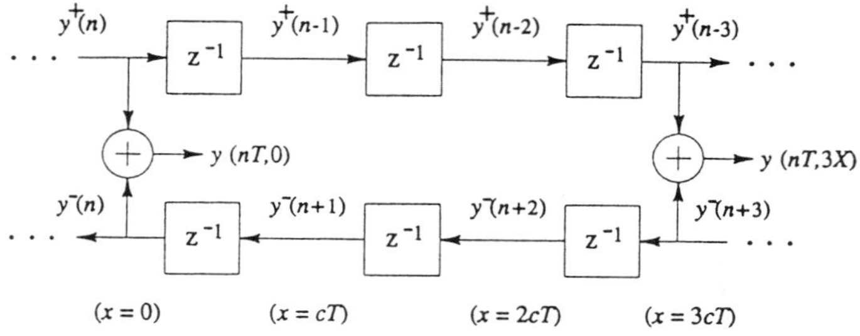

FIGURE 2. Digital simulation of the ideal, lossless waveguide with observation points at X=0 and X=3X=3cT. The symbol "Z^{-1}" denotes a one-sample delay. (from [14])

Nowadays, many researchers are studying waveguide models [14]. These simulates the propagation of sound vibration. The objects of application are plucked strings, winds, and so on. The synthesized sound is as high a quality as that of a natural instrument, and a model is now being fine-tuned for individual instruments. In some models [15], a nolinear term has been introduced, making the model rather complicated.

10.4. Abstract Model

FM synthesis. This is such a popular synthesis model, that even those who are not interested in music know it by name. Synthesis formulation is as follows: (analogue form, from [4])

$$y(t) \quad = \quad \mathrm{A} \sin(\omega_c t + \mathrm{I} \sin \omega_m t) \qquad \mathbf{10.4.1.}$$

This is expanded into the equation below which makes the model easier understand in the frequency domain.

$$\begin{aligned} y(t) = \mathrm{A}\{ & J_0(\mathrm{I}) \sin(\omega_c t) \\ & + J_1(\mathrm{I})[\sin(\omega_c + \omega_m)t + \sin(\omega - \omega_m)t] \\ & + J_2(\mathrm{I})[\sin(\omega_c + 2\omega_m)t - \sin(\omega - 2\omega_m)t] \\ & + \cdots\cdots\cdots\cdots\cdots\cdots \\ & + J_i(\mathrm{I})[\sin(\omega_c + i \cdot \omega_m)t + (-1)^i \sin(\omega - i \cdot \omega_m)t] \\ & + \cdots\cdots\cdots\cdots\cdots\cdots \} \end{aligned} \qquad \mathbf{10.4.2.}$$

The spectrum of the equation is shown in Fig. 3. The theorey given here appeare in the beginning of a modulation theory textbook. However, in applications to telephone or radio transmission systems, the value of the carrier and modulation frequency are quite different, while in music these might be quite similar. The purpose of the basic formulation is to generate sidebands, scattering energy in ω_c to create appropriate harmonics or inharmonics. In this sense, FM synthesis is categorized as spectral shaping synthesis. There is no general analysis algorithm because the model is highly nonlinear, although the model could be used as an analysis/synthesis model under very restricted parameter ranges. In musical applications, no single formulation above is used. Instead, feedback, multi carrier formulation, or some other combined and complicated forms are used. Musicians have developed several combinations of FM forms and values of the parameters for particular instruments by hand. In experiment, researchers use those empirical values as an initial value of parameter estimation.

Granular synthesis. The basic concept of granular synthesis is that any sounds can be composed of auditory units or "grains". Usually, the time

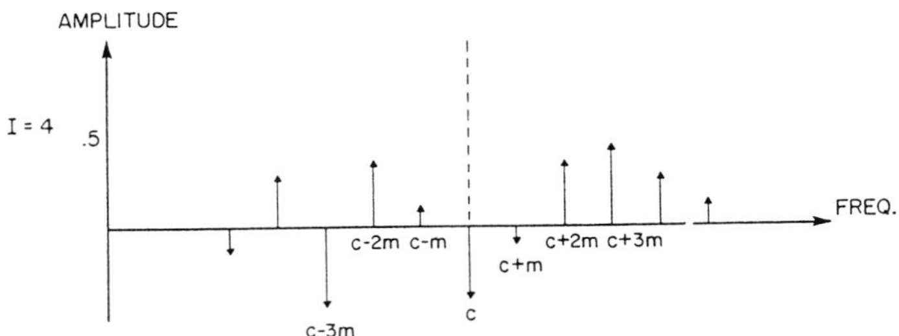

FIGURE 3. Plot of Eq. (6) with phase information included (the modulation index is 4). The bars extending downward represent spectral components whose phase differs by $\pi/2$. (from [4])

duration of a grain is about 5 to 10 msec. Gabor proposed this basic concept in ref. [16]. Bastians expanded this concept mathematically [?]. Xenakis was the first composer to apply granular synthesis to compose a piece. Roads adopted it in using a short-time sinusoidal with an envelope as a grain [?; ?]. In synthesis, these grains are patched together according to the spectral patterns of each time frame, about 10 to 60 msec. Analysis/synthesis is discussed in ref. [18]. Unfortunately, researchers and musicians in computer music have not yet treated this model as an analysis/synthesis model. The usage of these two is completely different. While Road's method is more the analysis/synthesis type, Xenakis' method has no intention of synthesizing given natural sounds, and is completely musical. Not very many researchers are making use of granular synthesis nowadays.

Other techniques are wave table control and wave shaping. These are not intended for analysis/synthesis, but strictly for creative synthesis. Wave shaping is a spectral model similar to FM synthesis. It can generate any spectral shape. It involves several modifications of spectral shape, including scattering one harmonics to create many sidebands [19].

10.5. Creative Synthesis and Application to Computer Music System

The sound synthesis research field in computer music accepts not only the analysis/synthesis method, but also the creative synthesis method. The terminology is defined not as a technical classification, but rather as the attitude related to the use of each model; whether or not it aims to synthesize attractive sounds as sound materials for computer music. In such a synthesis there are no ever-existing physical or perceptual objects to be resynthesized. Any synthesis model can be a creative synthesis model, which is rather an instrumental use.

Once a synthesis model is given, users are free to manipulate the parameters. One important task for artists is to determine how those parameters are modified to express a wide range of creative sound classes. At the same time, researchers or engineers have to present their own models to musicians in a way in which they can easily modify parameters. For that purpose, an application system for synthesis models has to meet the following requirements:

(a) The final model should have reduced data formulation. The fewer, the better.
(b) The original model should at least be based on a spectral model. If it is based on an analysis/synthesis model, all the better.
(c) The user interface for manipulating the synthesis parameters should be friendly.
(d) Real-time operation is recommended.

Requirements 1 and 2 are for a synthesis model and the rest are for application systems. To satisfy these specifications, several music systems and computer languages have been developed, such as Music V and UPIC. Recentry, IRCAM (Institut de Recherche et Coordination Acoustique/Musique) has developed a real-time DSP board on the NeXT computer called ISPW (IRCAM Signal Processing Workstation) for sound synthesis [20]. It has two i860 co-processors and runs at 40 MHz with application software called MAX. ISPW is gaining wide-spread popularity all over the world.

"O^t*kinshi*": A sound generation and performance system. The author has been developing a sound generation, modification, and performance system called "O^t*kinshi*" [21] on a NeXT computer, written in Objective-C. It makes use of speech information processing techniques. The block diagram of the system's software is shown in Fig. 4. The system consists of three parts; 1) sound generation, 2) sequencer, and 3) user interface.

Sound generation

The system's fundamental functions include wave generation by fomulas, time-variant digital filter processing, additive synthesis, FM source generation, sampling frequency conversion, formant vocoder, and LPC synthesizer. Various types of noise and distortion are also programmed in, including phase, clipping, and noise correlated distortion. Fig. 5 shows an example of a sound generation display.

Prosody control includes intonation changes by pitch, power, and duration of speech. The system described here regards prosody control as used in human speech dialog as musical expression, and integrates it into its model.

Sequencer

The sequencer plays the generated sounds, presenting them either in sequence or mixed. Performance may be either automatic or manual. Two modes are

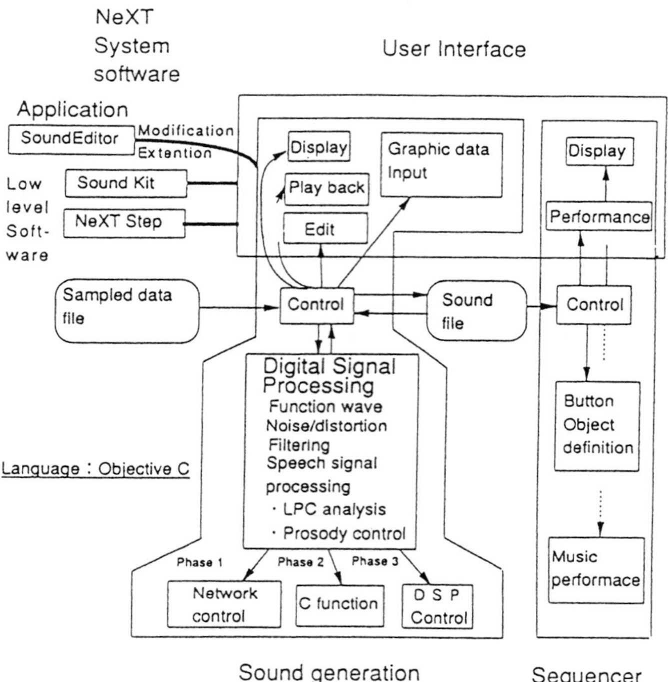

FIGURE 4. 4 Block diagram of "*O*^{t}*kinshi*"

considered here.
1. Manual performance (instrument mode)
Similar to an instrument keyboard, each sound object, represented by a button on a display, generates a predefined sound when pressed.
2. Automatic performance mode:
The duration of the sound is represented by the length of the button. By placing them in a time/timbre plane, a notation similar to that of a score is established. Performance is automatic along the time axis.

User interface

Sound manipulation involves four processes: 1) file I/O, 2) generating/editing, 3) sound output, and 4) characteristics display. Numbers 1 through 3 are related to both sound generation and sequencer, while number 4 is related only to the former. The user interface requirements here are as follows.

(a) Sound representation at any level required by a user.
(b) Graphical input of time sequence data
(c) The ability to move around among each manipulation process as quickly as possible.

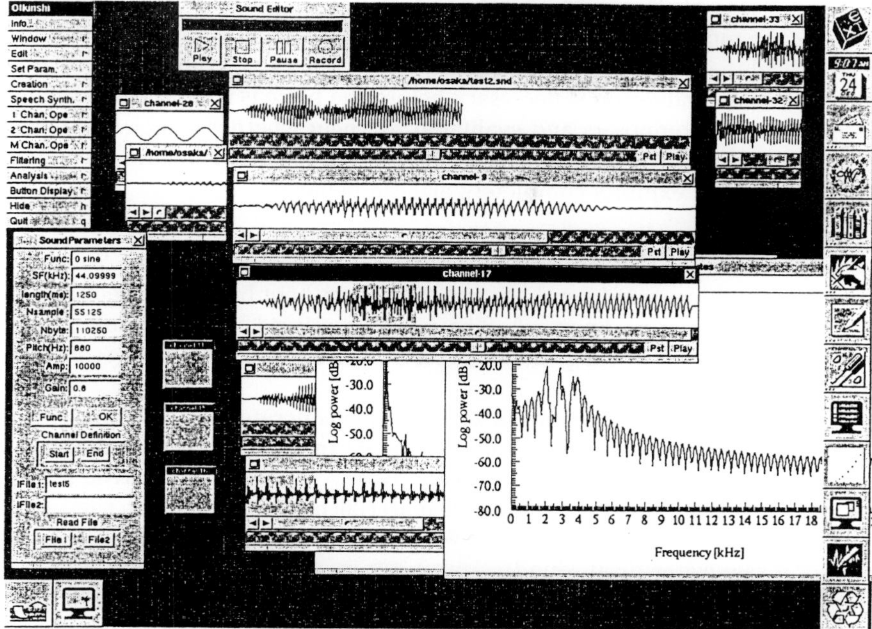

FIGURE 5. An example of the "sound generation" display in "O^t*kinshi*"

For requirement 1, sounds are represented as button objects. At the lowest level, they are displayed as waves or spectra. At the highest level, a button represents a musical phrase. A hierarchical structure is preserved in an object. Three buttons in Fig. 5 represent different sounds. By double clicking these, it changes into graphical representation seen as seen in other channels. For requirement 2, time sequence parameters, such as power envelopes, time-variant filter cutoff frequencies, or wave data, are input with a mouse, using a rubber band/spline function. For the third requirements, minimal mouse movement is necessary when moving to another manipulation process. For example, sound output is done by clicking the small button attached to the button representing a sound object.

This system is still under development. DSP use and integration with ISPW are two items for further study.

10.6. Evaluation of Creative Synthesis

Evaluating creatively synthesized sound is very difficult. Unlike the evaluation of speech quality in a standard telephone system for example, an ordinary audience cannot share one evaluation for a creatively synthesized sound. The value of creatively synthesized sound does not depend upon how new or complex the model is. Creative synthesis becomes valuable if it is given a role in a musical piece and the piece acquires its own identity from among several other pieces. If evaluation is necessary before the piece is composed, it should be presented to composers and evaluated by them whether or not they want to use the sound in their own pieces. Therefore, the author believes that this type of synthesis exhibits completely artistic behavior.

Examples of creative sound synthesis in a musical piece. Some examples of creative sound synthesis will be shown here based on the author's own piece, "Shizuku no kuzushi". The piece premiered at Xebec hall, Kobe, in an Computer music independent concert, in August 1991. A newer version was performed at ICMC'93 in Tokyo.

This piece inherits the concept of "musique concrète." The composer believes that a great deal of musical systems lie in the timbre of a sound, as is true in pitch-oriented musical systems. Here, "shizuku" in the title means a water drop, which is the raw sound material heard throughout the piece. "kuzushi" means variation, and the whole piece explores the possible variations of a raw water drop sound.

Several digital signal processing techniques are used to make those variations. The main processing techniques are time-variant digital filters, spectrum foldover distortion, and phase distortion caused by modulation. "O^t *kinshi*" involves all of these techniques. Fig. 6 shows filter cutoff frequencies for noise, which are used as sound materials of the theme in the middle section.

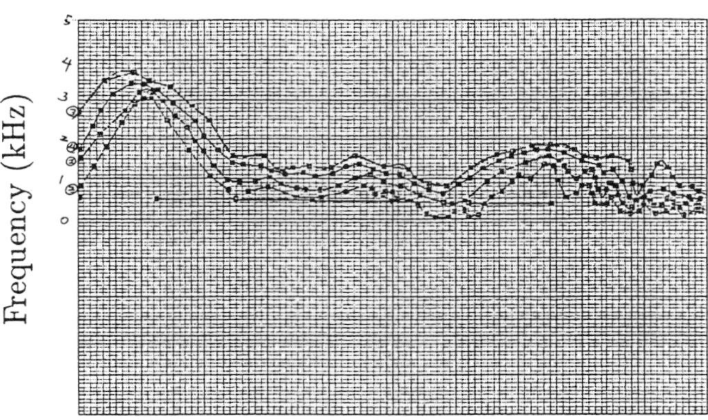

Time

FIGURE 6. Definition of time-variant filter cutoff frequencies in "Shizuku no kuzushi"

10.7. Future Direction of Sound Synthesis Study

Taking these trends into consideration, the author lists the following items as topics ofor further study:

(a) A new analysis/synthesis method with clarified physical characteristics and simple parameter representation
(b) Any abstract model showing the timbre range of synthesized sound, as well as the spectral characteristics
(c) Real-time implementation of sound synthesis system

10.8. Conclusion

Based on a brief introduction of the research areas of computer music, the author offered classifications of sound synthesis and described the attitudes related to its use in computer music. An overview of the sinusoidal, phase vocoder, FM, wave-guide, and granular synthesis models was given. These were shown as typical models of the analysis/synthesis, abstract, physical, and creative synthesis models respectively. Since the creative model is not interpreted as a classical framework of research, methods of evaluation were also discussed. Then we explored a new possibility for sound synthesis study. Although there are quite a few speech synthesis researchers in Japan, only a few are involved in sound synthesis. This is because computer music study, especially for the sake of art, is new to us. The author expects more researchers will come to the field, and thus sound synthesis, including creative synthesis, will be established as a new field.

References

1. Portnoff, Michael R. 1976. "Implementation of the Digital Phase Vocoder Using the Fast Fourier Transform," *IEEE Trans. Acoust., Speech, Signal Processing,* vol. ASSP-24, No. 3, pp. 243-248, June.
2. Mathews, M. V. 1969. "The Technology of Computer Music," Cambridge, Massachesetts, *MIT press.*
3. Risset, J. C. and Mathews, M. V. 1969. "Analysis of musical instrument tones," *Physics Today,* 22, No. 2, pp. 23-30.
4. Chowning, John M. 1973. "The Synthesis of Complex Audio Spectra by Means of Frequency Modulation," *Journal of the Audio Engineering Society,* vol. 21, No. 7.
5. Moorer, James A. 1977. "Signal Processing Aspects of Computer Music: A Survey," *Proceedings of the IEEE,* vol. 65, No. 8, pp. 1108-1137, Aug.
6. Roads, Curtis. 1978. "Automated Granular Synthesis of Sounds," *Computer Music Journal 2(2):*pp. 61-62.
7. Roads, Curtis, and Strawn, John . 1987. "Granular Synthesis of Sound," *Foundations of Computer Music,* Cambridge, Massachusetts. (updated version of [6])

8. Roads, Curtis. 1989. "The Music Machine – selected readings from computer music journal,"The MIT Press, pp.1-12.
9. McAulay, Robert J., and Quatieri, Thomas F. 1986."Speech Analysis/Synthesis Based on a Sinusoidal Representation," *IEEE Trans. on Acoust., Speech,and Signal Processing,*vol. ASSP-34, No. 4, Aug.
10. Flanagan, J. L., and Golden, R. M. 1966. "Phase Vocoder," *Bell Syst. Tech. J.,* Vol. 45, pp. 1493-1509, Nov.
11. Moorer, James A. 1978. "The Use of the Phase Vocoder in Computer Music Applications," *Journal of the Audio Engineering Society,* vol. 26, No. 1/2 , Jan./Feb.
12. Lansky, Paul. 1989. "Compositional Applications of Linear Predictive Coding," in *Current Directions on Computer Music Research,* edited by Mathews and Pierce, the MIT press.
13. Markel, J. D., and Gray, Jr.A. H. 1976 "Linear Prediction of Speech," in *Communication and Cybernetics 12,* Spring-Verlag.
14. Smith, Julius O. 1992. "Physical Modeling Using Digital Waveguides," *Computer Music Journal,* vol. 16, No. 4, Winter.
15. Vuori, Jarkko, and Välimäki, Vesa. 1993. "Parameter Estimation of Non-Linear Physical Models by Simulated Evolution - Application to the Flute Model," *Proceedings of the Int'l Computer Music Conf.,* 4P.11, pp. 402-404, Tokyo, Sep.
16. Gaobor, D. 1947. "Acoustical Quanta and the Theory of Hearing," *Nature,* 159, No. 4044, pp. 591-594, May.
17. Bastiaans, Martin J. 1980. "Gabor's Expansion of a Signal into Gaussian Elementary Signals," *Proc. of the IEEE,* vol. 68, No. 4, pp. 538-539, Apr.
18. Lienard, J. S. 1987. "Speech analysis and reconstruction using short-time elementary waveforms," *IEEE ICASSP'87,* pp. 948-951.
19. Brun, Marc Le. 1979. "Digital Waveshaping Synthesis," *Journal of Audio Engineering Society* vol. 27, No. 4, pp. 250-266, Apr.
20. Puckette, Miller. 1991. "FTS: A Real-Time Monitor for Multiprocessor Music Synthesis," *Computer Music Journal,* vol. 15, No. 3, Fall.
21. Osaka, Naotoshi 1992. "*O^tkinshi*":A Sound Generation and Performance System," *Proceedings of the Int'l Computer Music Conf.,* 4P.11, pp. 406-407, San Jose, California, Oct.

11. Virtual Revisiting of Architectural Masterpieces and the Problem of Lighting Simulation

Karol Myszkowski
Department of Computer Software, The University of Aizu,
Aizu-Wakamatsu City, Fukushima 965-80 Japan
(e-mail: k-myszk@u-aizu.ac.jp)

Summary.

One of the most successful applications of Virtual Reality is in architecture. This paper discusses exploring destroyed or unbuilt masterpieces of architecture, which could not be appreciated in other way but with the help of computers. The unbuilt Hurva Synagogue, designed by Louis Kahn, is considered as a case study of visualization based on physically accurate lighting simulation. Analysis of this presentation is used to frame more general remarks on adequate lighting calculations, storage and reconstruction of scene illumination, and image display, taking into account human perception.

Also, a practical solution used to render the Hurva Synagogue is outlined. A simple hierarchical algorithm is presented, exploiting the ray tracing technique and calculating ideal diffuse light path. The resulting distribution of illumination is stored in a triangular mesh structure, and used for interactive walkthrough animation. Perceptually based criteria for adaptive mesh subdivision, improving the quality of generated frames, are introduced. The proposed algorithms enable convincingly realistic visualization of the complex interactions of light in the Hurva Synagogue, which is illuminated predominantly by interreflected light components.

Keywords and Phrases: virtual reality, synthetic museum, global illumination, photorealism, ray-tracing, radiosity, adaptive meshing, walkthrough animation.

11.1. Introduction

Virtual Reality has tremendous potential, but systems that are available today leave much to be desired. One of the most successful applications of Virtual Reality is in architecture, which exploits walkthrough animation interactively driven by the user. The basic motivation of such systems is to present designs of architectural objects in a way comprehensible to customers, usually not expert in the field. A better understanding of the designers' ideas, and appreciation of the project details, impossible otherwise, can be achieved.

This paper presents results of the work on virtual reconstruction of architectural masterpieces. The most important technical problems to be solved are accurate modeling of the scene and real time display of high quality, realistic images. The true challenge is to trigger in the viewer's mind artistic impressions which correspond to the feelings evoked when observing a real object. Because of the subjective nature of such impressions, there is a danger that the original intentions of the architect are distorted even when subtle details of design are preserved. A partial answer as to whether the reconstruction succeeded can be given by viewers immersed in the virtual architectural masterpiece.

Revisiting great unbuilt or destroyed buildings of history, which cannot be appreciated in other way but with the help of computers, seems to be especially exciting. As the first target, the unbuilt, modernist Hurva Synagogue designed by Louis I. Kahn was chosen. Initial results have been already presented by the architect Kent Larson, who carefully reconstructed Kahn's design [16]. Larson describes the process of collecting informations on the Synagogue, preparation of the scene's model, and rendering still images. At present, a walkthrough animation displaying results of physics-based lighting calculations and sound simulation are also available.

In this paper, the Hurva Synagogue is used as the case for study of more general problems of adequate lighting calculations, storage and reconstruction of scene's illumination, and fast image display, taking into account human perception. Also, a practical solution developed to visualize the Hurva Synagogue is outlined.

11.2. General Objectives

The scope of this paper is view-independent realistic rendering, based on physically correct lighting simulation. In this work, exclusively diffuse interreflections are considered. Thus the results of lighting simulation stored in a mesh can be displayed during interactive walkthrough animation.

Real time image display rate can only be achieved by using specialized hardware. Further considerations are restricted to algorithms that rely on typical capabilities offered by graphic workstations. It means that the whole geometrical model must be polygonized. The triangle is chosen as the only possible geometrical primitive for reasons of efficiency, because graphic accelerators internally perform triangulation. Gouraud shading is a basic tool to reconstruct distribution of illumination over polygonal surfaces.

The shape of an architectural masterpiece is usually very complex. It means that geometrical models created by computer to reconstruct this shape consist of huge amount of polygons. The complexity of models requires carefully designed algorithms of lighting simulation and rendering.

11.3. Lighting Simulation

A majority of available virtual reality systems use very simple illumination models, restricted to primary lights. Visibility analysis resulting in shadows and calculation of the interreflected components of light are completely ignored. Such an approach cannot be afforded for visualization of architectural objects like the Hurva Synagogue, where play of intensive sunlight with concrete interior is an integral part of design. Light leaking into the building through narrow openings in the ceiling and gaps between the stone pylons only illuminates a small portion of the interior (Figures 1 and 2); the indoor scene is illuminated predominantly by complex interreflected components of light. The borders between illuminated and shadowed parts of the interior are very sharp and exhibit high contrasts of luminance (Figure 3).

From the standpoint of visibility calculations, the Synagogue is quite complicated, because of multi-layers structure of the building. In addition, pylons, concrete towers and walls tessellate the interior into multiple volumes (cells). Most of the cells are mutually visible, and interaction of light between them should be considered (Figure 4). Such scene characteristics, while not very common for ordinary buildings, are typical for interiors of architectural masterpieces.

Requirements and existing solutions. Various surfaces of the Synagogue have different impact on the global illumination of the interior, depending on their luminance, size, as well as location. Sorting of emitting surfaces (reflecting or radiating lighting energy) used by progressive radiosity algorithm [5] speeds up significantly the convergence of lighting calculations.

An emitter (shooter) of lighting energy usually significantly affects illumination of neighboring surfaces, while its influence on more distant surfaces is less important. The hierarchical algorithm presented in [13] adjusts the size of the planar shooters and receivers in the function of energy to be shot and the corresponding form factor value. In contrast to the non-hierarchical algorithm, the importance of all surface-surface interactions is similar (at least for given emitter) and bounded by a user-specified error tolerance.

Kok [1993] proposes a grouping algorithm for small surfaces, e.g., leaves of a plant, which usually are ignored as shooters because of negligible contribution to the scene illumination. The problem arises when such surfaces are energy receivers, because depending on the light shooting algorithm, some of them are not illuminated at all, or significant computational effort is required to consider every surface independently. Grouping small surfaces into "macro-patches" solves these problems. "Macro-patches" can also be efficiently considered as energy emitters.

Neumann *et al.* [1989] propose decomposition of the scene into smaller cells using virtual walls. Initially an independent lighting simulation for every cell is performed, and then interaction between cells is considered. Lighting energy gathered at virtual walls of a single cell is re-distributed to the neighboring cells. Non-Lambertian emitters should be considered, but storage of lighting spatial distribution based on spherical harmonics [28] solves this problem efficiently. When virtual walls coincide with opaque obstacles like true walls, ceilings, etc., energy exchange between cells is minimized, speeding up calculations. In the case of large scenes the influence of a single light emitter is usually local, affecting only neighboring cells. The scene decomposition is an efficient way to localize, i.e., significantly speed up lighting calculations while producing global solution, because of inter-cell energy exchange. For huge scenes that do not fit into computer memory, a cell by cell approach prevents swapping problems.

Shading artifacts are very often visible in the computer images when two surfaces meet, e.g., at room corners. The reason is that most of algorithms used to calculate form factors exhibit serious inaccuracies in the presence of singularities in formulations of the form factor [25]. Application of a closed-form solution for an arbitrary polygon and a differential element [1] in the proximity of singularity produces visually acceptable results, however it is only an approximate solution. This choice seems to be a reasonable trade-off between the cost of calculations and image quality.

Overview of applied algorithms. The hierarchical progressive light tracing algorithm was used for the lighting simulation in the Hurva Synagogue. However, for the sake of efficiency some modifications were introduced.

The hierarchical algorithm proposed by Hanrahan *et al.* limits significantly the number of light interactions comparing to the traditional radiosity. The main drawback of the algorithm is the amount of memory needed to store pre-calculated links between all interacting surfaces as well as quadtree structure used to describe hierarchy of these surfaces. In order to avoid the memory shortage a simple 3-level hierarchy algorithm was applied, whose performance is worse than the theoretical bound given for Hanrahan *et al.* algorithm, but which uses much less extra memory.

The lighting calculation consists of two phases. The first phase, based on the energy shooting schema [5], exploits the two highest levels of the hierarchical surface subdivision, i.e., groups of patches and patches. The grouping of patches is performed on the basis of uniform subdivision of space into voxels. All patches belonging to the same group should be quasi-coplanar (within a specified tolerance of the normal vector direction), and located in the same voxel (center of gravity of the patch is considered). The following light interactions are possible:

- group → group;
- group → patch (or patch → group for single patches that do not belong to any group);
- patch → patch.

The particular type of the light interaction is selected by comparison of the emitted luminous flux with the user-specified error bound. The decision is taken globally for all energy receivers inside the voxel instead of the single patch. For this purpose form factors are estimated taking into account voxel size and the distance between voxels, measured in the voxel units. The orientation of the receiver and intervening occluding surfaces are ignored. When interacting patches are located in the same or neighboring voxel, the patch-patch interaction is always chosen in order to prevent shading artifacts. The cost of the proposed error metric is negligible. Because of simplicity of this approach the choice of the interaction type is done on-the-fly, and storage of links between surfaces [13] is avoided.

As the result of the first phase the global illumination for every patch is calculated. During the second phase adaptive subdivision of patches into elements is performed. The algorithm corresponding to [4] approach is exploited. At this phase an energy gathering schema is used for the newly created elements.

Grouping of small, non-coplanar surfaces as suggested by Kok was not implemented; however, use of voxels is a good framework to perform grouping automatically, which originally was done manually [15].

The earlier-suggested decomposition of the scene into cells exploited for the lighting simulation is under development, and was not used for the Hurva Synagogue. Because of mutual visibility between the majority of naturally formed cells inside the Synagogue, the ratio of energy exchange between cells is high, which affects overall performance of the algorithm for this particular scene.

For some scenes, visualization of light reflected by mirror and illuminating diffuse surfaces is important. A practical solution of this problem for planar mirrors is presented in [28; 20]. The walkthrough animation exhibiting specular to diffuse light transfer is possible; both primary and secondary light sources are considered. In the case of the Hurva Synagogue this effect is not demonstrated, because reflectivities of all surfaces are approximated by Lambertian characteristic.

All presented lighting simulation algorithms were previously validated experimentally [19]. Comparison with the measurement data supplied by Toshiba Lighting Corporation reveals that maximum simulation errors fall into 10–15% range, depending on scene complexity. Comparison of simulation results with simple, analytically derived data resulted in a maximum error of 5%.

11.4. Storage and Reconstruction of Lighting Distribution

An accurate reconstruction of subtle and complex illumination details of the real world is a very difficult task. Taking into account human sensitivity to discontinuities of values and lower order derivatives in the luminance function, special attention should be paid to proper visualization of sharp shadow borders, regions of penumbra and high illumination gradients. The adaptive mesh subdivision techniques are usually applied to match mesh approximated illumination to the true lighting distribution. The main practical problem is reduction of mesh complexity, while preserving the quality of the images. To this end, the control of adaptive mesh subdivision should take into account basic properties of human perception, e.g., adaptation to various ranges of luminance, which leads to similar psychological sensations whether observing a real scene or the corresponding image on a computer display. The number of mesh elements depends mainly on the complexity of the lighting distribution, but also on the meshing algorithm.

Meshing requirements and existing solutions. It is assumed that the input mesh is "well-shaped", elements are distributed uniformly, vertices belonging to the same object are shared by neighboring triangles, with no t-vertices or t-edges [2]. Energy leaks and other negative shading artifacts introduced by implicit intersections and overlapping coplanar faces [2] can be neutralized in most practical cases by adaptive mesh subdivision algorithms. However, from the standpoint of efficiency, all these mesh features should be corrected at the preprocessing stage on the basis of purely geometrical considerations.

Below *a priori* and *a posteriori* meshing methods [6] are discussed in the context of visualization of complex architectural scenes.

A priori methods use purely geometrical considerations to split the mesh along principal discontinuities of the luminance function that result from the occlusion of the light sources by intervening objects. The quality of images produced using these methods [3; 17] is the best to date; however, only simple scenes were considered because of very high cost of calculations (Slater [1992] discusses the cost of Shadow Volume and Binary Space Partitioning algorithms, which are usually exploited by *a priori* methods). Discontinuity meshing is calculated for each light source independently, and the importance of generated shadow boundaries is not checked in the context of global illumination. Independent processing of each light source also precludes application of perceptually-based criteria of mesh subdivision. Furthermore, the spatial candle power distribution, nonuniform for real light sources, is ignored. At the intermediate stages of mesh subdivision many t-vertices are usually produced (The DM-tree algorithm is an exception [17].), affecting image quality when an immediate visual feedback is requested by the user during interaction. Applications of *a priori* algorithms in interactive systems that allow local mesh adaptation to frequent changes of illumination have not been reported to date. This group of methods is very promising, but still very far from being ready to use in practical applications involving complicated scenes.

In *a posteriori* methods the mesh is tuned when illumination of the surface at sample points is at least partially known. Published works on *a posteri-*

ori methods differ mainly in the error measure that controls adaptive mesh subdivision, e.g., Cohen *et al.* [1986] compare the difference of luminance between mesh vertices with the threshold value; Vedel and Puech [1991] add the use of gradients at sample points; Lischinski *et al.* [1992] evaluate the luminance at the centroid of an element and compare with the interpolated value. All discussed approaches tend to oversubdivide regions of luminance discontinuities. The uniform mesh subdivision exploited by these methods converges slowly to the luminance function. Also, some subtle shading details are missed. On the other hand, *a posteriori* methods are suitable to interactive applications; the local mesh corrections are easy to perform, and the image can be calculated immediately on the user's demand at any stage of calculations. Perceptually based mesh subdivision criteria, which exploit global (or direct) illumination can be applied.

Non-uniform mesh subdivision. For further consideration in our application we have chosen the *a posteriori* approach, which performs better for huge scenes and is more suitable to the user's interaction required when a scene model is prepared. We propose some extensions of the adaptive subdivision algorithm in order to decrease the number of mesh elements and improve the quality of shading.

Commonly used uniform adaptive subdivision is the best approach when no information about luminance function is available. However, our experiments show that it is worthwhile to acquire additional information (one or three sample points located on the edge) about the luminance function behavior in the regions where some discontinuities are detected during initial sampling. For such regions more sample points are generated; better knowledge of luminance distribution justifies inserting into the mesh sliver-like triangles. The resulting non-uniform mesh converges faster to the luminance function, reducing significantly the number of triangles comparing to traditional subdivision algorithms. The reusability of samples in the next iterations as well as the smaller number of mesh elements compensates for the additional cost of sampling each mesh element. Further gains in the number of mesh elements are obtained by error estimation criteria that prevent splitting when the luminance function is close to linear.

Degradation of triangular shape is justified exclusively in the proximity of shadow borders, or regions that exhibit non-linear changes of the luminance distribution. In all doubtful cases, including the case when a triangle is intersected by multiple shadow borders, subdivision at the middle of an edge is performed. The same approach is used when changes of illumination along the edge are nonmonotonic functions.

In the case of direct illumination, the cost of each sample is usually moderate (depending linearly on the number of primary lights). Distribution of resulting luminance exhibits many abrupt discontinuities, and the application of non-uniform triangle subdivision algorithm leads to fast convergence of the mesh reproduced luminance to the luminance function.

In the case of indirect diffuse light, the cost of each sample is very high (all important secondary light sources should be considered). On the other hand, the distribution of secondary illumination in Lambertian environment is rather smooth (sharp shadow borders produced by indirect light do not occur in practical scenes); application of non-uniform triangle subdivision is not justified in such circumstances, because the algorithm almost always chooses the splitting in the middle of the edge.

Sample points calculated in the middle of edges can be used by higher-order elements [17; 24] interpolating luminance function. This possibility has not been exploited because only linear interpolation is offered by standard graphic workstations.

Perceptually based mesh subdivision. The same absolute values of the luminance differences between sample points may have different impact on final image appearance, depending on scene illumination and observation conditions. Another problem is to map luminances of the real scene into the limited dynamic range of the display. In the case of the Hurva Synagogue both problems are handled by application of the Stevens curve [18] that maps the scene or display luminance (psychophysical space) to the corresponding brightness (psychophysiological space). Two sets of brightnesses B_s and B_d are calculated for a real scene and for a display device, respectively. Miller *et al.* found that B_s and B_d are visually equivalent when the ratio of every pair of elements of B_s is equal to the ratio of the corresponding pair of elements of B_d. The equivalence relation between B_s and B_d is used to determine the final RGB triples. Perceptually derived RGB values are compared against the threshold values controlling the mesh splitting.

Practical experiments show that shading artifacts can be significantly reduced by changing the level of mesh subdivision smoothly (gradually) in the regions of transition from complicated to simple luminance function. This means that some mesh splitting is also needed in saturated parts of the image, especially near a saturation border.

11.5. Texture Mapping

Nowadays texture becomes one of basic graphic primitives, which can be rendered very efficiently by dedicated hardware available on the more advanced workstations [12]. Application of textures enhances realism of visualized surfaces adding many fine details, and in many cases reduces the complexity of the geometric model.

Mesh-based lighting calculation requires many mesh elements to reconstruct subtle details of shading. On the other hand, the excessive number of polygons slows down rendering, impairing the sensation of interactivity when a user-navigated walkthrough in complex environment is performed. When distribution of illumination over a scene is to be quickly rendered, then the Gouraud shaded polygon becomes an inefficient drawing primitive, which can be successfully replaced by texture mapping.

Myszkowski and Kunii [1994] propose an application of texture mapping to reconstruction of surfaces shading in the scene regions where distribution of illumination is extremely complex. Mesh-based Gouraud shading is used to visualize remaining surfaces, exhibiting simple illumination, constituting usually a majority of the scene. As a result, many mesh elements can be eliminated, compared to traditional approaches, and image display can be done significantly faster. Also, improvement of shading quality is possible by recalculating illumination and storing results as textures in scene regions where a mesh-based approach produces shading artifacts. Experiments performed have shown that application of this idea pays off on high-end workstations, when hardware supported texture mapping is available.

One practical restriction is the size of texture buffer available on a workstation. In general, all textures displayed in the same frame should be stored in the texture buffer; otherwise memory swap can impair the speed of image display. In order to save memory a repeated texture pattern may be used. Also the number of bits describing a texture element (texel) should be minimized, which also speeds up image display [26].

Another severe restriction is simplicity of the hardware shading equation, which combines the luminance of the polygon and the color of the texture. Usually simple multiplication of the linearly interpolated polygon's color by the texel's color is performed just before a frame display. In the case of perceptually-based image display [18] the luminance should be filtered by the color of the surface prior to the mapping by the non-linear Stevens function.

The bump mapping technique would be very useful to visualize rough surfaces or even low reliefs; however this feature is not supported for real time image display. The reflection mapping technique can be used to render glossy surfaces. Appropriate images of the environment surrounding the glossy surface should be used as the reflection maps.

In case of the Hurva Synagogue, scanned photographs of concrete, travertine and wood were applied as three component (RGB) textures. Texture normalization was done to preserve correct scale to the real construction materials. Still images of the Hurva Synagogue exploit the bump mapping technique to visualize the roughness of the concrete and travertine surfaces. During the lighting simulation the reflectivity of textured surface is approximated as the average of the texture reflectivity.

11.6. Walkthrough Animation

Hardware graphics accelerators allow fast rendering of a scene using the Gouraud shading algorithm to display a mesh-stored luminance distribution. Smooth animation can be achieved when at least 20 frames per second are generated, which is usually impossible for scenes of even moderate complexity.

The new generation of graphics accelerators is designed as texture mapping machines, which reduces significantly performance penalties for texturing, e.g., SGI's *RealityEngine*^{2}. Gouraud shading and antialiasing are provided with no penalty at all. Observing these trends of graphic hardware development, the most important bottleneck of rendering is expected to be in visibility computation. It means that scan conversion hardware performing visibility calculations on the level of independent polygons should be supported by geometrical algorithms working on a higher level of hierarchical scene description.

The obvious approach is to eliminate quickly all objects outside the viewing frustum specified by the parameters of virtual camera (eye position, viewing direction, viewing and image twist angles [7]). This technique is very effective in architectural applications, where the viewer located inside the building usually can see only small fragment of the whole scene. A spatial subdivision is used to cull entire voxels rather than independent polygons to the viewing frustum [10; 8].

The next step is to remove polygons located inside the viewing frustum, but hidden behind opaque objects. Significant parts of the scene obscured by the walls, ceilings, etc. can be eliminated in architectural models. A practical algorithm exploiting object-space coherence, based on octree scene decomposition, was proposed in [11].

Further improvement of frame display rate can be achieved by the control of the **l**evel **o**f **d**etails (LOD) of the hierarchically stored mesh. A low resolution mesh is used for visualization of distant, small objects (a small number of pixels covered by each object), or when the view is changing rapidly. LOD can be adjusted dynamically in order to assure a fixed frame rate [27; 9]. The best result can be achieved when prediction of the system load is possible. In such a case LOD is changed smoothly, e.g., the level of details gradually decreases as a heavy system load in subsequent frames is anticipated. A technique suitable for a triangular mesh was presented in [23]. The vertex-clustering produces a series of 3D approximations that resemble the original object from all viewpoints, but increasingly reduces the number of faces. Another problem is to avoid sudden transition of the object from current LOD to the next one in the sequence of frames. Smooth transitions can be obtained with the help of a blending technique based on interpolation.

If a model of the scene does not fit in workstation memory, it has to be swapped to/from disk. The viewing frustum can be used to prevent unnecessary loading into memory of the fragments of the scene that are invisible.

The spatial hierarchy should be imposed onto the geometrical database, and culling against the viewing frustum may be performed for the compact navigational structure always stored in the memory. Temporal coherence of subsequent frames may be exploited to predict which portion of the scene is to be visible. On hardware platforms providing parallel processing capabilities, one of the processors can be assigned to pre-loading data needed for subsequent frames, replacing in the memory already invisible parts of the scene.

Only the culling of the objects outside the viewing frustum is performed during the display of the Hurva Synagogue.

11.7. Parallel Processing

Parallelization of the lighting simulation, meshing and image display algorithms is a natural way to increase efficiency of calculations and improve interactivity.

The concept of virtual walls dividing the scene into independent cells is very suitable for parallelized computations of architectural scenes. In the case of a single cell, shared memory techniques seems to be the most appropriate, because random access to all geometrical data may be required during visibility calculations. Immediate update of lighting data for patches assigned to one processor increases efficiency of the Gauss-Seidel iteration [6] calculated by other processors.

Meshing as a standalone operation is not calculation intensive. The main cost of adaptive mesh subdivision is related to lighting simulation, namely calculation of luminance at the sample point location.

The computational power during the architectural walkthrough is shared to control of navigation in the environment, culling the invisible portions the scene, selecting of the appropriate level of detail for visible objects, and controlling image generation by the hardware accelerator. In multi-processor environments all these tasks may be distributed between processors. Task assignment is a function of the scene complexity. For huge databases, culling operation is critical, while for scenes of moderate complexity, issuing drawing commands to the graphics hardware can be a bottleneck.

11.8. Results

The aforementioned perceptually-based mapping was used to express the scene's luminance values as RGB triples imposed by the display device. A special module was developed to adjust parameters required by the Stevens function [18]. The most important ones are the scene's minimum and maximum luminances and the range of luminance provided by the display device. The best visual results can be achieved by tuning Stevens curve parameters manually. Figure 1 demonstrates the user interface developed for this purpose. In the upper left window a reference image is available. The reference Stevens curve is shown in red in the upper right window. The bottom left image corresponds to the new, user-defined parameters for the Stevens curve, which is drawn in green in the upper right window. The parameters of the Stevens function strongly affect the appearance of images displayed during walkthrough animations.

Figures 2, 3, and 4 show the Hurva Synagogue from different viewpoints.

During the walkthrough animation, simulation of sound is also provided. When pre-recorded sound sequences (e.g., music, footsteps) are played, listening conditions are affected by the user's current position and orientation. Reverberation effects are also simulated. For the sake of speed of calculation, obstacles inside the Hurva Synagogue are ignored.

11.9. Conclusion

The virtual synthesis of the Hurva Synagogue has been discussed in this paper as a case study of physics-based rendering and walkthrough animation.

The general objectives of lighting simulation in a complex environment illuminated predominantly by interreflected light were presented. The critical factor is the accuracy of simulation, but the speed of calculations must also be applicable to real-life architectural scenes. Practical algorithms developed to meet these objectives were outlined.

The main requirement imposed on the storage of illumination is the reduction of the mesh complexity, while achieving good quality of visualization. The application of perceptually-based error measures to adaptive mesh splitting eliminates many redundant subdivisions without compromising the shading quality. Also, over-subdivision in regions of luminance discontinuity is significantly reduced by inserting sliver-like triangles into the mesh.

Real time image display is the most critical aspect of walkthrough animation in architectural environments. Brute-force display of the whole scene by graphic hardware accelerator is still too slow even for scenes of the moderate complexity. Spatial coherence of the model and temporal coherence of subsequent frames should be exploited to eliminate in advance non-visible objects. Parallelization of these calculations gives another tactic to eliminate image display latencies.

The speed of the image display seems to be the main problem encountered during the virtual visiting of the Hurva Synagogue. However, at the first instance the main goals of the project were the quality and realism of visualization, even at the expense of speed. Elimination of latencies between consecutive frames is the basic direction of future work on the project.

After completion of the project, the resulting system will be exhibited at the Museum of Modern Art in New York as a tool for virtual revisiting of architectural masterpieces.

Acknowledgements

The model of the Hurva Synagogue was provided by Kent Larson. All images of the Hurva Synagogue presented in this paper were created by Koji Tsuchiya using software developed by INTEGRA, Inc.

The author would like to thank colleagues from The University of Aizu, Oleg Okunev and Michael Cohen, for reviewing the manuscript. Special thanks go to Akira Fujimoto, who has always held an active, supporting role in the author's research. The author would like to thank Professor Tosiyasu L. Kunii for stimulating comments on this work.

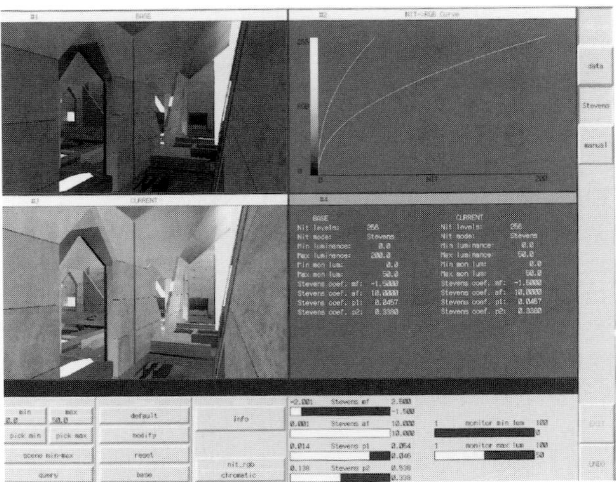

FIGURE 1. User's Interface developed to control perceptually-based mapping of a real scene luminances to RGB triples imposed by a display device.

FIGURE 2. View across Hurva Synagogue. In the foreground external stone pylons are visible.

FIGURE 3. View into inner sanctuary enclosed by four concrete towers.

FIGURE 4. Close-up view on concrete walls tessellating interior of sanctuary.

References

1. Baum D.R., Rushmeier H.E., Winget J.M.: Improving radiosity solutions through the use of analytically determined form-factors. Computer Graphics (SIGGRAPH'89 Proceedings), 1989, 23(3), 325-334.
2. Baum D.R., Mann S., Smith K.P., and Winget J.M.: Making Radiosity Usable: Automatic Preprocessing and Meshing Techniques for the Generation of Accurate Radiosity Solutions. Computer Graphics (SIGGRAPH'91 Proceedings), 1991, 25(4), 51-60.
3. Campbell A., Fussell D.: Adaptive Mesh Generation. Computer Graphics (SIGGRAPH'90 Proceedings), 1990, 24(4), 155-164.
4. Cohen M.F., Greenberg D.P., Immel D.S., Brock P.J.: An efficient radiosity approach for realistic image synthesis. IEEE CG&A, 1986, 6(3), 26-35.
5. Cohen M.F., Chen S.E., Wallace J.R., Greenberg D.P.: A progressive refinement approach to fast radiosity image generation. Computer Graphics (SIGGRAPH'88 Proceedings), 1988, 22(4), 75-84.
6. Cohen M.F., Wallace J.R.: Radiosity and Realistic Image Synthesis. Academic Press Professional, London. 1993.
7. Foley J.D., Van Dam A., Feiner S.K., Hughes J.F.: Computer Graphics, Principles and Practice, 2nd Edition. Addison-Wesley, Massachusetts. 1990.
8. Fujimoto A. Personal communication. 1993.
9. Funkhouser T.A., Sequin C.H.: Adaptive display algorithm for interactive frame rates during visualization of complex virtual environments. Computer Graphics (SIGGRAPH'93 Proceedings), 1993, 27, 247-254.
10. Garlick B., Baum D., Winget J.: Interactive viewing of large geometric databases using multiprocessor graphics workstations. Siggraph'90 Course Notes: Parallel Algorithms and Architectures for 3D Image Generation. 1990.
11. Greene N., Kass M., Miller G.: Hierarchical z-buffer visibility. Computer Graphics (SIGGRAPH'93 Proceedings), 1993, 27, 231-238.
12. Haeberli P., Segal M.: Texture mapping as a fundamental drawing primitive. In Fourth Eurographics Workshop on Rendering, Paris, 1993, 259-266.
13. Hanrahan P., Salzman D., Aupperle L.: A rapid hierarchical radiosity algorithm. Computer Graphics (SIGGRAPH'91 Proceedings), 1991, 25(4), 197-206.
14. Heckbert P.: Discontinuity meshing for radiosity. In Third Eurographics Workshop on Rendering, Bristol, 1992, 203-226.
15. Kok A.: Grouping of patches in progressive radiosity. In Fourth Eurographics Workshop on Rendering, Paris, 1993, 221-232.
16. Larson K.: Kahn's unbuilt Synagogue. Progressive Architecture. No. 9. 1993.
17. Lischinski D., Tampieri F., Greenberg D.P.: Discontinuity meshing for accurate radiosity. IEEE CG&A, 1992, 12(6), 25-39.
18. Miller N.J., Ngai P.Y., Miller D.D.: The application of computer graphics in lighting design. Journal of the Illuminating Engineering Society, 1984, 14(10), 6-26.
19. Myszkowski K.: A realistic image synthesis by bi-directional ray tracing method. PH.D. thesis, Dept. of Computer Science, Technical University of Warsaw (in Polish). 1991.
20. Myszkowski K., Wicynski K., Khodulev A.: Simulation of ideal specular light path by ray tracing. Machine Graphics and Vision journal issued by Polish Academy of Sciences, 1994, 3(1), 123-137.
21. Myszkowski K., Kunii T.L.: Texture mapping as an alternative for meshing during walkthrough animation. In Fifth Eurographics Workshop on Rendering, Darmstadt, 1994, 375-388.

22. Neumann L., Neumann A.: Photosimulation: interreflection with arbitrary reflectance models and illumination. Computer Graphics Forum, 1989, 8(1), 21-34.
23. Rossignac J., Borrel P.: Multi-resolution 3D approximations for rendering complex scenes. In Second Conference on Geometric Modeling in Computer Graphics, Genova, 1993, 453-465.
24. Salesin D., Lischinski D., DeRose T.: Reconstructing illumination functions with selected discontinuities. In Third Eurographics Workshop on Rendering, Bristol, 1992, 99-112.
25. Schroeder P.: Numerical integration for radiosity in the presence of singularities. In Fourth Eurographics Workshop on Rendering, Paris, 1993, 177-184.
26. Graphical Library Programming Guide. Document Number 007-1702-010, Silicon Graphics, Inc. 1992.
27. IRIS Performer Programming Guide. Document Number 007-1680-010, Silicon Graphics, Inc. 1992.
28. Sillion F., Arvo J.R., Westin S.H., Greenberg D.P.: A global illumination solution for general reflectance distributions. Computer Graphics (SIGGRAPH'91 Proceedings), 1991, 25(4), 187-196.
29. Slater M.: A comparison of tree shadow volume algorithms. The Visual Computer, 1992, 9(1), 25-38.
30. Vedel C., Puech C.: A testbed for adaptive subdivision in progressive radiosity. In Second Eurographics Workshop on Rendering, Barcelona. 1991.

12. Performance Facial Animation Cloning

Philippe Limantour
Medialab, 104 Av. du Pdt. kennedy, 75016 Paris and iMAGIS / IMAG*
- INRIA, BP 53, F-38041 Grenoble cedex 09, France

Summary.

This paper describes a method for cloning someone's face for performance facial animation by interpolation among various canonical expressions.

The proposed procedure allows the automatic real-time animation of both facial expressions and lipsynch of a textured 3D synthetic face. Moreover, as a video chromakey analysis is computed, the lipsynch is accurate and language independent.

Finally, the differential interpolation methodused is geometry independent as long as all the canonical faceshave the same topology. This allows the animation parameters to be directly applied to faces built the same way. We apply this property on testing the animation with a model that suits real-time constraints and afterwards using the same parameters on a more complex version for better rendering results.

12.1. Introduction

The face changes expression constantly, following the flow of the speech. The computer graphics animation of an accurate lipsynch is a complex process. This paper describes our experience investigating real-time video analysis tools for the automation of the lipsynch of areal-time computer graphics animated face. After a brief review ofthe previously done work in facial animation, we introduce our facial animation model. The following sections describe the videoextracted parameters and their use in the facial animation system. We then look closer at the lip animation specifications for solving the lipsynch problem. Examples of real-time facial animations performed using the described techniques are then presented.

---

* IMAG is a Research institute affiliated with CNRS,Institut National Polytechnique de Grenoble, and Université Joseph Fourier.

12.2. Background

Facial animation as part of Computer Graphics Animation is a three step process: modelling, animating, and rendering of a computer data representation of a face.

The face is a highly curved structure and is thus difficult to model. Polygonal representations are often created through interactive modellers, manual measurement on clay sculptures using 3D magnetic digitizers, such as the Polhemus, or through photogrammetry of stereo facial images.

Up to now, five techniques have been involved in animating faces: *key framing, parametrization, multi-target interpolation, video tracking warping,* and *physically-based modeling* [5]. Key framing [25; 26] is a technique derived from traditional animation [14]. It consists in completely specifying keys that can be interpolated, and is a long and data intensive process when to be applied on all the coordinates of the geometry. Parametrized facial models [22] allow the specification of a smaller set of variables, called parameters. The parameterscontrol all movement and change within the facial model. Keyframing is therefore applied to this small set of values, rather than directly to the three-dimensional geometrical information [6]. When a very realistic simulation of facial movements is needed, such as in surgical studies [23], parametrized models lack in precision control. Lance Williams introduced video tracking warping offacial faces [33]. Geoff Levner, and later on the whole research and development team, developed at Medialab amulti-target based real-time animation system called PORC *. The recent physically-based facial modellingapproach provides a more precise simulation of facial tissue and muscle mechanics [24; 29; 31]. Waters and Terzopoulos presented a method [32; 30] to model and animate such models, using adaptive deformable meshes applied to their two-layer physical model. Recently, Takaaki Akimoto, Yasuhito Suenaga and Richard S. Wallace developed an automatic system for creating a 3D facial model of a specific person using feature extraction from two images of the face [1].

12.3. Approach and Motivation

Our goal is to build a performance-driven graphics animation thatfollows the expressions of a real face traked in real-time. The real-time animation process is applied to a simplified synthetic head. We also need to be able to replay that animation to a more complex and texture-mapped version of the head to output a realistic post-rendered sequence. Using minimal geometric data allows real-time response and provides the user with a good feedback of the animation process. The dynamics involved [8] to modify a physical-model geometry are time consuming. Moreover, trying to apply the dynamics to

* Puppets Orchestrated in Real-time by Computer

another, say more detailed data set, is a difficult process; the result of the numerically solved dynamic system not always being the same when changing the level of detail and number of nodes. A differential parametric interpolation method has been chosen because it is an easy process to achieve in a real-time performance driven system, as further shown with outputs of the PORC program. The interpolation process is also very easy to apply with a different level of detail. All that is required is to keep the different percentages of expressions to be mixed. We already have used this animation system for the production of 3D series and virtual reality applications for the past three years [15; 16; 18; 27; 28]. Two years ago, we developed a lipsynched face of a robot called "Fabrika" with a method issued from cartoon animation techniques. The lipsynch data was acquired by listening to a prerecorded audio tape and infering mouth positions at specific frames – see the figure 1.

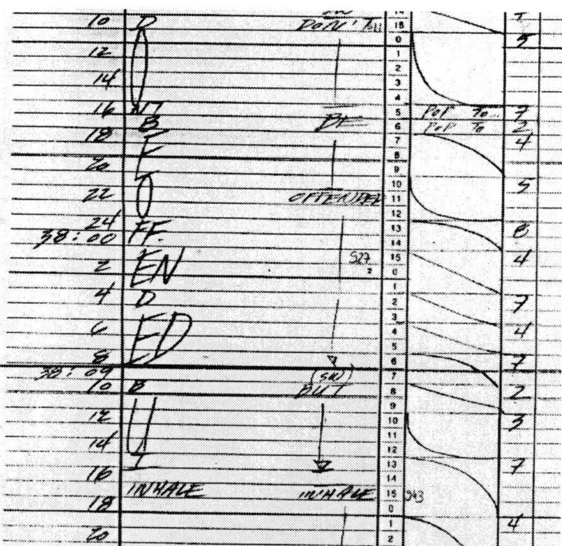

FIGURE 1. *Manual detection of phonems*

That method showed great precision but is time consuming. This paper addresses the problem of providing a method for performing real-time expression matching between a real face and a 3D computer graphics face. The work has been conducted with ICP† who developed a real-time chromakey video analysis of facial movements and provided us with accurate data for driving our model.

† Institut de la Communication Parlée, Grenoble

12.4. A Parametric Differential Interpolation Facial Animation

A neutral face object is deformed, according to the value of parameters, by interpolating between a set of canonical faces. Each canonical head represents an extreme facial expression, itself corresponding to the action of major facial muscles [9; 12]. The geometric interpolation used consists of point to point interpolation between different objects according to the value of a real parameter $\alpha \in \mathrm{Re}$.

The canonical objects are facial expressions meshes $\varepsilon_1^{\mathcal{F}}, \ldots, \varepsilon_n^{\mathcal{F}}$ with$n \in N$, of an animated face $\mathcal{F}$. The expression $\varepsilon_0^{\mathcal{F}}$ represents the neutral face $\mathcal{F}$. We are going to perform calculations on the 3D meshes defined by those cannonical data faces. The coordinates of a point P of a mesh ε_i will be referenced as $\varepsilon_{i_{px}}, \varepsilon_{i_{py}}, \varepsilon_{i_{pz}}$. $\varepsilon^{\mathcal{F}}$ will be the mesh of any given facial expression, and resulting of the interpolation process among the $\varepsilon_i^{\mathcal{F}}$ that deforms a neutral face $\mathcal{F}$.

Interpolation between two facial expressions. The usual keyframe interpolation method describes an animation as a sequence of interpolation computations between successive keys. Each key geometry must be modelled so that it takes into account the result of all the muscle actions at a specific frame of the animation. The work involved is then key-specific, and is performed many times in each minute of the final animation.

This calculus uses an interpolation variable $\alpha \in \mathrm{Re}$ an doutputs a deformed mesh $\varepsilon^{\mathcal{F}}$ of the face $\mathcal{F}$ that will be interpolated between two facial expressions $\varepsilon_i^{\mathcal{F}}$ and $\varepsilon_j^{\mathcal{F}}$.

$$\begin{cases} \varepsilon^{\mathcal{F}} = \varepsilon_i^{\mathcal{F}} & \text{if } \alpha = 0.0 \\ \varepsilon^{\mathcal{F}} = \varepsilon_j^{\mathcal{F}} & \text{if } \alpha = 1.0 \\ \varepsilon^{\mathcal{F}} = f_\alpha(\varepsilon_i^{\mathcal{F}}, \varepsilon_j^{\mathcal{F}}) & \text{if } \alpha \in]0.0, 1.0[\end{cases}$$

The linear interpolation algorithm giving the coordinates of the $\varepsilon^{\mathcal{F}}$ deformed face regarding points of the meshes of two expressions $\varepsilon_i^{\mathcal{F}}$ and $\varepsilon_j^{\mathcal{F}}$ is:

For each point P that samples the face geometry

$$\varepsilon_{px} = (1-\alpha) \times \varepsilon_{i_{px}} + \alpha \times \varepsilon_{j_{px}}$$
$$\varepsilon_{py} = (1-\alpha) \times \varepsilon_{i_{py}} + \alpha \times \varepsilon_{j_{py}}$$
$$\varepsilon_{pz} = (1-\alpha) \times \varepsilon_{i_{pz}} + \alpha \times \varepsilon_{j_{pz}}$$

Parametrisation. Starting from the previous example, we obtain a straightforward parametric model: *the interpolation variable α between two facial expressions parameterises a single deformation.* In our example, the *"jaw opening"* parametrisation has been derived by interpolating between the neutral face point mesh with a closed jaw and the point mesh of the face with a full opened jaw.

Parametrisation choice is of great importance in getting a convincing facial animation.

Multiple Differential Interpolation. The whole animation of a face is complex and is the result of blending several deformations [7]. The first part of the work must output a list of critical parameters and geometrical models. Starting from a neutral face $\varepsilon_0^{\mathcal{F}}$, the $\varepsilon_i^{\mathcal{F}}$, for $i \in 1, \ldots, n$ will stand for the set of n facial expressions using α_i parameters, thus defining the $\mathcal{F}$ face. We need to generalize the model to a calculus system that helps blending the n parameters influence. Using a differential interpolation method consists in blending any number of key facial expressions. Each expression is no longer a complex step of the animation process, but is to be seen as the unit vector basis $\varepsilon_1^{\mathcal{F}}, \ldots, \varepsilon_n^{\mathcal{F}}$ of the n allowable facial deformations. The deformed facial expression is then a linear combination of that vector expression basis; the combination variables are exactly theα_i parameters of the facial animation. Each $\alpha_i \in \mathrm{Re}$ may be seen as a parameter ranging from 0.0 to 1.0.

$$\begin{cases} \alpha_i = 0.0 & \text{The parameter is of no influence on the neutral face} \\ \alpha_i = 1.0 & \text{The parameter is of maximum influence and the face} \\ & \text{outputs the } \varepsilon_i^{\mathcal{F}} \text{ facial expression associated} \end{cases}$$

The equation giving the resulting influence of a set of n parameters$\alpha_1, \ldots, \alpha_i$ if then

12.4.1.
$$\varepsilon^{\mathcal{F}} = (1.0 - \sum_{i=1}^{n} \alpha_i) \times \varepsilon_0^{\mathcal{F}} + \sum_{i=1}^{n} \alpha_i \times \varepsilon_i^{\mathcal{F}}$$

Although this equation allows any combination of the α_i, care must be paid on the choice of the values in order to get a convincing and realistic animation, as further discussed.

12.5. Human Face Cloning by Chromakey Analysis

A virtual actor cannot achieve an "anthropomorphic quality" if his lips movements and his face expressions are not synchronized with the sounds [4].

When thinking of the natural complexity of the face, one must try to find an automatic way of achieving lipsynched facial animation. We have developed a recognition system ‡that recognizes phonemes within a recorded audio tape based on work by John Lewis [13; 17]. However, the automatic derivation of mouth movement from a speech soundtrack was not as accurate as the manual extraction described in paragraph 12.3, although is much faster to calculate, and is language and locutor dependent.

‡ work conducted by D.J. Sturman

ICP video analysis system. Christian Benoit and al. [2; 3; 4] at ICP developed a system that outputs facial parameters of a real speaker from two video images - a front anda side view. The system is able to run in real-time on an SGI IndigoWorkstation and extracts measures from chromakey contour detection. The parameters that may be extracted are shown in figure 2.

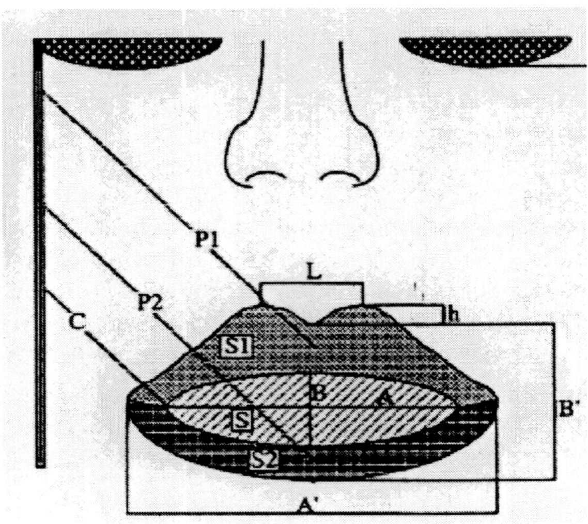

FIGURE 2. *Parameters extracted by ICP video analysis*

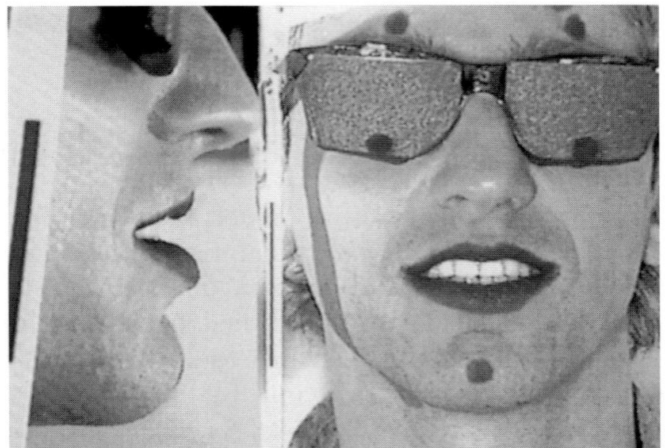

FIGURE 3. *Video views used for parameter extraction*

The figure 3 shows the two video views used for the analysis. The lips and some areas are blue painted on the skin to be later modified by a chromakey method. The blue color has been chosen because there are quite no blue component in the skin texture. ICP's system is language independent and may also be used to drive facial expressions other than lip synchronization.

Parameter use in Medialab's facial animation system. The ICP system is able to output parameters from a chromakey analysis. These parameters can be classified by the type of measurement made:

$$\begin{cases} \text{distance values } (mm) & \text{the L, H, A, B, A' and B' parameters} \\ \text{relative positions } (mm) & \text{the M, C, P1 and P2 parameters} \\ \text{surfaces } (mm^2) & \text{the S, S1, and S2 parameters} \end{cases}$$

Most of these parameters are correlated as one may foresee when thinking of the muscles action on the skin and flesh. Paul Ekman and Wallace V. Friesenhave developped the Facial Action Coding System [9; 10; 11]. FACS teaches how to recognize the Action Units – AUs – which are responsible for momentary changes in facial appearance.

The most important parameter for trying to clone a talking face is the M parameter that measures the jaw opening. The use of that variable is the simplest way of showing sound synchronisation by opening and closing the mouth of the clone. The measure of the M parameter, however, is not a direct measure of the jaw movements. The skin and flesh slide on the underlying bone under the control of the Chin Raiser – AU 17 of FACS.

The next step in building a more complex parameterisation consists in using the B, A', and C parameters. The B parameter will control the lips covering of the teeth – AU 10, Lip Raiser, and AUs 16+25, Lower Lip Depressors. The A' and C parameters will control the wideness of the mouth. You may see that A' increases when you push your lips forward – this is strongly correlated with a C augmentation. Those parameters describe what FACS calls the AUs 25, 26, 27 and AU 20, Lip Stretcher. When M, B, A', and C are used to control the deformations of the synthetic clone, the main expressions of the lower face are covered by the multi-target interpolation. However, the lips of the real speaker tend to stick together around the lips corners when he opens the mouth. This aspect is measured by the A parameter, or perhaps more by a function of the contact distance of the lips at each corner of the mouth $\eta = (\frac{(A'-A)}{2})$. In the next sections, we will use the ICP parameters within the multiple differential interpolation system we defined. We will use the α_M, $\alpha_{A'}$, α_B, $\alpha_C$which are the normalized versions of the M, A', B, and Cparameters. Normalization is computed from minimum and maximum values of the parameters, measured during a calibration period on the locutor.

Lip Sticking Constraint. Having the lips behing sticked is very difficult to obtain with a multi-target interpolation system because sticking may be involved in any combination of the other parameter values. Involving that effect will transform a open/close movement to a lip synchronisation expression by introducing subtle and natural deformations. We have developped a new deformation function that solves the problem of lip sticking at the corners of the mouth. In an usual multi-target interpolation system,the same parameter equally affects all the points of the object, as described in section 12.4. Our method computes a deformation that applies a different parameter value for each point. That parameter, hereafter called α_β, is automatically computed from a measure of the lips contact zone ηdefined in the section 12.5. We need to find a deformation that closes the mouth from each corner of the mouth toward the center by an η amount.

A good approximation function of $f(\beta)$ we have chosen is a gaussian function with maximum value of 1.0 and width A.

$$\begin{cases} \alpha_\beta = f(\beta) = 0.0 & \text{if } \beta \in [0.0, \eta] \cup [A' - \eta, A'] \\ \alpha_\beta = f(\beta) = \text{Gaussian}(\beta) & \text{if } \beta \in]\eta, A' - \eta[\end{cases}$$

α_β is 0.0 when the lips should be sticked, and goes smoothly to the opened value of 1.0 elsewhere. We will modify the mouth object according to the value of α_β.

The next step consists in taking into account both the α_β parameter and the expression parameters within the multi-target interpolation process. The deformation function has two more arguments: $\varepsilon_\partial^{calF}$ and ε_β meshes. ε_β is a copy [§] of ε_∂ that will further be filled with the deformation parameters α_β.

In the case of lip sticking, $\varepsilon_\partial^{\mathcal{F}}$ is the facial expression that results from the influence of all the parameters used to control the lipsynch.

$$\begin{aligned} \varepsilon_\partial^{\mathcal{F}} &= ((1.0 - \alpha_M + \alpha_B + \alpha_C + \alpha'_A) \times \varepsilon_0^{\mathcal{F}}) + \\ &\quad (\alpha_M \times \varepsilon_M^{\mathcal{F}}) + (\alpha_B \times \varepsilon_B^{\mathcal{F}}) + (\alpha_C \times \varepsilon_C^{\mathcal{F}}) + (\alpha_{A'} \times \varepsilon_{A'}^{\mathcal{F}}) \quad \textbf{12.5.1.} \end{aligned}$$

If no lip sticking would be implemented, $\varepsilon_\partial^{\mathcal{F}}$ would represent the facial expression to be rendered. The $\alpha_{A'}$ and α_C parameters act on mouth shape while the α_M and $\alpha_B$parameters deal with jaw and lips opening. When trying to automatically closing the lips we thus need to take those different actions into account. We define the $\varepsilon_\nabla^{\mathcal{F}}$ expression as the facial expression that results from the influence of the $\alpha_{A'}$ and α_C parameters. That expression will provide animation continuity by keeping track of the deformations that does not affect the closing of the mouth when we will force the lips to be sticked.

$$\varepsilon_\nabla^{\mathcal{F}} = ((1.0 - \alpha_C + \alpha_{A'}) \times \varepsilon_0^{\mathcal{F}}) + (\alpha_C \times \varepsilon_C^{\mathcal{F}}) + (\alpha_{A'} \times \varepsilon_{A'}^{\mathcal{F}}) \quad \textbf{12.5.2.}$$

[§] Same number of points, same topological connections between points to define the model facets, and same geometry

We are now able to compute the deformation we will write in the ε_β mesh. We have chosen to build the face so that the mouth goes along the x axis:

$$\varepsilon_\beta \equiv f(\varepsilon x_\partial)$$

We compute the deformation expression $\varepsilon^{\mathcal{F}}_\beta$ for each point $(\varepsilon x_\beta, \varepsilon y_\beta, \varepsilon z_\beta)$ of ε_β as

$$\begin{aligned} \varepsilon x_\beta &= f(\varepsilon x_\partial) \\ \varepsilon y_\beta &= f(\varepsilon x_\partial) \\ \varepsilon z_\beta &= f(\varepsilon x_\partial) \end{aligned}$$

We also need to define the $\varepsilon_{1-\beta}$ deformation as $\varepsilon_{1-\beta} \equiv 1.0 - f(\varepsilon x_\partial)$. The deformation that sticks the lips may then be applied as

$$\varepsilon^{\mathcal{F}} = (\varepsilon^{\mathcal{F}}_\partial \times \varepsilon^{\mathcal{F}}_\beta) + (\varepsilon^{\mathcal{F}}_\nabla \times \varepsilon^{\mathcal{F}}_{1-\beta}) \qquad \textbf{12.5.3.}$$

If the α_β parameter equals 0.0, the corresponding point of the $\varepsilon^{\mathcal{F}}$ facial expression results of the unique action of the $\alpha_{A'}$ and α_C parameters. W e then obtain a lips and mouth closed version of the face. If the α_β parameter equals 1.0, the corresponding point of the $\varepsilon^{\mathcal{F}}$ facial expression results of the action of all the parameters. Any value of α_β ranging from 0.0 to 1.0 interpolates the lip sticking to give a natural shape to the mouth.

12.6. Modelling the Neutral Face

The first step of the process consists in modelling a neutral face. The neutral expression is the result of a closed jaw and mouth with no specific muscle action, eyelids open. The way one builds the neutral face is of no real consequence in the described method. The important aspect of the neutral objectis that it drives the topology used for modelling the canonicalexpressions.

12.7. Cannonical Models

Each of the different face expressions must have the same topology. An easy way to achieve this constraint is to apply deformations on copies of the neutral face for modelling each expression. The different objects obtained can then be interpolated to find a specific facial expression, and texture-mapping may be applied. The textures are mapped using usual modelling tools. As the textures are attached to the facial geometry, their deformations will follow the computed facial animation. Figure 5 shows parameters mapping on canonical

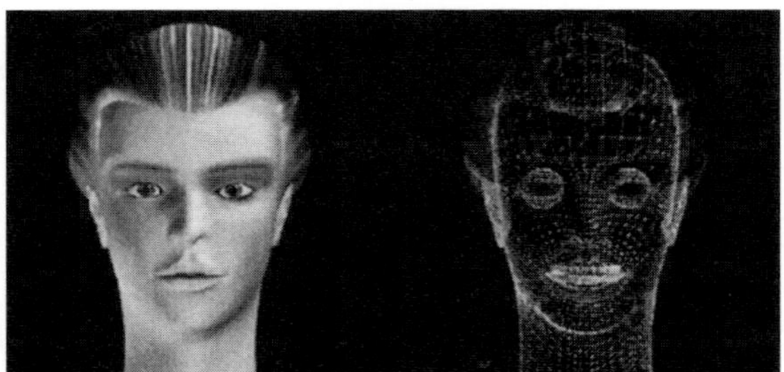

FIGURE 4. *Neutral texture-mapped and wireframe models*

geometries. The upper face is the neutral face. The lower face is the expression due to the full action of the α_M parameter. When $\alpha_M = 1.0$, the jaw is fully opened. The next face is computed for the value of $\alpha_B = 0.35$. The α_B parameter acts on vertical stretching of the lips. Finally, the lowest facial expression is mapped to the position of the corner of the mouth, $\alpha_C = 0.28$.

The image in figure 6 shows an example of a face obtained using intermediate parameters values. This face was computed with the parameters $\alpha_M = 0.3$, $\alpha_B = 0.35$, $\alpha_C = 0.28$. The face consists in 7390 polygons and uses five 256×256 textures – lips, eyes, eyelids and hair — and one 512×512 texture – the skin. The PORC software we developed computes that animation at about 27 frames/sec on an SGI Onyx 4 CPU Workstation.

The figure 7 shows an example of the animation of the α_M, α_B, and α_C parameters automatically extracted from a video analysis. One may understand how complex could the guess of such curves be for a human animator.

12.8. Conclusion

This paper has presented a new approach to facial animation by real-time mapping of parameters in interpolating canonnical expressions among a unit vectors basis. Moreover, the method can be applied to any kind of model,at any level of detail, allowing both a performance driven recording of the animation, and a more realistic post-rendering on a more complex model.

A second contribution of the paper is the ability of generalizing the interpolation animation to other close face shapes. This allows a bank of animations to be created easily by cloning and further applying records to different sequences. This is the point one needs when thinking of a use of facial animation in "syntheticsecretary" information assistance where a powerful and easy to use production tool will be needed.

A third aspect of that work is the ability of mixing prerecorded animations of a lipsynch while performance playing on facial expressions is added to the face. This technique allows adding sadness or happiness for example on a very accurate animation of the mouth movements.

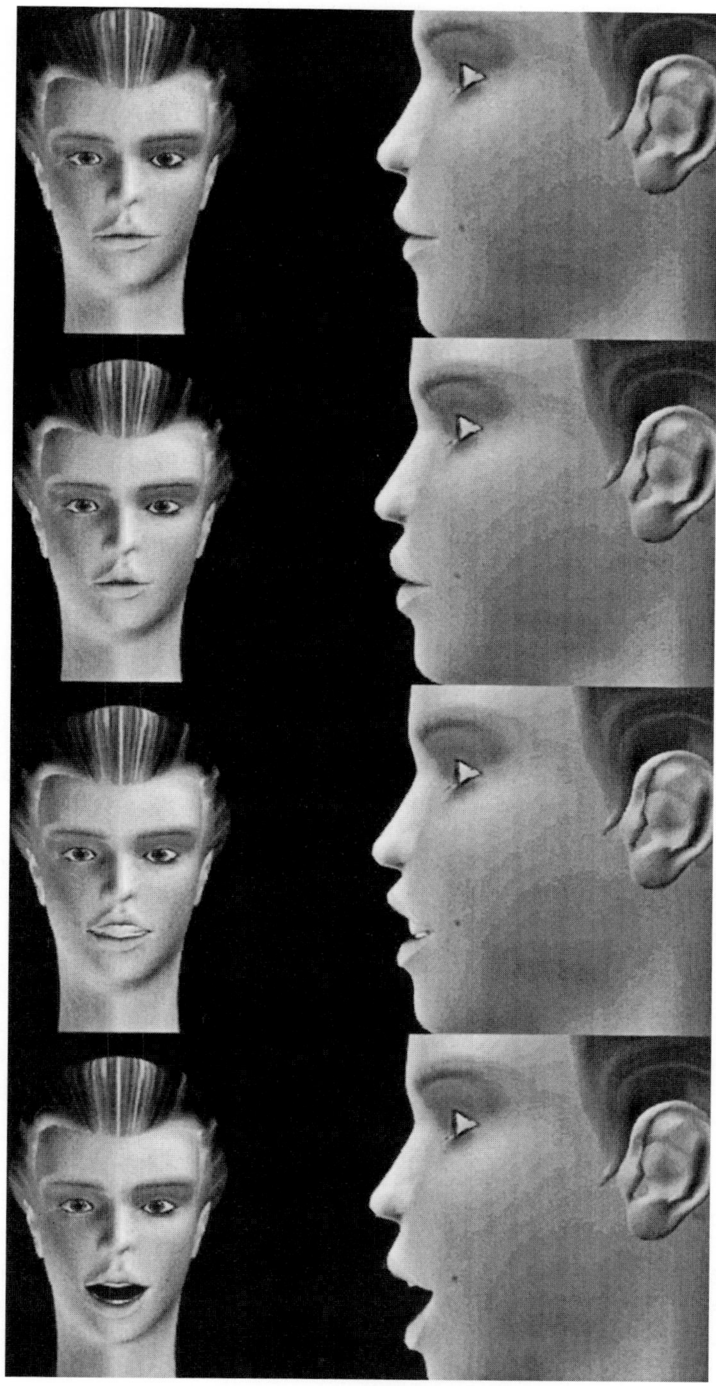

FIGURE 5. *Neutral and three canonical facial expressions*

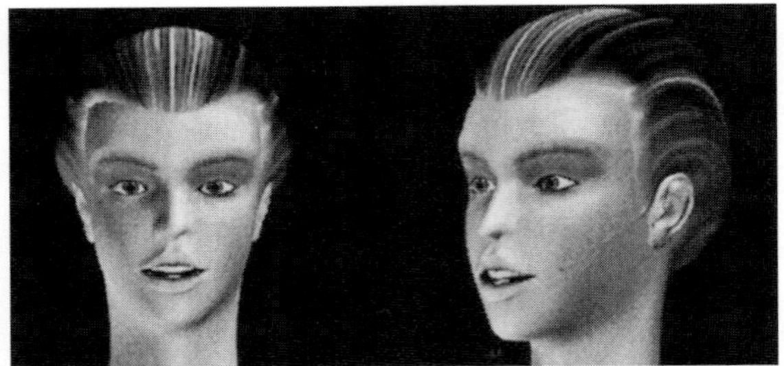

FIGURE 6. *Face computed with* $\alpha_M = 0.3$ $\alpha_B = 0.35$ $\alpha_C = 0.28$

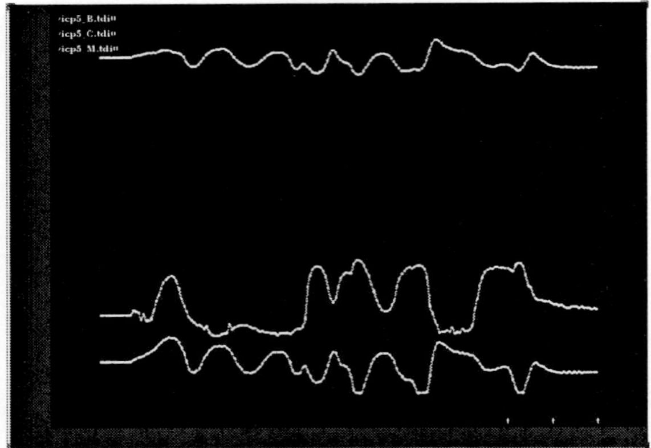

FIGURE 7. *The M, B, and C parameters extracted from a video sequence*

Future work would try to use a video analysis with light cameras directly attached to a person's head, thus also allowing the recording of head movements which are of primary importance in face expression. We intend to use that system in making a synthetic face that would be able of answering questions on a video phone server. A vocal recognition system will then drive the animation in selecting prerecorded sequences, while being able to adapt itself in the future to the facial expressions of the caller. Furthermore, that system couldbe used by someone to talk to someone else while not showing his real face, but using a different synthetic look depending on his mood.

Acknowledgements

I wish to thank François Garnier, Fabienne Rouaud and Jim Radford for having working with me on this project on conceiving the facial expressions data bases and finalising the real-time rendering. The work presented has been done on basis of all the Medialab research and development team efforts for the past four years. The PORC program on whichthe facial animation is running was originally written by Geoff Levner. Thank to the whole ICP team I have been working with, especially Ali Adjoudani, Christian Benoit, Thierry Guiard, and Tahar Lallouache.

References

1. T. Akimoto, Y. Suenaga, and R. Wallace. Automatic creation of 3d facial models. *IEEE Computer Graphics and Applications*, 13(5):16–22, septembre 1993.
2. Benoit C. The intrinsic bimodality of speech communication and the synthesis of talking faces. *Journal on Communications*, 43:32–40, July-Sept 1992.
3. Benoit C., Adjoudani A., Angola O., Guiard-Marigny T., and B. Le Goff. Perception, analyse et synthese de levres parlantes. In *Proceedings of Imagina'93*, fevrier 1994.
4. Benoit C., Mohamadi T., and Kandel S. The effects ofphonetic context on audio-visual intelligibility in french. *Journal of Speech & Hearing Research*, (to appear).
5. B. deGraf, M. Elson, F. Parke, B. Reevesand K. Waters, L. Williams, and B. Wivill. State of the art in facial animation. In *ACM SIGGRAPH'90 Course Notes*, volume 26, aout 1990.
6. S. DiPaola. Implementation and use of a 3d parameterized facial modeling and animation system. In *ACM SIGGRAPH'89 Course Notes*, volume 22, pages 20–33, 1989.
7. G.B. Duchenne. *Mécanismes de la physionomie humaine.* Baillère, 1876.
8. G. Dumont, M.P. Gascuel, and A. Verroust. Animation controlée par la dynamique – état de l'art –. Technical report, Rapport de Recherche INRIA 1405, avril 1991.
9. P. Ekman and W.E. Friesen. *Facial Action Coding System.* Consulting Psychologist Press, 1977.
10. P. Ekman and W.E. Friesen. *Investigators Guide for the Facial Action Coding System.* Consulting Psychologist Press, 1978.
11. P. Ekman and H. Oster. Facial expressions of emotion. *Annual Review of Psychology*, 1979.
12. H. Gray. *Anatomy, Descriptive and Surgical.* Bounty Books. Crown Publishers Inc., NY, 1977.
13. F. Parke J. Lewis. Automated lipsynch and speech synthesis for character animation. In *Proc. CHI'87 and Graphics Interface'87, Toronto*, pages 143–147, 1987.
14. J. Lasseter and S. Rafael. Principles of traditional animation applied to 3d computer animation. In *Proceedings of SIGGRAPH*, volume 21 (4), pages 35–44, juillet 1987.
15. G. Levner. Computer art: a technique for animation. In *Annecy 93, festival international du film d'animation*, june 1993.
16. G. Levner. Is vr technology really useful ? In *Proceedings of Imagina'93*, pages 173–178, juin 1993.
17. J. Lewis. Automated lip-sinc: Background and techniques. *The Journal of Visualization and Computer Animation*, 2(4), octobre-décembre. 1991.
18. Ph. Limantour. Virtual reality simulation. In *Proceedings of Imagina'93*, pages 123–133, février 1993.

19. Ph. Limantour. Real Time Facial Cloning. In *Proceedings of Imagina'94*, février 1994.
20. Ph. Limantour. Performance Facial Animation. *Fifth Eurographics'94 Workshop on Animation and Simulation*, Oslo Norway, Sep. 1994.
21. F. I. Parke. Parameterized models for facial animation. *IEEE Computer Graphics and Applications*, 2(9):61–68, novembre 1982.
22. F. I. Parke, K. Waters. *Computer Facial Animation.* A.K. Peters, Wellesley, Massachusetts, 1996.
23. S. Pieper, J. Rosen, and D. Zelter. Interactive graphics for plastic surgery: A task-level analysis and implementation. In *1992 Symposium on Interactive 3D Graphics*, pages 127–134. Special issue of Computer Graphics, ACM SIGGRAPH, 1992.
24. S.M. Platt and N.I. Badler. Animating facial expressions. *Computer Graphics*, 15(3):245–252, 1981.
25. W.T. Reeves. Inbetweening for computer animation utilizing moving point constraints. *Computer Graphics*, 15(3):263–269, aout 1981.
26. G. Stern. *GAS-A System for Computed-Aided Keyframe Animation.* PhD thesis, University of Utah, 1978.
27. H. Tardif. Character animation in real time. In *panel Proceedings of Siggraph'91*, 1991.
28. H. Tardif. Televirtuality link between paris and monaco by numeris. In *Proceedings of Imagina'93*, fevrier 1993.
29. D. Terzopoulos and K. Waters. Analysis of facial images using physical and anatomical models. In *IEEE Proceedings of ICCV Conference*, pages 727–732, 1990.
30. D. Terzopoulos and K. Waters. *Techniques for realistic facial modelling and animation*, pages 45–58. Springer-Verlag, 1991.
31. K. Waters. A dynamic of facial tissue. In *ACM SIGGRAPH'89 Course Notes*, volume 22, pages 145–152, 1989.
32. K. Waters and D. Terzopoulos. Modeling and animating faces using scanned data. *The Journal of Visualization and Computer Animation*, 2(4):123–128, octobre-décembre. 1991.
33. L. Williams. Performance-driven facial animation. In *Proceedings of SIGGRAPH*, volume 19 (4), pages 235–242, aout 1990.

Theme 3

Synthetic Factories

13. Towards the Synthetic Factories: Requirements and Components

Tsukasa Noma
Department of Artificial Intelligence, Faculty of Computer Science and Systems Engineering, Kyushu Institute of Technology, 680–4 Kawazu, Iizuka, Fukuoka 820, Japan (e-mail:noma@ai.kyutech.ac.jp)

Summary.
Making "factories" in virtual environments is a new research topic, but there has been a great latent demand for it. This paper analyzes the requirements for "synthetic factories," in particular, emphasizing the differences from typical applications of virtual reality. Then we introduce three components for synthetic factories: (1) an engineering animation system for assembly, (2) decompositive assembly simulation and its theoretical superiority, and (3) a system for visualizing processes in factories. Finally, we discuss the future research directions concerning synthetic factories.
Key words and phrases: synthetic factory, virtual reality, assembly, assemblability, visualization

13.1. Introduction

Recently research on virtual/synthetic worlds has been extensively conducted. In particular, many virtual reality (VR) systems for entertainment and industrial design have attracted a great deal of public attention. Compared with such typical VR applications, however, little attention has been paid to making "factories" in virtual environments though there has been a great latent demand and related work for it.

This paper discusses *synthetic factories*: making factories in virtual environments and utilizing them in many phases of production. In the next section, we analyze the requirements for synthetic factories. In particular, we emphasize the differences from typical VR applications. In the following three sections, three components for synthetic factories are introduced: An engineering animation system called ANIMENGINE is presented in Section 13.3, and Section 13.4 discusses decompositive assembly simulation and its theoretical superiority. In Section 13.5, we overview a system for visualizing processes in factories. Finally, we discuss the future research directions concerning synthetic factories in Section 13.6.

13.2. Requirements for Synthetic Factories

Graphics researchers made a great success of displaying objects realistically with their colors and other attributes. We can thus *preview* objects before making them. It seems that recent VR research enables us to *pre-experience* environments before they are realized. The primary purpose of synthetic factories should be to *pre-examine* the activities in factories and then to find problems before the operations are conducted in the real world.

Some may think that research on synthetic factories can be pursued on a similar line as the existing VR researches since there is an important property common between the two: *virtual environments.* Synthetic factories are, however, completely different from the current VR applications in two points: levels of view and evaluation methods.

Levels of view. One of the major differences between the existing VR applications and synthetic factories lies in *levels of view.*[1] In the current VR systems, at least in their spirit, users interact with virtual environments so that they can feel as if they exist in the environments. Users' view is thus limited to a single level. Although some VR systems have greatly changed the scales of view[11], their view is still a local one.

On the other hand, in synthetic factories, users cannot understand the activities in the factories only with a single local view. It is sure that local views are important for inspecting detailed aspects of production. More important in synthetic factories are, however, global views which enables us to grasp the whole activities in the factories.[2]

Evaluation methods. The other important difference between typical VR applications and synthetic factories are the evaluation methods used in the systems. In the existing VR systems, the primary evaluation methods are users themselves. For example, in case of evaluating some products with VR systems, users' intuition determines the evaluation. In addition to that, users evaluate VR systems themselves in case of entertainment-oriented VR systems including game machines. On the other hand, in synthetic factories, users cannot evaluate everything by themselves. Thus the systems should help users to make evaluation in many phases of production with sophisticated tools.

Requirements for synthetic factories. Based on the above discussions, systems for synthetic factories should satisfy the following requirements:

---

[1] In this paper, we use the term "view" in a wider (and more abstract) sense than the view specification in conventional computer graphics. It means an aspect from which the situations are observed.

[2] Ware and Osborne discussed three metaphors for specifying viewpoint in virtual environments: Eyeball in hand, Scene in hand, and Flying vehicle control[12]. The comparison between their discussions and ours would interest the readers.

1. The system should have multiple levels (aspects) of views, and the views should be integrated so that, for example, users can find problems from the combination of global views and local views.
2. The system should be furnished with sophisticated tools for helping users to make evaluations/decisions concerning the activities in factories.

13.3. ANIMENGINE: An Engineering Animation System

In 1985, we presented an engineering animation system called ANIMENGINE[8]. The purpose of this system is to help designers find and solve the problems encountered in the design process through animations of assembly simulation.

The system was designed based on the following requirements:

1. *Exact and unambiguous display of objects*:
   Objects in engineering animation are parts, modules, and units of production and assembly machines such as robots. It must be possible to distinguish the different objects in a picture unambiguously. So the style of display must make this possible. This is more important than making the pictures realistic. Also, the parts must look solid. Line drawings do not convey the impression of solid working parts. For an engineer to gain an understanding of the three dimensional motion of the animation, it is much easier if the pictures have a solid appearance.[3]
2. *High-speed and automatic production of engineering animations*:
   An engineering animation is also a way of communicating between designers, engineers, and workers. It needs to be produced as fast as possible so as to encourage their communication. In addition, engineering animations are usually produced by designers who are not professional animators. For this reason, an engineering animation system should work automatically.
3. *Lower host dependency and cost saving*:
   An engineering animation system must be constantly available during the design process. There is little point in having a fast system if you have to wait to use it. Typically, several work stations will share a central host computer and these must not put too large a load on the host. The work stations should be inexpensive too.

For historical reasons, the system was developed on a 2D graphic display connected with VAX750. We developed some special display techniques for speeding up the display processes on the 2D display, but most of the techniques as well as the third requirement above are out of date because of the rapid improvement of graphics devices.

[3] The reference to line drawings came from historical reasons. In 1985, many cartographic displays were in use for realtime display.

To date, many similar assembly/robot simulators have been developed on much improved devices, and with the progress of graphics hardware/software, the first and second requirements have been satisfied more and more.

Such systems are of much use in both design and production planning phase. Most of the existing systems, however, supply only a local view to users. The next step for the systems is the integration with multiple levels of views.

13.4. SYDEM: An Approach to Computer-Aided Assemblability Testing

To design assembly products, we need to test their *assemblability* (capacity for being assembled). This section presents an approach to computer-aided assemblability testing called *SYDEM*, which stands for *CIM through SYstematic DEcomposition of Manufacturing*[4]. In Subsection 13.4.1, we overview the related results of assemblability and classify assemblability into two categories. Subsection 13.4.2 introduces our decompositive approach and its theoretical superiority.

13.4.1. Assemblability

Russell et al.[9] pointed out that the parts and products designed for economical manufacturing could reduce the manufacturing cost. Lund and Kahler[6] also discussed the importance of rational design for assembly. Their proposal is, however, based on the empirical facts such as "decreasing the number of components." What they proposed is not how to decide the assemblability of an assembly but how to improve the design for better assemblability.

Miyakawa and Ohashi[7] developed a method for evaluating the assemblability of an assembly from its drawings, prototypes or samples. Although their method can express the degree of the assemblability as a value, it does not distinguish between manual and automated assembly.

Ishida, Minowa and Nakajima[3] directly treated the assemblability as disassemblability (capacity for being disassembled), and Takase and Nakajima presented an algorithm for testing the assemblability from Feature Descriptor[10]. Although this approach can determine the potential assemblability, it also ignores the environmental conditions. They decided whether an assembly can be separated into two units simply by examining whether the two units do not collide with each other through a path. In the actual manufacturing, automated machines may collide with components and/or other machines. Hence, with this method, we cannot decide the assemblability in some environment.

Based on the above discussions, we classify the notion of assemblability into the following two categories:

1. *Potential Assemblability:*
   Capacity for being assembled potentially. This relates to collision avoidance between moving components.
2. *Environmental Assemblability:*
   Capacity for being assembled in a specified environment. In this case, collisions are between not only components but also other obstacles such as robot hands, arms, and supports.

To apply the assemblability test to actual manufacturing, it is necessary to decide the environmental assemblability. In addition, since the evaluation of environmental assemblability depends on the facilities of plants where the products are assembled, it is impossible for designers to decide the appropriateness of the design of an assembly unless the information of the manufacturing facilities are provided. In the rest of this section, assemblability denotes the environmental assemblability.

13.4.2. Testing Assemblability

This subsection is devoted to our approach to testing assemblability. Our approach repeatedly utilizes the collision-free path-finding method (e.g. [2]). Depending on the purposes, automated generation and manual input of paths are both useful.

The following steps summarize our plan for testing the assemblability and/or finding the order of assembling in a given environment:

1. Store the data of an assembly as a set of components and relations among them in a computer (e.g. [5]).
2. Simulate a disassembly step where a component is going to be separated from the final assembly composed of all the components.[4] This disassembly utilizes the collision-free path-finding method. If this decomposition is successful, simulate the next disassembly step where another component is to be removed from the subassembly composed of the rest of the components; otherwise, with back tracking, another decomposition sequence is searched.
3. Repeat the step 2 until
   a) the disassembly sequence reaches the successful disassembly step where two components are separated, or
   b) all of the possible disassembly steps are tried.

   The case (a) is that the assembly has assemblability, and the case (b) indicates the impossibility of assembling.

Our evaluation of computational complexity tells that, in the worst case, the number of examined assembly steps in a decompositive simulation is

[4] Each step of the simulation is performed as not that of disassembling but that of assembling.

$O(n^2)$, while the number of steps in a compositive simulation is $O(2^n)$. The decompositive assembly simulation is thus superior to the compositive simulation from the theoretical viewpoint.

In general, we tend to simulate in the order actually occurred. Also in the assembly simulation, it is natural to perform a depth-first search in a compositive order. But in this case, our intuition is wrong, and decompositive simulation is superior to compositive one. It tells us that we need to develop sophisticated tools whose capacity partly exceeds the human intuition/power for the development of synthetic factories.

13.5. Process Visualization

In synthetic factories, users want to know how the factories work from global views. This section presents a process visualization system for visualizing the activities in factories[1]. Our approach has the following three steps:

1. Users specify the data concerning how the factories work.
2. The system visualizes how the synthetic factories work based on the specification.
3. The users see what happens in the synthetic factories and find (and solve) the problems.

Thus our approach relies heavily on human intuition[5], and contrasts with approaches based on operations research (OR)[6]. In Subsection 13.5.1, we present an underlying process model, and Subsection 13.5.2 introduces our visualization method.

13.5.1. Process Modeling

The whole activities in a factory can be viewed as a process which consists of events and (temporal) constraints between them. The substance of an event is described by a set of attributes. The temporal relationships between events are represented by relationships between the characteristic time points of two events, e.g. between the start time of an event and the end time of another event. Let A, M, and B be a set of event attribute descriptors, a set of characteristic time point descriptors, and a set of temporal relation descriptors, respectively. Event attribute descriptors are, for example, agents, actions, and objects. Typical characteristic time point descriptors are start time and end time. Temporal relation descriptors are, for instance, *simultaneous* or *behind 5 minutes.*

A process is formally defined as follows:

[5] This is because men often take a wider view than machines.

[6] Typical OR approaches are linear programming, simulation, PERT/CPM, and sequencing.

Definition 1 (Process)
A process P is a triplet, $P = (E, \alpha, C)$, where
1) E is a set of events,
2) $\alpha : E \to 2^A$ is the event attribute function, and
3) $C \subset M \times E \times M \times E \times B$ is a set of temporal constraints.

From the above definition, the substance of a process e is a set of attributes $\alpha(e)$. A temporal constraint $c = (m_1, e_1, m_2, e_2, b)$ denotes that the temporal relation between the characteristic time point m_1 of an event e_1 and the characteristic time point m_2 of an event e_2 is b. For example, $(start, e_1, end, e_2, simultaneous)$ signifies that the starting of e_1 and the ending of e_2 occur simultaneously.

13.5.2. Process Scheduling

In the previous subsection, a process is defined in an abstract manner. To visualize it, we need to derive a concrete time schedule of event occurrences.

Duration estimation. For the scheduling, the duration of each event should be estimated somehow. We thus assume that estimators can evaluate the durations of events. However, because these durations are *approximated suggestions* by duration estimators, they need to be adjusted via negotiation with other durations. To enable the negotiation, durations are estimated not simply by estimated constants, but also by the functions that indicate how much the actual durations may deviate from the estimated constants. Let us call such functions *duration estimation functions.*

Formally a duration estimation function is given below:

Definition 2 (Duration Estimation Function)
A duration estimation function φ is a function,

$$\varphi : \boldsymbol{R} \to \boldsymbol{R} \cup \{\infty\} \tag{1}$$

where $\varphi(d) = \infty$ $(d < 0)$.

For example, the typical forms of duration estimation functions are as follows:

$$\varphi(d) = \begin{cases} k(d - d_0)^2 & (d \geq 0) \\ \infty & (d < 0) \end{cases} \tag{2}$$

Types of inter-event temporal constraints. Inter-event temporal constraints can be classified into three: equality constraints, inequality constraints, and estimation constraints.

1. *Equality Constraints:*
   An equality constraint is one that a time point t_j is *exactly* Δt later than another time point t_i. Note that Δt can be minus. This constraint is translated into an equality:

$$t_i + \Delta t = t_j. \tag{3}$$

A typical equality constraint is that the start/end times of two events are exactly the same. In such a case, $\Delta t = 0$ in the above equality.

2. *Inequality Constraints:*
   An inequality constraint is one that can be translated into an inequality:

$$t_i + \Delta t \leq t_j. \tag{4}$$

This type of constraint is used for requesting that a particular time point should not exceed a given limit.

3. *Estimation Constraints:*
   An estimation constraint is one that a time point t_j is *approximately* Δt later than another time point t_i. This constraint is translated into an *estimation constraint function.* A typical estimation constraint function is:

$$\psi = k(t_j - t_i - \Delta t)^2. \tag{5}$$

Scheduling as an optimization problem. The duration estimation functions and estimation constraint functions mentioned above represent the unlikelihood or unimportance of the corresponding durations and time delays. To schedule a process appropriately, we need to minimize the functions. But they are interrelated and in general, we cannot minimize all the functions derived from a process simultaneously. We may assume that the sum of all the functions in a process represents the unlikelihood or unimportance of the whole process. The scheduling of a process thus comes down to the optimization of the sum of the functions in the process.

First, let $\tilde{\varphi}$ be a modified estimation function that is obtained by replacing d by $t_j - t_i$ in φ. (t_i and t_j are the start time and end time of the event whose duration is estimated by φ.) Let $\boldsymbol{t} = (t_1, ..., t_n)$ be a vector of start/end times of events in a process and (if necessary) other significant points of time. Note that an instance of $\boldsymbol{t}$ can be identified with a particular schedule of the process. Let P, Q and R be a set of duration estimation functions, a set of estimation constraint functions, and a set of equalities/inequalities, each of which is derived from a given process.

An optimal schedule of the given process is formally defined as follows:

Definition 3 (Optimal Schedule)
An optimal schedule of the process is $\mathbf{t} = (t_1, ..., t_n)$ *which minimizes the total estimation function* Φ *given below:*

$$\Phi = \sum_{\varphi \in P} \tilde{\varphi} + \sum_{\psi \in Q} \psi, \tag{6}$$

satisfying all the elements of R.

Thus the process is visualized based on the derived schedule. Then users observe how the synthetic factories work and find/solve the problems in the process.

13.6. Discussions

In this paper, we discussed the two requirements of synthetic factories: levels of view and evaluation methods, and three sample components are introduced. Each component has its purpose and works well to some extent. However, it is still doubtful whether synthetic factories will work well enough with these components. This is because the whole activities in factories are too complex and interrelated for users to grasp. To overcome this difficulty, "integration" will be the key issue for the future research on synthetic factories, and such researches will be the first step to handling complexity in synthetic worlds.

Acknowledgments

ANIMENGINE system is part of my MSc work, and I am deeply indebted to my adviser, Prof. Tosiyasu L. Kunii, for his assistance. SYDEM is also due to the work with Prof. Kunii and Dr. Kyu-Jae Lee. The process visualization system is the result of the joint research with Prof. Naoyuki Okada, Prof. Jun-ichi Nakamura, Dr. Moon R. Jung, and Dr. Hiromi Baba. I am grateful to them all for their cooperation.

References

1. Baba, H., Noma, T., Jung, M.R., and Okada, N., "Event Modeling for Process Visualization," In: Chua, T.S. and Kunii, T.L. (eds.), *Multimedia Modeling, Proc. MMM '93*, World Scientific, pp. 31–43, 1993.
2. Brady, M., "Artificial Intelligence and Robotics," *Artif. Intell.*, Vol. 26, No. 1, pp. 79–121, 1985.
3. Ishida, T., Minowa, H., and Nakajima, N., "Detection of Unanticipated Functions of Machines," In: *Proc. Int'l Symp. on Design and Synthesis*, pp. 21–26, 1984.
4. Kunii, T.L., Noma, T., and Lee, K.J., "SYDEM: A New Approach to Computer-Aided Design of Assemblies and Assemblability Testing," In: Kunii, T.L. (ed.), *Visual Computing, Proc. CGI '92*, Springer-Verlag, pp. 469–479, 1992.
5. Lee, K. and Gossard, D.C., "A Hierarchical Data Structure for Representing Assemblies: Part 1," *Comput. Aided Design*, Vol. 17. No. 1, pp. 15–19, 1985.
6. Lund, T. and Kahler, S., "Design for Assembly," In: *Proc. 4th Int'l Conf. on Assembly Automation*, pp. 333–349, 1983.
7. Miyakawa, S. and Ohashi, T., "The Hitachi Assemblability Evaluation Method (AEM)," In: *Proc. 1st Int'l Conf. on Product Design for Assembly*, pp. 15–17, 1986.
8. Noma, T. and Kunii, T.L., "ANIMENGINE: An Engineering Animation System," *IEEE Comput. Graph. Appl.*, Vol. 5, No. 10, pp. 24–33, 1985.
9. Russell, G.A., Boothroyd, G., and Poli, C., "Design for Manufacturability," In: *Production Research and Technology, Proc. 8th NSF Grantee's Conf.*, pp. M1—M7, 1981.

10. Takase, H. and Nakajima, N., "A Language for Describing Assembled Machines," In: *Proc. Int'l Symp. on Design and Synthesis*, pp. 600–605, 1984.
11. Taylor II, R.M. et al., "The Nanomanipulator: A Virtual Reality Interface for a Scanning Tunneling Microscope," In: *Proc. SIGGRAPH '93*, pp. 127–134, 1993.
12. Ware, C. and Osborne, S., "Exploration and Virtual Camera Control in Virtual Three Dimensional Environments," *Comput. Graph.*, Vol. 24, No. 2, pp. 175–183, 1990.

14. Virtual Manufacturing – Concepts and Effects on Manufacturing in the Future –

Kenjiro T. Miura
Realistic Modeling Laboratory, Department of Mechanical Engineering, Shizuoka University, Hamamatsu City, Shizuoka 432, Japan
(e-mail:ktmiura@eng.shizuoka.ac.jp)

Summary.
The concept of virtual manufacturing, or virtual factory is to model and simulate manufacturing systems including design, machining process, assembly lines, and robots in addition to products on computers to create, analyze, improve them by using the technology of virtual reality. One of the main merits of such a simulation technology is that we do not have to deal with products and manufacturing systems separately since they are modeled as objects in a uniform manner.

In this paper, we discuss significance of the concept of virtual manufacturing and its impacts on manufacturing system designs in the future as well as technical problems to be solved to realize virtual manufacturing.

Key words: virtual manufacturing, concurrent engineering, parallel processing, mesh subdivision, vertex label assignment, dynamic interaction

14.1. Introduction

The concept of virtual manufacturing, or virtual factory is to model and simulate manufacturing systems including design, machining process, assembly lines, and robots in addition to products on computers to create, analyze, improve them by using the technology of virtual reality. One of the main merits of such a simulation technology is that we do not have to deal with products and manufacturing systems separately since they are modeled as objects in a uniform manner.

In a conventional design of manufacturing systems, for example, transfer machines and robots are designed separately, or ones are designed after the others have already been designed without pursuing optimum designs of both of them simultaneously. Virtual manufacturing is one of key concepts for concurrent engineering(simultaneous engineering) that makes an open computer-aided environment for the development of products or systems where all persons in the project can do cooperative works with any other persons.

In this paper, we discuss significance of the concept of virtual manufacturing and its impacts on manufacturing system designs in the future as well as technical problems to be solved to reaplize virtual manufacturing.

14.2. Conventional Design's Problems

We show the relationship between a solution space and constraints from design to manufacturing for a conventional design in Fig.1 [3]. The solution space at a lower stream of the design process is wider than that at its upper stream since the designer may not be able to know what constraints the manufacturing process will confront.

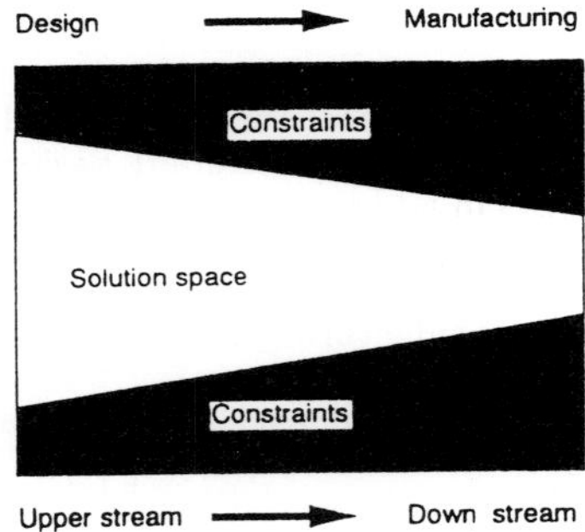

FIGURE 1. Solution space in conventional design flow

Figure 2 [3] show an example of the conventional design's problem explained above. Design (a) should be changed to design (b) in order to reduce the number of positioning for welding. If the designer understood the welding process, he would select design (b) even at lower stream of the design process.

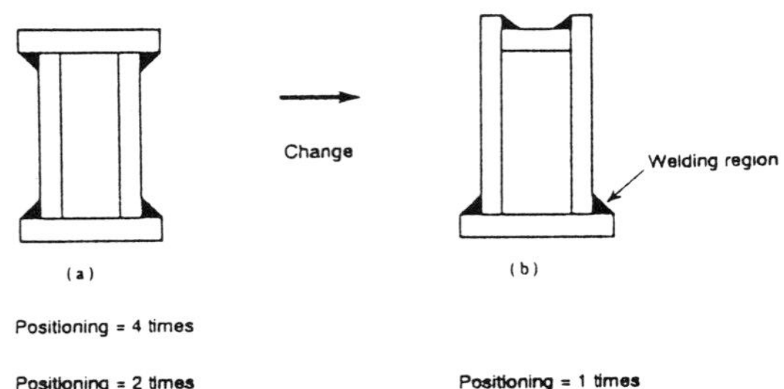

FIGURE 2. Reduction of the number of positioning

14.3. Concurrent Engineering

The concept of concurrent engineering(simultaneous engineering) was proposed in DARPA(Defense Advanced Research Project Agency)'s project, DICE(DARPA's Initiative in Concurrent Engineering) in 1988. According to this project, the definition of the CE is "an open computer-aided environment for the development of products or systems where all persons in the project can do cooperative works with any other patrons". This environment will make the relationship between a solution space and constraints from design to manufacturing that shown in in Fig.3 [3]. Information on design will flow from manufacturing to design as well as from design to manufacturing and constraints will be distributed evenly along design and manufacturing processes. We will get a rectangular solution space depicted in Fig.3.

Virtual manufacturing is necessary to realize the CE because of the following reasons:

- to communicate through visualization
- to know any other's jobs in any stage of design process
- to simulate unexpected manufacturing environments.

Especially, when we design a manufacturing system for products without much design experiences like micro machines or buildings in space, virtual manufacturing will be a strong tool to design efficient manufacturing systems.

The problems for the realization of virtual manufacturing are:

- physically-based simulations
- high computational requirements
- inherent parallelism.

In order to solve the above problems, we think parallel processing will be a key technology. By increasing the number of processors, we can achieve high performance. Graphics and computational geometry programs appear to have much inherent parallelism. One of the biggest obstacles to achieve high performance is communication and synchronization overheads. We have to minimize these overheads and allocate works suitably among processors.

14.4. Researches at the University of Aizu

Towards the realization of virtual manufacturing, two researches using parallel processing at the Shape Modeling Laboratory of the University of Aizu are introduced here. One is a mesh subdivision method based on vertex label assignment and a simulation of dynamic interaction between rigid body [4] [6].

Mesh Subdivision based on Vertex Label Assignment.

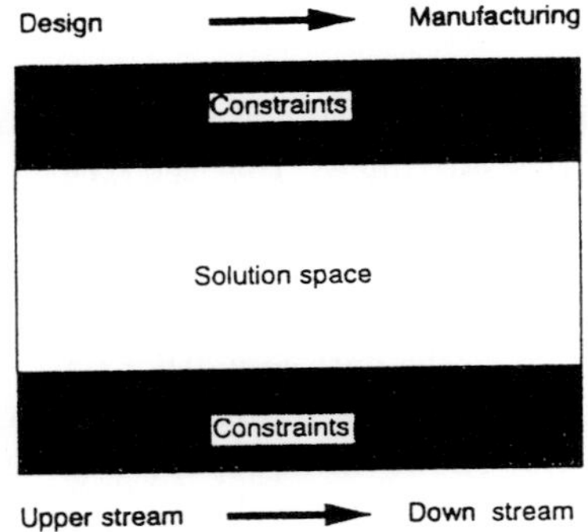

FIGURE 3. Solution space in CE

Definition of the problem. We obey almost the same definitions and notations used in Cheng et al.[2]. However, the problem we would like to solve is a little bit modified as follows. Given a regular quadrilateral network **P** and a subdivision mesh $\mathbf{P}^*$ of **P** such that

(R1) Each specified face f of **P** is subdivided into at least $9^{S(f)}$ subquadrilaterals.

(R2) The shape of faces generated in $\mathbf{P}^*$ is regular, i.e. faces of $\mathbf{P}^*$ are not too long or too narrow.

(R3) The resultant subdivision mesh $\mathbf{P}^*$ is amenable to local modification, i.e. changing the size or shape of some of the faces without affecting the remainder.

(R4) The number of faces generated in $\mathbf{P}^*$ is minimal over all subdivision meshes of **P** satisfying the goal(R1).

In the next section, we will show a solution to this problem that meets all the above goals (R1)-(R4).

Parallel mesh subdivision algorithm. The algorithm is based on five types of elementary subdivision procedures. These procedures will subdivide a given quadrilateral $f = v_1v_2v_3v_4$ into several subquadrilaterals.

1) one_v:only one vertex is labeled 1 or more

This procedure generates four subquadrilaterals $f_1 = q_1q_2q_3q_4$, $f_2 = r_1r_2r_3r_4$, $f_3 = s_1s_2s_3s_4$ and $f_4 = t_1t_2t_3t_4$, and assigns a label to each of their vertices (see Fig. 4).

The new vertices are defined as follows.

$$\begin{aligned} q_1 &= v_1,\ r_2 = v_2,\ r_3 = s_3 = v_3,\ s_4 = v_4, \\ q_2 &= r_1 = \frac{2v_1 + v_2}{3},\ q_4 = s_1 = \frac{2v_1 + v_4}{3}, \\ q_3 &= r_4 = s_2 = \frac{3v_1 + v_2 + v_3 + v_4}{6}. \end{aligned}$$

Labels assigned to the new vertices are defined as follows.

$$\begin{aligned}
Lab(q_1) &= Lab(v_1) - 1, \\
Lab(q_2) &= Lab(r_1) = Lab(q_1), \\
Lab(q_3) &= Lab(r_4) = Lab(s_2) = Lab(q_1), \\
Lab(q_4) &= Lab(s_1) = Lab(q_1), \\
Lab(r_2) &= Lab(r_3) = Lab(s_3) = Lab(s_4) = 0.
\end{aligned}$$

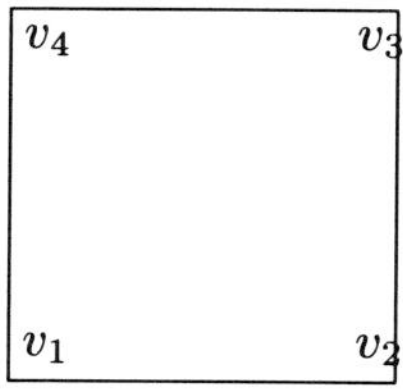

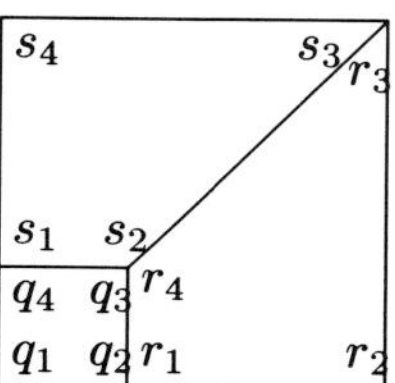

FIGURE 4. Only one vertex≥1

2) two_va:two adjacent vertices are labeled 1 or more

This procedure generates seven subquadrilaterals $f_1 = q_1q_2q_3q_4$, ..., and $f_7 = x_1x_2x_3x_4$ as shown in Fig.5. The new vertices and their labels are defined as follows.

$$\begin{aligned}
q_1 &= v_1,\ r_2 = u_2 = v_2,\ u_3 = x_3 = v_3,\ w_4 = v_4, \\
q_2 &= r_1 = \frac{2v_1 + v_2}{3},\ w_3 = x_4 = \frac{v_3 + 2v_4}{3}, \\
s_4 &= w_1 = \frac{v_1 + 2v_4}{3},\ q_4 = s_1 = \frac{2v_1 + v_4}{3}, \\
q_3 &= r_4 = s_2 = t_1 = \frac{3v_1 + v_2 + v_3 + v_4}{6}, \\
r_3 &= t_2 = u_1 = \frac{v_1 + 3v_2 + v_3 + v_4}{6}, \\
t_3 &= u_4 = x_2 = \frac{v_1 + v_2 + 3v_3 + v_4}{6}, \\
s_3 &= t_4 = w_2 = x_1 = \frac{v_1 + v_2 + v_3 + 3v_4}{6},
\end{aligned}$$

$$\begin{aligned}
Lab(q_1) &= Lab(v_1) - 1,\ Lab(w_4) = Lab(v_4) - 1, \\
Lab(q_2) &= Lab(r_1) = Lab(q_1), \\
Lab(q_3) &= Lab(r_4) = Lab(s_2) = Lab(t_1) = Lab(q_1),
\end{aligned}$$

$$\begin{aligned}
Lab(q_4) &= Lab(s_1) = Lab(q_1), \\
Lab(s_4) &= Lab(w_1) = Lab(w_4), \\
Lab(s_3) &= Lab(t_4) = Lab(w_2) = Lab(x_1) = Lab(w_4), \\
Lab(w_3) &= Lab(x_4) = Lab(w_4),
\end{aligned}$$

other new vertices are labeled 0.

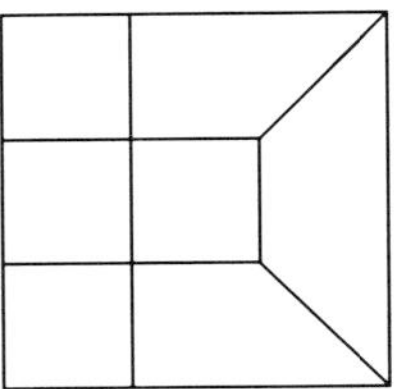

FIGURE 5. Two vertices≥1 (adjacent type)

3) two_vd:two diagonal vertices are labeled 1 or more

This procedure generates seven subquadrilaterals shown in Fig.6. Similarly,

$$\begin{aligned}
q_1 &= v_1,\ r_2 = u_2 = v_2,\ x_3 = v_3,\ s_4 = w_4 = v_4, \\
q_2 &= r_2 = \frac{2v_1 + v_2}{3},\ u_3 = x_2 = \frac{v_1 + 2v_3}{3}, \\
w_3 &= x_4 = \frac{2v_3 + v_4}{3},\ q_4 = s_1 = \frac{2v_1 + v_4}{3}, \\
q_3 &= r_4 = s_2 = t_1 = \frac{3v_1 + v_2 + v_3 + v_4}{6}, \\
r_3 &= t_2 = u_1 = \frac{v_1 + 3v_2 + v_3 + v_4}{6}, \\
t_3 &= u_4 = w_2 = x_1 = \frac{v_1 + v_2 + 3v_3 + v_4}{6}, \\
s_3 &= t_4 = w_1 = \frac{v_1 + v_2 + v_3 + 3v_4}{6},
\end{aligned}$$

$$\begin{aligned}
Lab(q_1) &= Lab(v_1) - 1,\ Lab(x_3) = Lab(v_3) - 1, \\
Lab(q_2) &= Lab(r_1) = Lab(q_1), \\
Lab(q_3) &= Lab(r_4) = Lab(s_2) = Lab(t_1) = Lab(q_1), \\
Lab(q_4) &= Lab(s_1) = Lab(q_1), \\
Lab(t_3) &= Lab(u_4) = Lab(w_2) = Lab(x_1) = Lab(x_3), \\
Lab(u_3) &= Lab(x_2) = Lab(x_3), \\
Lab(w_3) &= Lab(x_4) = Lab(x_4),
\end{aligned}$$

other new vertices are labeled 0.

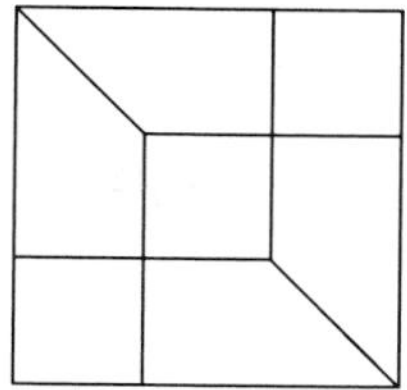

FIGURE 6. Two vertices≥1 (diagonal type)

4) three_v:three vertices are labeled 1 or more

This procedure generates eight subquadrilaterals shown in Fig.7. Similarly,

$$\begin{aligned}
q_1 &= v_1,\ s_2 = v_2,\ w_3 = y_3 = v_3,\ x_4 = v_4, \\
q_2 &= r_1 = \frac{2v_1 + v_2}{3},\ r_2 = s_1 = \frac{v_1 + 2v_2}{3}, \\
s_3 &= w_2 = \frac{2v_2 + v_3}{3},\ x_3 = y_4 = \frac{v_1 + 2v_4}{3}, \\
t_4 &= x_1 = \frac{v_1 + 2v_4}{3},\ q_4 = t_1 = \frac{2v_1 + v_4}{3}, \\
q_3 &= r_4 = t_2 = u_1 = \frac{3v_1 + v_2 + v_3 + v_4}{6}, \\
r_3 &= s_4 = u_2 = w_1 = \frac{v_1 + 3v_2 + v_3 + v_4}{6}, \\
u_3 &= w_4 = y_2 = \frac{v_1 + v_2 + 3v_3 + v_4}{6}, \\
t_3 &= u_4 = x_2 = y_1 = \frac{v_1 + v_2 + v_3 + 3v_4}{6},
\end{aligned}$$

$$\begin{aligned}
Lab(q_1) &= Lab(v_1) - 1,\ Lab(s_2) = Lab(v_2) - 1, \\
Lab(x_4) &= Lab(v_4) - 1, \\
Lab(q_2) &= Lab(r_1) = Lab(q_1), \\
Lab(q_3) &= Lab(r_4) = Lab(t_2) = Lab(u_1) = Lab(q_1), \\
Lab(q_4) &= Lab(t_1) = Lab(q_1), \\
Lab(r_2) &= Lab(s_1) = Lab(s_2), \\
Lab(r_3) &= Lab(s_4) = Lab(u_2) = Lab(w_1) = Lab(s_1), \\
Lab(s_3) &= Lab(w_2) = Lab(s_2), \\
Lab(t_4) &= Lab(x_1) = Lab(x_4), \\
Lab(t_3) &= Lab(u_4) = Lab(x_2) = Lab(y_1) = Lab(x_4), \\
Lab(x_3) &= Lab(y_4) = Lab(x_4),
\end{aligned}$$

other new vertices are labeled 0.

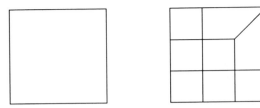

FIGURE 7. Three vertices≥1

5) four_v:all vertices are labeled 1 or more

This procedure generates nine subquadrilaterals shown in Fig.8. Similarly,

$$\begin{aligned}
q_1 &= v_1,\ s_2 = v_2,\ z_3 = v_3,\ x_4 = v_4,\\
q_2 &= r_1 = \frac{2v_1 + v_2}{3},\ r_2 = s_1 = \frac{v_1 + 2v_2}{3},\\
s_3 &= w_2 = \frac{2v_2 + v_3}{3},\ w_3 = z_2 = \frac{v_1 + 2v_3}{3},\\
t_4 &= x_1 = \frac{v_1 + 2v_4}{3},\ q_4 = t_1 = \frac{2v_1 + v_4}{3},\\
q_3 &= r_4 = t_2 = u_1 = \frac{3v_1 + v_2 + v_3 + v_4}{6},\\
r_3 &= s_4 = u_2 = w_1 = \frac{v_1 + 3v_2 + v_3 + v_4}{6},\\
u_3 &= w_4 = y_2 = z_1 = \frac{v_1 + v_2 + 3v_3 + v_4}{6},\\
t_3 &= u_4 = x_2 = y_1 = \frac{v_1 + v_2 + v_3 + 3v_4}{6},
\end{aligned}$$

$$\begin{aligned}
Lab(q_1) &= Lab(v_1) - 1,\ Lab(s_2) = Lab(v_2) - 1,\\
Lab(z_3) &= Lab(v_3) - 1,\ Lab(x_4) = Lab(v_4) - 1,\\
Lab(q_2) &= Lab(r_1) = Lab(q_1),\\
Lab(q_3) &= Lab(r_4) = Lab(t_2) = Lab(u_1) = Lab(q_1),\\
Lab(q_4) &= Lab(t_1) = Lab(q_1),\\
Lab(r_2) &= Lab(s_1) = Lab(s_2),\\
Lab(r_3) &= Lab(s_4) = Lab(u_2) = Lab(w_1) = Lab(s_1),\\
Lab(s_3) &= Lab(w_2) = Lab(s_2),\\
Lab(y_3) &= Lab(z_4) = Lab(z_3),\\
Lab(u_3) &= Lab(w_4) = Lab(y_2) = Lab(z_1) = Lab(z_3),\\
Lab(w_3) &= Lab(z_2) = Lab(z_3),\\
Lab(t_4) &= Lab(x_1) = Lab(x_4),
\end{aligned}$$

$$Lab(t_3) = Lab(u_4) = Lab(x_2) = Lab(y_1) = Lab(x_4),$$
$$Lab(x_3) = Lab(y_4) = Lab(x_4),$$

other new vertices are labeled 0. The overall structure of the algorithm is

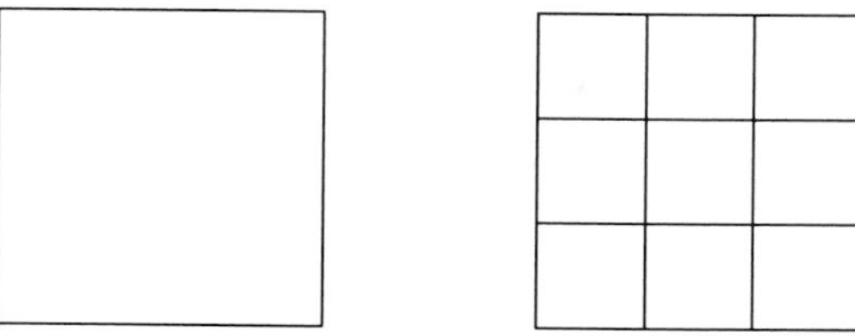

FIGURE 8. All vertices≥1

given in Fig.6. A procedure, subdivide(g) in Phase 2 is defined in Fig.7.

Algorithm PMS:Parallel Mesh Subdivision
{input:a regular quadrilateral network **P** and a subdivision level assignment **S** on **P**}
{output:a subdivision mesh **P*** of **P**}

Phase 1:[Construct the vertex label assignment **L** of **P** with respect to **S**.]

PARDO for each vertex v of **P** **do**
$L(v)$:=max$\{S(f)—f\in F, v$ is a vertex of $f\}$
DOPAR

Phase 2:[Subdivide the faces of **P** in parallel.]

PARDO for each face g of **P** **do**
subdivide(g);
DOPAR

Figure 10: Parallel mesh subdivision

```
subdivide(g:quadrilateral);
    begin
      if(Lab(v) > 0 for only 1-v v of g)then
        begin
            one_v(g, g1, g2, g3, g4);
            sibdivide(g1);
            sibdivide(g2);
            sibdivide(g3);
            sibdivide(g4);
        end
      else if(Lab(v) > 0 for 2-ad-v v of g)then
            ...
    end;{subdivide}
```

Figure 11: Procedure *subdivide*

See Fig.11-12 that illustrate the mesh generation for 2-D grids with different number of faces and subdivision levels.

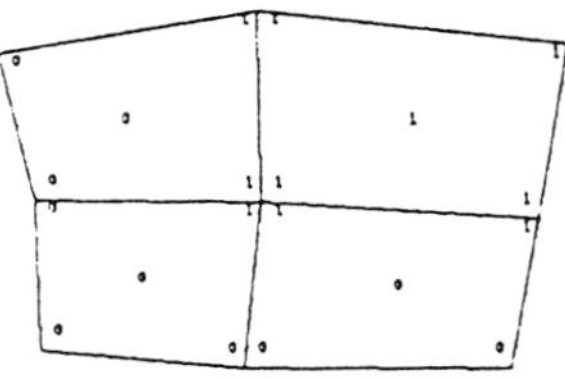

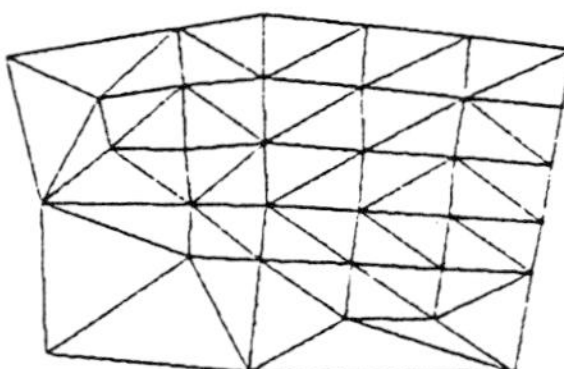

FIGURE 11. Example No.1

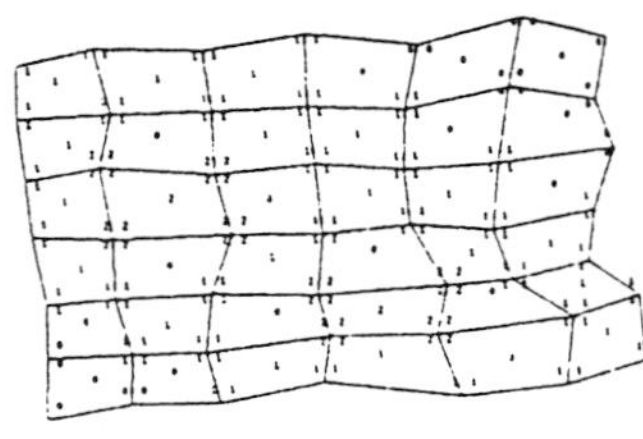

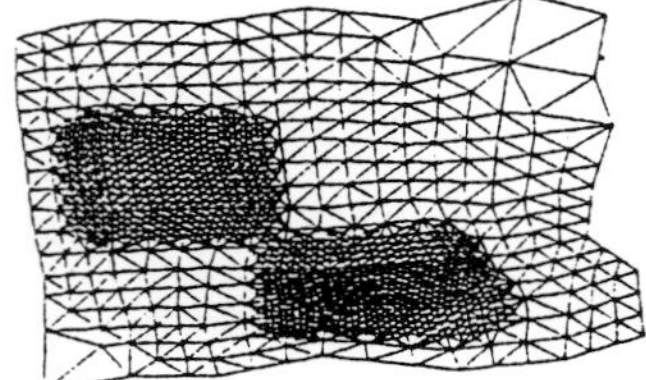

FIGURE 12. Example No.2

Simulation of Dynamic Interaction between Rigid Bodies.

Methods of collisions modeling. Lately the different kinds of movement of objects and an interaction between them have been proposed for robotics and modeling a large number of problems to explain structural, physical and chemical properties of the matter. This simulation includes not only the lows of physics but takes into account interactions of objects. Simulation of the geometric collisions between rigid bodies is computational expensive and it is important to calculate as close as possible to real time. Buzbee[1] presents a detailed estimation of operations number needed to obtain reliable results of plasma simulation and outlines that Particle in Cell problems can be solved on the computers whose time performance is about 1GF. With the advancement in hardware technology implementation of the parallel computers for solving such problems seems very attractive. The main advantage of parallel computers is the possibility to increase number of processors when dimension (number of particles, for example) of problem increases. In the present paper we describe software algorithm for computing dynamic process which simulate motion of the center of mass and rotation motion about the center of mass of the bodies under external forces and collisions among objects with implicitly defined surfaces. Our software algorithm is not quite ordinary for traditional computer graphics and introduces the next concepts:

- we use discrete-event approach to advance state of the system. The discrete event approach means a changing of the state in the defined time moments when the event takes place. And a global time step is a time interval for advancement from event to event;
- geometrical sharing of data space (or subdivision on patches each of which belongs to one processor);
- nearest-neighboring strategy of collision determination are reasonable for calculations;
- ability to create complex objects from simple ones keeping the type of the representation is supported by using R-functions;
- particles can follow global rules and don't ignore each other;
- efficient collision - detection algorithm is used;
- rigid body physically based interaction is implemented.

Rigid body motion is well studied and in this paper we do not deal with details of object motion. Algorithm is opened for including different forces that influence the motion of the objects and they are independent of searching of intersections.

Parallel algorithm description. In the outside physical world there are a lot of initially simple geometrical forms which can produce interesting complex forms in accordance with some rules. Unfortunately, a simulation of geometric collision is computational expensive and an implementation of the parallel computer to calculate the dynamic interaction of colloidal particles close as possible to real time seems to be very attractive. This work is an attempt to find out approach to solve the problem.

Let us formulate problems. Let 3D domain is given and it has M*K*L cells. Each patch contains a group of cells. Procedure begins by placing N "simple" forms or particles randomly into cells. We want to study motion and geometrical collisions as functions of the time and of forces influencing particles. Global state $S(t)$ of the system at time t is the vector $s_1(t)$, $s_2(t)$, ...,$s_N(t)$, where $s_i(t) = (r_i(t), v_i(t), w_i(t), f_i(t), b_i(t))$ and $r_i(t)$, $v_i(t)$, $w_i(t)$ are the center position vector , the velocity and the angular velocity vectors respectively. $f_i(t)$ is some function which defines time-dependent surface of the particle (this function will be described below). $b_i(t)$ is a spherical bounding box which contains all points of a surface defined by $f_i(t)$. Bounding box location is defined by the vector $r_i(t)$. We suppose that a number of particles in the system can be changed and depends on a character of interaction between particles. We suppose also that periodic boundary conditions are stated. A chained list of pointers is implemented for storing a state vector and characteristics which define a type of interaction between particles. This form of storage lets us avoid an accumulation of rubbish on the processors. The space-sharing approach is implemented, it means that parallel execution is achieved by dividing 2D domain into patches both horizontally and vertically. Boundary cells require inter-processor communications. The current dynamic state is changed from event to event . An event is either :

- collision of two particles;
- intersection of cell boundary by the mass center of a particle;
- case when one of sizes of a bounding box exceeds sizes of a cell.

Many phenomena of the physical world are by nature of the earest- neighbor type and "nearest-neighboring" strategy has been used as a conception for discrete event simulation. It means that a state of each element of a cell is defined by corresponding state of each element of the nearest eight cells for L = 1. Such approach we name "cellular automata" approach. The main purpose of the presented algorithm (simplified OCCAM-2 language code is given in Fig.14) is to provide calculations with high rate of parallelism. Folds denote basic stages of communication and computation in the algorithm.

In the actual program named.interface is a subroutine which works in a parallel with the computational part of program and provides dynamical allocation memory. Fold *memory allocation* changes the data type from one data type to another. Folds *input, output* produce parallel an input to receive data and an output to send the values from four directions for the nearest eight neighbors or the "Host" processor. Fold generation includes procedures to start each cell to generate new state, to calculate rendering data and to send them for representation on the screen. Signal stop is sent into internal channel *fr.sys* for reallocation of memory by *named.interface* subroutine.

To prevent a processors from going idle between the moment of receiving data from neighbors and the moment of calculating a next state we use the data buffer. The problems of parallel data input/output and computations have been solved by using "blinking" buffers. It is important to notice that the processor receiving data checks only the tag glued to the data packages and if the data is sent to this processor it will be sent by internal channel for the processing, otherwise it will be loaded into the free transit data buffers and then will forward to the next processor. The input and output processes are given a higher priority and such a logic let us to reach minimal loss in performance.

```
PAR
    named.interface(fr.sys, etc.)
    SEQ
        ... memory allocation
        PRI PAR
            PAR
                ... input
                ... output
                ... generation
        fr.sys ! stop
```

Figure 14: Simplified "OCCAM-2" algorithm

Control or synchronization of the event set is provided by "Host" processor on the base of information received from processors. Advancement of the system state is performed by two steps. First step is prediction to determine the state vector using a current dynamic state defined by virtual values of $r_i(t)$, $v_i(t)$ and $w_i(t)$. On this step we use linear approximation of motion and a simple condition that the distance between the centers of bounding boxes equals the current diameter of bounding box. In the each time substep we compute potential interaction of bodies. The algorithm examines intersection of bounding boxes and then if such case takes place the "shapes" are checked for intersection. Naturally, only particles in the neighboring cells have to be checked. In such a manner we can detect a collision event. If this event takes place and if character of interaction defines particles union, particles are united with a new complex shape particle generation. Additional examination is taken to check center mass crossing event when particles change cell membership. This case is defined by particle center crossing a patch or cell boundary.

Next computing overhead is an event when a size of a bounding box becomes bigger than a size of a cell. It requires rebuilding of a cell grid.

Unfortunately random accumulation of particles on one processor can lead to the non-uniform loads of processors. This event requires reloading of particles among processors. The "Host" processor makes a decision about reloading taking into account a time load of each processor and if time histogram is not uniform, e.g. a maximum time load of one processor exceeds a minimum time load of another one by appointed value, new division of the region into rectangular patches is done. Being collected on the "Host" processor global state vector is distributed between processors. To provide new data distribution a dynamic memory reallocation is performed.

The second step is numerical solving the set of the ordinary differential equations with the definite time increment. For the numerical integration of the system of second order differential equations of the center mass motion we use simple numerical Runge-Kutta method and for the Euler equations in the principal axis we apply simple Euler method.

Particles geometry and collisions. To define geometric object with virtually any surface the implicit function representation is used. Both simple and complex objects are represented by inequality:

$$f(x, y, z) \geq 0$$

where f - a real continuous function of Cartesian coordinates of a point. The function has negative values for points outside an object, positive values for inside points and zero values for points on a surface. Two conjunct colloidal particles can be described by the set theoretical union. Analytical definitions of such operations in the form of so-called R-functions have been studied by Rvachev [5] and applied to geometric modeling in [4].

Detection of the collision point of particles is summarized to an approximate solution:

$$p^* = argmax\{G(p_i) : p_i \in \mathbf{P}\}$$

where

p_i - rectangular point coordinates ,

$\mathbf{P}$ - admissible domain,

$G(p_i) = f_1 \wedge_\alpha f_2 \ldots \wedge_\alpha f_N$,

$\wedge_\alpha$ - the symbol of R-conjunction,

N - number of bodies.

The numerical algorithm is proposed for detection of the admissible domain. Searching of the admissible domain P is performed through the intersection test of the couples of bounding boxes. We use the next scheme:

- bounding boxes are projected onto three coordinate planes;
- projection intersections are determined in each plane;
- rectangular domain such as all points of intersection belongs to it is determined.

Coordinates X_b,Y_b, Z_b define the size of the admissible domain. If this admissible domain is empty we have the case when search of the collision point is out of use. Searching of intersection of boxes pair is performed rapidly but computation of intersection point of "shapes" pair is a time consuming operation. For finding intersection points it is reasonable to use random LPτ

points as an initial values for simple quadratic process of finding coincidence points. These points are placed randomly in the nodes of regular rectangular grid.

The quadratic process employs three values of $G(p_i)$. Accuracy of a solution pi depends on some acceptable term about nearness to the solution. In our case we complete trials as soon as we find zero or positive value of the function G or reach assigned number NU of treats which depends on step value H. The grid step H along coordinates axes X_b, Y_b, Z_b is assigned according to needed accuracy. Besides these points are used for calculation of value $G(p_i)$. If the value of this function ≥ 0 we have the case of intersection. Figure 14 illustrates the worst case. In this case NU treats will be done.

FIGURE 14. An implicit surface is defined by $f(x, y, z) = 0$. Worst case of finding of collision points.

A general solution for the collision of two arbitrary rigid bodies involves solving a set of 15 linear equations in 15 unknowns as described. These equations we solve by Householder method, which possesses high numerical stability. We use the matrix expansion into orthogonal and triangular.

Examples. In this work the comparison the parallel speed of particle moving simulation and rendering with that of a serial computer and benchmarking were not done because the special work is a desirable in future. The question of benchmarking is not so simple as it appears at a first glance. The calculation speed depends on number of processors, number of cells, number of particles, sizes, velocities and shapes of initial and colloidal particles. Therefore, it is difficult to find a "common" example for evaluating the time performance. We suppose to devote the special investigation for evaluating the solution. And here we present only rendering results of dynamical behavior of particles. Figure 15 illustrates the sequence of being glued and colliding particles generated with our algorithm. It presents collisions of noisy block (which surface is time-dependent because of randomly being glued small spheres) with torus and noisy ellipsoid. The small sphere having collision point with the noisy block is glued to it by the blending union operation. The solid noise texture is generated on the surface of the block and the ellipsoid by the Gardner algorithm. All bodies have changeable orientation in the space and interact with each other as rigid bodies.

Our software algorithm simulates 1320 steps for 35 small spheres and generates 440 ray traced images with 250x250 resolution and with anti-aliasing in 13 hours on one T800 transputer which achieves the instruction throughput of 1.5 Mflops.

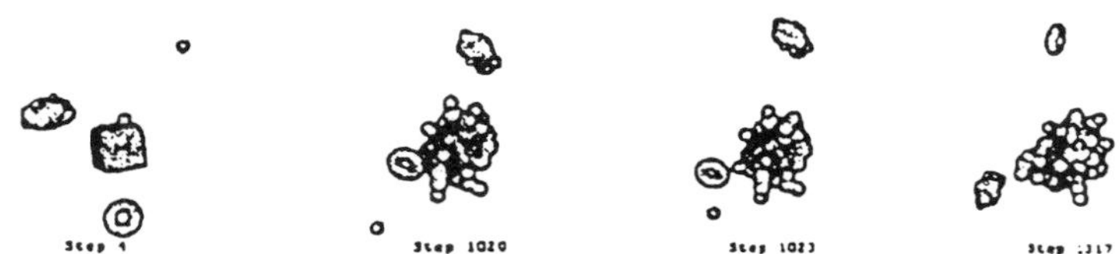

FIGURE 15. Sequence of being glued and colliding particles

14.5. Conclusions

The concept of virtual manufacturing is expected to give strong impacts on manufacturing as well as manufacturing system designs in the future. However, in order to realize virtual manufacturing, there are lot of problems to solve, i.e., time-consuming physically-based simulation, high computational requirement, exploration of inherent parallelism, etc. We have explained the importance of the research on parallel processors towards the realization of virtual manufacturing. Two researches are introduced based on parallel algorithms at the Shape Modeling laboratory of the University of Aizu, FEM mesh generation based on the vertex label assignment and simulation of dynamic interaction. These research will be basic techniques for virtual manufacturing. We will continue our researches on parallel processors to realize virtual manufacturing environments where high-quality products will be designed and actual manufacturing processes will be made highly efficient.

Acknowledgement

The author would like to thank Professors V. Savchenko at the University of Aizu for their help to write this paper.

References

1. Buzbee BL (1988) A Plasma Simulation and Computing Problems of Nuclear Physics. In: Kowalik JS(Ed.), High-Speed Computation. Radio & Swjis Publisher, Moscow, pp 384-391

2. Cheng F, Jaromczyk JW, Lin JR, Chang SS, Lu JY (1989) A Parallel Mesh Generation Algorithm based on the Vertex Label Assignment Scheme. International Journal for Numerical Methods in Eng., Vol.28, pp 1429-1448.
3. Fukuda S (1993) Concurrent Engineering(in Japanese). Baifu-kan.
4. Pasko AA, Savchenko VV, Adzhiev VD, Sourin AI (1993) Multidimensional Geometric Modeling and Visualization based on the Function representation of Objects. University of Aizu Technical Report 93-1-008.
5. Rvachev VL (1974) Methods of Logic Algebra in Mathematical Physics. Naukova Dumka Publisher, Kiev.
6. Savchenko VV, Pasko AA (1993) Simulation of Dynamic Interaction between Rigid Bodies with Time-dependent Implicitly Defined Surfaces. Proceedings of the 6th Australian Transputer and OCCAM User Group Conference, Brisbane, Australia, pp 122-129.

Theme 4

Synthetic Communication

15. Virtual Space Teleconferencing System – a Synthetic Teleconferencing System

Haruo Takemura* and Fumio Kishino†
ATR Communication Systems Research Laboratories, 2-2 Hikari-dai, Seika-cho, Soraku, Kyoto 619-0237 Japan

Summary.

A virtual environment, which is created by computer graphics and an appropriate user interface, can be used in many application fields, such as teleoperation , telecommunication and real time simulation. Furthermore, if this environment could be shared by multiple users, there would be more potential applications.

Discussed in this paper is a case study of building a prototype of a cooperative work environment using a virtual environment, where more than two people can solve problems cooperatively, including design strategies and implementing issues. An environment where two operators can directly grasp, move or release stereoscopic computer graphics images by hand is implemented. The system is built by combining head position tracking stereoscopic displays, hand gesture input devices and graphics workstations.

Our design goal is to utilize this type of interface for a future teleconferencing system. In order to provide good interactivity for users, we discuss potential bottlenecks and their solutions. The system allows two users to share a virtual environment and to organize 3-D objects cooperatively.

Key words: Virtual reality, communication with realistic sensations, virtual space teleconference, shared workspace, networked virtual environment.

15.1. Introduction

"*Teleconferencing with realistic sensations*" aims at allowing smooth and intricate communications among users by reproducing various aspects of face to face conferencing. One method for achieving this is a virtual conferencing room created by virtual reality technology. Moreover, if we regard this virtual conferencing room as a shared workspace among users, an environment can be formed where users can cooperatively solve various problems.

---

* presently at Nara Institute of Science and Technology, Nara Japan
† presently at Osaka University, Osaka Japan

In order to achieve "Teleconferencing with realistic sensations," the concept of virtual teleconferencing is proposed [4]. As shown in Figure 1, a "virtual teleconferencing" system creates an image of a conference room (virtual conference room) using computer graphics in real time. It also constructs images of the remotely located conference participants. Users of the system can talk to each other or proceed with the conference with the sensation of sharing the same space. There are many problems to be solved however, before this system can be realized. Some of them are now being studied at our laboratories [2; 7; 6].

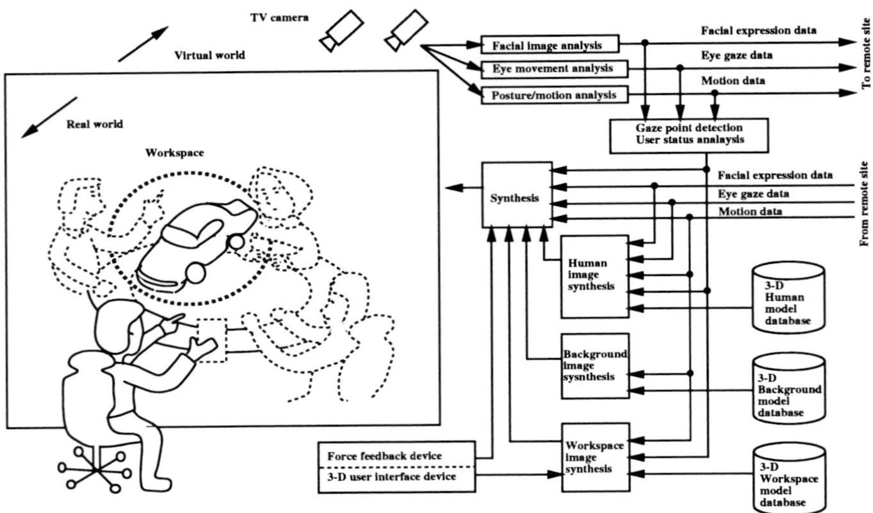

FIGURE 1. Virtual Space Teleconferencing

A virtual workspace for virtual teleconferencing is to be generated by computer graphics. "Virtual manipulation" is a facility enabling users to interact with the virtual environment. Users can cooperatively work on tasks such as city planning or modeling a new car. In such a case, it is desired that users be able to handle objects in a virtual environment just as they do in a real environment without a sense of incompatibility. If this can be achieved, users can collaborate in various ways without any prior training of teleconferencing operations.

However, there are not many reports on cooperative environments created by virtual reality. Ishii et al. pointed out the importance of shared work environment for cooperative work, although their approach is not based on a virtual environment or computer-generated environment [3]. Codella et al. implemented a demonstration system of a multi-person virtual world [1].

This paper first reviews and classifies networked virtual environments according to the level of sharing. Second, implementation issues of the networked virtual environments are discussed. Third, a prototype system of a *Virtual Space Teleconferencing System* is described.

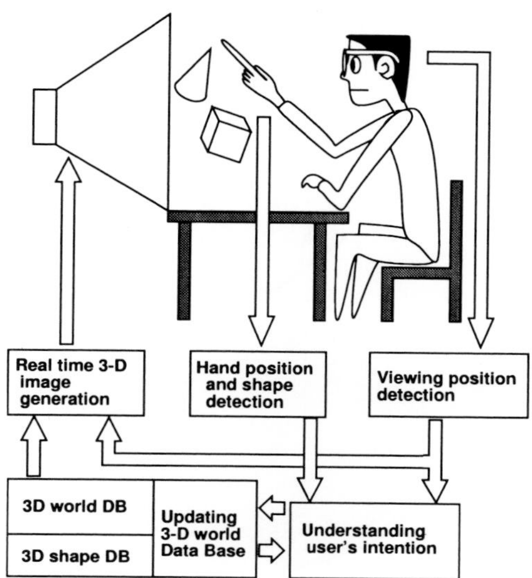

FIGURE 2. Typical Non-networked Virtual Environment

15.2. Networked Virtual Environment Classification

Figure 2 shows an overview of a typical non-networked virtual environment. If it is possible to create truly realistic virtual world which is precisely modeled on a real world by using computer vision and computer graphics technologies and also is possible to create virtual human being who is reproduction of receivers, such virtual world can be shared and used for two-way or multipoint communication and can make users feel as if they are really coexisting with their communication partners. By connecting more than two of the equipments in Figure 2, a networked virtual environment is configured as illustrated in Figure 3 and can be used for such a purpose. Users of the system can talk to each other or proceed with a conference with the sensation of "sharing the same space." Characteristics of virtual space teleconferencing are shown in Table 1 in comparison with conventional video teleconferencing characteristics.

A networked virtual environment (NVE) can be classified into 4 categories.

FIGURE 3. Shared virtual environment

Table 1. Characteristics of virtual space teleconferencing

Items	Virtual space teleconferencing	Conventional video teleconferencing
Motion parallax	Participants can observe a stereoscopic CG image according to the eye-position allowing the viewer to get a motion parallax effect.	Impossible.
Eye contact	It can be easily realized.	Difficult.
A sense of immersion	Participants feel as if they are actually in the conference room.	Impossible.
Cooperative work in a common space	Participants can cooperatively manipulate virtual objects in the conference room.	Impossible.

Level 1 Basic features of this level includes a facility to access a networked or remote virtual world database (VWDB). The VWDB can be shared among the sites that access the VWDB. Modification of the VWDB is not allowed. The status of other sites is not displayed in VE, i.e., one can not know what the other users are doing in the VE. This type of NVE is equivalent to an on-line database retrieval system Users do not modify the database but merely access and refer to the database. A virtual museum is one possible application of this level. The advantage of this level of NVE is that the communication can be one way from the VWDB to the local site.

Level 2 In addition to the level-1 NVE, the status of each site is distributed to the others. This information can be used to display an image of other users in the same VE. In this case, a bidirectional data path exists between each local site and the VWDB. User can not only share the environment but also know about the other users. This level can be used for communication media, a virtual community etc. However, it can not be used for a cooperative work environment among users, because no local site is allowed to modify the VWDB or shared environment.

Level 3 In addition to the level-2 NVE, independent VWDB modification is allowed. For example, an operator is allowed to modify the properties of a virtual object, such as position, color, shape. However, VWDB modification which results from operations at multiple sites, such that two people simultaneously try to change the shape of a single object, is still not allowed. This limits the mutual interaction between two users. For example, at this level, two operators can not hold the same virtual object at the same time. When the system allows independent modification of the VWDB, concurrency control of the VWDB becomes an issue. This level can be used for a cooperative work environment, as each site can share VWDB, can acquire the status of the other site(s) and can modify the VWDB cooperatively. The simplest implementation is that only one client is allowed to perform an modification. The entire database is locked during the operation.

Level 4 In addition to level-3 features, mutual operation is allowed. Mutual operation is an operation on the VWDB that results from control from multiple sites. For example, mutual interaction is the situation that arises when more than two operators cooperatively change the properties of a single object, or when objects controlled by more than two operators collide. In this case, more sophisticated concurrency control over the VWDB is required. However, this is the most flexible structure for NVE.

For a virtual space teleconference system, at least, level-2 NVE is required to enable users to communicate with each other. Thinking of ease of implementation and cooperative work operation, we have chosen to use Level-3 NVE for our Virtual Space Teleconferencing system.

15.3. Implementation Considerations

Figure 4 shows a processing outline for a non-networked VE. Basically, it includes components to handle three main processes: 1) Acquire user's status, 2) Update virtual world database (VWDB), 3) render images or provide other output (e.g. tactile feedback, etc.). Even in this case, when each sensor has a different sampling rate, the entire processing loop is effected by the slowest input device, as shown in Figure 4. A typical glove type input device such as the DataGlove [8] has an sampling rate of 60Hz. A 3-D position sensor [5] has a sampling rate of 30Hz, when measuring two 3-D positions (usually head position and hand position). To upgrade system performance, using shared memory is effective (Figure 5). The input process continuously acquires data from the sensors. The output process simply reads in the data from shared memory and returns the value. Simple semaphore locking can be used for shared memory control. By using this structure the system can use different cycle times for acquiring data from sensors and reading data from sensors.

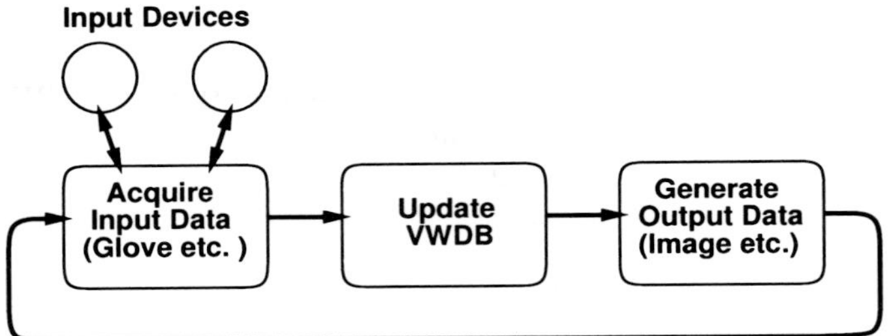

FIGURE 4. Non-networked VE processing architecture

When considering a level-3 the NVE following problem must be considered:

Consistency: Each site must share the status of the virtual world, which changes according to operations performed at multiple sites. Therefore, there must be a mechanism to maintain consistency.

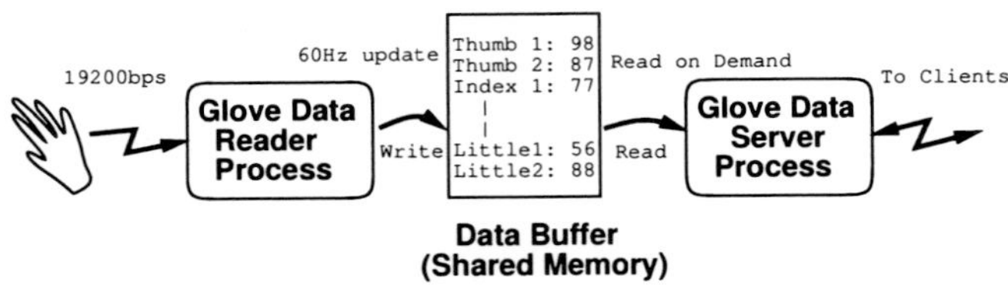

FIGURE 5. Data acquisition server architecture

The simplest way to maintain the consistency of a distributed virtual world database is to restrict manipulation, such that only one site at a time can perform operations to alter the status of the virtual world, such as grasping, rotating or translating an object. This mechanism can easily be implemented by token passing. The site that has the token is allowed to manipulate objects in the virtual world. When there is no need for manipulation, the token is passed to the next site However, this mechanism obviously narrows the possibilities of cooperative work. When N sites are used, a single site is the source of the actual operation and the other N-1 sites are present with the results of the operation.

Another way to solve this problem is assuming that an operation on one object does not interfere with an operation on another object. By making this assumption, it is possible to allow N different sites to simultaneously manipulate N different objects. The results of the operations at each site are collected at the master site and then redistributed to all sites. Our prototype system uses this method.

Mutual exclusion: If users simultaneously try to alter the status of the virtual world, contradictions may arise. For example, two users may simultaneously try to grasp the same object and translate it in different directions. These operations must be prohibited to avoid inconsistencies in the virtual world status.

Mutual exclusion to avoid simultaneous manipulation of the same object must also be incorporated. If the system has a master site at which all requests for an operation are concentrated, this can be accomplished by simply assigning a priority to each request. When two sites request an operation at the same time, the master site allows an operation by the site with the higher priority. Objects being manipulated are marked in order to prohibit manipulation by another site.

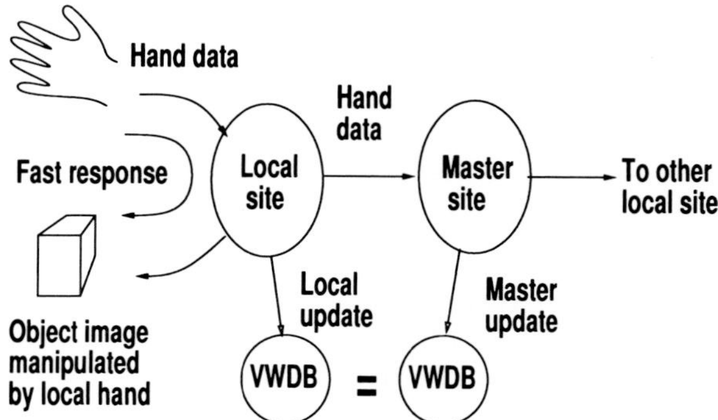

FIGURE 6. Local loop for fast response

Interactivity: In order to provide good interaction, the system must respond to users' reactions as quickly as possible. Unlike a single user system, interactivity in a cooperative work environment is affected by the time required for data transmission. Therefore, any processing that can be performed locally must be selected and implemented at each local site. Distributing redundant data to each site may significantly reduce the communication load between two sites and improve system response. In particular, the following strategies are actually used:
3-D shape data of objects in the virtual environment are distributed to each local site. A user's head position is also measured locally. Using this head position data and 3-D data, a 3-D scene can be rendered locally. Thus, a user at a local site experiences minimum delay in image generation based on one's head position.
When a user grasps an object in the virtual environment, the lag between one's hand motion and object motion is minimized by locally binding the hand position data and object position (Figure 6). At the same time, hand position data is transmitted to the master site to update the master virtual world database, the updated database of which is then distributed to other local sites. This local binding does not cause any inconsistency in the virtual world database provided that each object in the virtual world is manipulated by a single hand at any one time.

15.4. Virtual Space Teleconferencing System

Two of the systems in Figure 2 were used to implement a cooperative work environment.

This implementation structure has the following characteristics:

- Each site can rapidly generate a CG image, because a copy of the data for the image generation is distributed to each site.
- Gesture understanding and database updating are performed only by VWDBM. Therefore, it is relatively easy to implement a mutual exclusion facility, such as prohibiting two users from simultaneously grasping the same object.
- Once the "Virtual World Data Base" are distributed to each site, there is relatively little data traffic.

When the communication link between the two sites have a lag, users get slow response in their their operations. To examine the communication overhead of the prototype system, several types of measurements were made. First, Table 2 shows the communication speed between two workstations used for the prototype system. As is evident from the table, the overall rate is much better when remote procedure call (RPC) is not used. However considering the fact that using RPC makes it easy to support different types of workstations, we have used an RPC-based server-client architecture. Table 3 shows

Table 2. Measured communication throughput between two workstations

Method	TCP Protocol	UDP Protocol
With RPC	132 two-way / sec (264K byte/sec)	143 two-way /sec (285k byte/sec)
Without RPC	206 two-way / sec (411K byte/sec)	208 two-way /sec (416K byte/sec)

* 1K byte data are send/recived bwtween two IRIS340 VGX workstations using 10Mbps Ethernet. The network were shared and user by 80 workstations during the mesurement.

Table 3. System Servers

Name	Description	Data direciton and size
Tracker server	Spools and distributes data from 3-D tracker	c → s None s → c 416 byte/request
Glove server	Spools and distrbutes data from DataGlove	c → s None s → c 40 byte/request
Gesture server	Handshape-to-Gesture conversion	c → s 44 byte/request s → c 4 byte/requiest
VE server	Maintains Master VWDB for update loop when down loading VWDB for a local copy	c → s 76 byte/request s → c 12 + 326 × (No. of Sites) + 28 × (No. of Moving OBJ) Size depends on VWDB size

a list of implemented servers. Figure 7 shows the RPC relationship between severs and clients. Table 4 shows which server or client runs on which work station. Also, Table 4 shows the measured cycle time of the prototype system. Regardless of the size of the VWDB, the communication cycle times are quite stable and low enough to maintain the system's quick response time.

Using The System. Figure 8 shows two users facing each other and manipulating the CG image of a space shuttle, located between the two users. An image of the remotely located person is regenerated by computer graphics and displayed on the screen. A 70-inch CRT projector is used as an image output device for a *viewing position tracking stereoscopic display,* which is a system for measuring user eye position and generating perspective projection images based on real time measurement. A user who wears a stereo viewer and a DataGlove can directly grasp the virtual object and perform such manipulation as translation and rotation. Some of the objects in the scene are fixed and some can be moved based on the constraints given to the object.

Neither the 3-D cursor nor the computer graphics hand is displayed. The operation, locating one's hand where the object is perceived to be and grasping it, determines the target of the operation. In comparison with the method which uses an indirect pointer such as a cursor, this method is superior because it does not require users to learn how to operate cursor control devices and allows intuitive operation.

Table 4. Server distribution and system processing cycle speed

System	Servers running
IRIS 4D340VGX	VE server, gesture-server(for-all), tracker-server(for site A) , glove-server(for site A), video-lab(Facial expression detection)
IRIS Crimson/RE(site B)	VE client, glove-server(for site B), tracker-server(for site B) (Rigid face images only)
IRIS Crimson/RE(site A)	VE client (CG human image with facial expression and body motion)

Simple VWDB (Sigle cubic objects displayed)							
Site A Processing	min.	max.	ave.	Site B Processing	min.	max.	ave.
VW rendering	0ms	1ms	0.2ms	VW + face rendering	40ms	50ms	17ms
CG human image	60ms	70ms	65ms				
Communication	10ms	40ms	21ms	Communication	10ms	40ms	20ms
Total cycle time	70ms	110ms	88ms	Total cycle time	60ms	110ms	37ms

Complicated VWDB (many objects with aproximately 10,000 polygons in total)							
Site A Processing	min.	max.	ave.	Site B Processing	min.	max.	ave.
VW rendering	60ms	120ms	74ms	VW + face rendering	120ms	140ms	129ms
CG human image	60ms	200ms	83ms				
Communication	10ms	80ms	21ms	Communication	10ms	60ms	22ms
Total cycle time	140ms	300ms	181ms	Total cycle time	130ms	180ms	151ms

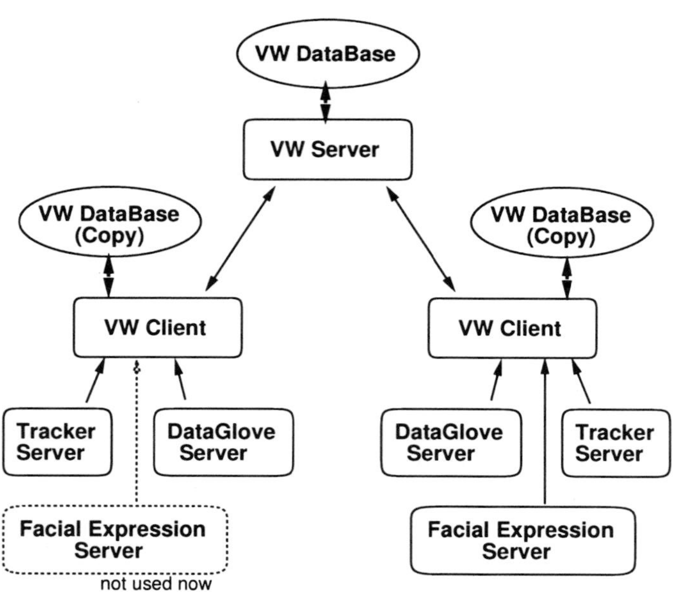

FIGURE 7. Distributed processing architecutre for the system

A 3-D model of a user at site B is constructed using a wire frame model mapped by color texture and is displayed on the 3-D screen at site A. To realize real-time detection of facial features at the site B, tape marks are attached to the facial muscles, and the marks are tracked visually. To detect movements of the head, body, hands and fingers in real-time, magnetic sensors and a DataGlove are used. When the movements of the participant are reproduced at site B, the detected results are used to drive the nodes in the wire frame model. Although CG generated human images are not rich in expressions, the image of the conference partner is nevertheless very useful and plays an important role in cooperative work.

FIGURE 8. Virtual space teleconferencing system

15.5. Summary

A teleconferencing system using a networked virtual environment is described. Implementation issues of the networked virtual environments are discussed. Specific design criteria of the system, such as concurrency and interactivity control have also been described. A prototype of a *Virtual Space Teleconferencing System* is implemented based on the above considerations. By distributing redundant data to each local site, the data traffic between two sites is relatively light. However, the implementation limits the operation of virtual objects. To give a more free interaction to the user will be the next step of our approach.

Acknowledgments

The authors wish to thank Dr. N. Terashima - President of ATR Communication Systems Research Laboratories, and Dr. K. Habara - Executive Vice President of ATR International (Chairman of the Board of ATR Communication Systems Research Laboratories), for their thoughtful advice and encouragement on this research. The authors also wish to thank their colleagues who voluntarily took part in discussing this study.

References

1. Christpher Codella, Reza Jalili, et al. Interactive simulation in a multi-person virtual world. In *CHI '92 Proceedings*, pages 329–334. ACM Press, 1992. Monterlay.
2. Koichi Ishibuchi, Haruo Takemura, and Fumio Kishino. Real time hand shape recognition and its application for man-machine interface (in japanese). In *Proceedings of IEICE conference 1991 Autumn*. Institute of Electronics, Information and Communication Engineers, 1991.
3. Hiroshi Ishii and Nahomi Miyake. Toward an open shared workspace. *Communications of the ACM*, 34(12), December 1991.
4. Fumio Kishino. Communication with realistic sensation(in japanese). *3-D image*, 4(2), 1990.
5. F.H. Raab, E.B. Blood, T.O. Steiner, and Jones H.R. Magnetic position and orientation tracking system. *IEEE Trans. on Aerospace and Electronics system*, AES-15(5):709–718, 1979.
6. Haruo Takemura, Akira Tomono, and Fumio Kishino. A usability study of virtual environment. In *Proceedings of the 6th Human Interface Symposium*, pages 577–582. The Society of Instrument and Control Engineers, 1990. Tokyo.
7. Haruo Takemura, Akira Tomono, and Yukio Kobayashi. A study of human computer interaction via stereoscopic display. In *Proceedings of HCI '89*, pages 496–503. Elsevier Science Publishers, 1989. Boston.
8. T.G. Zimmerman and J. Lanier. A hand gesture interface device. In *CHI+GI '87 Proceedings*, pages 189–192. ACM Press, 1987.

16. Real Time Image Processing and Real Time Image Rendering for Televirtuality Application

Philippe Quéau
Instutut National de l'Audiovisuel, 4, Avenue de l'Europe, 94366, Bry-sur-Marne, France (e-mail: phil@ina.fr)

Summary.
Televirtuality is a concept expressing the merging of telecommunications and computer graphics. This technique allows the creation of "virtual communities" based on networked virtual worlds and virtual agents. These "agents" or "clones" are 3D computer generated images of the real persons involved in the network communication . This paper will adress the key issue of the development of an efficient interface between the real world scenery and its virtual equivalent, and more precisely the real time analysis of human body and its translation into computer generated models.
Key words: Televirtuality, virtual communities, real time image processing, facial synthesis.

16.1. Introduction

Televirtuality allows interactive computer images to be distributed on commuted narrow band networks (ISDN network at 64 kbits / sec or even the telephone network in certain cases), endowed with all the functional possibilities of computer graphics images. The relatively low cost of televirtuality is due to the fact that it is not the images themselves that are transmitted, but just the symbolic data required for their synthesis by the terminal with which communication has been established. Contrary to wide band networks (optical fiber, coaxial cable), which transmit the raw images (characteristically tens of millions of octets per second), televirtuality networks merely transmit the essential information. All the intelligence is in the terminals which must regenerate the image thanks to models they already possess, and symbolic data received in real time.

This new approach gives rise to two main consequences. On the one hand, it is henceforth possible to communicate in real time with quality "images" on inexpensive telecommunications networks. On the other hand, the functional possibilities of computer graphics work stations can be exploited to create "virtual" work spaces, sites of symbolic encounters allowing spatially and possibly temporally remote dialogue, by ensuring one's representation via synthetic clones, in other words, computer generated puppets abstractly or realistically representing each collaborator's "viewpoint". It is thus possible in Paris to comment with a Tokyo based colleague on the possible evolution of a carcinogenic tumor in keeping with various treatment options, to manipulate protein structure or to jointly sculpt a panel body model. The impact of televirtuality in the office environment will also be considerable. The representation of numeric data can but benefit from the passage to interactive, three-dimensional images.

16.2. Analysis an Suntesis of "Clone"

On of the most obvious lines of research followed up by televirtuality aims to give the most convincing illusion of a veritable picturephone conference. Televirtuality can serve as a backup to standard teleconference links, or even replace them completely, given the economic advantages, if a new cultural attitude makes this possible and "natural". Indeed, accepting on's representation by a computer-generated clone no doubt calls for evolution of habits regarding one's self-image. Nevertheless, it is already predictable that these virtual clones will become increasingly "realistic", thanks to computer graphics advances in fields like real-time texturing. Leading-edge research, notably that undertaken by the Japanese in NTT Laboratories and above all, in the ATR Communication Systems Research Laboratories consortium, has already developed the processing chain necessary for pseudo-realistic televirtuality applications. First, expression of the real speaker's face is analyzed using powerful image processing techniques based on optical flow analysis. Automatic extraction of characteristic facial features is thus possible, i.e., the labial commissures, the tip of the chin, the corner of the eyes, cheekbone position, etc. With the aid of these characteristic points analyzed in real time, it is possible to generate and animate a 3D computer face in wire-frame, i.e., structurally equivalent form. This face previously memorized data, which match the real face analyzed. Certain machines are already able to effect real-time grafting of various "photorealistic" textural elements corresponding to a real face onto the synthetic structure miming it, while faithfully adhering to expressions of the live person.

Televirtuality allows the creation of virtual environments that can be shared by multiple participants, linked up via a narrow bandpass telecommunications network. Indeed, as stated above, only the data necessary for generating images or ensuring their realtime update from the same database are in fact transmitted. This base is common to several workstations, capable of permanently regenerating a virtual universe that can be shared by several protagonists engaged in virtual communication. The problem of "compatibility" of the participants various representations and virtual viewpoints is thus raised. Contrary to objective reality, virtual spaces allow the coexistence of multiple competing realities, of different "visions of the world" associated with each participant.

16.3. Virtual Communities

The concept of televirtuality can be generalized with the notion of virtual communities [1] . Numerous individual virtual environments are thus "connected" to each other and "shared" by all network members. Low flow telematics networks, or even the standard telephone network, are the perfect vehicle for creating such virtual communities; the electronic mail and French Minitel systems constitute alphanumeric prefigurations of this type of network.

The Habitat project set up in 1985 by Lucasfilm Games in association with Quantum Computer Services in the San Francisco region was the first to create a multiple participant environment. Several thousands pf players represented as 2D "Avatars" were able to meet up in a virtual world for a kind of gigantic role-playing game, potentially lasting for years, based on graphics computers displaying the action as it evolved.

The Habitat experience did not seek to emphazise "rendering" but rather participants' group behavior, hence the pursuit of common ends. One of the lessons of this experiment was heightened awareness regarding notions of spaces of collaboration. These collective, symbolic spaces were continuously built up by various "objects" the Avatars procured or exchanged in view of a common aim, for example, to unravel the mystery surrounding several particularly impemetrable Habitat regions.

The future "virtual" Minitel displaying virtual 3D computer graphics and calling on televirtuality techniques will allow the transmission of virtual messenger services, where other people can be encountered by adopting a realistic or imaginary synthetic "virtual body". Communication with other people linked to the virtual messenger service will take place via the voice, gesture, bodily attitudes and facial expressions of the virtual alias representing each participant.

16.4. The "Cluny" Televirtuality Experiment

During the IMAGINA'93 session devoted to "televirtuality", a groundbreaking televirtuality experiment has been organized on the initiative of INA. Several partners have joined forces for this operation : Medialab for the synthesis of virtual images and real-time management of interactions with the database, IBM for providing the database representing a reconstitution of the Cluny Abbey, France Telecom for NUMERIS links between Paris and Monte

[1] P. QUÉAU. *Le Virtuel: Vertus et Vertiges*, Champ Vallon, Seyssel (1993)

Carlo, and Silicon Graphics for making graphic calculators available. The operation has also received the backing of the Ministry of National Education and Culture.

Two participants wearing stereographic display helmets and located respectively in Paris and Monte Carlo, have "virtually" met up in the Cluny Abbey. They were able to talk to each other, wander through the abbey together, and point out architectural details.

Two other televirtuality experiments have also been organized. ZKM from Karlsruhe has presented a "Televirtual Chit-Chat" between Karlsruhe and Monte Carlo. INA has presented a demonstration of televirtual "Tangram" between Bry-sur-Marne and Monte Carlo.

The object of the televirtuality link between Paris and Monte Carlo was to illustrate the concept of televirtuality by an experiment combining immersion in a virtual world and communication via a standard digital network. The experiment shows two users linked to the Numeris communications network can evolve and interact in a given virtual environment.

The two users could see each other through their representation in the shared universe. They perceived this universe on the screens of a stereoscopic helmet fitted with position tracking sensors, enhancing the impression of immersion. They could hear each other thanks to a parallel telephone link, and move around in this universe with a 3D mouse.

Two Silicon Graphics 440 VGXT machines were available for the experiment. These two machines were connected to the Numeris network by a series link. On each machine, a program developed at Medialab [2] ensured the representation of worlds, and management of interactions and communication. This program called PORC (Puppets Orchestrated in Real time by Computer) calculates and displays the image of the world as a local observer sees it at a rate of not less than 10 frames per second. User interactions with the scene are transmitted to the program by the intermediary of input/output peripherals on the machines (3D mouse, position trackers, etc.) exchange information concerning the two users (current position, direction of gaze, status of the input/ output peripherals solicited, etc.), and information concerning the actual scene (attributes of the constituent objects, etc.).

Choice of this configuration ensures that information transmitted on the Numeris network represents a low data volume and can be exchanged sufficiently fast to comply with the constraints of real time (for this application, these constraints are characterized by response time of about a tenth of a second). For examble, 100 inventories of 4 octets are exchanged at a rate of 20 times per second on the Numeris network, at 64 kbits / sec.

---

[2] H. Tardif, Character animation in real time. *Proceeding of SIGGRAPH'91*, Las Vegas, NV (1991)

16.5. Towards a General Real Time Analysis / Synthesis Televirtuality System

The concept of televirtuality has many potential applications . Its main strong points are twofold: the very cheap coding system and the possibility for numerous participants to share a virtual environment, be it "realistic" (a factory, a brain...) or "symbolic" or "imaginary" (artistic and games environments, abstract informations...) and to allow the virtual community of agents to "fly" freely among the virtual world, and to interact with it.

Although the animation of virtual clones is no longer just a dream, current drawbacks limit possible applications (contact device, sensor, head immobilization in front of the camera, etc.).

At the Televirtuality Laboratory of INA, we are currently developing a real-time facial animation analysis/synthesis chain which imposes few constraints. This study has been elaborated for a televirtuality context: several physically distant persons intervene in a common virtual environment via their synthetic representatives. They are thus able to share a virtual community, enter a virtual visiophone, follow a visioconference, access telework operations, or even join in multiparticipant game.

The system can be broken down as follows:

(a) Video input
(b) Real image analysis: extraction of characteristic parameters
(c) Symbolic interpretation of parameters
(d) Transfer of these parameters to a remote machine
(e) Animation of the symbolic or realistic computer graphics clone
(f) Video output

The video image processing is designed to extract real control parameters. This chiefly consists of identifying head movements and mouth deformations.

For the realistic model, parameters corresponding to facial muscle movements derived from the analysis are interpreted in terms of muscular intensity.

Only parameters necessary for synthesis of the clone image are transmitted via the network or telephone line.

The computer graphics clone may be either symbolic, in which case it is based on a geometric model, or realistic, in which case it is endowed with a muscular basis. In the latter case, the facial surface is represented by a network of springs. Each muscle is modeled by forces, and muscular deformations are calculated by solving dynamic equations for the given system (face/force). The muscular deformations are then precalculated to obtain a system capable of real-time evolution. Finally, facial texture is mapped onto the polygonal representation of the face.

FIGURE 1. The Cluny Abbey Televirtuality Experiment at IMAGINA'93, ©IMAGINA

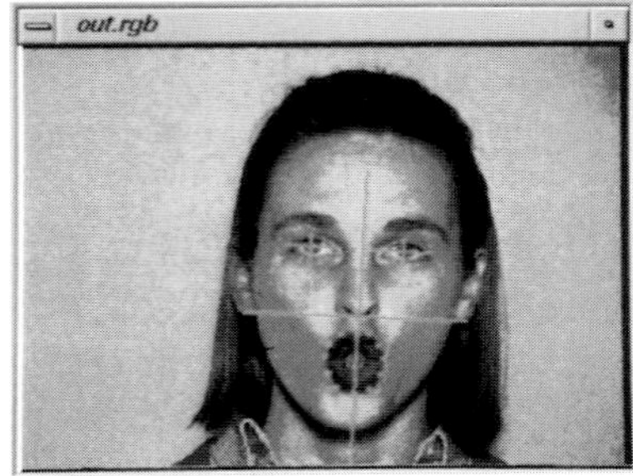

FIGURE 2. Real Time Facial Characteristics Extraction, ©Project Televirtuality, INA

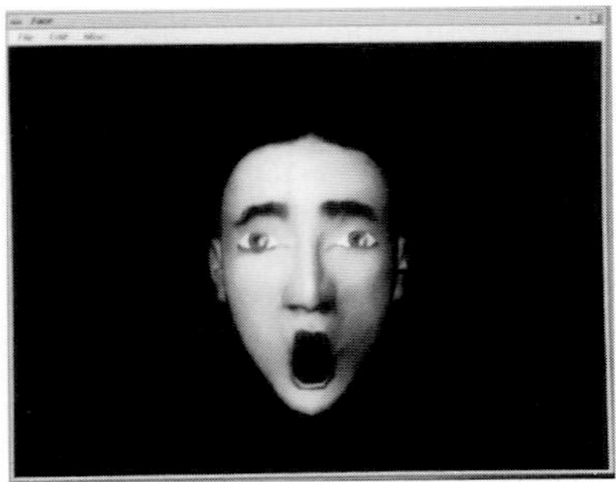

FIGURE 3. Real Time Facial Synthesis, ©Project Televirtuality, INA

Theme 5

Synthetic Perception

17. Towards a Complete Representation by Means of Computer – The Instrumental Communication Interface Concept –

Annie Luciani, Claude Cadoz and Jean Loup Florens
Association pour la Création et la Recherche, sur les Outils d'Expression, Laboratoire d'Informatique Fondamentale et d'Intelligence Artificielle, INPG -46 av. Félix Viallet 38031 Grenoble Cedex, France (e-mail:luciani@lifia.imag.fr)

Summary.

This paper deals with a project in progress called I.C.I. - Instrumental Communication Interface. This project is supported by the IMAG Institute, which is the Grenoble Computer Science Institute, and by the French Ministère de la Culture. Two of its major aims are artistic creation and man-machine Communication. We will discuss about the fundamental motivation of this new way of communicating and creating with computers, that is the concept of Complete Representation. We will present our technological developments of ICI and our scientific and artistic results: the physical modelling of objects, the force feedback gestural transducers, the real time simulation allowing the user to act on a physically simulated object and to perceive it by its synthetic visual, acoustic and tactilo-proprio-kinesthetic behaviours.

Note: A video tape containing all the concepts and the experiments described in the paper is available at the ACROE laboratory.

Key words: Image synthesis, Sound synthesis, Physical models, Animation, Force feedback, Gestural feeling, Virtual Realities, Virtual Worlds

17.1. The Concept of "Complete Representation"

The term of Virtual Realities, or Artificial Realities, is interesting but it does not represent the contemporary deep evolution, due to the computer, in our representation tools.

We believe that what is happening now in the field of computer uses cannot be fully rendered by the term of Virtual Realities.

As a matter of fact, the virtual as well as the realistic, are not a product of contemporary technologies. Our only way to access reality has been through "virtualities", through "images": those produced by our senses, to begin with retinian and cochlear images, and those produced by the various observations and representation tools made by man such as telescopes, microscopes, microphones.

For us, the term of representation is stronger than virtuality because we always communicate, understand, create, through virtualities, (more generally, representations).

What is happening today is a new stage of the evolution of our means of representation but with an unprecedented speed and depth.

The breakthrough is that the representations can be "total", "complete". What is new is not in the term "virtualities", nor in the term " realism", nor in the term "representation", but in the term "complete": we can see and hear these representations; but also, we can touch them. In addition, they can be dynamic, and even varying themselves; finally, they can act directly on man or on the natural universe.

We have now at our disposal the basis of a kind of general "acting language"; general in the sense that it is independant of the perceptual modalities but it can produce all of them: visual, acoustic, and gestural perceptions, and it can receive our gestural actions.

We think that this evolution -this "acting language" or "total representation"- is equivalent to the birth of writing.

This new computer representation tool is characterized by three aspects:

Make all the signified sensitive. In the past, symbolic representations were to be distinguished from the representations capable of addressing perception. Today it is possible to generalize and make sensitive entities that are a priori not sensitive. The computer appears as a universal tool for sensitive representation.

A multisensorial representation. For the first time, the sensitive representations produced are multisensorial. In the past, images and sounds were on separate supports and were processed independently. Today, the signifier appeals to several sensorial modalities at the same time: sight, hearing, tactilo-proprio-kinesthetic perceptions. As a matter of fact, until now, our senses have been considered as compartmentalized. Each separate sensorial modality can be used in man-computer interfaces. The tools for the use of each of them are available, and in multimedia tools, they are superimposed, with a specific process for each one. We can now take one further step forward and speak of multisensoriality. The perceptual system is a global system in which various modalities collaborate and, even though they can be distinguished, the whole is more than the sum of the components. Multisensoriality and multisensorial synthesis can and must be considered as a whole. And thus the usual communication media (either the sound or the visual signals) can be replaced by a supramodal entity that is none of the three main modalities (sight, hearing, and touch) but can produce all of them, providing consistant correlation between the three communication signals. Thus it is possible to produce synthetic sounds, images, and gestural signals that are not juxtaposed but correlated in a genuine manner. The objective is to obtain a greater authenticity of the representation and a greater efficiency of action.

The last characteristic of this multisensorial representation is the rise of gestures as a full modality. Historically, sound synthesis for auditive perceptive modality appeared first, then appeared image synthesis for the visual perceptive modality. Both are merely sensorial modalities. Gesture is a sensorimotor modality. Action is necessary for perception. This requires transducers that are technologically more difficult to design and build because they must couple motors and sensors, they are multidimensionnal and they convey energy. These are the reasons why gesture was introduced in computers after sound and image synthesis.

A behavioural representation. An image, a photograph or a sound are only phenomenological events. And only visible or acoustic information are printed on a film or a magnetic tape. All that is connected to their potential transformations and interactions with other objects or with human beings is lost. This is why it is impossible to have a gestural perception of an object only represented by a visual image. Today, what can be synthesized and represented is a multimodal entity, that is the physical object underlying our perceptions. And, precisely because it is physical, this physical object can produce the consistant signals stimulating the perceptions. Only physical objects produce perceptions. This is the reason why physical modelling is the next step after visual, acoustic and geometric modelling. This physical model is the supramodal entity that we introduced before.

17.2. Acting with Feeling

The Force Feedback Principle. In the natural perception-action situation, objects are not only perceived by the user by sight and hearing. In the same time that we are acting on an object, we are feeling it by our proprio- tactilo-kinesthetic perception. The specificity of the proprio-tactilo-kinesthetic channel -called in this paper in an abbreviate form "the gestural channel"- is to be a sensori-motor channel. The visual and acoustic sensorial channels convey a specific modality of perception which is the exteroception and they are essentially only perceptive channels. On the contrary, the gestural channel combines actions and proprioceptions. To gesturally perceive objects, you can touch and act on them. One consequence is that the gestural channel is not only a channel which conveys information but it conveys also energy. The user will be informed of the object's behaviour if he displaces or deforms it, in other words, if he spends physical energy.

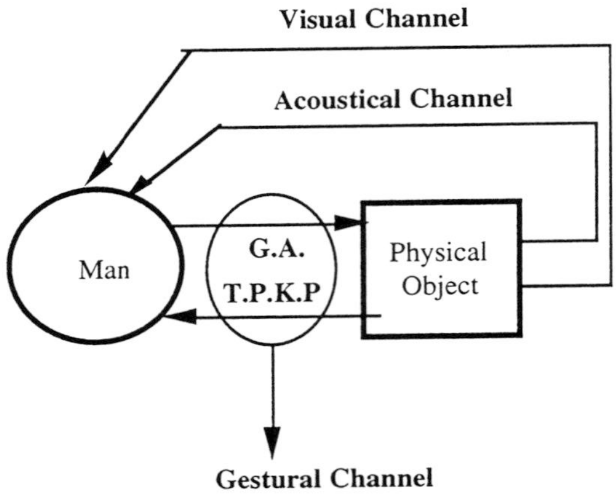

FIGURE 1. The natural intrumental communication. The gestural channel is a sensorimotor communication channel

Let us call "intrumental gestures" the gestures applied on an instrument. These gestures are defined by the physical parameters exchanged between the operator and the objects, such as velocities, displacements and forces.

In a computer context, the device which will convey the instrumental gesture must combine in a specific mechanical structure, sensors and motor organs. Sensors have to capture the physical parameters of the instrumental gestures. Motors have to produce signals conveying the proprio-tactilo-kinesthetic perceptions, enabling the actual fingering of the instrument to be synthesized. According to general considerations on physical systems, there are two dual ways to support gestural computer communication: the sensors can be displacement sensors and then the motors will provide forces, and vice-versa, the sensors can produce forces and then motors will then produce positions. Speeds and accelerations can be calculated from displacements. The first case concerns the force feedback concept and the adequate computer tranducers are the force feedback gestural transducers.

To synthesize gestural perceptions, the forces produced from a simulated physical object are sensed by the user through the force feedback gestural transducers. To have a genuine sensation of the physical existence of the object through gestural perception, the input positions representing the actions and the output forces, representing the response behaviour of the object must be correlated in accordance with specific dynamic contraints. One of these major constraints is a temporal constraint: to have the sensation of a hard collision between hand and a rigid object, the bandwith of the input-output loop must be at least 1 kilohertz and it is also the bandwith needed to restitute a dry friction between a simulated rough surface and a human finger.

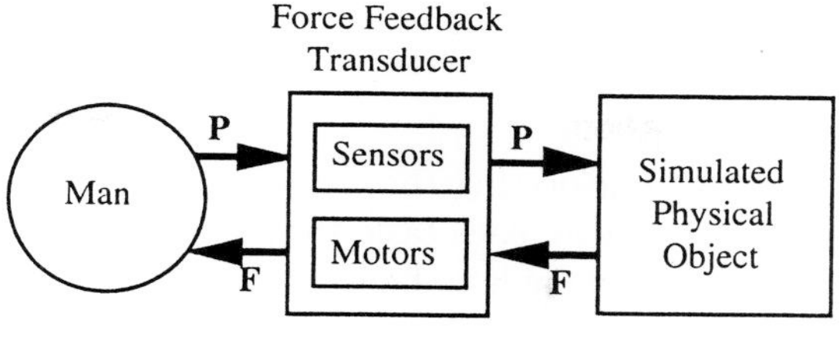

FIGURE 2. The force feedback principle and the force feedback transducer

The ACROE force feedback gestural transducers. ACROE has introduced in 1978 the force feedback principle in a computer sound synthesis context [3]. Its first force feedback prototype was a 1D stick performing large scale displacements (50 cm), large feedback force (60N peak) with high dynamic performance (at least 1kHz). With this device and an analog computer, we realized some experiments, as for instance a highly rigid virtual wall or a highly realistic rack rail with hard notches and holes. The second step of ACROE was in the obtention of compacity [4]. The second prototype had the same dynamic characteristics but in a smaller size, about 15cm*15cm*20cm. Our last prototype [7] -called CRM as Force Feedback Modular Keyboard ("Clavier Rétroactif Modulaire" in french)- has about the same range of dynamic characteristics but in the same range of size, it has sixteen degrees of freedom. The breakthrough is simultaneous in compacity, versatility of the external morphology and in the high number of degrees of freedom. An international licence covers its modularity principles as well as its motor technology, specially developed to achieve the today's desired performances.

The three contemporary challenges for force feedback gestural transducers are:

- Compacity: the size of the device must enable its use in interactive computer workstations and not only in industrial offices. The technological problem is then that, as the intensity of the feedback force is correlated with the size of the eletromechanical components, how can we have a high feedback force in a small bulk?
- Modularity: The human physical system -fingers, hands, arms and body- is a deformable system able to present a great number of configurations. In consequence, gestural tasks require various configurations of the instrument, in terms of number of degrees of freedom as well as in terms of their assembly and the geometry of the device. How can we have the most versatile device morphology?
- Dynamic behaviour: feeling a rigid object during a hard collision or feeling the gestural texture of a surface when we move on it, requires about 1 kHz

bandwith for the input-output loop of the gestural signals. How can we obtain this dynamical properties with the force amplitude and the modularity given before?

There are two ways of answering these questions: the first is to design a specific force feedback device for each task, the second is to design elementary electromechanical components able to be assembled. That is the choice made for the CRM device.

The CRM device is built from two basic components: the sliced sensor-motor module and the covering. The sliced sensor-motor module is composed of one displacement sensor, one flat mobile coil and one flat magnet. The slice is sized according to a piano or alphanumeric keyboard key thickness (about 1,5 cm large). All the coils are independent. The internal friction force and the mass of the coil are low, achieving good dynamic performances. A high electromechanical power is obtained thanks to the addition of the magnetic fields of each module. Various mechanical coverings can be mounted on the coil axes providing various external morphologies. We mounted three kinds of coverings: a piano keyboard, a 1D stick, a 2D stick (see photograph 1).

Gestural feeling experiments. An important research field is to try to restitute gestural feeling in a computer context [1], [2], [8], [9]. One of the first experiment we carried out was the restitution of feeling between a finger and a rough surface. The rigid surface and the dry friction between the surface and the manipulation point has been physically modelled and implemented in our real time simulator. For this experiment, the CRM has been equipped with a 2D stick covering. In a first step, the user does not touch the surface. He goes towards the surface and feels the hard collisions between his finger and the rigid surface. His finger cannot penetrate into the simulated surface. Afterwards the finger moves on the simulated surface and feels the dry adherence. The greater the pressure is, the more the surface is adherent causing rough sliding.

17.3. Gestures and Sounds

All physical objects are deformable objects, even if the deformations are not perceptive. Some deformations are perceptible by gestural perception, others by sight, others by hearing. Others are perceptible only by their consequences, such as fractures.

By means of physical modelling, all the deformations of objects can be reproduced, whether they are visual gestural or acousic deformations. Sounds can be considered as the acoustic perceptible effect of a physical deformation of a physical object caused by external forces or displacements. These forces can be either natural forces, or artificial forces produced by manufactured motors, or human forces. The case of human physical intervention is probably the more subtle type of the instrumental relationship between a man and a physical object. Can we imagine to produce such complex information as a cello timbra variation without such a complex physical phenomenon as a precise dry friction well controlled by a human complete gesture?

With the CRM and physical modelling, we have reproduced the situation of a cello play (gesture and sound) [10]. The string and the dry bowed friction between the gestural transducer and the string is simulated by a physically based model. The user manipulates the force feedback stick, built from the CRM force feedback device. He bowes the string and the friction produces acoustical deformations producing the sound of a cello. The player feels the friction and the pressure on the string. The experiment proves that without force feedback, we cannot play cello. Without collision and contact perception, the player presses too hard on the string, such as a bad player causing very hard saturation and deformation. Without the feeling of the friction, the player cannot control the relation between the velocity and the pressure of the bow causing unpleasant creakings.

The technical questions raised by these experiments are:

(a) To have a sufficient restitution of the gestural perception, the input displacements -Force output loop- must run at 1kHz per degree of freedom. It is very high in comparison with current works in force feedback and it needs specific computers and computer architectures.
(b) The simulation of the rough surface or the string with dry friction must run at 44,1 kHz to produce sounds, which is the bandwith of acoustic deformations.
(c) The real time synchronization process between the gestural loop and the simulated scene is highly dependent on temporal constraints such as the delay between the gestural samples and the related acoustic deformation samples. This delay must not exceed 1 ms.

17.4. Gestures and Images

As said before, movements can be produced by various kinds of forces applied on physical objects. Motions in animated pictures are only the perceptible deformations of physical objects. These external forces can be gravity, wind, turbulences but they can be human gestures as in the marionette paradigm. In the first case, the animator tries to control motions by means of control parameters. In the second case, it is the gestures themselves, in others words, the cause of the motions, which is the way to control the motions. In this way, we can introduce in computer animation, the concept of Instrumental Playing and as in the marionette paradigm or in the musical situation, the concept of performance animation. In this case, the physical object has two roles: firstly, it produces the animated images and secondly, it plays the role of an intrument which transforms the human gestures in images in motion.

Photograph 1 shows a physically based model of a plastic paste [12]. Firstly, this paste has physical properties of plasticity and fractures. Secondly, the animator kneads the paste by means of two force feedback sticks. He can give a shape to the paste. He can break it and stick it back. During the gestural action, he feels the physical resistance of the paste. The gestural input-outputs are sampled at 1 kHz which is also the calculation step of the simulation of the plastic paste.

Having force feedback gestures, having physical modelling for acoustic deformations, having physical visual deformations, with a synchronization process which respects the temporal constraints working on the complete physical object, we modelled multisensorial physically- based objects [?].

17.5. Physically Based Models

As the aim is also to have a large variety of simulated physically-based icons, we have designed since 1984 a computer formalism, called the CORDIS-ANIMA system [4], [5], [14], [11], which combines a physically based modeller and a physically based real time simulator.

The fundamental choices of this modeller-simulator is the particle physics paradigm, based on the physical interactions between punctual masses. In this formalism, a physical object or a set of objects are modelled and simulated in real time as a set of punctual masses linked by centered interaction chains. The most basic ones are linear elasticity and viscosity combined by finite state automata processes, allowing the description of any kind of non-linear interactions. Between masses, interactions can be put in parallel, and the conjunction of these two functionalities allows the creation of very complex interactions. By these means, we can create any kind of deformable materials (rigid, elastic, plastic, friable...), of complex materials (pastes, soils, woods, metals, sand, muds ...) and of complex object assemblies (articulated objects, collisions, dry friction, adherence, sticking...)[12]. With the choice of punctual physics, an object or a scene is calculated as a great number of few simple algorithms able to run in parallel performing real time simulation. Any physical object or set of objects is represented by a network composed of two kinds of components: the mass component and the interaction-without-mass component (Figure 3).

With this modeller-simulator, we have modelled different kinds of physical objects, different kinds of physical interactions between objects, but also physically-based models of non- physical objects -called physically-based metaphores- such as physically based menus and widgets with force feedback pointing, moving and grasping.

Photograph 2a and 2b show a physically based model of a dynamic dune of sand[16]. The simulation restitutes the dynamical behaviour of fine granular material with avalanches and internal collapses. In the same way, photograph 3a and 3b show a physically based model of piles of rocks with structured

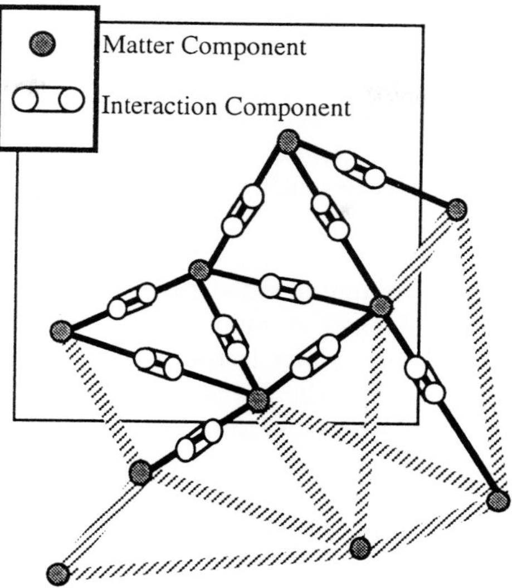

FIGURE 3. A Cordis-Anima network. The grey component is the matter component and the white component is the interaction-without-mass component.

avalanches. Photograph 4a and 4b show the deformations of a physically based model of a surface of water on which pebbles are thrown.

17.6. Physically Based Icons

Computer widgets can be represented, not only visually but also physically. This is done by giving them a weight, a resistance to displacements, attractive behaviour... The gestural feeling unloads the visual perception and this permits to have more complex man-computer interfaces. The CRM device has been used in man-machine interface to physically point, pick and grasp physically based widgets. Photograph 6 shows physically-based widgets handled by means of the CRM force feedback gestural device. The operator gesturally feels the limits of the window. He finds the paper basket, located on the lower right corner, without seeing it (the paper basket is not visualized). He feels the frontiers when he changes the menu areas. The use of the physical modelling and the force feedback interaction improves the pointing and the moving and simultaneously relieves the visual activity of the user.

17.7. Conclusions

The I.C.I. has a specific position in the field of Virtual Realities [13]. It represents the vis-à-vis type of interaction with virtual worlds, in which virtuality is a modality of reality. On the contrary, the immersion paradigm tries to completely replace the real world by a synthetic world, breaking down natural perceptions. But the sense of evidence of a virtual object cannot only be achieved by the realism of the images. The gestural perception is an essential component of world's realism. And if we equip men with gestural force feedback transducers, we alter very much their natural skills. Probably the skill of the "immerged man" will decrease, reducing the interest of the immersive situations. On the contrary, it is a very interesting perspective for us to use all our skills in complex computer aided tasks with all the simulation and representation tools and all the communication media mentioned above. For us the first important acquired fact is the necessity of tools that be more capable of communicating than the previous tools, particularly on the same modalities, that are perceptive modalities. The second important point is the rise of the instrumental communication as a complementary mode of communication next to the symbolic more usual computer communication. All human activities proceed probably from both. For us, artistic creation such as music is the best example.

Note: The works presented here and the patent of the CRM are supported by the french MINISTERE de la CULTURE

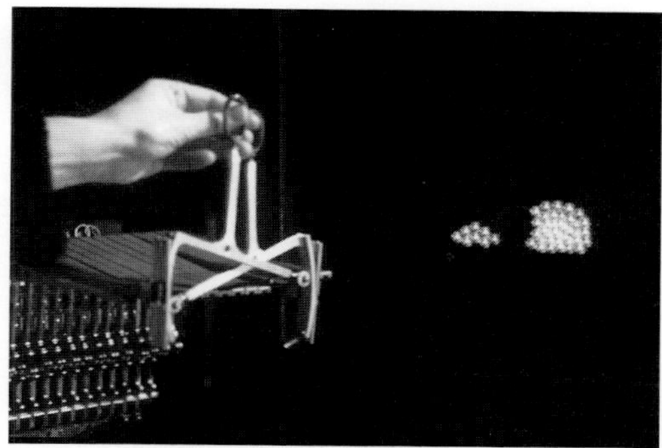

Photograph 1 - Real time kneading a simulated plastic paste with gestural feeling

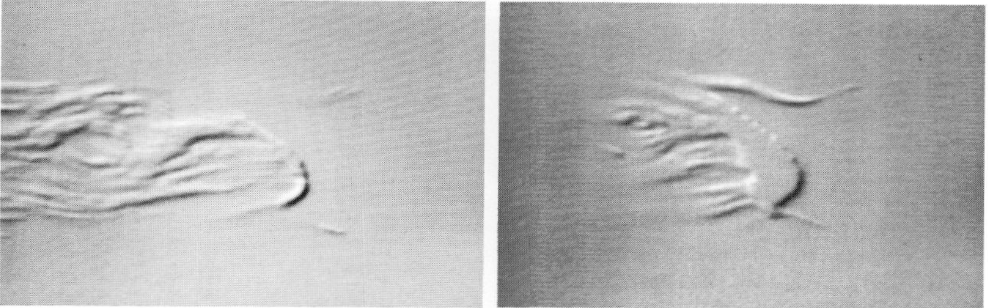

Photograph 2a & 2b - Physically-based animation of fine sand dunes

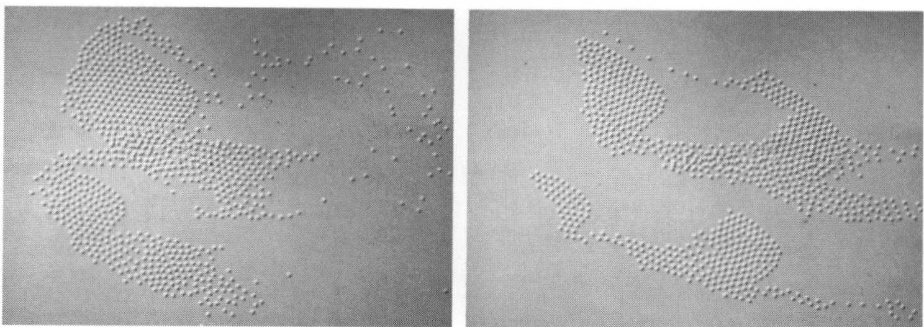

Photograph 3a & 3b - Physically-based animation of piles of small rocks

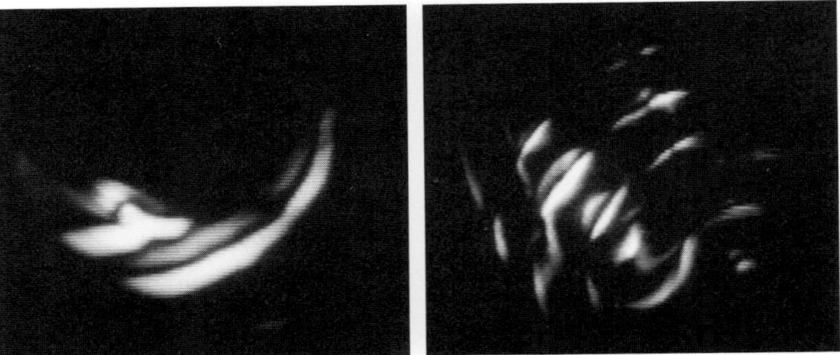

Photograph 4a & 4b - Physically-based animation of a surface of water

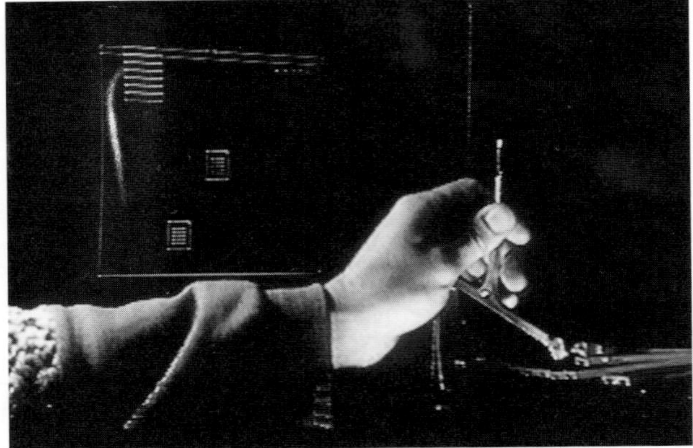

Photograph 5 - The ICI in man-machine symbolic interaction - The wigdets are physically based models and the user feels them gesturally.

References

1. Batter, J.J., Brooks, F.P., Jr. 'GROPE-I - A computer display to the sense of feel', Information Processing, Proc. IFIP Congress 71, 1971, 759-763.
2. Atkinson, W.D., Bond, K.E.,Tribble, G.L., Wilson, K.R. 'Computing with feeling', Comput. and Graphics, 1977, 2.
3. Florens, JL, 'Coupleur gestuel rétroactif pour la commande et le contrôle de sons synthétisés', PhD Thesis, 1978, INPG-Grenoble.
4. Cadoz, C., Luciani, A., Florens, J.L. 'Responsive input devices and sound synthesis by simulation of instrumental mecanisms: the CORDIS system', Jour. of Computer Music, Vol 8, No 3, 1984
5. Luciani, A., Cadoz C., "Modélisation et animation gestuelle d'objets: le système ANIMA", CESTA, Actes du 1er Colloque Image, 1984
6. Boff, K, Kaufman, L, Thomas, J, "Handbook of Human Perception and Human Performance", 1986, Ed John Wiley and sons, N.Y..
7. Cadoz, C, Lisowski, L., Florens, J.L. ' Modular Retroactive Keyboard', Computer Music Journal , 1990, 14(2).

8. Brooks, F.P., Ouh-Young, M., Batter, J.J., Kilpatrick, J. 'Project GROPE ; Haptic Displays for Scientific Visualization', Computer Graphics, 1990, 24, No 4.
9. Minsky, M, Ouh-young, M, Steele, O, Brooks FP, Behenski, M, 'Feeling and seeing: issues in force display', Computer Graphics, 1990, 24(2).
10. Florens, JL., Cadoz, C., 'Modéles et simulations en temps réel de cordes frottées' 1er Congrés Français d'Acoustique - SFA - Editions de Physique - Lyon Avril 1990.
11. Luciani, A, Jimenez, S, Cadoz, C, Florens, JL, Raoult, O 'Computational Physics: A Modeler-Simulator for Animated Physical Objects', Proceedings of Eurographics Conference, 1991, Vienna, Austria.
12. Luciani, A, Jimenez, S, Raoult, O, Cadoz, C, Florens, JL, 'An unified view of multitude behaviour, flexibility, plasticity and fractures: balls, bubbles and agglomerates' - Modeling in Computer Graphics, 1991, 54-74, Springer Verlag Ed.
13. Rheingold, H, Virtual Reality, 1991, Secker & Warburg Ed.
14. Cadoz, C., Luciani, A., Florens, J.L. 'CORDIS-ANIMA: A Modeling and Simulation System for Sound and Image Synthesis - The General Formalism', Computer Music Journal, 1993,10(1), 19-29, M.I.T. Press. Reprint of Proceedings of Physical Modelling, Musical Creation and Computer, MSH France 1990
15. Uhl, C., Florens, J.L., Luciani, A., Cadoz, C. 'Hardware Architecture of a Real Time Simulator for the Cordis-Anima System: Physical Models, Images, Gestures and Sounds', Proc. of Computer Graphics International '95, 1995, Academic Press. - RA Ernshaw & JA Vince Ed., 421-436.
16. Luciani, A., Habibi, A., Manzotti, E. 'A Multi-scale Physical Models of Granular Materials', Proc. of Graphics Interface '95, 1995, pp.136-146.

18. Virtual Space Decision Support System Using Kansei Engineering

Junji Nomura, Kayo Imamura and Noriko Enomoto
Matsushita Elecric Works, Ltd, Osaka 571, Japan

Mitsuo Nagamachi
Department Of Industrial & Systems Engineering, Hiroshima University, Higashi-Hiroshima 724, Japan

Summary.
A new paradigm for relationship between humans and computers has been called artificial reality, virtual reality or cyberspace. Using three-dimensional computer graphics, interactive devices, and high-resolution display, a virtual world can be realized in which one can pick up imaginary objects as if they were physical world. Using this technology and Kansei Engineering, Virtual Space Decision Support System has been developing in Matsushita Electric Works. Kansei Engineering is defined as a "translation system of a customer's favorite or image into real design components "(Nagamachi, 1986) can be used for the customers to design furniture which just they image and experience them in virtual space. And in future, it will be able to deal with whole of house, then customers can design their house and check the housing performances such a light, sound, vibration, temperature, air and living-space amenity. This paper details Kansei Engineering and Virtual Space Decision Support System.

18.1. Introduction

The changing needs and values of today's consumer has had a significant impact on the the sales and manufacturing process. A customer must get the necessary goods in the required quantity when needed. But when the goods desired by many users are diversified, the manufacturer has a difficult time coping with the increased workload. Changing only the production system cannot deal entirely with the situation: the corresponding sales system, including marketing, distribution, and information services, must also be improved.

Computer technology is advancing at a rapid rate. The development of a total production system incorporating CAD, CAM, and CAE is now possible. This technology also permits movement from mass production to the production of a variety of goods in small quantities. At present, however, most computer-aided manufacturing is geared towards mass production, unable to handle one-of-a-kind products. The specifications of these products should be easily changed to accommodate individual customer's needs. To execute this concept, Kansei Engineering production system is necessary with a knowledge-based expert system at its core. Using virtual reality (VR) (Rheingold 1991) technology, the virtual space decision support system (VSDSS) (Imamura 1991) lets users design virtual products and experience them while in virtual space. VR is defined by three elements (HDTV 1990): three-dimensional computer graphics technology, interactive interface devices with multi-function sensors, and high-resolution displays.

Studies of this computer environment are being done by NASA Ames Research Center (Fisher 1986), the MIT Media Lab (Sturman 1989), the HIT Lab (Jacobson 1991), the University of North Carolina (Airey 1990), the University of Tokyo (Hirose 1989), the University of Tsukuba (Iwata 1990), and the ATR Communication System Institute (Kishino 1990). An example of one commercially available VR system is from the VPL Corp., Redwood City, California.

18.2. VSDSS (Virtual Space Decision Support System)

A decision support system (DSS) can be characterized as an interactive system which helps the decision-maker solve non-structured and semi-structured problems by means of data and models (Simon 1960). On the assumption that decision making is best performed by a human being, the computer-based system increases the human's judgment and problem solving ability (Anthony 1965). Since the origin of "compute" consists of com- (together) and putare (to think), one could say a natural use for the computer is decision support. According to Gorry and Morton (1971), a DSS is an information system that easily supports decisions in business management. The strategic information system (SIS) by C. Wiseman (1988) and the information system by M.Porter (1985) demonstrate that a DSS is indispensable for concrete operation of business management strategy. DSS has been expressed clearly by S.Morton (Gorry 1971) in the 1970's. Many applications to various fields have been studied and many applied cases have been reported. But in each case, the developed systems were limited by the ability of the available computers and interface equipment. Because of these limitations, the developed system was different from the original concept of DSS. The spread of the personal computer, development of computer network technology, and development of multi-media technology now make a new DSS possible.

Problems with Current DSS. Even if enough computer technology is available, the system will still need much development if the problem we wish to solve is large and nonconstructive. Moreover, problems can occur if the goals of the project are changed or the system becomes difficult to use. These problems are caused by the poor interface ability of computer and peripheral equipment. There is not only a man-machine interface but also a man-model interface and a man-method interface. Together we call these problems the 3M-Interface Gap.

There are three types of interface gaps: the Model interface gap, the Method interface gap, and the Machine interface gap. The Model interface gap is a knowledge-level gap between the computer's model base and the user. This gap prevents the user from understanding the structure of problems shown by the model. For example, a gap would exist if a user working with Interpretive Structural Modeling (ISM) (Warfield 1974) cannot easily understand or manipulate the ISM chart.

The Method interface gap occurs when analysis, simulation, or optimization based on the model gives Table 1. 3M-Interface Gap and VSDSSreal world. In the case of the multiobjective optimization problem, it is difficult for the decision maker to deal with the real problem after he recognizes the limits of multiattribute utility theory or recognizes what the optimal solution derived from such as theory means.

Finally, the Machine interface gap occurs between the developed system and the user. The word "keyboard allergy" is symbolic of this gap. The system will not work properly if the operation is complex and difficult, even if problems related to the Method interface gap and the Model interface gap are solved.

Solving The Interface Gap. The most important theme for DSS developers in the future is how to reduce or resolve this "3M" (model, method, machine) interface gap. VSDSS is a system which supports decision making in virtual space by applying VR technology. It resolves the 3M interface gap. The construction of the interface system, which is impossible in physical space, can be done by means of a virtual panel, virtual touch keys, and virtual multi-windows in the virtual space. An example of the system developed to eliminate the 3M Interface Gap using VSDSS is indicated in Table 1. Figure 1 shows the difference between DSS and VSDSS.

18.3. Kansei Engineering

Kansei Engineering is defined as "a translation system of a consumer's image or feeling into the real design components"(Nagamachi, 1986). Namely, when a customer expresses his image toward a object using adjective, detail design items (for instance, object style, color, material, size and so on) are selected throught the Kansei Engineering procedure, and using this outputs, a designer or planner can design the object.

The Kansei Engineering Procedure is;

Table 1. 3M-Interface Gap and VSDSS

3M-Interface Gap	Example of the system development in VS-DSS
Model Interface Gap	By creating the information retrieval space in the virtual space, the objective system is shown in three dimensions. Input/output into the detail retrieval space concerned with each factor or explanation of the contents is performed by means of a voice input/output system, a virtual panel and virtual touch keys.
Method Interface Gap	Developing such system, the limiting value search process and its result can be experienced in the virtual space, while performing optimization; (in case of simulation - its process state). Moreover, developing such a system enable alternative plans to be recognized and experienced through the five senses such as sight, hearing, touch and others.
Machine Interface Gap	Developing a function that allows interaction with the objective system by the person concerned in the virtual space by means of a voice input/output system, virtual panel and virtual keys.

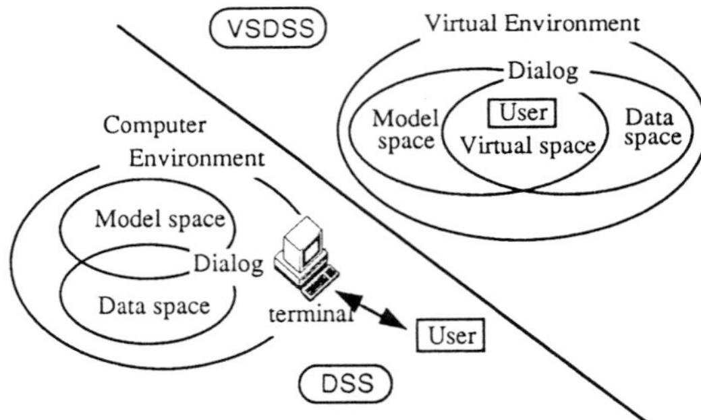

FIGURE 1. Relationship within DSS and VSDSS

Step1. Collecting the adjective words collect many adjective words which have relation to the object domain.

Step2. Assessing slides or pictures on SD scales Make pair these adjectives in a good-bad fashion for the SD (or good's Semantic Differentials) scales. Then assess many slides or pictures related to the object domain on these SD scales.

Step3. Eliciting effective adjectives from collected adjectives Calculate the assessed data at Step2 by factor analysis or principal component analysis, and obtain the semantic factorial structure of adjectives on the related design domain. And elicit adjectives which have a close relation to the object domain from the collected adjectives.

Step4. Subdivideing the object design into the design components subdivide the object design on the slides into detail design components, then classify each component into category according to it's quality. For example, L-style (category) layout (component), mahogany (category) cabinet (component).

Step5. Geting the relevancy between an adjective and qualitative data at Step4, analyze by Hayashi's Quantification theory Type 1, which is a kind of multivariate regression analysis dealing with qualitative data (Hayashi, 1976). The results of this analysis means relevancy between an adjective and each design component.

18.4. Application of VSDSS Using Kansei Engineering to the PS/US System

Production and sales activities start with the planning of sales and stock production. After evaluating the results of manufacturing, assembly, and sales of these products, business planning is performed again. These are cyclic and systematic activities. Conversely, the consumer must make various decisions about the product he wishes to purchase. The type and time of delivery has a significant impact on whether the user will purchase the goods:

(a) The product is bought when it can be obtained immediately.
(b) The product is bought only when it can be obtained by specified date.
(c) The product is bought regardless of its date of delivery.

A can of soda in a vending machine is an example of (1). But the soda which is bought in a cooperative store by joint purchase is an example of (2). Custom-ordered soda that is desperately needed is an example of (3). Planning on the assumption of (3) is sufficient with simple information processing. But planning on the assumption of (1) requires complex information processing.

In case of (1), it is necessary to decide production planning on the basis of sales planning information which is uncertain. Moreover, the quality of the planning accuracy has an effect on the business accounts. In this case, it is very important how to draft the production, sales and stock planning from information that is as uncertain after processing as before. For sales of type (1), it is necessary to develop an expert system on production, sales and stock planning (Nomura 1990) with a simulation function and optimization function for the various demands.

The (2) pattern is a special case. It is very rare that products manufactured according to a standard specification are delivered on the appointed date of delivery. It is common that such products are manufactured according to the customer's specifications. Since these specifications differ among every customer, it is necessary to develop a design support and performance estimation system for the customer together with the development of a CIM production line and a standard part order/stock system. In the case of standardized parts, it is possible to decide to purchase after looking and touching the parts at the showroom.

But when a product is to be designed by a customer, it is very important that he is able to estimate or experience it. Current design systems are tailored for the specialist and are not well suited for the intentions of the ordinary consumer. Therefore it is quite possible that the customer cannot imagine the completed state of the system. For example, many problems with constructed houses frequently occur since the buyer could not properly imagine the completed home.

How well is the room lit after changing the lighting equipment, or how well is the car noise attenuated after inserting sound-proofing material into the wall? Although these products can be seen in the showroom or reports can state "10 decibels are decreased according simulation results," it isperformance estimation and the suspected experience are in fact what the user will experience. Please refer to Figure 2 and Figure 3. By using VSDSS to produce products most suitable for the individual customer, construction of a new production and sales unification system (PS/US) becomes difficult to actually feel what these mean. VSDSS is a decision support system that ensures the possible.

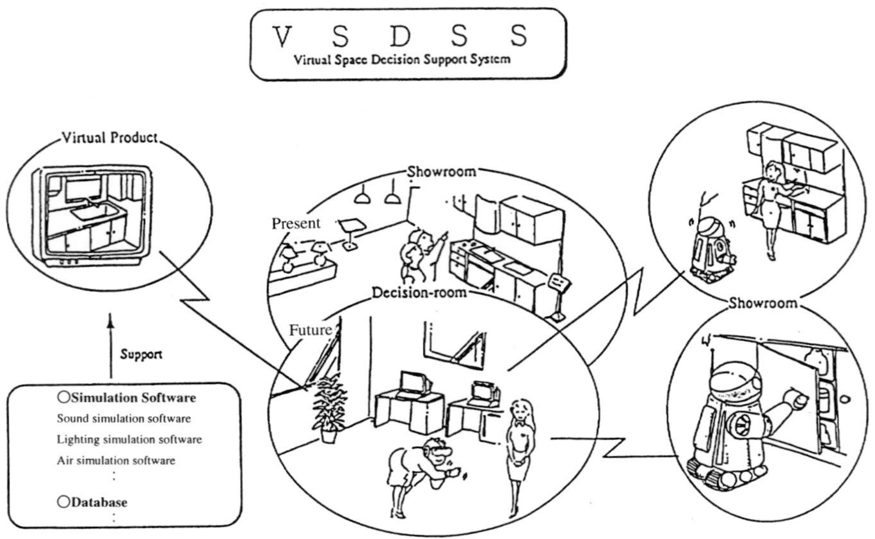

FIGURE 2. VSDSS

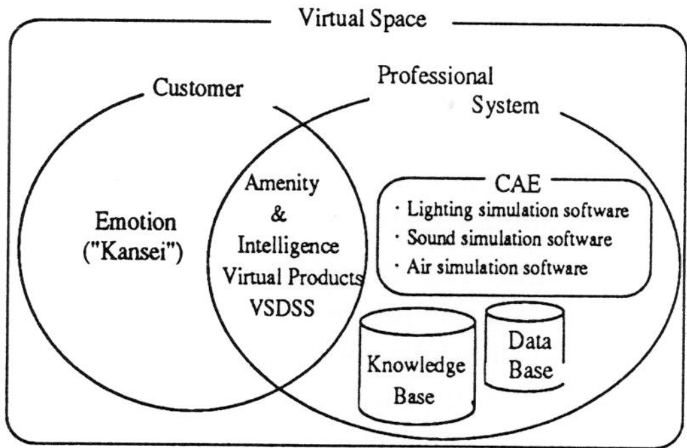

FIGURE 3. Customer-Oriented Decision Support System

Desktop Showroom. The showroom is the point of contact between the customer and the manufacturer. It must contain elements of display, consultation, advisement, and so on. A vast display space and many salespeople are required to display our various products at Matsushita. Since the number of showrooms are limited due to expense, the contact points between the manufacturer and the consumer are reduced. Moreover, it is difficult to display our 30,000 different products in combination with standard parts as well as large-scale products such as our system kitchen. Therefore, we are studying the desktop showroom concept as shown in Figure 4.

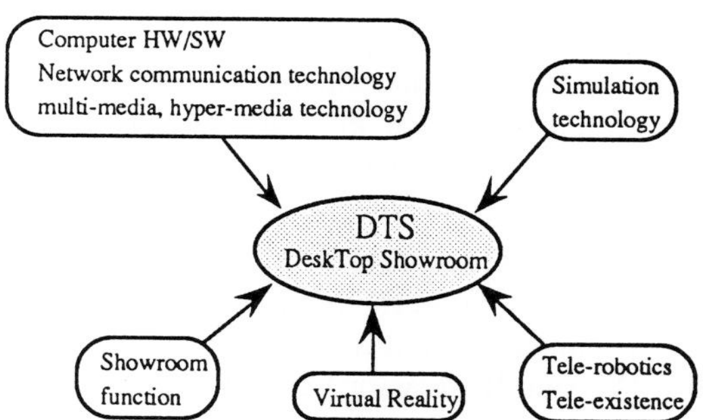

FIGURE 4. Desktop Showroom

The desktop showroom is applied with VR, telerobotics, and multi-media technology, and provides a display without display-space or geographic limitations.

Space And Geographic Limitations. The desktop showroom would eliminate space and geographic limitations by immersing the customer in a virtual showroom, where he can see actual product images or hear real salespeople speak. For example, the products displayed in Shinjuku, Tokyo can be seen by a customer using the desktop showroom at Takamatsu, Kagawa Prefecture as if he were casually walking through the remote showroom. To maintain these situations, VR, telerobotics, and multi-media technology must be applied. Thus, the display space and expense can be kept to a minimum.

Living Environment Design. This type of house-design simulation, which we might call the "inhabitant-participation" simulation process, is being developed through the New Industrialization House Production Technology and System Development Project, by the Ministry of International Trade and Industry (MITI). This project investigates the lighting, sound and vibration, heating, and air environments of the house. A pseudo-experience VR subsystem using three-dimensional HDTV and screen projection is also being investigated. These sub-systems estimate the results so that the living performance can be estimated in the design process and the resident can judge its performance level.

With current design systems, a resident may discover many unexpected problems after constructing his own house. The current design system causes many troubles after the fact. The high-quality living environment design and the pseudo-experience estimation system will correspond to the resident's needs more accurately.

Application to the PS/US System. One of our strong products lines is the "System Kitchen." a custom planned and built kitchen using Matsushita's cabinets and applicaes. The customer can choose from over 30,000 kitchen products and an infinite number of possible kitchen layouts. Since he must make many detailed and difficult the user erroneous results. If an objective problem is expressed as a mathematical model, there exists a gap between the meaning of these mathematical methods and their relationship to the decisions when selecting his new kitchen, it was natural to apply VSDSS and Kansei Engineering technology to this sales process.

System Kitchen Overview. The overview of the "system kitchen" production and sales unification system (Nomura 1990) is shown in Figure 5. The kitchen planning process is detailed in Figure 6. We developed a prototype VSDSS system called ViVA (Virtual Reality for Vivid A&i space system) which allows our customers to pseudo-experience their custom kitchen before purchasing it. When an interested customer comes to the showroom, the kitchen planner first explains the kitchen products' descriptions using catalogues and exhibits. Figure 7 shows the presentation of a sample kitchen to a customer by the kitchen planner. Figure 8 shows one of sample kitchens in our showroom.

The kitchen planner next draws a rough layout according to the desires of the customer. The customer can experience a similar pre-existing kitchen using the ViVA system if he wishes. Then a floor plan, an elevation view, a perspective drawing, and a written estimate are created on a CAD system

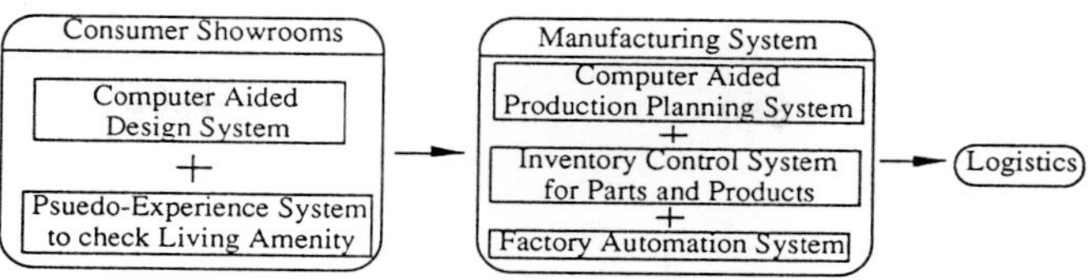

FIGURE 5. Consumer-Oriented Integrated manufacturing System

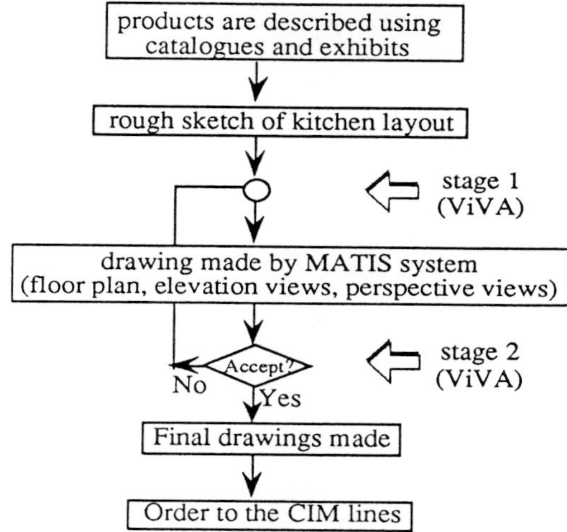

FIGURE 6. System Kitchen Planning Process

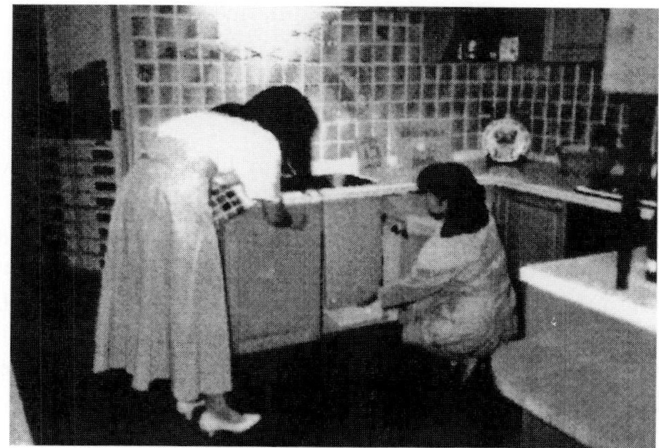

FIGURE 7. Presentation of Sample Kitchen to Customer

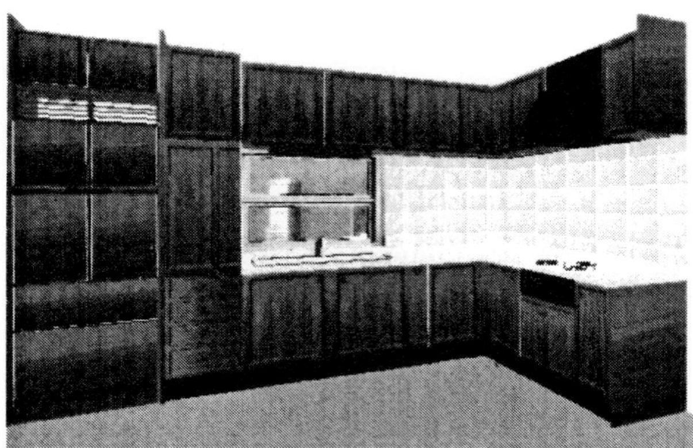

FIGURE 8. System Kitchen

based on the rough sketch. These three types of drowings are shown in Figure 9. The customer's own kitchen plan can be translated into a ViVA database within a week. The next time the customer comes to the showroom, he can experience many aspects of his own kitchen. The customer can check his own kitchen and decide if it matches his own idea of how the kitchen should be. Once the customer approves his kitchen design, final approval and appliance drawings are made and the order is sent to the CIM line.

In a current planning system without the ViVA pseudo-experience system, the customer can only see floor and elevation plans without getting a "feeling" for the kitchen. Sometimes there are many discrepancies between the system kitchen actually manufactured and the customer's original idea. The ViVA system helps eliminate these mistakes that are often made. With ViVA, the following items can be experienced in the virtual kitchen:

(a) The arrangement of cabinets and appliances.
(b) The general feeling of available space.
(c) Overall ergonomic design: The user can open and close cabinet doors, turn on faucets, move goods in the pantry, etc.

MATIS/ViVA Overview. Originally, system kitchen planning was done on a Sun-based CAD system called MATIS (Matsushita Amenity Total Interior System). The MATIS database includes approximately 30,000 of Matsushita's kitchen products as well as data on previous and current customers. This customer data include fields for room dimensions, cabinet placement, standardized parts information, special order information, etc.

After drawing the plan on the MATIS system, the two-dimensional picture is first translated to a three-dimensional layout to be experienced in the ViVA system. Figure 10 shows the dataflow from the MATIS system to the ViVA system. An interactive conversion program called Starch running on a Silicon Graphics Iris can be used to convert this monochrome, wireframe data to

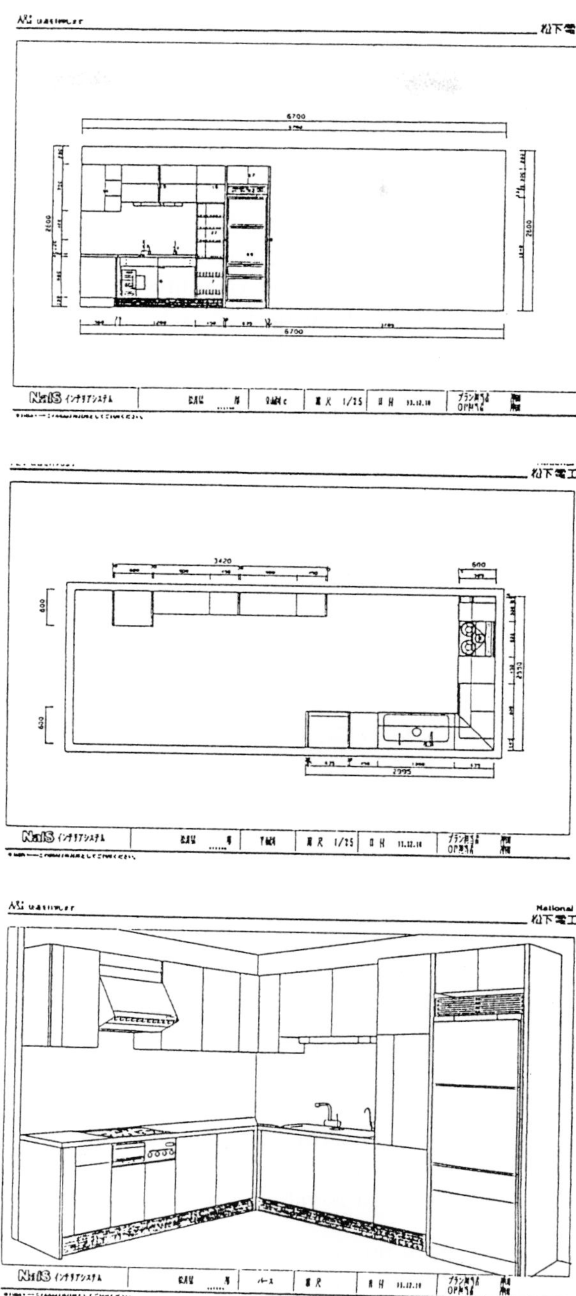

FIGURE 9. Floor, Elevation, Perspective Views

the ViVA format. If the desired product has not yet been converted to the ViVA format (remember, there are over 30,000 possible products) or it is a special-ordered product, Starch is used to edit the product and add color or special constraints.

Once the products have been translated to three-dimensions, the Wringer program is used. This program combines the products converted by Starch and the room dimensions described by the MATIS file. As each wall is created, the products are placed upon it one by one. The output of Wringer is a Swivel file and an Isaac file used by a VPL RB2 system. The Isaac data file is used to render the virtual kitchen on a Silicon Graphics Iris, and the Swivel file is transferred to a Macintosh, where it it read by a VPL program called Body Electric. Body Electric manages the behavior of the virtual world by controlling the renderer and linking in real-world data such as head and hand positions. The customer can now experience his own virtual kitchen. A sample of what the user sees is shown in Figure 11.

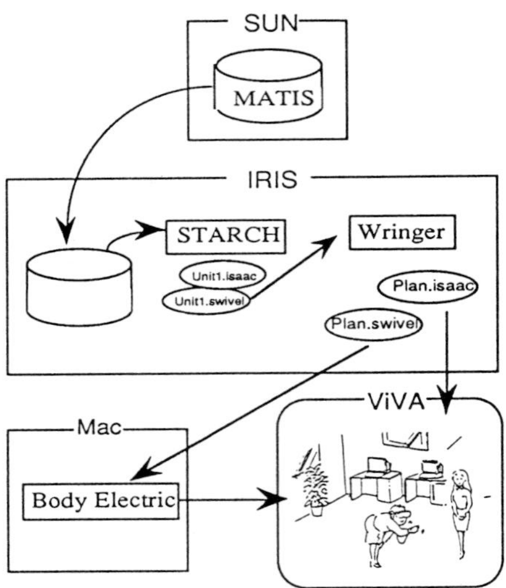

FIGURE 10. Dataflow from MATIS to ViVA

Virtual Kitchen System using KANSEI Engineering Overview. As the next version of ViVA system, Kansei ViVA system is being developed (stage1-type system on Figure 1) This system is valid to the follwing customers' types:

(a) The customers who have no idea of the kitchen
(b) The customers who are in confusion because they saw many catalogues and exhibits

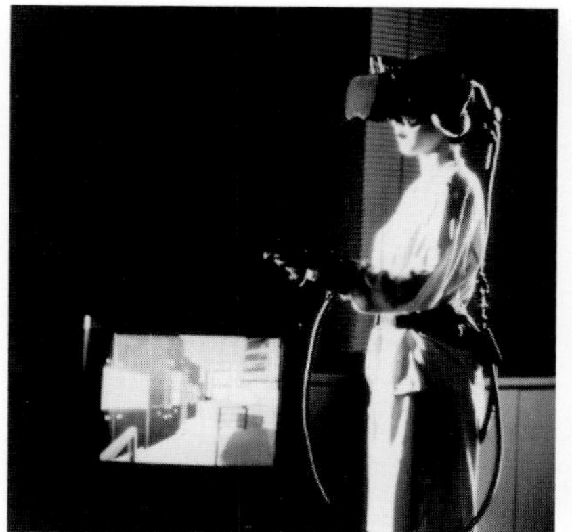

FIGURE 11. Sample Virtual World Views

(c) The customers who cannot imagine what the size of their kitchen space (usually, kitchen looks smaller than actual size in showroom because the height of the room in showroom is higher than housing one).

Using this system, vagueness and confusion of customer's image are cleared. So we expect that this system can decrease the number of the consultation between a planner and a customer (usually it repeat 4 or 6 times, sometimes over 10 times), and decrease the time of the consultation (usually it takes 2 hours, sometimes over 4 hours). The ViVA system using Kansei Engineering is detailed in Figure 8. First, customer inputs the field for room dimension and height of customer who use kitchen as restriction conditions. Next, he inputs lifestyle of his family and his image toward the kitchen in adjective words as Kansei conditions. Then the Kansei ViVA system identifies the kitchen plan in detail (for instance, kitchen layout, cabinet color, floor color, counter height and so on) using Kansei Engineering, and selects the kitchen plan used before similar to his kitchen plan the ViVA database. We gathered over 200 of adjectives and 18 items featured lifestyle. After experience, customer can change the wall size, cabinet arrangement, cabinet color and so on of the similar kitchen plan into his own kitchen plan. Figure 14 shows the relation between Kitchen design and adjecive words.

Living Amenity Simulation System Overview. Current ViVA system and Kansei ViVA system are dealing with kitchen space. In the future, we wish to develop to model an entire house. Figure 15 shows such a system. This development is joined with the project which is a 7-year plan since 1989 called "Technology Development Project for New Industrialized Houses" under the Ministry of International Trade and Industry. The aim of this project is to develop a system which achieves new housing for the coming 21st century. For the implementation of the project, research and development is being proceeded by "The New Industrialized House Production Technology and Sys-

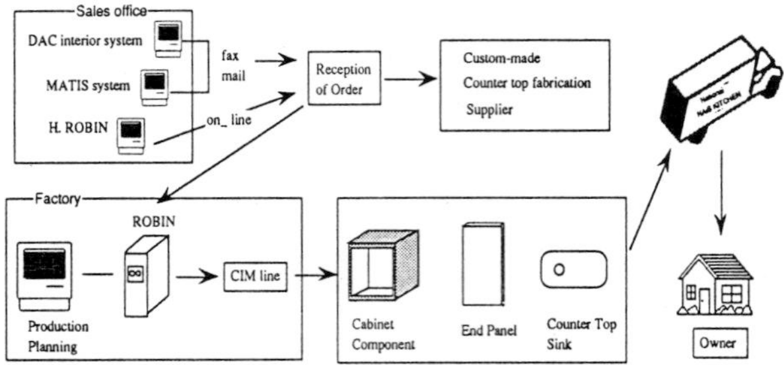

FIGURE 12. CIM Overview for System Kitchen

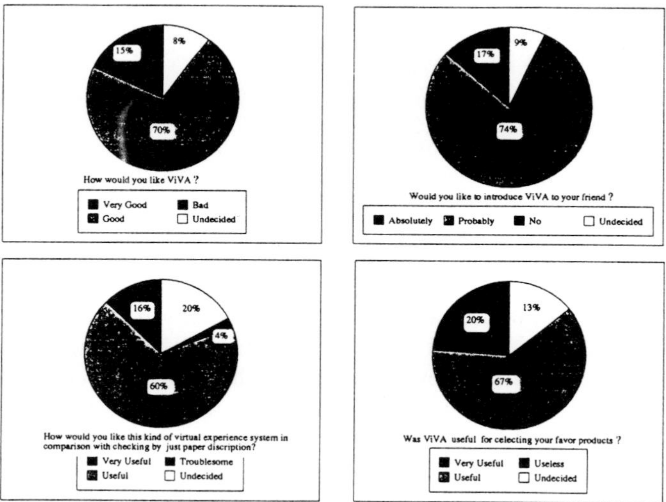

FIGURE 13. ViVA User Surver Results

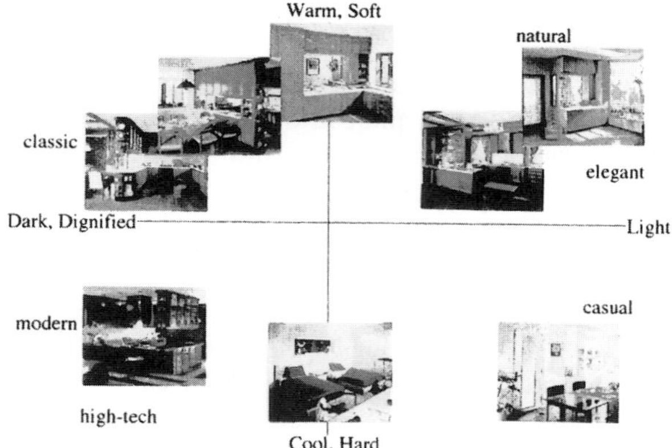

FIGURE 14. The relation between kitchen design and adjective words

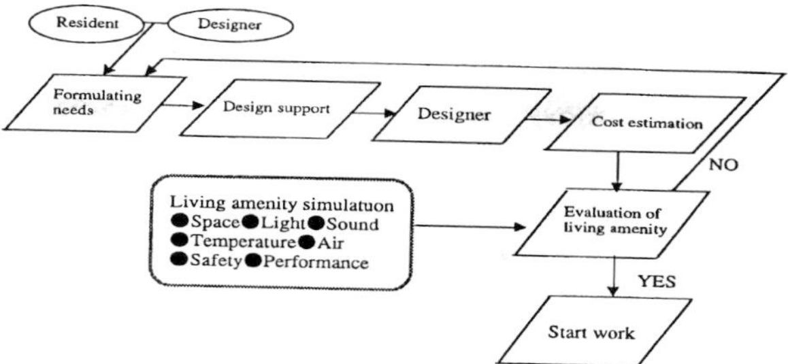

FIGURE 15. A House Planning Process

tem Development Technology Research Association(WISH21)". MEW takes charge of development of "resident participation" amenity simulation system in this project. Using this system, resident can experience and evaluate housing performance such as light, sound, vibration, temperature, air and so on.

18.5. Conclusion

This paper described about Kansei Engineering and the Virtual Kitchen System. As indicated in this paper, current system kitchen simulation system is valid. And Kansei ViVA system could cover gap which arose between customer and kitchen planner in their consultation, and decreased consultation-time to a certain extent. In future, Kansei ViVA system will be developed which can deal with the Kansei information in a broad sense. Namely, advanced Kansei ViVA system will be able to deal with customer's "amenity" such as favorite lighting effect, comfortable temperature and so on.

References

1. Airey J, Rohlf J, Brooks F (1990) Towards Image Realism with Interactive Update Rates in Complex Virtual Building Environments, University of North Carolina at Chapel Hill TR90-001.
2. Anthony R (1965) Planning and Control Systems: A framework for Analysis, Harvard Businees School,Division of Research.
3. Fisher S, McGreevy M, Humphries J, and Robinett W (1986) Virtual Workstation: a Multimodal,Stereoscopic Display Environment. SPIE Intelligent Robots and Computer Vision.
4. Gorry A, Morton M (1971) Framework for a Management Information System, Sloan Management Review.
5. Hirose T (1989) Creation of Artificial Reality; System/Control/Information, Vol.33, No.11(in Japanese).
6. HDTV & The Quest for Virtual Reality (1990) ACM SIGGRAPH.

7. Imamura K, Ohata H, Nomura J (1991) Virtual Space Decision Support System. The 1991 Spring National Conference of ORSJ (in Japanese).
8. Iwata H (1990) Artificial Reality to Walk in The Large-scale Virtual Space, Human Interface, Vol. 5 (1990) (in Japanese).
9. Jacobson R (1991) Televirtuality : "Being There" in the 21st Century, Human
10. Kishino F (1990) Feeling Communication, Three-Dimensional Image, Vol.4, No.2, (in Japanese).
11. Nagamachi M (1986) A Study of Custom Consultation System in Terms of Knowledge Engineering, Human Interface, Vol.3.
12. Nomura J (1990) Expert System on Production, Sales, and Stock Planning, Logistics Software National Conference (in Japanese).
13. Porter M (1985) Competitive Advantage: Creating and Sustaining Superior Performance, New York: Free Press.
14. Rheingold H (1991) Virtual Reality. Summit Books, New York, Tokyo.
15. Simon H (1960) The New Science of Management Decision, Harper & Row, Publishers, New York.
16. Sturman D, Zeltzer D, Pieper S (1989) Hands-On Interaction with Virtual Environments, AGMSIGGRAPH/SIGCH.
17. Warfield J (1974) Toward Interpretation of Complex Structural Model, IEEE, SMC-4-5, September, 1974.
18. Wiseman C (1988) Strategic Information Systems, Richard D. Irwin, Inc.

19. Quantity of Presence: Beyond Person, Number, and Pronouns

Michael Cohen
Spatial Media Group, Human Interface Lab, University of Aizu, Aizu-Wakamatsu, Fukushima-ken 965-8580, Japan
(*e·mail*: `mcohen@u-aizu.ac.jp`)

Summary.
Alternative non-immersive perspectives enable new paradigms of perception, especially in the context of frames-of-reference for musical audition and groupware. MAW, acronymic for **m**ultidimensional **a**udio **w**indows, is an application for manipulating sound sources and sinks in virtual rooms, featuring an exocentric graphical interface driving an egocentric audio backend. Listening to sound presented in such a spatial fashion is as different from conventional stereo mixes as sculpture is from painting. Schizophrenic virtual existence suggests sonic (analytic) cubism, presenting multiple acoustic perspectives simultaneously. Clusters can be used to hierarchically organize mixels, [sound] **mix**ing **el**ements. New interaction modalities are enabled by this sort of perceptual aggression and liquid perspective. In particular, virtual concerts may be "broken down" by individuals and groups.

Key words and Phrases: binaural directional mixing console, CSCW (**c**omputer-**s**upported **c**ollaborative **w**ork) , **f**rames **o**f **r**eference , groupware, mixel ([sound] **mix**ing **el**ement) , **p**oints **o**f **v**iew , sonic (analytical) cubism, sound localization, spatial sound.

19.1. Introduction

"Traditional" immersive VR systems feature a HMD (**h**ead-**m**ounted **d**isplay) that tracks the user's position, adjusting visual and audio displays accordingly. Because of the intimate coupling between control and display in such a system, there is a sense of framelessness, of being inside the projected world. This intimacy is not without its cost, however, as it implies a strict mapping between each user and the respective displays. To enable potentially useful modalities like omniscient views and shared or overlaid displays, different **c**ontrol/**d**isplay conventions are needed that relax the mapping between user and presence, applied, for instance, to desktop or 'fishtank' VR systems. This chapter explores the philosophical distinction between egocentricism and exocentricism, especially as blurred by emerging technologies.

19.2. Duality and Synthesis of Self/Other: Beyond Person

In any kind of display, there is a constant tension between the realism of the presence and one's unwillingness to suspend disbelief. As the realism of the presentation increases, one becomes increasingly, if subconsciously, willing to accept immersion, enabling an egocentric impression. Exocentricism, in contrast, is an awareness that the display derives from a perspective different from where the user imagines themself to be. The egocentric nature of a display is not an inherent quality of the presentation, but a subjective willingness of the user to project their perceptual center to the point-of-view of the display. A few examples demonstrate:

- A good movie or book is absorbing partly to the extent that the attendee or reader projects themself into the story or scene. Immersed in a compelling situation, the subject loses their identity (empathy and vicariousness are projected egocentricism), only to be brought back to an awareness of their actual place by a crunch of popcorn or jangle of a telephone, reasserting an exocentric perspective.
- A subject in a spatial sound experiment, presented with a stereo signal simulating a directionalized channel, was unable to perceive a single object; he couldn't (let himself) ignore the fact that the headphones were actually playing separate sounds to each ear. For him, the egocentric display was hobbled, reduced to its exocentric shadow by an overzealous self-consciousness.
- A classic example of an exocentric display is a map. If someone allows themself an imagined out-of-body (but not out-of-mind) experience, flying above the landscape to see the world the way it is portrayed in the map, then the map has become an egocentric display. (This is especially easy to accept if the map is replaced by or superimposed upon an aerial photograph of the same area.) One can slide back and forth along a spectrum between egocentric and exocentric impressions or perspectives.
- A networked Formula 1 racing simulator arcade game, Sega's "**V**irtua **R**acing," allows each driver to switch between four perspective modes:
  cockpit (Figure 1 top), in which the visual presentation is as if the user were inside the car, including the dashboard, top of the steering wheel (including driver's hands), and rearview mirrors;
  follow (Figure 1 bottom), in which the driver's perspective is just behind and above the vehicle, tracking synchronously;
  float, in which the camera position is well above the car, still orienting 'up' on the display with 'forward' from the driver's point-of-view; and
  fly, in which the monitor tracks the car as if from a blimp, clearly showing one's own car in the context of the field.

  Even though the simulator's 'radio buttons' select a predetermined degree of immersion, drivers may switch modes during a race, and the visual dis-

FIGURE 1. Sega Virtua Racing

play slides seamlessly between them, by zooming, focusing, and soaring the virtual camera through the computer graphic raceway. Further blurring the sampled/synthesized distinction, monitors for spectators show live video of the drivers, panning shots of the lead car, static shots of strategic curves, and instant replays of crashes [7].

For conversational groupware systems, the notion of egocentric and exocentric frames of reference can be reconciled with grammatical person. In sliding from an immersive (subjective) perspective to an "exmersive" (objective) perspective, the user transforms from a 1st person to a 3rd person. If all participants are represented by separate icons, a user could adjust another's virtual position as easily as her own, blurring the self/other distinction. Reflexive and imperative operations are thereby cast as special cases of transitive commands. By projecting the metaphorical world onto an external and egalitarian medium, the 1st and 2nd persons have become special cases of the 3rd.

19.3. Shared and Split Perception: Beyond Number

Most discussions of virtual presence are about its quality– degree of individual resolution and interactivity [18] [36]; here its *quantity* is elaborated. Once it is admitted that any display can be egocentric, given appropriately imaginative users, the issue of multiple simultaneous or overlaid egocentric perspectives, or multifocal virtual presence, can be addressed. One's perceptual center need not be unique or singular, just as the effects of one's actions need not be limited to a single place.

These split or shared perceptions can be thought of as violating the "one [sensory] sink to a customer" rule inherent to immersive systems; each user may have an arbitrary number of dedicated virtual sensor instances, and the mapping between sinks and users may be one→many, many→one, or many→many.

Imagine this experiment: A user is connected to a hand position sensor, which drives, via telerobotics, a pair of identical manipulators, playing separate instruments — a harpsichord and a grand piano, in arbitrarily different locations. (This experiment is easily simulated by using a MIDI configuration, say, to fork-drive multiple voices.) The user can be said to have a presence in multiple places.

Now imagine the dual of this multiple effector situation, multiple sensory locations. This notion is related to the idea of multiple cooperating agents in a telepresence environment [35]. Different modalities can superimpose separate channels in different ways, outlined later.

The opposite situation, multiple users sharing a single sensor instance, can also be useful: "This is interesting; share it with me..." Mass broadcast media like radio and TV employ this one→many mode (made explicit by first-person movies like "84 Charlie Mopic"). Of course they lack the control of VR systems, but interactive television (suggested by zapping movies whose simultaneous parallel broadcast of multiple characters' stories allows viewers to follow alternate threads) and call-in shows blur this distinction.

19.3.1. Video

There are several ways of presenting multiple video channels simultaneously. Distributed camera systems can present multiple views at once. Visual su-

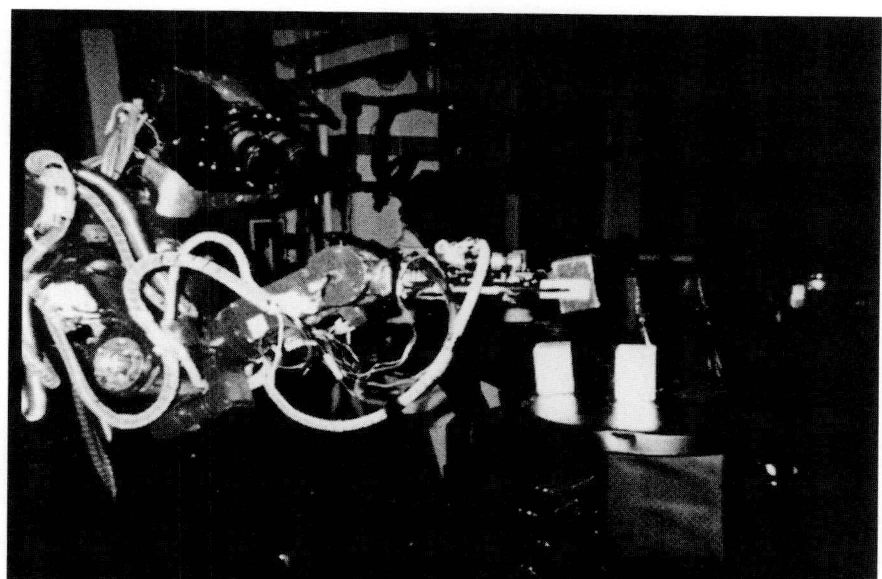

FIGURE 2. RCAST Telerobot

perposition is achieved by tiling strategic perspectives, like security monitors, or by embedding a view in a less important section ("picture in picture"). It is difficult in general to use translucency to overlay opaque scenes, except in special circumstances. Split-screen television and cinematographic techniques are common. Montage offers a time-domain multiplexed worldview, as one's perceptual center flitters from place to place, which may or may not correspond to a character's location. Music videos, for example, often composite or crossfade visual scenes. Analytical cubism, as developed by Braque and Picasso, presents multiple visual perspectives on a scene simultaneously.

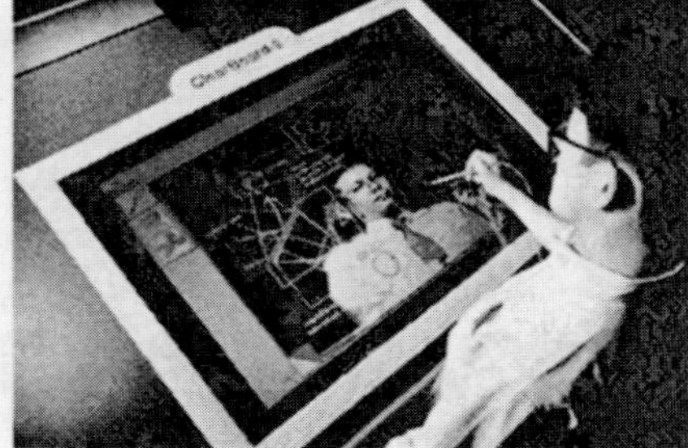

FIGURE 3. Clearboard-2: shared multilayer drawing tool

HUDs (**h**ead-**u**p **d**isplays) are used in airplanes to throw navigation, tracking, and status information onto the windshield. Half-silvered mirrors can be used to view translucent images. Clearboard (Figure 3) [22] [23] uses superimposed translucent viewing planes for teleconferencing with video of the conferees plus a shared whiteboard; different focal distances can help distinguish the layers. [27] superimposed real and virtual images by using a virtual image as a mask for a real, or by rendering a virtual image as a (non-occluding) wireframe. "Mirror-type" VR systems like Mandala [43] (Figure 4) can combine CG and (chroma-key captured) sampled signals, overlaid on arbitrary background graphics.

FIGURE 4. Vivid Mandala

Visual "augmented reality" describes the superposition of computer-generated imagery on top of a see-through display [4] [41]. The dual of augmented reality is augmented virtual reality, manifested in the video domain by texture mapping camera-captured images on polygon models, as suggested by Figure 5 [21].

Presenting different signals presented to separate eyes (of which using computer graphics to simulate stereopsis is a special case) is also possible. While future generations of users might be able to mentally integrate or perceptually multiplex separate scenes presented to each eye, binocular views, augmented with status information tucked into a corner of a display (as in Private Eye [1] or ScopeHand [39]), seems like the most we can expect for the near future.

FIGURE 5. Hirose Lab Virtual Dome

19.3.2. Audio

Video is not the only modality in which multiple displays may be superimposed. For example, multiple tactile or temperature channels can be simultaneously experienced, by presenting them to different hands.[1] Similarly, dichotic experience involves simultaneous presentation of separate audio scenes to each ear. More directly, an arbitrary number of audio channels may be simply added and played diotically, the same composite signal at each ear. Audio entities, unlike visual, do not occlude (although masking can be thought of as audio occlusion). It is usually straightforward to overlay sonic landscapes, monaurally or stereophonically, as in a mixer. In particular, stereo sources– real (or mic'd via a dummy head) or artificial (binaurally spatialized)– may be simply added.

Using such a scheme, distributed microphone systems can superimpose auditory scenes. Musical recording can be thought of as presenting sound as if the listeners had their ears near all the respective instruments, even though the tracks might have been laid down in separate (acoustically isolated) rooms and at different times.

One could share or swap ears with another user, and listen to oneself as a distal source. This is also not terribly exotic: singers often amplify their voice, and musicians want to be able to monitor a live performance from the perspective of the audience, the same way people look in a mirror.

Augmented reality in the audio domain can superimpose computer synthesized sounds upon natural, using some non-exclusive sound presentation

[1] This recalls the adaptation parlor trick of immersing opposite hands in baths of hot and cold water, then plunging them together into tepid, to consequent cognitive confusion.

like loudspeakers or open-ear headphones [9]. For instance, the author has perceptually thrown a ringing sound to a location occupied by a muted telephone, recalling [26]'s visual analog of projecting a picture of a room on the same space after it was painted white. **P**ublic **a**ddress, or sound reinforcement, systems are a common example of augmented audio reality.

This kind of superposition potential is manifested in MAW (acronymic for **m**ultidimensional **a**udio **w**indows), an audio windowing system with a visual map and auditory display: an interface for manipulating iconic sound sources and sinks in virtual rooms, deployed as a binaural directional mixing console. MAW is suitable for synchronous applications like teleconferences or concerts, as well as asynchronous applications like voicemail and hypermedia [5] [6] [13], which can be thought of as equivalent (because of spatial data models) to cyberspace [45], as diagramed by Figure 6.

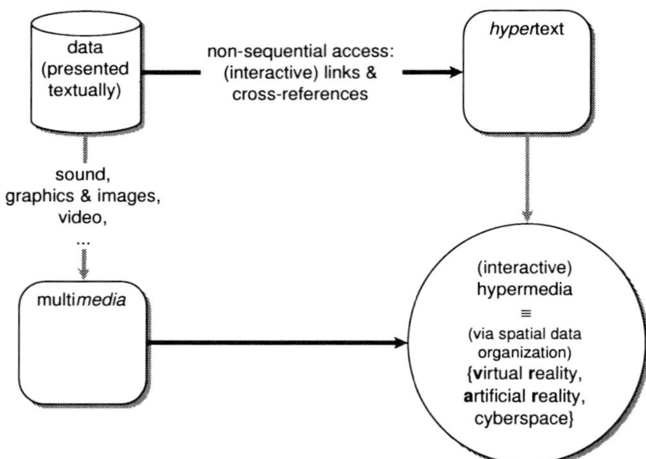

FIGURE 6. Hypermedia: *hyper*text × multi*media*

MAW's main view is a dynamic map of iconic sources and sinks in a virtual room. A source is a sound emitter; a sink is a sound receptor, a delegate of a human listener in a virtual room. (In a teleconference, an icon might represent both a source and a sink.)

Source→sink directionalization can be performed by a DSP (**d**igital **s**ignal **p**rocessing) module which convolves the digitized input streams with HRTFs (**h**ead-**r**elated **t**ransfer **f**unctions) that capture directional effects [42]. This spatialization enables auditory localization, the identification of the location of a source, which can be used for "the cocktail party effect." The use of such effects might be used in a concert to 'hear out' an instrument, virtually and perceptually pulling it out from the mix, or for sub-caucusing in a teleconfer-

	Icon	
	Source:	Sink:
Function	radiator	receiver
Direction	output	input
Instance	speaker (human or loud-)	listener (human or dummy-head)
Include	solo	confide
Exclude	mute/conceal	deafen/blind

Table 1. $^{s}OU^{rce}_{Tput}$ and $^{s}IN^{k}_{put}$

ence. Listening to sound presented in this spatial fashion is as different from conventional stereo mixes as sculpture is from painting.

Audio window icons may move around each other and the virtual room. For example, if a sink rotates (exocentrically visually, perhaps driven by a chair tracker [11]), the apparent sonic location of the source revolves (egocentrically acoustically) accordingly. The sinks and sources may wander around, like minglers at a cocktail party, or upon the stage during a concert, hovering over the shoulder of a favorite musician. Background music may be brought into the perceptual foreground.

19.3.3. Shared Perspective: Sink Fusion

Illustrating a one→many mapping of sinks to users (as in broadcasts), [10] allowed two users to synchronously adjust the position of multiple sources and a single shared sink in a virtual concert, as if they were simultaneously director and (singleton) audience. (For graphical displays, such inter-user consistency is called "[relaxed] common view," since the various users might zoom or scroll their room windows differently.) This style presentation blurs the distinction between composer, performer, and listener, as hypermedia blurs the distinction between author, publisher, and reader.

19.3.4. Split Perspective: Sink Fission

Some systems support multiple visual windows, each featuring a different perspective on a scene. In flight simulators, for example, these might be used to display (egocentric) views out cockpit windows, and/or views from a completely different location— high above the airplane, for example, looking down (exocentrically): a virtual 'out-of-body' experience. Since audition is omnidirectional, perhaps audio windows can be thought of as implicitly providing such multiperspective capability, audio sources being inherently superimposable. MAW further generalizes multipoint audio perspective by allowing users to fork their presence, as explained below:

Schizophrenia. A simple configuration typically consists of several icons, representing distributed users, moving around a shared space. Each icon represents a source, the voice of the associated user, as well as a sink, that user's ears.

MAW's graphical windows correspond to virtual rooms. Using the `cut` / `paste` idiom as a transporter or 'wormhole,' one may leave a room and beam down into others. Such a control mechanism can be used to focus selectively on various sources. If several rooms were interesting, it would get tiresome to have to bounce back and forth.

Allowing users to designate multiple sinks effectively increases their attendance in conference. A user may simply fork themself (with `copy` / `paste`, for instance), leaving one clone hither while installing another yon, overlaying soundscapes via the superposition of multiple sinks' presence. Such a 'schizophrenic' mode, enabling replicated sinks in same or different conference rooms, explicitly overlays multiple audio displays, allowing a teleconferee to leave a pair of ears in one conversation, while sending other pairs to side caucuses.

This feature can be used to sharpen the granularity of control, as separate sinks can monitor individual sources via selective amplification, even if those sources are not repositionable; just as in ordinary settings, social conventions might inhibit dragging someone else around a shared space. One could pay close attention to multiple instruments in a concert without rearranging the ensemble, which would disturb the soundscape of the icons that personify other users in the shared model.

Autofocus. The apparent paradoxes of one's being in multiple places simultaneously can be resolved by partitioning the sources across the sinks. If the sinks are distributed in separate conference rooms, each source is directionalized only with respect to the sink in the same room. In the case of autothronging, or multiple sinks sharing a single conference room, an autofocus mode can be employed by anticipating level difference localization, the tendency to perceive multiple identical sources in different locations as a single fused source. (This is related to the precedence effect, or "rule of the first wavefront" [2].) Rather than adding or averaging the contribution of each source to the multiple sinks, MAW localizes each source only with respect to the best (loudest, as a function of distance and mutual gain, including focus and orientation) sink.

Figure 7 illustrates this behavior for a top-down view of a conference (top row) with two sinks, represented by icons (distinguished by shaded rings), and two different sources, represented by a square and a triangle. In the absence of room acoustics, multiple sinks perceiving a single source is equivalent, via "reciprocity" or symmetry, to a single sink perceiving multiple identical sources. Therefore the exampled scene can be decomposed source-wise into two additive scenes (second row), each single sink combining the parent sinks' (shaded) perceptions of the respective sources. These configurations reduce (third row), via 'autofocus' level difference anticipation, to the respective sinks and only the loudest source. The loudest source is typically the closest, since the respective pairs of sources are identical, the chorus of phantom sources being a manifestation of the multiple sinks. Finally (bottom row), the additive scenes are recombined, yielding the overall simplified percept.

Say, for example, that a listener wanted to pay special attention to an ensemble's drum and rhythm guitar, while preserving the configuration of the instruments. Besides tradition and mnemonics, one reason for not just rearranging the instruments around a singleton sink is to maintain consistency with other listeners, distributed in time and (both physical and virtual) space. Using MAW, the user could fork themself, as in Figure 8, locating one instance inside the drum, and the other doppelgänger near the rhythm guitar.

Sonic Cubism. The experience of being in multiple places simultaneously, like all virtual situations, may define its own rules. A psychophysical interpretation, as elaborated above, however, is important as an interface strategy, making the system behavior consistent with users' intuitions, artificial but accessible. Other schemes are possible, like adding or averaging source→sink transmissions, or disambiguating fancifully by focusing sinks on more distant sources. The overlaid existence suggests the name given to this effect: sonic (analytic) cubism, presenting multiple simultaneous acoustic perspectives. Being anywhere is better than being everywhere, since it is selective; MAW's schizophrenic mode is distilled ubiquity: (groupware-enabled) audition of multiple objects of regard.

19.3.5. Non-atomic Sinks and Sources: Clusters

Clusters are hierarchically collapsed groups of objects [32]. MAW features such a cluster utility for organizing spatial sound objects. By bundling multiple channels together (like the drums in Figure 8), a composite timbre is obtained. Clusters have two main purposes:

conservation of spatializer resources Postulating a resource manager, like a switching matrix on either side of the spatial sound processor [15] along with dynamic allocation of spatializer channels, a source cluster feature organizes separate input streams that share a single spatializing channel. One application might involve zooming effects. Distant sources would not be displayed; but as it approaches, a cluster would appear as a single point; only to disassociate and distribute spatially as it gets closer. Such variable **l**evel **o**f **d**etail ("LOD") allows navigation in arbitrarily large spaces, assuming bounded density of point sources. Alternatively, with limited spatializing resources, a user might chose to group a subset of the (less important or less pleasant) channels together, piling them in a corner or closet.

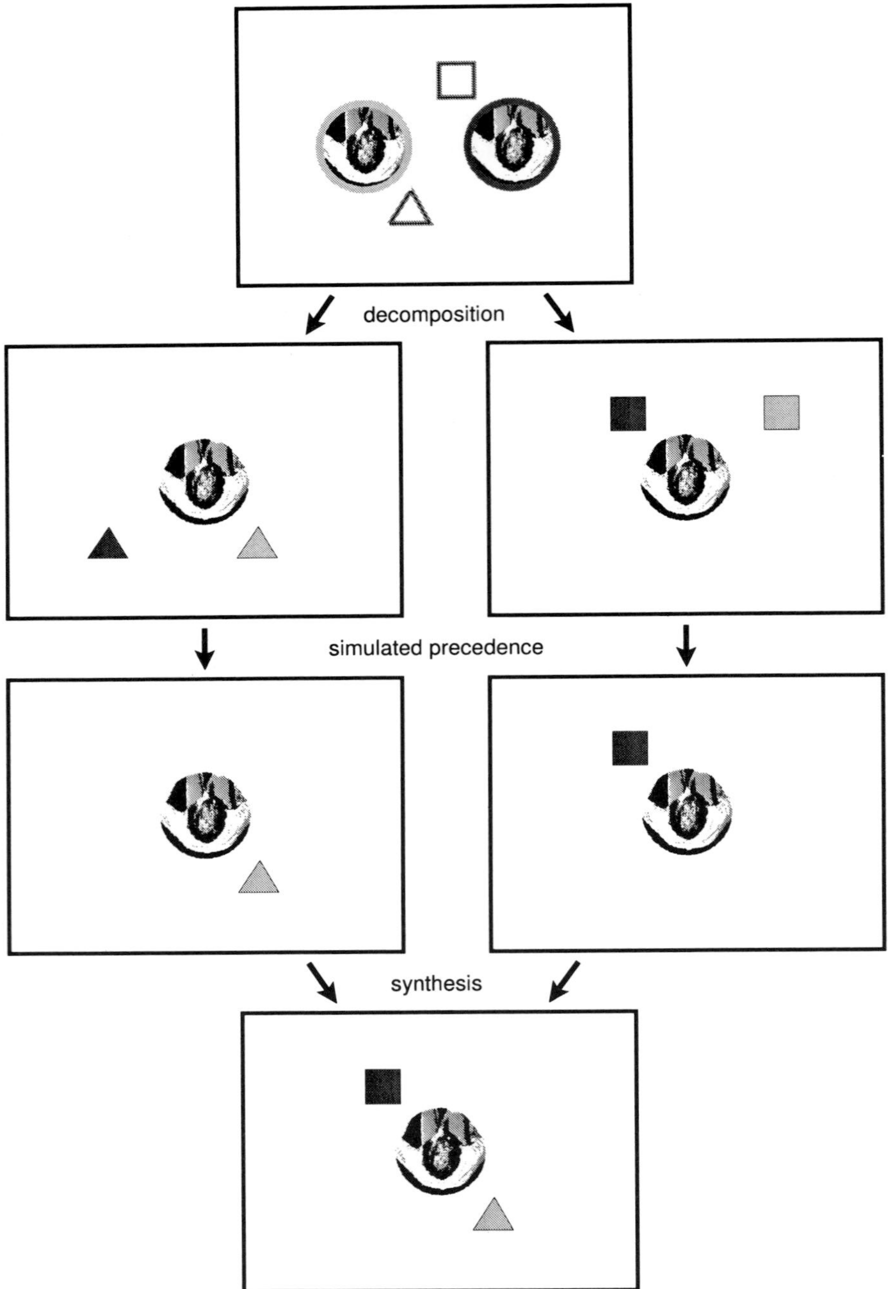

FIGURE 7. Sonic cubism: schizophrenic mode with autofocus

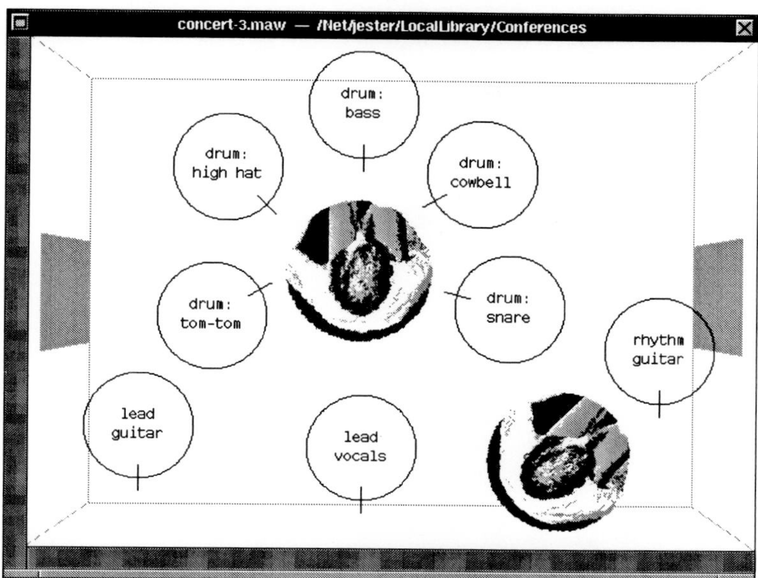

FIGURE 8. Virtual concert: multiple sinks and exploded clusters (generalized multi-focus audio fish-eye)

logical organization of hierarchical structure In the context of a concert, individually recording (or mic-ing or synthesizing) individual instruments, presenting each of the channels to a binaural directional mixing console like MAW, and mixing them at audition time, rather than in "post-production" (as tracks and subgroups), allows the instruments to be rearranged by the listener [38]. One could grab an orchestral cluster, for instance (shown as part of the concert in Figure 9), explode it to separate different instruments, and drag one of those instruments across the room. Successive differentiation can go right through concert → orchestra → section → instrument and actually break down the instrument itself. Such a superdecomposition aspect of the cluster feature could allow, for example, a user to listen to spatially separate strings of a guitar (assuming a hexaphonic pickup for performance, or decoupled tracks for digital synthesis), or different components of each string's sound. Even more radical decompositions than the partitioning suggested by Figure 9 are possible, enabled by advanced workstation musical capability [24] and such techniques as physically-based modeling [44]. A generalized approach, ultimately fractal, assumes limitless levels of zooming or analysis.

Atomic sources, the leaves of the tree in Table 9, are called "mixels,"—acronymic for '[sound] **mix**ing **el**ements,' in analogy to pixels, taxels (tactile elements), texels (texture elements), or voxels (volumetric elements, a.k.a.

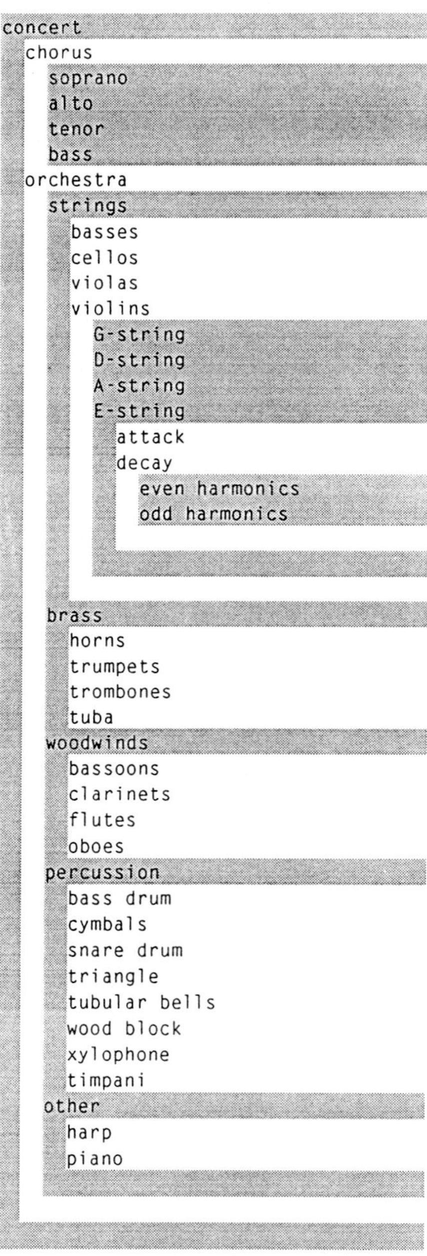

FIGURE 9. Concert decomposition

boxels)— since they form the raster across which a soundscape is projected, defining the granularity of control and degree of spatial polyphony. While eventually such decompositions might be dynamically performed, using some equivalent of subtractive synthesis, the current audio window system requires anticipation of the atomization, assuming *a priori* assembly of the finest-grained mixels.

Unclustering can be likened to viewing the sources through a generalized fish-eye lens [17] [31] [29], which spatially warps the perception of the localized sources to enlarge an area of focus and shrink everything else. That is, when the user indicates a direction of special interest, the sources in that direction effectively approach the user and recede from each other in perspective.

19.4. Grammatical Blur: Beyond Pronouns

An example of a many→many sink:user mapping is a virtual concert in which the audience shares a distribution of sinks: each user hears the same thing, but multiple sinks are used to increase the granularity of audition [12] [14].

point of view	person	intimacy	object	distance	mode	perspective
exocentric	3rd	public	other	distal	transitive	objective
vicariousness, empathy	2nd	social, multipersonal	familiar	medial	imperative	
telepresence, autoempathy		remote self				
immersive	1st	personal	self	proximal	reflexive	subjective
egocentric						

Table 2. Points of View

Grammatical constructions like the taxonomy in Table 2 could not anticipate exotic forms of reference, like shared, multiple or reciprocal existence. In an exocentric system, all icons in a dynamic map are potential sensation sinks, and designations associated with pronouns become very fluid. For example, say I choose to think of "my location" in a shared virtual environment as where my voice or instrument comes from, as perceived by some other users. For the purposes of a teleconference or concert, it is philosophical whether the various iconic sinks are thought of as

- multiple manifestations of a singleton ("I" [or lowercase 'i'], or perhaps the Rastafarian "I and I" [16]),
- a plural deployment of self ("we," inclusive or exclusive, editorial or royal, ...),
- another user's position ("you" or "thee," singular or plural ["y'all" or "ye"], "he" or "she"),
- a many-eared eavesdropper ("it"), or
- an army of dedicated robot listeners ("they").

19.5. Conclusion

Questions about whether or not non-immersive systems are pure 'virtual reality' are really besides the point; what's important is that they enable a computer-enhanced view of the world that is useful and interesting. Such "deconstructions of the body," not in a literary sense, but in a literal sense, as in interfaces developed by [25], relax sink↔user mappings. The extension of an exocentric perspective beyond a multimedia interface is a (possibly multiple or shared) projection of the user into the virtual world. Discussions about workstation-oriented "desktop-" or "fishtank-VR" usually involve issues like cost, constraints on movement, ergonomic engineering (sensor lag, update rates, display resolution), "simulator sickness" [20], and user recalibration, but philosophical differences are deeper.

We generally think of our centers of consciousness and perception as residing together, in a single place inside the head attached to our body. But by sidestepping subjectivity of the 1st person, non-immersive systems can augment (instead of simulate) reality. For some applications, an exocentric presentation is more convenient than an egocentric or immersive one. To get a global perspective, for instance, a map is more useful than an immersive display. Down-scaling enables a quicker overview than possible with an immersive world, and humans are quite good at conceptualizing 3-space from projections.

It is important to note that the advantages of non-immersion are not limited to 2D "gods' eye" views. The argument that a map is like a omniscient perspective on an immersive world fails, since the location of the subject, usually thought of as unique, is not above the terrain, but in it. Participatory and experiential $\not\Rightarrow$ inclusive [30] [28]!

Explicitly distinguishing the domain of the ([virtual] conference, concert, cocktail party) inhabitants from the observing point of view has benefits not afforded by even aerial perspective in immersive systems:

- A user perceives, and can manipulate, themself in the context of the colloquia.
- A user can perceive everyone else in the conference at once. In a groupware environment, others can run but they can't hide. There is no possibility, for instance, of the immersive trick of one user hiding inside another's head. Users might not want to (have to) turn around to see who is approaching from behind.
- Exocentric interfaces allow multipoint audio perspectives. It is hard to imagine how multiple instances of self might be implemented effectively in an immersive system.

Audio window metaphors apply to full 3D graphical interfaces and earprints (HRTFs) as well. Rather than encase the user in a HMD and glove/wand configuration, we can augment the telephone and stereo, using the computer as a map. Using such a full spatial model, music can be we spatialized according to a helical structure of scale [33] [34]. The harmony and melody of a song can be perceived by separate sinks, using the audio cubism idiom to normalize the octave, as suggested by Figure 10 [19].

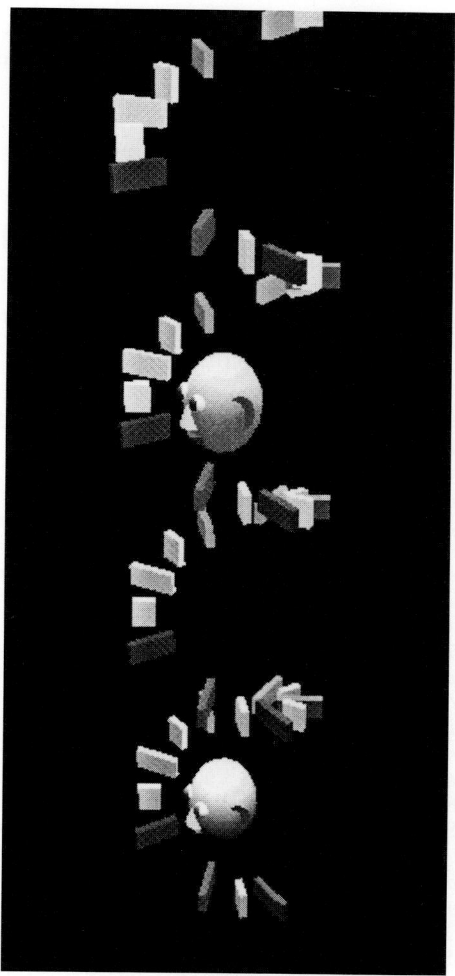

FIGURE 10. Octave normalized by separate sinks for harmony and melody

Such schizophrenic modes can be thought of as forking reality, rather than cloning self. The perception of telepresence is auto-empathy, imagining how oneself would feel elsewhere. New interaction modalities are enabled by this sort of perceptual aggression and liquid perspective, as style catches up with technology.

Acknowledgments

This research has been supported in part by grants from NTT Human Interface Laboratories and the Fukushima Prefectural Foundation for the Advancement of Science and Education.

References

1. Allen Becker. High resolution virtual displays. pages 27–34, 1992.
2. Jens Blauert. *Spatial Hearing: The Psychophysics of Human Sound Localization.* MIT Press, 1983. ISBN 0-262-02190-0.
3. Albert S. Bregman. *Auditory Scene Analysis: The Perceptual Organization of Sound.* MIT Press, 1990. ISBN 0-262-02297-4.
4. T. P. Caudell and David W. Mizell. Augmented reality: An application of heads-up display technology to manual manufacturing processes. In *HICSS: Proc.* **H***awaii* **I***nt.* **C***onf. on* **S***ystem* **S***ciences.* IEEE, January 1992.
5. Michael Cohen. Integrating graphical and audio windows. *Presence: Teleoperators and Virtual Environments*, 1(4):468–481, Fall 1993.
6. Michael Cohen. Throwing, pitching, and catching sound: Audio windowing models and modes. *IJMMS: the Journal of Person-Computer Interaction*, 39(2):269–304, August 1993. ISSN 0020-7373.
7. Michael Cohen. Cybertokyo: a survey of public VRtractions. *Presence: Teleoperators and Virtual Environments (Special Issue on Pacific Rim Research)*, 3(1):87–93, Winter 1994.
8. Michael Cohen. Besides immersion: Overlaid points of view and frames of reference; using audio windows to analyze audio scenes. In Susumu Tachi, editor, *Proc. ICAT/VRST:* **I***nt.* **C***onf.* **A***rtificial Reality and* **T***ele-Existence/Conf. on* **V***irtual* **R***eality* **S***oftware and* **T***echnology*, pages 29-38, Makuhari, Chiba; Japan, November 1995. ACM-SIGCHI(TBD), SICE (**S**ociety of **I**nstrument and **C**ontrol **E**ngineers), JTTAS **J**apan **T**echnology **T**ransfer **A**ssociation), and NIKKEI (**Ni**hon **Ke**izai Shimbun, Inc.).
9. Michael Cohen, Shigeaki Aoki, and Nobuo Koizumi. Augmented audio reality: Telepresence/VR hybrid acoustic environments. In *Ro-Man: Proc.* 2nd IEEE *International Workshop on* **Ro***bot and Hu***man** *Communication*, pages 361–364, Tokyo, November 1993. ISBN 0-7803-1407-7.
10. Michael Cohen and Nobuo Koizumi. Audio window. In *Den Gaku.* Tokyo Contemporary Music Festival: Music for Computer, December 1991.
11. Michael Cohen and Nobuo Koizumi. Iconic control for audio windows. In *Proc. Eighth Symp. on Human Interface*, pages 333–340, Kawasaki, Japan, October 1992. 1411.
12. Michael Cohen and Nobuo Koizumi. Audio windows for virtual concerts. In *JMACS: Proc.* **J***apan* **M***usic* **A***nd* **C***omputer* **S***cience* **S***ociety Meeting*, pages 27–32, Tokyo, February 1993. No. 47.
13. Michael Cohen and Nobuo Koizumi. Putting spatial sound into voicemail. In *NR94: Proc. 1st International Workshop on* **N***etworked* **R***eality in TeleCommunication*, Tokyo, May 1994. IEEE COMSOC, IEICE.

14. Michael Cohen and Nobuo Koizumi. Audio Windows for Virtual Concerts II: Sonic Cubism. In Susumu Tachi, editor, *Video Proc. ICAT/VRST: Int. Conf. Artificial Reality and Tele-Existence/Conf. on Virtual Reality Software and Technology*, page 254, Makuhari, Chiba; Japan, November 1995. ACM-SIGCHI (TBD), SICE (Society of Instrument and Control Engineers), JTTAS (Japan Technology Transfer Association), and NIKKEI (Nihon Keizai Shimbun, Inc.).
15. Michael Cohen and Lester F. Ludwig. Multidimensional audio window management. *IJMMS: the Journal of Person-Computer Interaction*, 34(3):319–336, March 1991. Special Issue on Computer Supported Cooperative Work and Groupware. ISSN 0020-7373.
16. Richard Dennison, Michio Ogata, and Mike Pawka. Rasta/patios dictionary. `http://www.willamette.edu/~tjones/languages/rasta-lang.html`.
17. George W. Furnas. Generalized fisheye views. In *CHI: Proc.* ACM *Conf. on Computer-Human Interaction*, pages 16–23, Boston, April 1986.
18. Richard M. Held and Nathaniel I. Durlach. Telepresence. *Presence: Teleoperators and Virtual Environments*, 1(1):109–112, 1993.
19. Jens Herder and Michael Cohen. Project report: Design of a helical keyboard. In *ICAD: Proc. Int. Conf. Auditory Display*, Palo Alto, CA, November 1996.
20. Lawrence J. Hettinger and Robert B. Welch. *Presence: Teleoperators and Virtual Environments*, Summer 1992. 1(3).
21. Michitaka Hirose and Kensuke Yokoyama. VR Application for Transmission of Synthetic Sensation. In Susumu Tachi, editor, *ICAT: Proc.* Int. *Conf. Artificial Reality and Tele-Existence*, pages 145–154, Tokyo, July 1992.
22. Hiroshi Ishii. Translucent multiuser interface for realtime collaboration. *IEICE Trans. on Fundamentals of Electronics, Communications and Computer Sciences* (Special Section on Fundamentals of Next Generation Human Interface), E75-A(2):122–131, February 1992. 0916-8508.
23. Hiroshi Ishii, Minoru Kobayashi, and Jonathan Grudin. Integration of interpersonal space and shared workspace: Clearboard design and experiments. *TOIS:* ACM *Trans. on Information Systems (Special Issue on* CSCW *'92)*, 11(4):349–375, July 1993.
24. David Jaffe and Lee Boynton. An Overview of the Sound and Music Kits for the NeXT Computer. *Computer Music Journal*, 13(2):48–55, Summer 1989.
25. Myron W. Krueger. *Artificial Reality II.* Addison-Wesley, Reading, MA, 1991. 0-201-52260-8.
26. Michael Naimark. Elements of realspace imaging: A proposed taxonomy. In *Proc. SPIE/SPSE Electronic Imaging Conf.*, San Jose, CA, 1991. Vol. 1457.
27. Eimei Oyama, Naoki Tsunemoto, and Susumu Tachi. Remote manipulation using virtual environment. In *ISMCR: Proc. Int. Symp. on Measurement and Control in Robotics*, pages 311–318, Tsukuba Science City, Japan, November 1992. Society of Instrument and Control Engineers.
28. Randy Pausch, Tommy Burnette, Dan Brockway, and Michael E. Weiblen. Locomotion in virtual worlds via flight into hand-held miniatures. In SIGGRAPH *Proc.*, LA, CA, July 1995.
29. Ramana Rao, Jan O. Pedersen, Marti A. Hearst, Jock D. Mackinlay, Stuart K. Card, Larry Masinter, Per-Kristian Halvorsen, and George G. Robertson. Rich interaction in the digital library. *Communications of the ACM*, 38(4):29, April 1995.
30. Warren Robinett. Synthetic experience: A proposed taxonomy. *Presence: Teleoperators and Virtual Environments*, 1(2):229–247, 1992.
31. Manojit Sarkar and Marc H. Brown. Graphical fisheye views. *Communications of the ACM*, 37(12):73–84, December 1994.

32. Doug Schaffer, Zhengping Zuo, Saul Greenberg, John Dill, Shelli Dubs, Mark Roseman, and Lyn Bartram. Navigating hierarchically clustered networks through fisheye and full-zoom methods. *TOIS:* ACM **T***rans. on* **I***nformation* **S***ystems*, January 1996.
33. Roger N. Shepard. *The Psychology of Music*, chapter Structural Representations of Musical Pitch, pages 343–390. Academic Press, December 1982.
34. Roger N. Shepard. Demonstrations of circular components of pitch. 31(9):641–649, September 1983.
35. Thomas B. Sheridan. Progress and challenge in human telerobot control. In *ISMCR: Proc.* **I***nt.* **S***ymp. on* **M***easurement and* **C***ontrol in* **R***obotics*, pages 19–29, Tsukuba Science City, Japan, November 1992. **S**ociety of **I**nstrument and **C**ontrol **E**ngineers.
36. Thomas B. Sheridan. Musings on telepresence and virtual presence. *Presence: Teleoperators and Virtual Environments*, 1(1):120–125, 1993.
37. Julie Stanfel. Mandala: Virtual cities. In SIGGRAPH *Computer Graphics Visual Proc.*, page 208, Anaheim, CA, August 1993.
38. Gavin R. Starks and Ken N. Linton. A 3-D Stereo Processing Tool. In *AES: Proc.* **A***udio* **E***ngineering* **S***ociety Conv.*, Amsterdam, February 1994. 3830 (P9.1).
39. Gen Suzuki and Takashi Kouno. Virtual collaborative workspace. In *ICAT: Proc.* **I**nt. **C***onf.* **A***rtificial Reality and* **T***ele-Existence*, pages 119–125, 1992.
40. Susumu Tachi, Hirohiko Arai, Taro Maeda, Eimei Oyama, Naoki Tsunemoto, and Yasuyuki Inoue. Tele-existence in real world and virtual world. In *ICAR: Proc. Fifth Int. Conf. on Advanced Robotics*, pages 193–198, Pisa, Italy, June 1991.
41. Pierre Wellner, Wendy Mackay, and Rich Gold. Communications of the ACM, July 1993.
42. Elizabeth M. Wenzel. Localization in virtual acoustic displays. *Presence: Teleoperators and Virtual Environments*, 1(1):80–107, 1992.
43. Susan Wyshynski and Vincent John Vincent. Full-body unencumbered immersion in virtual worlds. In Alan Wexelblat, editor, *Virtual Reality: Applications and Explorations*, chapter 6, pages 123–144. Academic Press, 1993. ISBN 0-12-745046-7.
44. Yamaha Corp. *VP1 Virtual Acoustic Synthesizer*, 1994.
45. Michael J. Zyda, David R. Pratt, John S. Falby, Chuck Lombardo, and Kristen M. Kelleher. The software required for the computer generation of virtual environments. *Presence: Teleoperators and Virtual Environments*, 2(2):130–140, 1994.

20. The STV-Synthetic TV System

Armand Fellous
Director of the "Laboratoire 3D", I.N.A., 4, Avenue de l'Europe
94366-Bry/Marne, France (e-mail: armand@ina.fr)

20.1. Introduction

The STV-SYNTHETIC TV system is a technology designed to allow Computer Graphics (CG) users to mix *coherently* their images with images coming from real shootings, or alternatively to allow film-makers to include CG elements in their live shootings. To make it clear, one can imagine the two opposite paradigms: real actors in virtual backgrounds, virtual actors in real backgrounds. However in practice, the distinction of these two extreme situations is not relevant, and we deal usually with sceneries where the same element is sometime real, sometime virtual.

By coherency, we mean *geometrical* coherency, which is only part of the overall visual coherency that the combined images must exhibit. Geometrical coherency means correct positionning of virtual elements w.r.t. real elements, correct modelisation, frame after frame, of the virtual camera (used by the 3D software) w.r.t. the real camera. In short, consider the following example: one wants to see a 3D CG generated building in its future real environment. Geometrical coherency implies that in the resulting combined sequence, the building will be at the right place and will keep it stable as the camera moves.(see fig.1)

This defines, evidently, a necessary condition for the realistic aspect of the result, but this condition is not sufficient: all other aspects of visual coherency are to be considered (lights, shadows, reflections, textures,...). Until now, empirical methods prevail for these and the results rely heavily on the experience and talent of the 3D CG designer.

20.2. Dynamic Coupling and Initializing

Conveniently, let us described the situation as such: there is two cameras system, furnishing each a part of the image; one - virtual - pointing to a

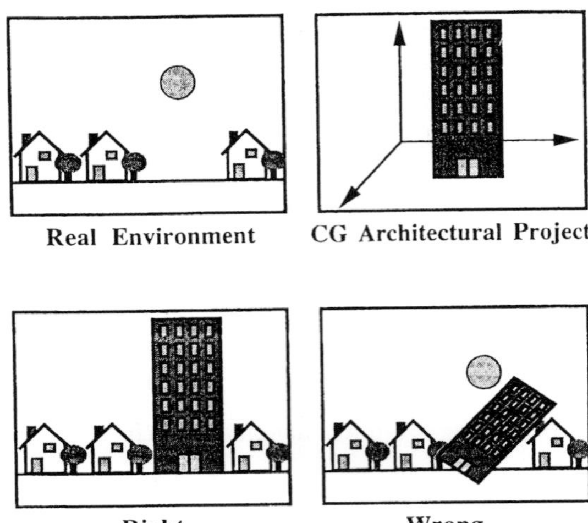

Fig 1: Geometrical Coherency

virtual world already set in a computer, the other - real- pointing to some place in the real world.

System(1): (real camera, real world)
System(2): (virtual camera, virtual world).

Using masks, we combine the images coming from these two systems, which result in a hybrid image. In order for this hybrid image to look realistic, coming from a unique world, the two camera systems must be dynamically coupled. What does this mean?

In order to simplify, consider first the following more usual situation:

System(1): (real camera, real world)
System(2): (real camera, real world)

We assume that the two real cameras are perfectly identical, equiped with perfectly identical optical instruments. These two cameras are placed on the same kind of articulation system (allowing, for example, horizontal and vertical panning and traveling and elevating movements,...), so that we may say that the two camera systems are perfectly identical.

We may say that these camera systems are dynamically coupled if, for each image of the shooting,

- all parameters of both lenses (zoom, focus, iris,...) are set to the same values,
- the image acquisition devices (video or film) are kept identical and
- the articulated systems supporting the cameras undergo exactly the same changes during the movement.

Dynamic coupling can be obtained mecanically by using, for example, a system of rods. A cameraman manipulates one of the shooting systems and the other system follows. We say, in this particular case, that the second system is slaved to the first. Other systems are motorized, therefore, the camera man works from a control pannel, sending, simultaneously, the same instructions to both cameras.

The coupled systems may produce an image seemingly filmed by only one camera from a unique world, but, unfortunetly, this is not sufficient to make what we see of this unique world understandable. This is naturally because dynamic coupling just insure the equivalence of the internal parameters of both systems, and we have to take into account external parameters as well.

Here's an example using two coupled systems, (1) and (2).

The system(1) is filming someone on a blue background sitting on a blue cube and a red vase on another blue cube. System(2) is filming the set with a chair and a pedestal table. The hybrid image is obtained by inlaying the person and the vase to the set with the chair and pedestal table, a technique called chroma-key: all that is blue in the image produced by system(1) is replaced by what is found at the exact same place in the image produced by system(2). (see fig.2, where the vase is omitted)

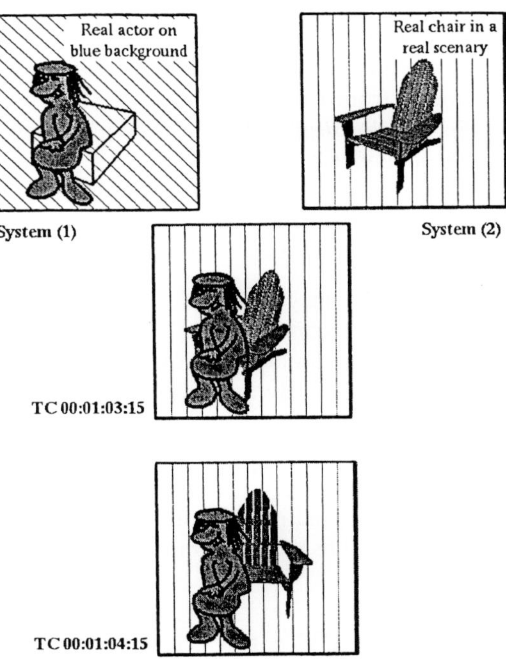

Fig 2: Dynamic Geometrical Coherency

How can we make sure that, when both cameras are joined in action, the person will stay, in the resulting image, sitted firmly on the chair and the vase placed on the pedestal table, and, that neither one of them will be travelling through the set?

The answer is obvious. If at any precise moment both systems occupy the same relative position w.r.t. their own space, due to dynamic coupling it will be so for the remaining of the application. This implies, as a first condition, that the respective positions of the two blue cubes must be exactly the same as the respective positions of the chair and pedestal table, which we shall assume now: this condition is called

– *spatial coherency of the two spaces.*

Furthermore, the cameras systems have to occupy the same position w.r.t. their respective spaces, an operation we call

– *initialization.*

When system(1), for example, is slaved to system(2), we proceed initialization as such: once system(2) is positioned in its world, we move system(1) through its' own world while observing the composed image, until... the person is sitting in the chair and the vase is placed on the pedestal table! This could imply a lot of measuring and mathematical calculations, instead of trials and errors. When the result has been achieved, we are *relieved* and say that the coupling of system(1) and system(2) is *initialized*. The use of the word *initialization* comes from the fact that, since there is coupling, the initial coherence existing at the beginning of the sequence implies a coherence throughout the entire sequence.

We should remember, from what has been mentionned, that, if the person slides from the chair or the vase from the pedestal table while the camera is in movement, it could be for any of the following reasons;

– both systems are not sufficiently identical,
– the dynamic coupling is not good enough,
– the chair or table's position should be re-examined,
– the initialization is not sufficiently accurate.

On the other hand, when the person stands firmly sitted on the chair, and the vase on the pedestal table, we can say that:

– all has been sufficiently well realized, or that
– all which seemed inacceptable has been cut while editing.

20.3. STV-Synthetic TV Procedure in a Nutshell

By replacing the couple (real camera, real world) of system(2) used in the previous example with the couple (virtual camera, virtual world), you find the STV-SYNTHETIC TV system. This system was developped by INA as part of the EUREKA 283 project in co-operation with TDI(France), TELSON(Spain) and VIDEOTIME(Italy). Since TDI has joined the Wavefront Group (USA), it has been replaced by SYSECA(France). More precisely, the system being developped so far by INA is a dynamic coupling in which the virtual camera is slaved to the real camera. The identity of both systems symbolizes that the virtual system(2) is a sufficiently precise replica of system(1).

This is the result of an extensive study done on the real system(1), during a laboratory operation called system calibration, involving a series of precise mesures (parameterization) taken on the mecanical parts and on the images produced.The precision level we have taken as our standard implies that distortions of the real lens, actually used, are replicated in the corresponding 3D CG generated images.

20.4. The System Decelopped by INA

There are two complementary versions of the STV system. The first one is called the OffLine system, while the second one is called the OnLine system. Note that the OffLine system is contained in the OnLine system.

Each of these two versions of STV represents a different trade-off between the two concurrencing qualities: interactivity versus freedom in the camera movements. OffLine system is weakly interactive but is universal in many aspects, camera displacements are totally free, and no special limitation exists in the choice of the camera system. On the opposite, OnLine system gives maximum interactivity, but restrains camera to guided movements (excluding camera on shoulder for instance). Maximum interactivity means here that the cameraman has a real time control of the combination of the real scene and the virtual one. This will be best understood after the description of the OnLine architecture.

The OffLine system. In this version, the required equipement consists in a camera, a calibrated and sensed lens. This can be either a fixed focal lens, or a zoom. Furthermore, an electronic device, called ZIF, is fixed on the camera and records the data coming from the sensors of the lens (one for the zoom, one for the focus and one for the iris) on the soundtrack of a video tape recorder (VTR), which can be included in the camera (combo type video camera) or portable. In the case of 35mm film camera, we use a portable VTR, which records also the video signal coming from the video viewfinder on the camera. (see fig.3). When lens manipulation is motion controlled from a computer, the ZIF device can be avoided and the data are taken from the computer.

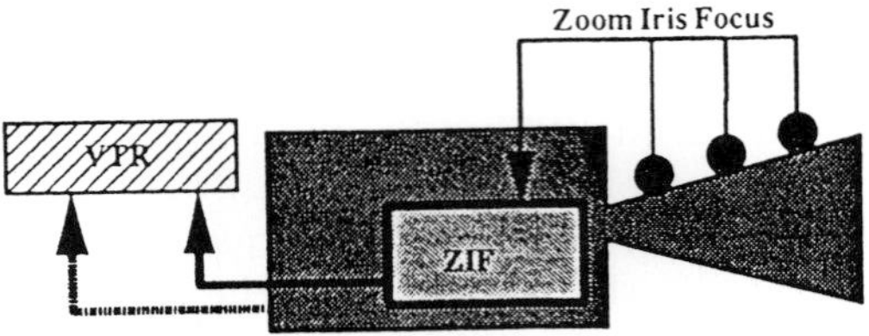

Fig. 3: The OffLine STV System

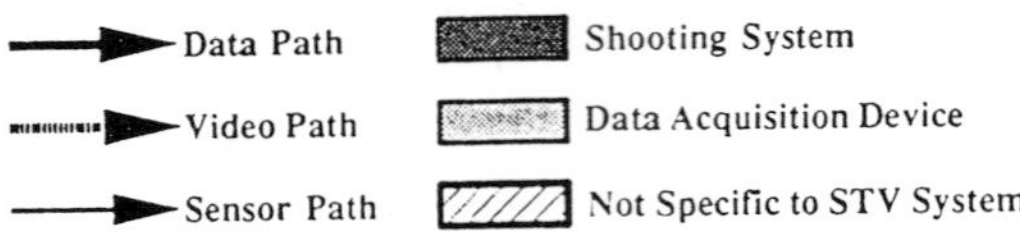

After shooting, these data are transferred onto a graphic workstation, where they are processed by the STV software in order to compute the relevant camera parameters. This is done through an interactive software, where the operators, with the help of some automatic procedures, tracks 3D measured points visible in the shot images. This implies that before, or after the shooting, the software is provided with this 3D information; most currently, these measurements are achieved with the help of geometers' instruments.

Finally, the user gets all the needed informations on the camera parameters values of the actual shootings, and can compute, with any kind of 3D software (such as Alias, TDI, SoftImage,... or proprietary software) the corresponding virtual images. STV software includes specific tools to post-process these images, so that they show all the distortions existing in the real images. This guarantees an exact geometrical matching between the two sources of images.

The OnLine system. In this version, we use a graphic worstation directly linked to the real camera system to display, in real time, during the shooting, a (possibly simplified) view of the desired 3D elements: since this image can be mixed with the real image, the cameraman is able to see, in real time, what the final composite image will look like at the end. For this reason, the system has been sometime described as a mixed camera, looking simultaneously at the real world and at the virtual world in the memory of a computer.

As previously mentionned, camera movements are restricted to guided movements. Presently, we are supporting, in the standard configuration, on top of the zoom, focus and iris of the OffLine version:

- Pan and tilt
- Traveling along rectilinear rails. Elevation can be added, but is subjected to variable hardware implementations.

The standard pan-tilt head is a Sachtler Video80, which is designed to handle cameras up to 80kg. We install sensors on this head, for the pan and tilt axis, with a standard resolution of 1/400 degree. Traveling is composed with specially designed rails and platform, that reach both goals: precision and portability for outside use. Each rail is 1.5m long. The resolution of the traveling sensor is configurable and is usually set to 0.1mm.

Data coming from the lens (zoom, iris,focus) are, as in the OffLine version, handled by the ZIF device, but are also transmitted to the CAB (Central Acquisition Box). The CAB handles the data coming from the other axis (pan, tilt, elevation and traveling), sends all the data to the graphic workstation in real time, and records them onto two VTR soundtracks. It is worth to mention that the sampling of the sensors is synchronized with the time-code. (see fig.4)

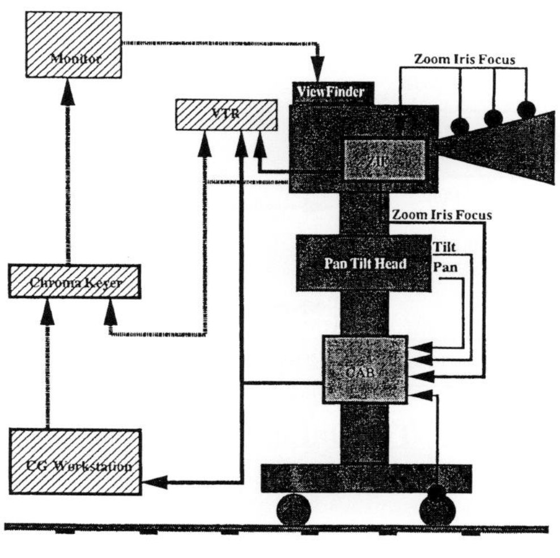

Fig. 4: The OnLine STV System

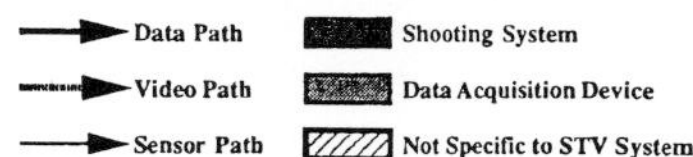

STV softwares offer a fully interactive user interface and a methodology which mimics closely customary way of shooting.

To each sequence is associated an ASCII script file, that describes the virtual world, and the animations that may occur in it. These animations may have been previously prepared, but may be interactively generated, in real time, during the actual shooting as well.

Before each sequence, a simple procedure of initialization (cf.supra) must be undertaken, in order to determine the initial position of the camera system in the surrounding world. This position becomes then the home position of the virtual camera system in the virtual world and remains the same for all the subsequent shots. As soon as the initialization is done, the cameraman may be provided with a coherent mixing of the real and virtual images, in his viewfinder. This functionnality is the most striking feature of the OnLine version, since it allows for dynamic framing during the shooting of virtual animations. This is clearly illustrated in the example production with Renault "Racoon". (cf.infra)

STV OnLine Production Unit. The standard OnLine Production Unit that we use, for services, at INA, involves more equipements than the list above, because it includes a video mobile van (see fig.5), which results in considerable savings in time (and risks), and avoid tedious manipulations and connections problems with other existing equipments. This is evident for outside use and helps a lot for indoor studio shootings as well.

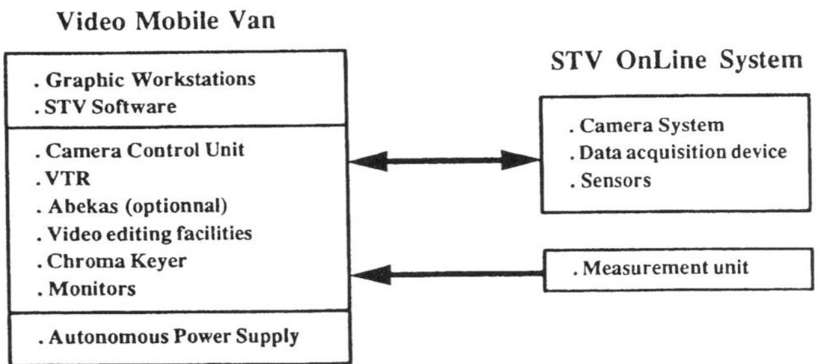

Fig. 5: The OnLine STV Service

20.5. Some Production Examples

After some experimental shootings done at INA, the first real application was, in 1992, the film "RACOON", for which the Design Dept. of Renault (french car industry) used our system. It is worth to notice that, apart from communication gain, the goal of the shootings was to build a database of images, where Renault could insert new prototypes at their earliest phase of conception with maximum realism. Since "Racoon", we have been doing more shootings for Renault, this time in an urban context.

Since then, the concept of accurate motion camera tracking started to be more and more understood and desired by the 3D CG European production companies when dealing with real/virtual mixings. As a consequence, there is a growing demand for services at the STV system produced by INA, for both OffLine and OnLine versions. Hopefully, a commercial version of the system will be available within 1994.

20.6. Further Extensions

The work developped so far at INA by the Laboratoire 3D constitutes the kernel of many possible applications, one of them being the STV system, a tool for program production. Among the other, we can quote:

a) Motion tracking
Put several fixed marks on any object (at least 3 marks, whose position on the object is known), and film this moving object with one STV camera, then you can determine the 3D path (position and orientation) of this object.
Alternatively, using two STV cameras filming the same 3D moving point allows to reconstitute the 3D path (position) of this point along the time. This is true, naturally, for any number of points moving simultaneously, but independantly, in the same space.
The advantage of this tracking system over some other traditionnal tracking system, is the ability to move the camera(s) (zoom,focus,pan,tilt,...) thus allowing to widen the area which the moving target is bound to. To the owner of a STV system, these motion tracking capabilities require only additionnal software.

b) "Augmented reality"
Our interest on this topic is very new. It deals with the following general question: an image is coming from a real camera. The information contained in this image can be sometime very complex and hard to extract and analyse properly by human observer; this can be because the shooting conditions are bad, or because the scene itself is confusing.
Real time 2D techniques for enhancing the interesting parts of the images are well known, and largely used. With some STV-like techniques, we think that real time 3D techniques could be used as well: by superimposing "comprehensive" schematic drawings on the real image. Fields of application includes, by evidence, tele-manipulation of robots operating in hard environments, and many medical areas.

21. Teaching the English [r] sound to Japanese Through Sound and Image Understanding

Hisako Murakawa
The University of Aizu, Aizu-Wakamatsu City, Fukushima 965-80, Japan

Summary.

Japanese have studied English for years; however, they cannot accurately produce some English sounds. Students have difficulty emulating articulation such as tongue movement while producing the [r] sound. Textbooks explain this articulation in various ways using exterior facial views in lieu of interior views of the mouth and its sound producing organs.

The University of Aizu's Center for Language Research utilizes a multimedia computer workstation system in its Language Media Laboratory. Its functions include (1) voice analysis, (2) voice analysis transfer, and (3) student guidance. Voice analysis involves recording voice data and displaying voice patterns and pitches. Voice analysis transfer allows data to be sent to the teacher's console. Student guidance allows the teacher to monitor the students' activities and provide audiovisual guidance. Using this system, students can visualize their pronunciation and compare it to that of a native speaker.

The purpose of this chapter is to suggest the development of an ideal pronunciation training software using: (1) three dimensional (3-D) graphic displays of the ideal interior facial movement involving the tongue, jaw, and lips; (2) superimposed 3-D images of the inaccurate portion of the speakers articulation organ movements.

Key words: phonetics, pronunciation, methodology, articulation

21.1. Introduction

Although Japanese people have been making a great effort for years to master the four English language skills: listening, speaking, reading, and writing, they still have great difficulty communicating in English with native speakers of English. Pronunciation is especially difficult.. Several factors cause Japanese speakers this difficulty with the English pronunciation. These include: psychological and linguistic reasons as well as a lack of effective language teaching software and hardware. The first psychological reason is the fact that most Japanese abandon trying to improve their pronunciation. Psychologically they firmly believe that pronunciation is difficult and there is no way of improving it no matter how hard they try. This negative belief may lie in the disapointing results of long periods of effort made by Japanese and foreign teachers under Japan's English education system. Because of increasingly difficult high school and university entrance examinations, Japanese junior and senior high school teachers emphasize reading and writing, using the grammar- translation method to prepare for these examinations. Even though some universities have recently included listening skills in the entrance examination, the listening and the speaking of English are still being neglected. The "Oral Approach," a teaching method introduced by Palmer in 1922, has been used over the years to try to improve the English listening and speaking ability of Japanese students. Charles Fries came to Japan in 1956 when the English Language Exploratory Committee (ELEC) had just been organized. The ELEC invited Einar Haugen and Ernest F. Haden as ELEC counselors. The progam they helped to develop was to train junior high school English teachers in the principles and techniques of the "Oral Approach" and to improve their own individual language skills, with special emphasis on aural-oral English. In connection with this "Oral- Approach" effort in schools by many foreign and Japanese teachers, there appeared phonograph records, tape recorders, and instructional programs in English on television and radio. Still, however, too few Japanese can speak, pronounce, or understand English with ease.

Another psychological reason is that Japanese are afraid of making mistakes. Japanese are not accustomed to expressing themselves freely in either Japanese or English. Therefore, they are timid and fearful that they will make mistakes. They may feel it a disgrace to admit ignorance in the classroom, especially if this relates to the inability to produce the same English sounds that children can produce fairly accurately.

The second inhibiting aspect in English pronunciation arises from the natural differences existing between a native language and a target language. No sound features between the two languages are equivalent nor are the loudness of the voice, the rate of speaking, the pitch of the vocal tone, the articulation, or the breathing mechanism the same. For example, the Japanese phoneme /r/ differs from the English /r/. Japanese people confuse the English /r/ and /l/ in the words, "read" [rid] and "lead" [lid] for the Japanese flap sound [rid]. Japanese also replace the English vowels [æ] in the word "hat," [a] in "hot,"[ʌ] in "hut,"and [ɝ] in "hurt," with the single Japanese sound [a]. The Japanese may pronounce, "I have a hot (hat)," "The hot (hut) is made of wood," "He hot (hurt) his back." Thus, native speakers of English may have difficulty understanding what the Japanese are trying to say.

Allophonic variation in English is represented in various sounds in many various environments. The English voiceless fricative sound [s], for example, in any environment has a stronger and longer duration than the Japanese [s] sound. The duration of the Japanese [s] sound, which occurs in the initial, middle, or final positions, is weak and short in duration, and often is not perceived clearly by English speaking people. Japanese do not have to produce the Japanese [s] strongly; therefore, Japanese are expected to understand a sentence or a word without perceiving the Japanese [s] sound. The sceintific analysis of the duration of the [s] identifies the differences between the duration of the Japanese and English [s] sounds. As a result, Japanese often may not produce the [s], esepcially when they produce a cluster as seen in the word "style" [stal], though they think they are producing the English [s] clearly. Japanese may produce [tal] which sounds like the word "tile". This allophonic problem leads to a phonemic problem.

Another pronunciation problem is rate of speaking. In particular the relative duration of successive syllables in an utterance in English differs from the Japanese. The Japanese language is syllable-timed, meaning all syllables are produced at the same duration. Therefore, Japanese produce a syllabic vowel and a syllable consisting a consonant and vowel at the same rate, as seen in "aka" (red) which is composed of two syllables. The first syllable "a" and the second syllable "ka" are pronounced at the same rate. This indicates that the duration of the Japanese consonant is very short. As a result, native English speakers will not be able to perceive the Japanese consonants clearly.

The Japanese intonation pattern also differs from that of English. The Japanese affirmative sentence is produced by beginning with pitch level 3 and ending with pitch level 1, while the English pitch level is produced using a 231 pitch level sequence in the sentence. For example, the Japanese will pronounce "Amega futte imasu" (It is raining), while English speaking people will produce "It is raining." This intonation pattern affects the Japanese when they try to speak English, such as "It is raining." The first part of the sentence is pronounced strongly with pitch 3 and then gradually the pitch will fall to pitch 1. The change from high pitch to lower pitch affects the ability of native English speakers to perceive the last part of the sentence clearly. They hear "It is" distinctively, but not "raining" distinctively.

In spite of long periods of effort by both foreign and Japanese teachers, the large majority of Japanese adults still experience a sense of frustration when they try to understand the English spoken by native speakers, or try to make themselves understood in English. In particular, Japanese feel that pronunciation which is related to listening and speaking skills, is their weakest area of learning and teaching the English language. Foreign and Japanese language teachers are aware that serious Japanese pronunciation problems exist; however, they are still searching for answers to these pronunciation problems.

The purposes of this chapter are to present various currently available methods and techniques of teaching and learning the pronunciation of the English /r/ sound; to view the acoustic features of the /r/ sound produced by native English speakers using the analyzer in the Language Media Laboratory (LML) of the University of Aizu, Fukushima, Japan; to introduce an ideal model of the English /r/ sound; and finally to suggest the development of ideal pronunciation training software as an effective learning and teaching tool.

21.2. The English Semivowel: [r]

The English semivowel /r/ sound is an elusive sound for Japanese to grasp perhaps because it is difficult to describe accurately, difficult to perceive, and definiable by what it is not, rather than by what it is. However, the /r/ sound is one of the most frequent sounds in the English language. English language learners, teachers, researchers, and phoneticians around the world have been greatly interested in this /r/ sound simply because it has been considered one of the most difficult sounds for non-native speakers of English to master. Many textbooks and other teaching and learning materials emphasize the importance of mastering this /r/ sound and the difficulty for non-native speakers to produce /r/ accurately [6],[8],[13],[17],[20]. Undoubtedly the world's English language learners have difficulties as described in these references. French learners of English habitually use a uvular trilled /r/ or /g/ quickly to form the glide /r/, and Spanish learners produce a tongue-tip trilled /r/ instead of the English /r/ [2],[4],[5],[7]. Prator and Haycraft state that Japanese and Chinese have difficulty in the distinction between /r/ and /l/ and in producing both also [6],[15]. It is worthwhile then to find effective techniques to facilitate the production of the English /r/ sound. For this reason, the traditional or general teaching techniques or methods for learning and teaching this sound need to be reexamined.

21.2.1. Various instruction of the /r/ sound

Many technical pronunciation books and textbooks give various instructions for articulating the /r/ sound; however, whether or not these instructions are effective and appropriate for Japanese learners is an issue to discuss.

Not touching the roof of the mouth. A commonly emphasized articulatory explanation is that the tip of the tongue must not touch anything. Bronstein states that the tip and blade of the tongue are turned upward, toward the hard palate, the tip pointing to (but not touching) the area immediately behind the alveolar ridges [2]. Tiffany and Carrell explain that the tongue must not touch the roof of the mouth [19]. Fisher describes that the central part of the tongue is tensed and raised toward the palate and the tip of the tongue varies in its articulation, being either lifted toward (but not touching) the hard palate or drawn back somewhat from the lower teeth [4]. Orion explains that a learner should raise the tip of his tongue towards the upper gum ridge but should not touch it and the tip of his tongue should not touch anything. Under these instructions which emphasize "not to touch anything," Japanese learners usually try not to touch the entire tongue to the upper palate nor to anywhere else. In order to raise their tongue without touching anything, they have to lower their jaw as widely as when producing the [a] sound; therefore, it is very difficult for them to move their tongue to the sounds which follow, such as a vowel or a consonant. For example, when a Japanese learner tries to produce [r] in "ran," [rid] in "read," or [rand] in "round," he or she produces the [r] and the following vowel with the mouth open; therefore, his or her [r] sound is extremely ambiguous because he or she is trying so hard to "not touch anything." It takes a while to open the jaw only slightly from their position, so if a learner tries not to touch the tip or front of the tongue to the alveolar ridge or palate, the [r] sound may be heard differently by native English speakers.

Curling the tip of the tongue. Another confusing instruction to Japanese learners for producing the [r] sound is to curl the tip of the tongue toward the back of the mouth. Bowen gives instructions as follows: "The tip is curled high toward the back of the mouth, but not touching anywhere" [1]. Kreidler also gives an instruction stating that the tongue is curled [9]. The Japanese are aware that they have to curl their tongue or the tip of the tongue, but yet they should not touch the tip of the tongue to anypart of the mouth. This is one of the most difficult instruction for them to follow. As a result, they end up opening their mouth too much to produce the [r] and the following vowel. Thus,the [r] sound produced may again be different from the native English speaker [r].

Pressing the sides of the tongue against the upper back teeth. Many linguists, and scholars in Teaching English as a Second (Foreign) Language recommend pressing the sides of the tongue against the upper back teeth. Although Orion emphasizes the instruction of "not touching," he also adds this advice [10]. Rivers and Temperley also recommend having the back of the tongue low and the edges of the tongue against the back part of the tooth ridge [16]. Japanese learners are greatly confused when they read this instruction because it contradicts the instruction of "not touching the tongue." When they try to press the sides of their tongue against their upper back teeth, they tend to touch the tip of the tongue to the upper palate or upper part of the mouth. As a result, they produce the Japanese flap sound or struggle to place their tongue in the right place.

Making a narrow groove in the tip of the tongue. Some scholars suggest making a somewhat narrow groove in the tip of the tongue. Although Kreidler recommends curling the tongue to produce the [r] sound, he gives a description of the [r] sound as follows: "The whole body of the tongue is pulled back and bunched up, with a slight groove in the very tip" [9]. Potter and Kopp suggest to moving the tip or blade of the tongue forward from an elevated position near the center of the palate towards the alveolar ridge [14]. If Japanese learners follow Potter and Kopp's description, they will be able to make a groove automatically. Singh explains the articulatory components involving the lips and tongue as follows: 'The lips are rounded and the tongue contacts with the alveolar ridge with smooth central opening [18]. O'Connor says that the tip of the tongue is curled backwards and upwards in the mouth so that it is quite close to the highest part of the palate, but not so close as to cause friction as the air streams out [12]. His explanation seems easy to follow and it gives the idea that the learner needs to make a narrow space between the palate and the central part of the tongue. As a result, the tip of the tongue touches the palate but the central part of the tongue does not touch the palate. However, his instructions still do not give satisfactory articulatory explanations because they do not describe how much space (groove) the learners should make between the palate and the tip of the tongue.

Rounding and unrounding the lips. Another sound feature of the [r] sound is rounded lips. O'Connor [12], Singh [18], and Potter [14] say that the lips are somewhat rounded to form the [r] sound. On the other hand, some say that the lips are slightly open [10],[16]. Rounding and unrounding the lips are obviously important components of the articulation of the [r] sound.

From all these instructions, several questions will be raised. How can a learner and a teacher know the ideal [r] sound? Why is it important to make a narrow groove? What is the best size of the space to make to produce the correct [r] sound? In other words, how much does a learner have to raise his tongue to make the narrow groove? What is the relationship between rounded and unrounded lips in producing the [r] sound? None of the instructional materials cited state the detailed information needed to answer these questions.

21.2.2. Acoustic Features of the /r/ sound

The acoustic features of the /r/ sound have been given and explained by many phoneticians. As the articulators move from the positions required during the steady-state portions of the semi-vowels to the positions required for the following vowels, the filter functions of the vocal tract change in dynamic fashion. O'Connor explains changes in the frequency of F1 (the first formant) are the result of a complex interaction of changes in laryngeal height, place of articulation, degree of vocal tract construction, changes in pharyngeal volume, and lip rounding. Changes in F2 (the second formant) appear to be largely controlled by changes in the place of articulation and the degree of vocal tract constriction. F3 (the third formant) appears to be primarily related to the degree of lip rounding [12]. O'Connor suggests that the first two formants are somewhat similar for /l/ and /r/, but F3 undergoes a marked upward shift in frequency during /r/ while it remains relatively constant during the production of /l/ [12]. He therefore suggests that the low resonance frequency for F3 is associated with lip rounding [12]. Fant describes F1 as determined largely by the volume behind the constriction, F2 as a half-wave length dependent on the resonance of the interior cavities (primarily controlled by the tongue position) and F3 as substantially dependent upon resonances in the anterior mouth cavity (in front of the alveolar constriction, and therefore controlled largely by the lip configuration) [3]. Potter's visible patterns as shown in Figure 1 help clarify the sound features described above. He explains as follows: "The [r] from which and to which the glide [r] moves can be made from a steady state position. F1 (termed "bar" by Potter) is on or very near the baseline. F2 and F3 are in close proximity, a little below the center of the pattern. The group of [r] sounds are the only sounds in the language that have F2 and F3 in this position. Since the glide [r] is made as the articulators move from this [r], beginning at the position of the vowel resonances, F2 and F3 may curve in parallel, as in "read," or they may separate as in "road." Whether or not they stay together, depends upon the relative positions of the resonance formants of the vowel to which or from which the [r] glides" [14]. Because Potter does not give even approximate frequencies to identify these three formants, it is difficult to relate each formant appearing in Figure 1 to his descriptions of the three formants. However, it is possible to view the relationships between the descriptions and each formant very briefly. The first formants of the [r] in "read" and 'road' presented in Figure 1 appear near the baseline, which means that each F1 has a low frequency. This may be the result of the volume behind the constriction. The second formants of the [r] of these two words may indicate the tongue position. Since the tongue is lifted to make a narrow groove, they appear in the areas of low frequencies. The sceintifically calculated size of the groove is unknown; however, it is possible to view F2's characteristics by comparing the areas of F2s of the vowel [i] and [o]. The second formant of the [i] appears much higher than that of the [r] in "read" because the tongue position is in a high place in the pattern, while the second formant of the [o] appears low because the tongue position when articulating the [o] in "road" is low. The third formant of the [r] indicates lip rounding. The characteristic of the third formant of the [r], rounded lips, is possibly recognized in the pattern in Figure 1. The third formant of the [r] appears in the area of low frequencies; therefore, the formant of the [r] may be considered to reveal rounded lips. Figure 2 gives the voice patterns produced by one of the American faculty at the University of Aizu and shows a similar pattern of the three formants. After this American faculty member produced the word "read" [rid], the tongue position was shown though it was impossible to see the tongue position when he articulated. A very narrow groove was observed and lip rounding was observed when he actually produced [rid]. Obviously, these two tongue positions, which occured at different times, might not be exactly the same; however, in Figure 3, the patterns of all of his [r] sounds, similar to those of Potter's, are shown because the three formants of the [r] appear in the lower area of frequencies.

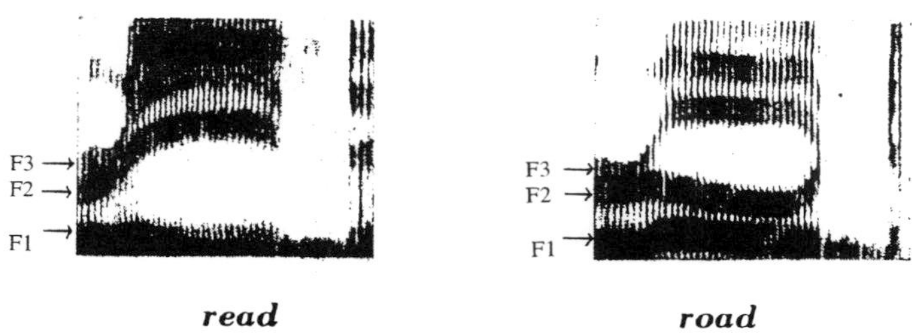

FIGURE 1. Potter's visible patterns of the [r] in the words "read" and "road".

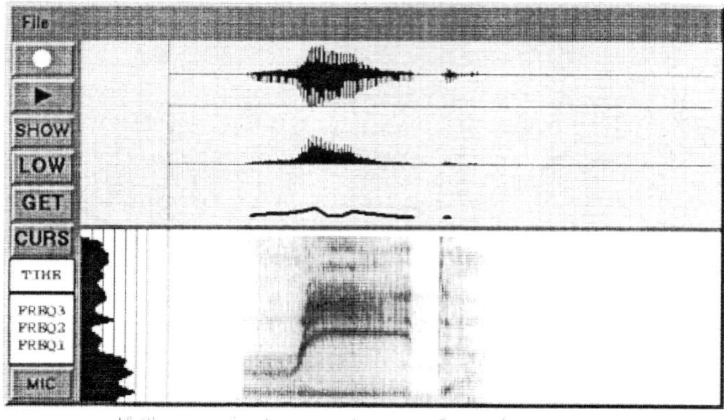

FIGURE 2. A voice pattern of the word "read" produced by one of the American Faculty at the University of Aizu.

21.3. A Model of the Ideal American [r] Sound in the Initial Position

Various [r] sounds in the initial position are produced by native English speakers. It will be very difficult to define an ideal [r] sound because of regional variations, idiolect variations, and language learners' proficienty levels. However, it is extremely difficult for Japanese learners, especially beginners, who try to practice English pronuncnaition without leaving a model of the [r] sound which they can imitate. Some of the Japanese intermediate and advanced learners who have been trained in listening to and producing English may not be interfered with by the Japanese sound features; however, it will also be difficult for them to practice English pronunciation without being familiar with the ideal [r]. Moreover, teachers need to be knowledgeable about the features and articulation of the [r]. If teachers are not able to explain to the students how the [r] sound is articulated, but require the students to repeat after them, neither teacher nor student will be able to gain satisfactory results from the students. Teachers probably will have to select the [r] sound produced by various English speaking people as a model.

21.3.1. Various [r] sounds

This section presents various [r] sounds produced by native speakers of American English. The main focus in observing these [r] sounds are based on the three formants and the duration of the sound. All voice data were analyzed using an analyzer in the University of Aizu LML, whose functions will be explained later.

The [r] sound appearing in the voice pattern. Figure 2 presents a voice pattern of the word "read," produced by one (T.O.) of three male American faculty (T.O., S.L., and K.C) of the Center for Language Research at the University of Aizu. In order to present the characteristics of the [r] sound vividly, T.O. exaggarated his pronunciation of the word so that the three parallel formants of his [r] sound appear clearly in the voice pattern. This voice pattern is similar to a visible pattern of the [r] presented by Potter in Figure l. Moreover, the [r] in the initial position produced by a TV announcer in the word "real-time" appears in the same area. The three formants move parallel from left to right and appear low along the baseline.

The [r] sound appearing in different environments. Many phoneticians present the frequencies of the three formants to introduce the features of the [r] sound. The frequencies of the [r] formants vary depending on the phonetic environment and also on the speaker's pitch level. Because of a wider range of frequencies of each formant, it has been very difficult to define the [r] sound in terms of frequency domains. However, phoneticians, scientists, and others have been wording toward an objective description of the [r] sound.

Both Gimson and Fant give the range of each [r] sound formant. Gimson states that F1 appears between 120 and 600 cps, F2 between 840 and 1560 before [i,e,], 840 to 1200 cps before [ɔ], and 600 to 1200 cps before the vowels [o,u], and F3, which provides an essential regulation cue, 840-1920 cps before [i,e,] and less than 1680 cps before [o,u] [5]. Fant reports that for non-palatalized [r], F1= 500 pcs, F2=1000 cps, and F3=1800 cps. For palatalized [r], F1=400 cps, F2 =1500 cps, and F3=2200 cps [3]. Both sources indicate that the three formant frequencies before high front vowels are higher than those before low back vowels. There are, however, slight differences between Gimson's and Fant's data. Gimson gives a wider range for each formant depending on the environment. There is a difference of 480 cps for F1, 720 cps for F2, and 600 cps for F3. Furthermore, the range between F1 and F2 is approximately 720 to 960 cps before front and back vowels, and between F2 and F3 approximately 240 to 720 cps before front vowels. For non- palatalized [r], Fant's data show the difference between F1 and F2 as 500 cps, and between F2 and F3 as 800 cps. Between F1 and F2 1100 cps, and between F2 and F3, 700 cps.

Three American faculty of the Center for Language Research recorded the [r] occuring before various vowels, as shown in Figure 3. Table 1 provides the frequencies of the three formants of the [r] sound produced by these three American faculty. The ranges of the first, second, and third formants are from 341 cps to 493 cps, from 835 pcs to 1139 cps, and from 1518 cps to 1784 cps, respectively. The average frequencies of the [r] spoken by T.O. are: F1= 393 cps, F2= 930 cps , and F3=1675 cps . The average frequencies of the [r] spoken by K.C. are: F1= 450 cps, F2=1153 cps, and F3=1675 cps. The average frequencies of the [r] spoken by S.L. are: F1= 398 cps, F2=1110 cps, F3= 1660 cps. T.O.'s F2 frequencies are lower than those of K.C. and S.L., while the three speakers'F1 and F3 frequencies almost are the same.

Table 1. The Frequencies of the Three Formants of the [r] Sound Produced by Three American Faculty

Names		read [i]	rid [I]	red [ɛ]	ran [æ]	rod [a]	raw [ɔ]	road [o]	root [u]	Average
T.O.	F3	1670	1708	1746	1784	1632	1518	1632	1708	1675
	F2	987	987	949	911	949	911	835	911	930
	F1	417	417	417	379	379	379	379	379	393
K.C.	F3	1784	1632	1746	1670	1632	1594	1670	1670	1675
	F2	1177	1063	1177	1253	1063	1101	1139	1253	1153
	F1	341	493	531	417	493	455	455	417	450
S.L.	F3	1670	1670	1670	1670	1670	1632	1632	1670	1660
	F2	1139	1063	1101	1139	1063	1139	1101	1139	1110
	F1	417	417	341	417	417	417	341	417	398

(cps)

Comparing these three faculty's data with Gimson's and Fant's data, only T.O.'s F2 frequencies before the high front vowels [i,I,ɛ] are lower than those before low back vowels [ɔ, o, u]. The other two speakers' frequencies do not differ in environments before high front vowels or low back vowels. Fant gives F2 and F3 friequencies for palatalized [r] as 1500 cps and 2200 cps. However, the averages of these three speakers are 1064 cps, and 1670 cps. Apparently, Fant's data indicate that the F1 and F3 of the [r] sound appear lower in frequencies.

Various durations of the [r] sound. The duration of the [r] sound varies depending on a speaker's speech rate and also on whether the words were read separately or in a sentence. The slower a speaker speaks, the longer the duration of the [r] sound. Table 2 presents all the durations of the [r] pronounced in individual words read by three American faculty. These words and the [r] in different environments are shown in Table 3. The duration of the [r] sound produced by T.O. and S.L. are almost the same, with a difference of only 8 msc. The average duration of the [r] sound produced by T.O. and S.L. is 140 msc and 148 msc respectively, while K.C.'s is 84 msc. Obviously, T.O. and S.L. read words more slowly than did K.C.. If these three faculty had read these words in sentences at a natural speed, the duration would be very differ-

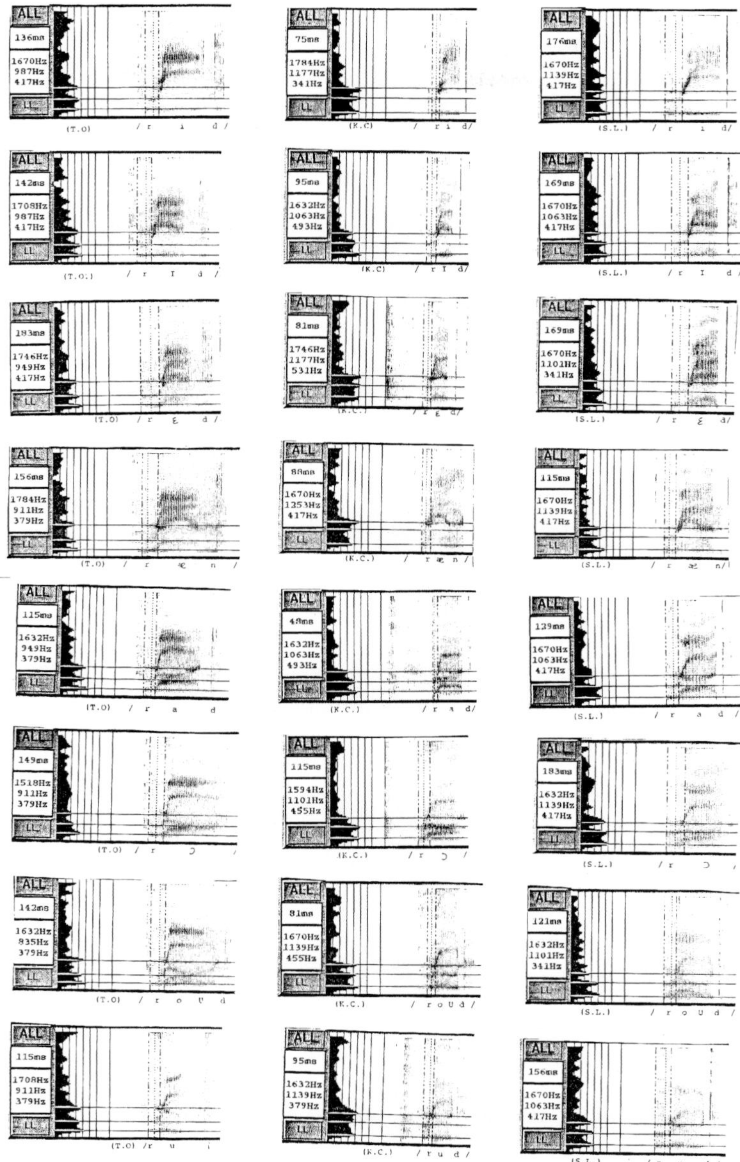

FIGURE 3. Voice patterns of the words "read," "rid," "red," "ran," "raw," "road," and "rude."

ent from these data. The long duration of the [r] will help Japanese learners to perceive the [r] sound more accurately than the short duration, while native English speakers will recognize [r] sounds occuring in any environment at any time.

Table 2. Duration Taken from Three American Faculty

Words	T.O.	K.C.	S.L.	Average
read	136	75	176	129
rid	142	95	169	135
red	183	81	169	144
ran	156	88	115	119
rod	115	48	129	97
raw	149	115	183	149
road	142	81	121	114
root	115	88	115	106
rude	115	95	156	122
Average	140	84	148	

(msc)

Table 3. The Words and the [r] in Different Environments

1.	[r]	+	[i]	read
2.	[r]	+	[ɛ]	rid
3.	[r]	+	[æ]	red
4.	[r]	+	[æ]	ran
5.	[r]	+	[a]	rod
6.	[r]	+	[ɔ]	raw
7.	[r]	+	[o]	road
8.	[r]	+	[u]	rude

21.3.2. A model of the ideal [r] sound

As previously mentioned, Japanese teachers who teach English pronunciation need a model of the ideal [r] sound. With it, the teachers will be able to teach the [r] sound effectively and students will be able to understand the articulatory movement of the [r] and practice it effectively, if they know how to place the tongue, how to round the lips, and how to make a narrow groove in the mouth. Voice patterns and approximate formant frequencies are available for viewing the [r] sound. However, no precise relation between the frequencies of the three formants and articulatory movements has been presented, such as the relation between rounded and unrounded articulation with a narrow and wide groove. If a narrow groove is important, then the question will be the size of the groove. T.O., who was asked to demonstrate the tongue placement for producing the [r] sound, showed the width of the groove in this mouth– approximately two to three centimeters long and eight centimeters wide. Of course, it was impossible to observe the groove while he began to articulate the words. Both Potter's and the three American faculty's [r] sounds probably suggest a model of the ideal [r] sound as follows: the tongue should be raised towards the upper palate, the sides of the tongue should press the back part of the teeth, and the lips should be rounded. In addition to these articulations, Japanese students need to prolong the [r] sound when they practice production, and to listen as much as possible to the [r] sounds having a short short duration.

21.4. The Development of the Ideal Pronunciation Training Tools

Instruments used to analyze the sounds of speech are available at U.S. and Japanese universities offering programs in speech and hearing studies. Tape recorders, oscilloscopes, and the sound spectrograph developed in 1940s have been used for research purposes. The oscilloscope makes sound waves visible for analysis, but it is very difficult to view individual features of the sound. Currently, the computer can be programmed to extract and display signal parameters, for example the peak signal amplitude or the fundamental frequency. Therefore, the acoustic phonetician can study duration, frequency, intensity, formant patterns, or transitions of speech signals with greater flexibility than was formerly possible. However, until now computerized sound spectrographs have been used exclusively research, not for practicing or teaching pronunciation.

21.4.1. The Language Media Laboratory English Education System

The Language Media Laboratory (LML) English Education System was developed at the University of Aizu to facilitate the interactive study of pronunciation as well as conversation. In the future, this system will be expanded into a multi-media education system. The language software and lab materials developed by Sony under the author's direction, contain a series of graded lessons and show moving images and sounds of prerecorded speakers. These allow students to speak and then manipulate sound voiceprints, sound spectram, and so forth. The main functions of the system related to voice analysis are presented below.

Voice analysis in the LML. On the SUN workstation installed in each student's booth (64 total in two labs), both student and AV voices are recorded and are analyzed on a graphical display of voice patterns and pitches. The results of the analysis of two voices can be displayed at the same time as shown in number 3 in Figure 4. Figure 5 shows a screen of voice analysis applications. Although the top and bottom voice analysis applications are the same in the function and operation method, a student can operate them separately. On the screen, there are four areas: envelope display, power display, pitch display, spectrum display. A student selects voice input from four different sources, such as the headset microphone, an AV device (Laser disk player, VHS video deck, 8mm video deck, or television and BS tuners (satelite TV), the LL system, or from the student desk monitored in the video window. A student records voice input; the maximum recording time is 3.3 seconds. A student has to select from three analysis modes: for people with low voices (generally men), for people with high voices (generally women), for people with particularly high voices (generally children). A student can display three different cursor bars: (1) frequency measurement cursor bar (three horizontal cursors), (2) frequency transverse cut display cursor bar (one vertical cursor), and (3) continuation time measurement cursor bar (two vertical cursors). A students can display three horizontal frequency measurement cursor bars and one vertical frequency cut display cursor bar transversely. At the same time, he or she can display the frequencies at the positons of the horizontal cursor bars in the frequency display area and make transverse display of the frequency at the position of the vertical cursor bar. He or she can move each cursor bar with the mouse to change the freqeuncy measurement position or transversely cut the display position. A student can read the duration time and the three frequencies.

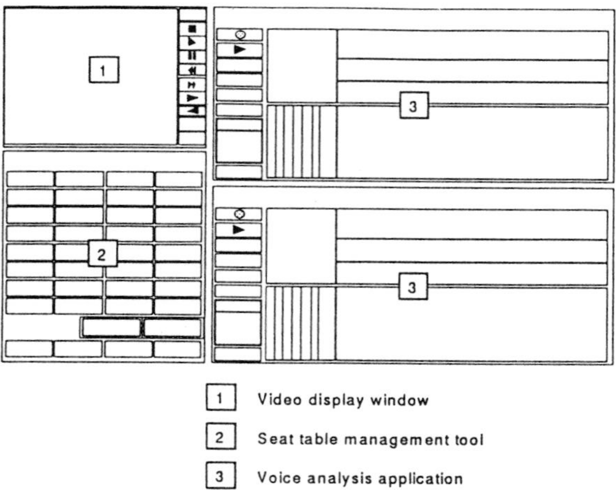

FIGURE 4. Applications in Display

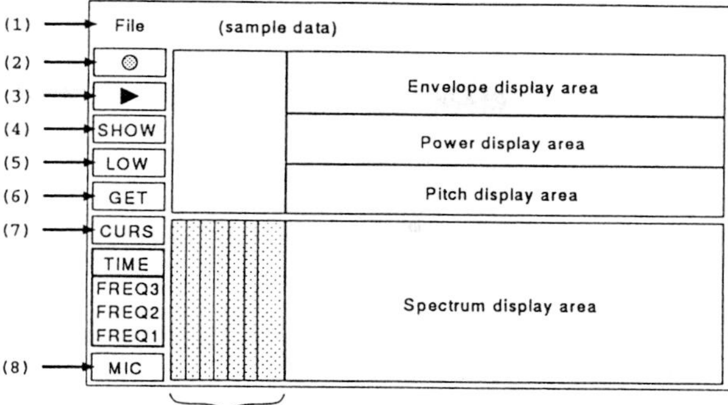

Spectrum transverse cut display area

(1) File pulldown menu
(2) Record button
(3) Play button
(4) Analysis start button
(5) Analysis mode change button
(6) Getdata button
(7) Cursor bar display button
(8) Input voice source selection button

FIGURE 5. Voice Analysis Application

Transfer function of voice analysis results. Voice data analyzed by students can be called up on the workstation screen and voice data analyzed by the teacher can be shown to students. A console monitor allows the teacher to listen in on students' efforts, as well as interact with them via the headsets and gather statistics on progress. Voice data can be sent to all of the students' desks from the master console. The teacher can send voice data for both voice analysis applications, only the top voice analysis application, or only the bottom voice analysis application.

Printing function of voice analysis results. Both the teacher from the master console and students from their booth can print their voice data. The same print data as the voice analysis data printed by a student can be saved in a buffer for batch printing at the master console. The teacher can save students' data in five buffers and printed data can be saved a maximum of five times during one lesson.

AV device control function. A student can stop or pause video play, replay the video at normal speed, stop, rewind at high speed, and slowly reproduce the video at a quarter of the normal speed. A student can reproduce video slowly only for the laser disk function. This function is very effective for the students to observe the articulatory movements.

Laser index search viewer screen. To teach English pronunciation, the laser disk teaching material titled Pronunciation Training System developed by the Kawai Instrument Company, is in the LML. The laser index search viewer enables students to make an index search of a laser desk. If the student double clicks the desired index entry, an automatic search is made of the corresponding portion of the laser disk, which is then played. When the corresponding portion has been reproduced playing stops automatically. Further teaching material will also be installed in this manner in the future.

Reading model voice data. The LML system provides model voice data which can be read for reproduction and analysis. The model voice is classified for each phonetic symbol. The model voice data are read and an envelope is displayed on the screen. The students of the University of Aizu study computer science and engineering; therefore, model voice data based on approximately 550 technical words which are commonly used in this area are installed in the file. The students can compare their pronunciation with these model voice data. The Pronunciation Training System includes techniques of articulation, allophones, words, sentences, and dialogues spoken in daily conversation as well.

21.4.2. Three dimensional (3-D) graphical displays of ideal interior facial movements in virtual reality

Although the University of Aizu provide a highly computerized education system in teaching and learning English pronunciation interactively, more effective tools need to be developed for both teachers and students. The facial movements presented in the laser disk series Pronunciation Training System show only the movement of the mouth from the front of the speaker and the tongue movement in animation from the side of the speaker. This animation gives only an approximate representation of the tongue's movement. Therefore, it is very difficult for students to articulate English sounds exactly, because interior articulatory movements are impossible for teachers to show to the students. Students can see the teacher's jaw and lip movements clearly but cannot see the tongue movement at the same time as the jaw and lip movements. Once an ideal [r] sound has been established as a model, a 3-D virtual reality graphical display of all articulatory movements performed while producing the [r] would allow students to see and hear every aspect of the articulation simultaneously.

21.4.3. Superimposed 3-D images of the inaccurate portion of the speakers articulation organ movements.

When the students emulate the articulations shown in the 3-D graphical display of the ideal [r] sound, they probably will not know whether or not their movements are accurate. If a 3-D image of the inaccurate portion of the student's articulation were superimposed over the model, the student would be able to understand what precisely they were doing wrong. Because the Japanese have had amazing difficulty producing the [r] sound, one of the most important English sounds, for more than 150 years, such tools will be extremely useful for them when they try to produce a satisfactory and understandable [r] sound.

21.5. Conclusion

This paper has presented the unique English pronuncition problems experienced by the Japanese. One of the most serious problems is posed by the English [r], which is difficult to describe scientifically. The frequency domain of this sound has yet to be correllated to the articulatory movements made in producing it. Voice patterns of native English speakers are providing insight into the features of the [r], but further detailed analysis of this sound is still needed. Eventually, this analysis will lead to the development of 3-D graphical displays in virtual reality of the production of this sound (and others). Such a tool would allow learners to finally hear, see and "feel" correct English pronunciation.

References

1. Bowen, J. Donald, Patterns of English Pronunciation, Rowley: Newbury House Publishers, Inc., 1975, p. 52.
2. Bronstein, Arthur J., The Pronunciation of American English: An Introduction to Phonetics, New York: Appleton-Century-Crofts, Inc., 1960, p. 121.
3. Fant, G., Acoustic Theory of Speech Production, The Hague: Mouton, 1970.
4. Fisher, Hilda B., Improving Voice and Articulation, Boston: Houghton Mifflin Company, 1975, p. 301.
5. Gimson, A.C., An Introduction to the Pronunciation of English, New York: St. Martines Press, 1970, pp. 207-211.
6. Haycraft, Brita, The Teaching of Pronunciation, London: Longman, 1984, p. 108.
7. Hook, Robert and Judith Rowell, A Handbook of English Pronunciation, Edward Arnold, 1982, p. 72.
8. Kawabe, Shunichi and Yukio Kotani, Eigohatsuon to Katsuyo Goi, Tokyo: Tokyo Denki University Press, 1991.
9. Kreidler, Charles W., The Pronunciation of English, New York: Basil Blackwell, 1989, p.42.
10. Orion, Gertrude F., Pronouncing American English : sounds, Stress, and Intonation, New York: Newbury House Publishers, 1988, p. 176.
11. O'Connor, J.D., A Course of English Pronunciation, London: The British Broadcasting Corporation, 1979, p. 15.
12. O'Connor, J.D., et al., "Acoustic cues for the Perception of Initial /w,j,r/ on english," Word, Vol. 13, pp. 24-43.

13. Otsuka, Takanobu et al., American Pronunciation for the Japanese, Tokyo: Naundo, 1968.
14. Potter, Ralph K., George A. Kopp, and Harriet Green Kopp, Visible Speech, New York: Dover Publications, Inc., 1966.
15. Prator, Clifford H., Jr. and Betty Wallace Robinett, Manual of American English Pronunciation, New York: Holt, Rinehart and Winston, 1972, p. 96.
16. Rivers, Wilga M. and Mary S. Temperley, A Practical guide to the Teaching of English as a Second or Foreign language, New York: Oxford University Press, 1987, p. 159.
17. Takamoto, Sutesaburo, Aural-Oral Approach to Modern English, Tokyo: Naundo, 1977.
18. Singh, Sadamand, and kala S. Singh, Phonetics Principles and Practice, 2nd ed. Austin: Pro.ed, 1982, p. 209.
19. Tiffany, William R., and James Carrel, Phonetics: Theory and Application, New York: McGraw-Hill Publishing Company, 1977, p. 346.
20. Torii, Yoshitsugu and Naomichi kaneko, Eigo no Hatsuon, Tokyo: Taishukan, 1979, pp. 132-133.

Theme 6

Applications to Real Worlds

22. A Geological Model for Landscape Simulation

B. Peroche and P. Roudier
Ecole Nationale Supérieure, des Mines de Saint-Etienne, Département Informatique, 158, cours Fauriel, 42023 Saint-Etienne Cedex 2, France

M. Perrin
Ecole Nationale Supérieure des Mines de Paris, 60, Boulevard Saint-Michel, 75006 Paris, France

Summary.
This paper describes an original approach to terrain evolution in landscape synthesis. In order to create some realistic landforms, we simulate geologically contrasted terrains and apply deterministic erosion processes to them. This allows us to relate erosion at any point of the model to local geological parameters. Any height field may be chosen as an initial topographic surface. Small perturbations may be introduced to avoid unpleasant regularities. A 3D model defines the geological parameters of each point according to elevation. Our method is iterative: at each step, rock removal and possible alluvial deposition are computed on each point of the land surface. The available erosion laws simulate mechanical erosion, chemical dissolution and alluvial deposition. The geology and the morphology of the resulting landscapes and the river network are created at each iteration. Landsurfaces can be visualized at the final stage, by a rendering algorithm including natural texture mapping. The stream network and the ridges may also be visualized.

Key words: Geological Modelling, Erosion and Deposition Simulation, Landscape Rendering.

22.1. Introduction

Generally speaking, artificial landscape creation is concerned with producing both realistic and attractive pictures of landforms. In contrast to previous approaches, we assume that this can be obtained in a more efficient way through modelling which takes into account geological parameters and laws. Our approach consists in using a geological description of the terrain and a geological simulation of the evolution of the corresponding land surface. It is thus a potential tool in studying quantitative erosion and producing artificial landscapes representing mountainous regions.

The principle of erosion simulation may be summarized as follows. We start from an initial land surface that may be represented by any height field. Making use of a 3D geological model, definite geological parameters are assigned to each node. There are of importance to further landscape evolution. This initial surface is then modified through an iterative method that simulates geological processes. At each iteration, the available erosion laws make it possible to simulate terrain creep and wash, chemical deposition as well as alluvial deposition according to local geological parameters. So, at each step, a new land surface and corresponding river network are created. These correspond to a particular stage in the landscape evolution. At the final step, a classical rendering algorithm is proposed for visualizing the resulting land form. The Z-buffer technique takes into account the geological specificities of the land surface. In order to improve the realism of the rendering natural textures obtained by a spot noise method are mapped onto the surface. The river network and the ridges may also be visualized.

In this paper, we first summarize previous work performed in landscape synthesis. Afterwards, the main principles of our geological model and the terrain representation at the geometrical and lithological [1] level are presented. The different geological processes are detailed in part three. We next present the rendering algorithm and in particular, the method for creating natural textures and visualizing the stream network and ridges. Finally, we comment on the resulting landscapes and conclude with suggestions for possible future work.

22.2. Previous Work

Creating synthetic images of landscapes usually involves two distinct procedures: modelling and rendering. A first approach to the problem consists of a procedural method using simple primitives texture mapping. It has been proposed by Marshall [11] who used some linear primitives as initial surfaces, and by Gardner [5], who used quadrics. In both methods, the resulting valleys do not really look very realistic since they are outlined by texture discontinuities at surface intersections. A second possible approach for creating realistic looking mountains uses well-known and efficient fractal techniques [3] [8] [9]. The resulting landscapes show accurate details and great realism but also a self-similarity character which is never observed in nature. In fact, different erosive processes operating on geologically ordered ground heterogeneities produce more variable landforms.

During the last decade, several models have also been developed by geomorphologists. Such modellings generally seek to check the effects of a limited number of erosional laws – which commonly imply mass balance calculations – on a land morphology in 2D (river profile) or in 3D (river network and land

[1] lithology is the geological science which describes the nature of various rocks

surface morphology) [4] [6]. The possible effects of geological diversification of the eroded terrain are hardly taken into account or are the object of very simplistic models [1]. There is no particular refinement in the visualization of the resulting land surfaces.

Recently, landscape modelling has been performed by trying to reproduce some actual geomorphological characteristics: landforms or networks. Kelley [7], for instance, creates terrains by first generating a stream network, adding successive tributaries according to a mass transfer law and then creating a landform by computing elevations starting from the network. This method provides an efficient way to model hydraulic erosion but there are some inconsistences between the river network which is fractal and the surface under tension which is not. There may be discrepancies between the drainage basin and the stream paths. Musgrave [10] proposed another model of simulation of simple hydraulic erosion and thermal weathering in a fractal height field. He creates a drainage network and valleys with talus slopes at their feet. A third method is proposed by Arques [2] who produces artificial landscapes and an associated stream network by modelling a planar map in which a fixed river network is introduced as a binary tree.

We notice, however, that in contrast to the approach that is be proposed in the present paper, none of these recent models takes into account possible geological heterogeneities of the ground and of the possible differential erosion that results.

22.3. Terrain Modelling

The classical method of representing terrains uses a height field. Many reasons justify this choice. It allows, for instance, the representation of a grid in a very simple way, fast techniques to have access to any point and the use of DMA[2] files for initial surfaces. This representation appears thus well adapted to defining the topology of our land surface. Furthermore, geological parameters may be easily associated with the elevation map by means of a 3D geological model. This allows defining a different lithology at each node.

Geometrical level. The land surfaces are described by means of a square or hexagonal height field. Each point of the grid has four or six equally distant neighbours. The use of an hexagonal grid is easier and makes the representation more accurate since each point has a greater number of neighbours. The dimension of the surface is specified by the number of points and by the distance between each node of the grid.

Nop particular shape is imposed on the initial surfaces which could even be entirely flat. In fact, we usually select an inclined plane that we disturb by a slight altitude perturbation in order to create a few irregularities. These

[2] Digital Mapping Agency

modifications allow the erosion process to start more quickly and to create a definite direction of flow. They also avoid obtaining unpleasant symmetries when geological differences between neighbouring points are small.

Lithological level. The lithological characteristics of the ground and underground (bedrock) have been simulated so that appropriate erosion laws may be applied during the iteration process. We assume that the geology consists of layered rocks that may have been deformed by various folds[3] and faults[4]. A geometrical model of geologically differential strata can be created, assuming naturally that each layer has different properties with respect to erosion. Folds and faults are both considered to be cylindrical deformations; folds respect the strata pile continuity while faults introduce local elevation discontinuities.

We will shortly sum up the main properties of the geological model that were previously published [12].

Geometrical model of folded and faulted geological terrains. Individual folds and faults are simulated by a geometrical transformation which is applied to the model. A deformation phase is defined as a purely geometrical operation which modifies the shape of the geological structure. Starting from an initial pile of planar strata S, a model M is built by applying n deformation phases Φ_i, one after another. The global deformation allows us to create a full geometrical model of deformed terrains.

An elementary deformation Φ_i results from the slipping of numerous material planes (which are different from the original layers), with respect to one another along a definite direction (fig. 1). The geometrical operations associated with the deformation phase Φ are *similar type transformations* (STT). Each STT is defined by a plane direction (*A axial plane*), a particular linear direction within the plane (*G slip direction*) and by a *profile function* $z = f(x)$. This specifies the magnitude of the offset between the various material planes.

If trirectangular coordinates $(Oxyz)$ are chosen so that Oz corresponds to the slip direction G and yOz to the axial plane A of a particular STT Φ, then such a transformation associates with each material point $M(x, y, z)$ a transformed point $M'(x',y',z')$ so that:

$$\begin{aligned} x' &= x \\ y' &= y \\ z' &= z + f(x) \end{aligned}$$

[3] a fold is a deformation of a layered stack in a particular direction

[4] a fault corresponds to an elevation difference between two areas of the land on either side of a fault plane

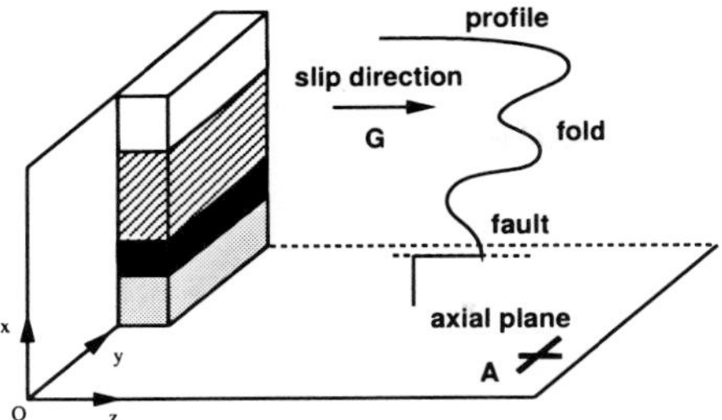

FIGURE 1. *Similar type transformation*

M may be also considered as the transform of M' through an inverse STT Φ^{-1} which has the same axial plane and the same slip direction as Φ but those profile function is $-f(x)$.

The profile function f defines the shape of the simulated deformation. It may be defined with the help of a mathematical function: a sine function allows simulating particular shapes of folds, a staircase function may define a fault and an oblique line a tilt of strata. It may be also defined manually by a string of segments drawn interactively.

The full 3D geometrical model that would result from the application of the n STT sequence is not actually built. The model remains virtual and is known through particular sections. The virtual 3D model is commonly visualized by a block-diagram where each layer is differencied by color (fig. 2 and 3).

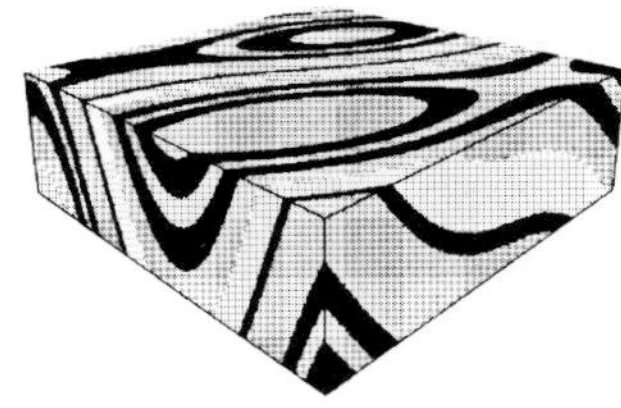

FIGURE 2. *Block-diagram representations: with two fold phases*

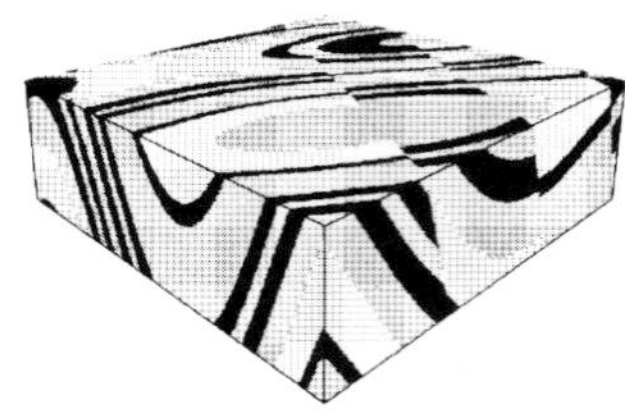

FIGURE 3. *Block-diagram representations: with two fold and one fault phases*

The number and the thicknesses of the strata may be modified. The model allows determining the lithological nature of any point of the land surface.

The bedrock representation. Each point P of the height field belongs to a given layer of the model. In order to determine this layer, we calculate, from the actual location of the point, its various positions by smoothing the deformation phases, in reverse order, one after the other.

Let us consider S_Φ the coordinate system $(Oxyz)$ connected with Φ. To find out the position of P within the initial stratification, the process performs the following operations:

- computing the coordinates M_n of P in the coordinate system S_{Φ_n} corresponding to the last STT (n) of the sequence.
- moving P by operating Φ^{-1} which anneals the effect of phase Φ_n,
- computing the coordinates M_{n-1} of P in $S_{\Phi_{n-1}}$,
- moving P by operating Φ_{n-1}^{-1},
- computing the coordinates M of P in S_{Φ_1},
- moving P by operating Φ^{-1},
- computing the coordinates M_0 of P in the coordinate system correlated with the initial stratification (world system).

These various operations are easily performed by applying appropriate transformation matrixes. At the end of the process, we obtain the location of the point within the chosen stratification and we thus associate the corresponding lithology.

In fact, each layer has four parameters which quantify its geological behaviour with respect to erosion and deposition processes: rock softness, porosity, permeability and vegetal cover. An altitude lowering of one particular point of the land surface may induce a change in its geological nature, since this corresponds to a modification of the location of the point in the 3D model.

The geological parameters. The above laws depend on the local values of the various geological parameters: K_d (rock softness), K_c (chemical dissolution), K_f (infiltration), K_v (vegetal cover). The following table shows some examples of coefficients values for common strata. These values range from 0 to 1. Alluvials have the same coefficients as river sands.

Stratum	Coefficients		
	K_d	K_f	K_c
Clays	0.90	0.10	0.30
Quartzites	0.10	0.30	0.30
Limestones	0.30	0.50	0.95
River sands	0.80	0.50	0.30
Granite	0.50	0.75	0.30

For the representation of the vegetal cover, we propose the following rules for the use of the K_v coefficient:

- $K_v = 0$
  - for every point whose altitude is greater than or equal to the snow level,
  - for any slope $\geq 60^o$ (where vegetal cover virtually does not exist),
  - for all the points which belong to river beds (these ones are defined according to the water height present at each point).
- $K_v = constant$ for any slope $\leq 30^o$.
- K_v is a linear function of the slope for values between 30° and 60°.

22.4. Simulation of Erosion and Deposition Processes

Many erosion and deposition processes operate on the land surface depending on various agents: rain water, ice and glaciers, wind... In the present paper, we only consider those processes that depend on running and infiltrated water. We assume that the flow of running water issued from any point of the land surface is entirely directed towards this point's lowest neighbour. Besides, when all the neighbours of a point have the same altitude (for instance in the case of a plateau), the flow direction is chosen arbitrarily .

The erosion and deposition processes may be viewed in the following way:

- each node of the grid receives the same quantity of rain water;
- part of this water is held by the vegetation and evaporated; the rest gets to the ground;
- a part of the water which gets to the ground percolates through the soil; another part flows towards the lowest neighbour (if it exists), as running water.
- the running water removes some rock detritals which is then deposited along the slopes or in the basins;

– the infiltrated water partly dissolves underground rocks.

These processes are performed from point to point, from upstream to downstream, down to the base level. All the flow paths form the stream network which can be considered as a graph. Such a representation allows examining all the points that are located upstream of a particular point, before considering itself.

The simulation of these processes also supposes that a *base level* is defined. It corresponds to the level below which a land surface cannot be reduced by running water. It can be considered as "local" (closed basin) or "global" (sea level) and can be modified by terrain lowering or raising.

Erosion laws. The above mentioned laws are issued from simplified geomorphological theories [4]. They are quantified with reference to the grid describing the land surface. During one erosive cycle, each of these processes induces variations of the altitude of nodes. Since we have been mostly concerned by performing 3D modeling of the eroded land surface within reasonnable computing times, we have chosen rather simple and empirical formulations of the erosion laws. We compute no accurate mass blance, the total amount of dissolved matter and the major part of the detritals being simply drained out of he model.

Gravity creep law. We suppose that, at any point, gravity creep is proportional to the slope magnitude and to rock softness. The small resulting landslide induces a lowering of the altitude z_g at the given point P. If P is not a low point, the elevation of its lowest neighbour is increased by the same quantity. This phenomenon modifies the elevations but does not produce detritals.

$$z_g = K_d \tan(\theta)$$

K_d: rock softness coefficient,
θ: angle between the segment joining P to its lowest neighbour and the horizontal plane.

Law of detritus removal by running water. The removal of rock fragments by running water wears away the land surface. The quantity of detritals S produced at each point depends on the amount of running water coming from upstream and on an erosive coefficient proportional to K_d. The quantity q of running water resulting from rain water fallen on a particular point is:

$$q = [1 - (K_f + K_v)]W$$

and the quantity of detritals produced is:

$$S = \alpha K_d \tan(\theta) q$$

q: quantity of running water,
W: amount of rain water,

K_f: infiltration coefficient,
K_v: vegetal cover coefficient.

At any point in a stream, the amount of detritals is defined according to the total running water, accumulating all running water coming from upstream. We must add to this quantity the total amount of the detritals produced upstream that has not been deposited as alluvials. The total amount of detritals at any point i of the stream is thus expressed by:

$$S^i = \alpha \sum_{j=1}^{i} K_d^j \tan(\theta^j) \sum_{k=1}^{j} q^k$$

$\tan(\theta^j)$: slope at point j,
K_d^j: rock softness coefficient at point j.

Taking the expression of q into account, we get the final formula:

$$S^i = \alpha W \sum_{j=1}^{i} K_d^j \tan(\theta^j) \left[j - \sum_{k=1}^{j} (K_f^k + K_v^k) \right]$$

This law induces a lowering $z_w = S^i$ of the altitude of point i. The amount of detritals S^i is supposed to have been put in suspension in the running water coming from i. It may thus be subject to alluvial deposition downstream according to the sedimentation law which will be emphasized below.

Chemical dissolution law.. We consider that the amount of infiltrated water q' at each point depends on a local infiltration parameter K_f. We have thus:

$$q' = K_f q$$

Dissolved matter may be expressed by:

$$z_c = \gamma K_c q'$$

K_c: coefficient of chemical dissolution,
q': amount of infiltrated water at the given point,
γ: coefficient which allows to specify the importance of chemical dissolution with respect to mechanical erosion.

The lowering induced by chemical dissolution is considered to be equal to z_g.

Alluvial deposition law. Alluvial deposition occurs when running water gets to a low point or when the amount of sediment exceeds the transport capacity of the stream. This last condition depends on the flow rate and thus on the local slope. There is no sedimentation when $\frac{S}{q} \leq \frac{r}{\cos\varphi}$. Otherwise, we deposit at the point, the height h_s of detritals which results in an increase z_d of the altitude of the point:

$$z_d = h_s = q\frac{r}{cos\varphi}$$

and a quantity $S - h_s$ of sediment is carried down.

φ is the angle between the vertical line and the normal to the surface at the point,

r is a transport coefficient which estimates the proportion of deposited and suspended detritals.

Alluvial deposits correspond to a specific geologic layer which is superposed upon the initial 3D model. In the case of basins, the model fills them as much as possible in order to prevent generating disconnected streams.

Cumulating all these laws provides the altitude change of each grid point. At each step, the new altitude is given by:

$$\boxed{z' = -z_g - z_w - z_c + z_d}$$

22.5. Rendering

The rendering of the eroded land surfaces is performed independently of the modelling process. A hidden lines algorithm which includes natural textures mapping and artificial visual effects is available.

Z-buffer algorithm. The shading process of the z-buffer algoritm produces hilly landforms. So, in order to visualize the outlines of the landscape, a different shading is used on either side of the ridge lines. The ridges are defined as the lines connecting all the points which have no upstream antecedent.

The stream network may be visualized in order to improve the realistic appearance. Is is created starting from definite points of the graph. In fact, all the points of the surface belong to the stream network but only some of them are selected for visualization. These correspond to the most important tributaries. All of the tributaries are fitted by a B-spline technique and two triangles are created for each section between two points of the interpolation. The width of the triangles is calculated in proportion to the depth of the points in the graph. In order to avoid these new triangles cutting any triangle of the land surface, the altitudes of the new vertices are calculated according to the elevations of the surface.

Textures. In order to improve the realistic look of the landscapes, natural textures are mapped onto the land surfaces. The creation of these textures is realized with the help of a spot noise method [13]. Spot noise is synthesized by addition of randomly weighted and positioned spots. This technique provides local control and is well-suited for texture design. The relationships between the features of the spot and the features of the texture are straight forward.

Thanks to these principles, various natural textures are created. Different sizes and shapes of spots are used to characterize various kinds of textures. These correspond to the different kinds of natural cover which exist in mountainous landscapes: grass lands, deciduous forests, coniferous forests, alpine meadows, rocks and snow. These textures are mapped according to classical principles which allow assigning each of them to a particular area according to exposition, slope and altitude. The difference of textures between two neighbouring areas looks unpleasant. We reduce these visual effects by blending the textures at the boundaries of the concerned areas. In a final stage, a blue atmospheric effect and water texture are added.

The landscapes shown in figures 7 and 8 present some of these textures as well as the visualization of the ridges.

Resulting landscapes. Computed surfaces look like realistic landscapes such as those that can be observed in geologically contrasted mountain areas. It appears that the results bear a strong relation with geology. Some morphological features induced by geology such as peaks, plateaus, valleys, hills and fault scarps are very conspicuous. These various structures are directly related to the nature of the bedrock and give proof of the efficiency of the simulation. A small number of iterations (about thirty) allows easily creating various landforms. Starting from one height field, we can obtain numerous land surfaces by only varying the associated lithology. Further deformations of the geological model after having processed erosion may proceed to another erosion cycle. The stream network can also be easily visualized since it just corresponds to the flow lines of running water. These lines are already used within the erosion deposition procedure.

Figures 4 and 5 show the example of a landscape obtained after 50 and 100 iterations. The initial land surface (figure 6) is an hexagonal flat height field of 100x100 nodes, affected by a small perturbation. The geological model corresponds to layers of even but unequal thickness, which have contrasted physical properties. They are affected by two fold and by two fault deformation phases. All of the above described erosion and deposit processes have been implemented in the simulation. The results correspond to one possible evolution of the landscape. For clarity, the stream network is not visualized.

Simulation parameters

Number of steps: 50/100

Amount of rain: 1.

Chemical/Mechanical erosion ratio: 2.

Transport ratio: 0.9
No lowering or raising of base level

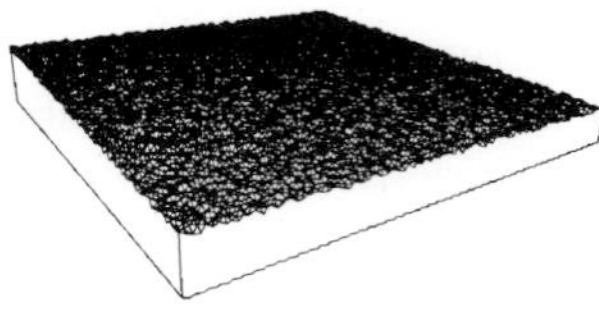

FIGURE 4. *Initial terrain*

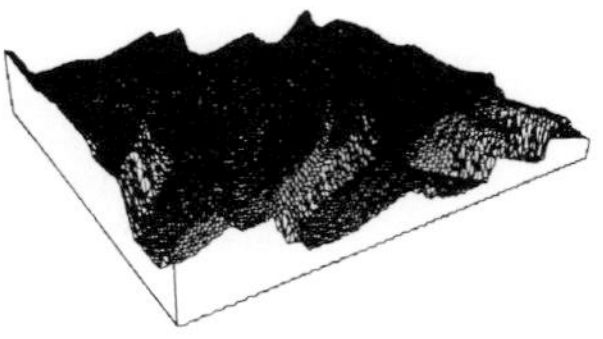

FIGURE 5. *Surface after 50 steps*

One could also think of using the results that we have presented to create computer animations of landscape evolutions.

22.6. Conclusion

We have presented a new method for creating artificial landscapes which is based on geomorphologic theories. Unlike previous works, the simulation of erosive and deposit processes takes into account the geological features of the terrain. This model allows to create some realistic looking landforms for

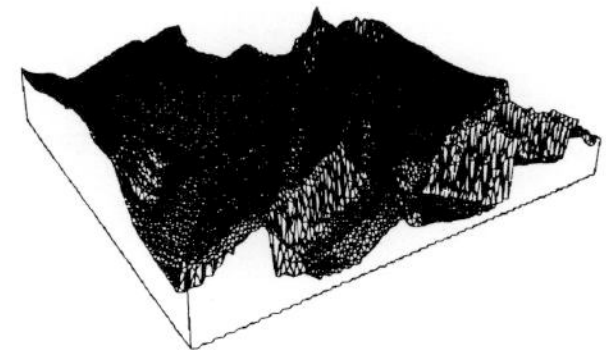

FIGURE 6. *Surface after 100 steps*

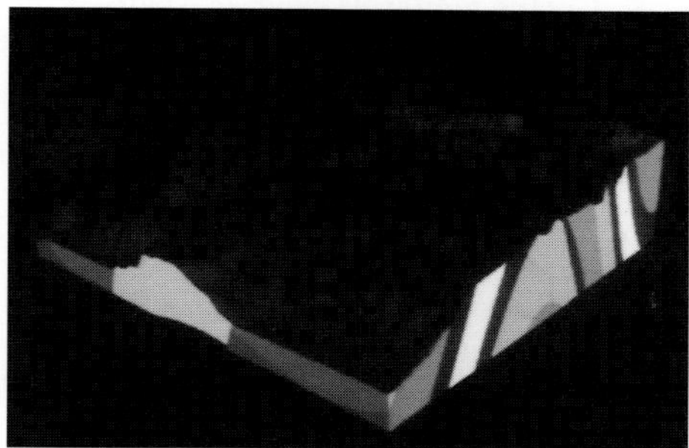

FIGURE 7. *Eroded landscape with bedrock*

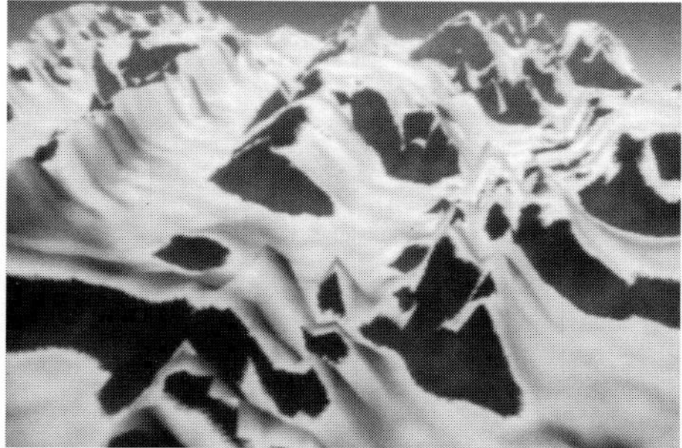

FIGURE 8. *Another eroded landscape*

mountain regions with geological outlines and stream network. The results show the efficiency of the simulation, even with a few number of iterations. The flexibility of the different laws and the variety of the geological bedrocks provide numerous modelling possibilities. Such modelling is an interesting mean of performing artificial landscapes which may be of interest in various disciplines, in particular environment sciences. It is also a potential tool for quantitative erosion studies. It may be subject to many extra refinements in the future.

Further work could be devoted to introduce other erosional processes like wind and glacial erosion. The latter could be welcome to get a hilly realistic representation of many mountain regions. Although, they may be more difficult to simulate in a simple way than rain water processes.

References

1. Ahnert Frank *Brief Description of a Comprehensive Three-Dimensional Process-Response Model of Landform Development*, Z. Geomorph. N.F./Supll. Bd 25, Berlin Stuttgart, September 1976, pp. 29–49.
2. Arquès D., Janey N. *Cartes planaires pour la synthèse d'images d'un relief à partir de son bassin fluvial*, MICAD, actes de la 11ème conférence, pp. 247–262, 1992.
3. Barnsley M. F., Devaney R. L., Mandelbrot B. B., Peitgen H. O., Saupe D., Voss R. F. *The Science of Fractal Image*, 1986, Peitgen & Saupe Editors, Springer Verlag.
4. Chorley R. J., Schumm S. A., Sugden D. E. *Geomorphology*, Methnen (Londres), 1984.
5. Gardner G. *Simulation of Natural Scene Using Textured Quadrics Surfaces*, Computers Graphics, vol. 18, no 3, July 1984, pp. 11–20.
6. Kirkby M. J. *A Two-Dimensional Simulation Model for Slope and Stream Evolution*, Hillslope Processes, A. D. Abrahams, Allen et Unwin, Boston 1986, pp. 203–222.
7. Kelley Alex D., Malin M. C., Nielson G. M. *Terrain Simulation Using a Model of Stream Erosion* Computers Graphics, vol. 22, no. 4, August 1988, pp. 263–268.
8. Mandelbrot B. B. *The Fractal Geometry of Nature*, W. H. Freeman & Co, San Francisco, 1982.
9. Miller G. *The Definition and Rendering of Terrain Map*, Computers Graphics, vol. 20, no. 4, August 1986, pp. 39–48.
10. Musgrave F. Kenton, Kolb C. E., Mace R. S. *The Synthesis and Rendering of Eroded Fractal Terrains*, Computers Graphics, vol. 23, no. 3, July 1989, pp. 41–50.
11. Marshall R., Wilson R., Carlson W. *Procedure Models for Generating Three-Dimensional Terrain*, Computers Graphics, vol. 14, no. 3, July 1980, pp. 154–162.
12. Perrin M., Cheaito M., Bonijoly D., Turmeaux T. *Visualizing Multifolded and Multifaulted Terrain Geometry Using Computer Graphics*, Japan Society of Geoinformatics, vol. 4, no.3, 1993, pp 330–339.
13. van Wijk Jarke J. *Spot Noise, Texture Synthesis for Data Visualization*, Computers Graphics, vol. 25, no. 4, July 1991, pp. 309–318.